RESEARCH AND THEORY
IN CURRENT ARCHEOLOGY

RESEARCH AND THEORY IN CURRENT ARCHEOLOGY

CHARLES L. REDMAN

EDITOR

A WILEY-INTERSCIENCE PUBLICATION

JOHN WILEY & SONS, New York • London • Sydney • Toronto

Copyright © 1973, by John Wiley & Sons, Inc.

All rights reserved. Published simultaneously in Canada.

Library of Congress Cataloging in Publication Data

Redman, Charles L
   Research and theory in current archeology.

   "A Wiley-Interscience publication."
   Bibliography: p.
   1. Archaeology—Addresses, essays, lectures.
2. Archaeology—Methodology—Addresses, essays,
lectures.   I. Title.

CC75.R42   1973   913'.031   73-6717
ISBN 0-471-71290-6
ISBN 0-471-71291-4 (pbk.)

Printed in the United States of America

10 9 8 7 6 5 4 3 2 1

PREFACE

Research and Theory in Current Archeology is an integrated collection of papers that presents a broad coverage of the positions, procedures, and controversies currently revitalizing the discipline of anthropological archeology. The emphasis of this volume is on the rapidly changing nature and future roles of archeology as seen by some of its outstanding practitioners.

This book is an expansion of the symposium "Archeology's Future: Roles and Relevance" presented at the 1971 meetings of the American Anthropological Association. Nine of the chapters were originally written as papers for this symposium (those by Rouse, Fritz, Trigger, Watson, Flannery, Taylor, Woodbury, Longacre, and Adams). The quality of the contributions by these participants and the enthusiastic response of the audience prompted me to expand this symposium into the present book. The central idea was to elicit new papers on current developments and future trends within archeology. I invited additional contributors to broaden the scope of coverage and the spectrum of opinions represented.

This volume is not intended to be a recounting of the current understanding of cultural history or a guide to the detailed procedures of field archeology. Instead it presents archeology as an active area of intellectual inquiry with all its important theoretical and methodological innovations.

Many authors and publishers have generously given permission to print excerpts from their works as they are used by the authors of the various chapters. I thank the American Anthropological Association for allowing us to reprint a revised version of a speech given by Robert J. Braidwood (chapter 3) from *Bulletins of the American Anthropological Association 3*, pt. 2 1972; the Society for American Archaeology for selections from *American Antiquity* (28:224, 1962; 29:440, 1964; 36:222, 1971; 36:259, 1971); the American Association for the Advancement of Science for excerpts from *Science* (172:1192, 172:1226, 174:264); and the Anthropological Society of Washington for reprinting a passage from *Anthropological Archeology in the America's* 1968 (p. 132). I also wish to thank various publishing houses and other journals for their permission to reprint excerpts. These include the University of Chicago Press, *Journal of Economic History, Economic History Review,* McGraw-Hill, and Addison-Wesley.

Many individuals have helped in the preparation of this book. My special thanks go to Bert Salwen, who originally stimulated me to organize the symposium, and to my wife, Linda, who aided me at countless tasks in all stages of preparation. My deepest gratitude goes to the contributors to this book. It is to these scholars and to the many others who have made archeology such a fascinating area of intellectual inquiry that I will remain forever indebted.

CHARLES L. REDMAN

University of California, Berkeley
January 1973

CONTENTS

ONE

APPROACHES TO CONTEMPORARY ARCHEOLOGY

Archeologists, like many other social scientists, are seriously re-evaluating their methods and goals and are demonstrating an increasing concern with the role of archeology in contemporary society. The contributions to this volume are an outgrowth of this development. The trend toward self-awareness compels the researcher to examine what he considers to be the nature of archeological inquiry and the fundamental tenets of his discipline. The four articles in this section outline different approaches toward the study of archeological remains and the intellectual divisions that these studies have created within the field. By explicitly examining these approaches and their results, we may be able to determine whether the espoused divisions within archeology are actually based on disagreements about theoretical matters, or about the methods employed, or result from the clash of personalities.

The first article by Charles L. Redman gives a short definition of archeology and concludes that the primary emphasis in current usage should be on understanding human behavior instead of the artifacts per se. The discussion includes three approaches to data recognition, data manipulation, and interpretive frameworks that are becoming productive aspects of contemporary archeology. It is suggested that the classification and functional interpretation of stone tools and other artifacts should be approached through a combination of statistical-morphological analysis and wear-pattern and edge-use analysis. The data gathered on the nature of archeological artifacts and sites should be investigated by using various forms of locational analysis that seek to discover and summarize the spatial patterning. A systems-theory approach that emphasizes the interrelatedness and complexity of processes is suggested as a promising interpretive framework for archeological data.

In the second selection, archeology is characterized by Irving Rouse as a distinct body of knowledge. The discipline can be divided into three alternate strategies for deriving knowledge from archeological data. The first type of research design in Rouse's system utilizes an "analytical" strategy. It consists of a series of techniques and methods for extracting and interpreting objects. The placement and collection of adequate samples are primary research objectives. The second type of archeologist employs a "synthetic" strategy and focuses on the people who produced the remains. He attempts to create a picture of the life and development of the people who are being studied. The third division in Rouse's scheme—"comparative archeology"—is a strategy that attempts to learn about the nature, behavior, and development of people in general. The problem to be investigated comes first; then the societies on which the problem is tested are selected. This comparative strategy depends more closely on utilization of a scientific approach and binds archeology closely with other social sciences.

Robert J. Braidwood's article is based on a lecture he delivered at the 1971 American Anthropological Association meetings in which he comments on the current state of archeology. Braidwood, in viewing the different current approaches to archeological research, suggests that there is room for both a nomothetic and a historical approach to prehistoric remains. He questions whether "new" archeology is actually new or is only a series of new idioms introduced to describe ideas already current in archeological research. Braidwood uses specific references to research carried out in Southwestern Asia, an area with its own unique set of opportunities and limitations. He suggests that theoretically sound research designs must be tailored to the practical realities of the situation and that, therefore, innovations pioneered in one region may not be applicable in another. Many restrictions imposed on archeological expeditions can be partly attributed to the continuing traffic in illegally excavated and smuggled antiquities. Southwest Asia has been especially hard hit by this problem, but other areas (such as Latin America) are also victims. Braidwood's pessimistic view of future research in these parts of the world is worsened by financial problems and the scanty nature of the available data. He suggests that the problems will require a restructuring of archeological research. Joint programs with local universities and institutions, greater participation in salvage efforts, and more attention to already assembled museum collections are the future directions of archeology in Southwestern Asia.

Kent V. Flannery's article is an outline of the direction that archeology has been taking during the past several years. He summarizes these developments as five phenomena or trends. The first phenomenon is the popularity that processual archeology has recently enjoyed. The second is the backlash against processual (or new) archeology. This is the reaction of young practitioners, who are very critical of processual studies, and of some of the original proponents of new archeology who have accepted the more established ways and positions. A third phenomenon is the reaction of several senior archeologists who have presented overviews of the discipline. These investigators suggest that processual archeology cannot be done until after the facts have been collected during a stage of cultural historical research. The fourth trend, according to Flannery, is the appearance of some bad examples of new archeology. And, finally, there is a methodological schism among the adherents of the new archeology. One group, whom Flannery calls the "law and order" archeologists, seeks general laws of human behavior by utilizing "If A, then B" assertions and testing them by statistical correlations. The other group uses what is called by Flannery the "Serutan" approach. This approach is based on a systems-theory framework and utilizes such techniques as simulation to determine why populations act the way they do.

1. RESEARCH AND THEORY IN CURRENT ARCHEOLOGY: AN INTRODUCTION

CHARLES L. REDMAN

Department of Anthropology
New York University
New York, New York

Miller Research Institute
Department of Anthropology
University of California, Berkeley

This volume includes original essays from a diverse group of archeologists who are concerned with what archeology is today and what it should be tomorrow. Their viewpoints represent a broad spectrum of current opinion within the field of anthropological archeology. However, they are not as directly applicable to archeology as practiced by scholars in such disciplines as Classics, Art History, or Near Eastern Languages.

Archeology is an eclectic field that encompasses varied approaches and subject matter. There are many different definitions of archeology, and most of them are viable. Each archeologist has his own view of the field that reflects his approach, training, abilities, interests, and financial backing. The only generally accepted criterion is that archeology is concerned with the past. However, today the question of *how* archeology is concerned with the past is receiving radically innovative answers, as I indicate below (see also Bert Salwen's Chapter 10 this volume).

Archeology is, of course, what archeologists do. But if we stop with this definition we sidestep the important methodological issue of explicit definition. Archeologists today are actually in the process of redefining the scope and role of archeology in our society.

Many archeologists agree that "Archeology may be simply defined as the systematic study of antiquities as a means of reconstructing the past" [Clark 1957: 17]. I shift the emphasis in this definition and broaden its scope—from the study of antiquities and the reconstruction of the past to the study of human behavior per se. Therefore, I define archeology as the systematic (i.e., scientific) study of the nature and cultural behavior of human beings through the examination and analysis of the material remains of their past activities.

These definitions differ in stress and approach. I think the main focus of archeology is human behavior instead of artifacts and the historical past. The study of artifacts and other aspects of excavated sites is only one of the many methods used to accomplish a better understanding of the great diversity and the complex processes that make up the human condition. It is the way in which archeologists go about studying the human condition that differentiates them from other scholars.

Clark's definition points out—as mine does—that human behavior is studied by archeologists through the examination of past remains, but his definition also restricts (as mine does not) the archeologist to the historical reconstruction of only prehistoric or past human behavior. Thus, his definition is transitional between the old one that would view archeology as the study of artifacts for their value as *objets d'art* and the current view that the main value of artifacts is that they constitute decipherable, systematic records of past human activities. When understood, these artifacts can help us to understand human behavior not only of the past but also as it is today.

One of the main goals of archeology *is* the historical reconstruction of past human behavior. But this historical reconstruction is subordinate to the task of understanding human behavior as such. No doubt, most archeologists—including myself—are committed to do an enormous amount of historical reconstruction because of the very nature of the records that we disturb and destroy in the process of studying them. But some archeologists will look more and more to these data for clues to the lawful behavior of human beings, and I predict, in the future, that most historical reconstruction will be done in the larger context of the definition of archeology that I give here.

Archeologists must confront a broad range of problems—and must solve many of them—to pursue their discipline successfully. This is shown here by the contributors who are concerned with innovations in the theoretical bases, advanced methods, and the efficient organization of archeological research. In the present article I discuss selected archeological topics that are matters of great concern and that illustrate recent advances in our field.

The information that archeologists utilize to understand (and to reconstruct) past human behavior is derived from man's material remains. These remains (or artifacts) have a form of their own and are spatially distributed. Aspects of their manufacture, their use, and how they were deposited are reflected in their form and distribution and the sites that contain them. Data on other, nonmaterial aspects of cultures are also preserved in the form and spatial arrangement of the archeological record. Consequently, one of the fundamental steps of archeological research involves an adequate description of the form and spatial interrelations of artifacts and archeological sites. An approach to artifact categorization and analysis is discussed in the beginning of this chapter. Then I deal with some of the methods of locational analysis that can be applied to settlement pattern studies.

Related to attempts to develop more rigorous and realistic methods for observing archeological material are efforts to formulate an effective interpretive framework for analyzing the results. Finally, I discuss a systems framework for interpreting archeological information. The three sections of this chapter reflect three of the major areas of inquiry and achievement in archeology today: data recognition, analysis, and interpretation.

APPROACH TO CLASSIFICATION AND TYPOLOGY

Archeologists, like all researchers, must develop methods for interpreting the empirical world they observe. This is the primary rule for all future work. The fundamental method of making any information usable is to categorize it. This basic step in research is necessary for any kind of communication or analysis and leaves its imprint on all subsequent work. These categories may be extremely broad to begin with, but they are refined as the research proceeds.

Artifacts are the primary source of archeological information, and it is through rigorous study of them that archeologists learn about prehistoric society. Archeologists assume that the patterned behavior and activities of human beings in social circumstances affect the ultimate form and systematic deposition of these artifacts. Consequently, we seek to understand the spatial distribution and the morphological patterning of artifacts that reflect the different varieties of patterned behavior of prehistoric peoples.

Like ethnographers, archeologists are interested not only in studying lifeways and social systems, but also in understanding their structure and functioning. To learn about social systems, ethnographers make a series of detailed observations on certain aspects of the behavior and communication of peoples. Archeologists must do the same for the people they are studying. The difference between the approach of ethnographers and archeologists is not a logical one but relates to the material examined. Archeologists must develop a more effective means of detailed observation and significant measurement to obtain from artifacts what ethnologists obtain from direct observation of behavior. As archeologists we are still discovering the multivaried significance of the material we work with, and we still have a long way to go to develop a complete means of measuring and studying this material. Methods of understanding the meaning of the form and distribution of artifacts are still at a preliminary level. A basic goal of most archeologists today is to find new ways of linking artifacts to their behavioral correlates. Once this is done, we must construct arguments that defend the inferences that link the material being studied with the interpretations drawn from the material.

Since archeologists do not directly observe the phenomena they are most interested in but observe only their remains, our investigations must focus on data recognition, categorization, and interpretation. Identification and classification have always been a central focus of archeological research because these results directly affect subsequent inferences and interpretations. We observe the archeological record through the categories we construct for artifacts, and these categories leave their imprint on our conclusions. There has been a recent tendency toward increasing the precision and scope of artifact classification and analysis by using computer-based statistical routines for clustering artifact attributes and for finding covariational patterning. Although these techniques hold great promise, they are only as good as the typological base on which they are built. Precision in statistical manipulation may obscure the faulty categories that are used as input data.

Consequently, I think that to derive the full benefit of developments in data manipulation it is necessary to formulate more effective means of recognizing and categorizing relevant artifact attributes and of identifying their function. Since these conclusions (like all conclusions from archeological reasoning) must be based on indirect observation of the artifact—not an observation of the act of using it—it is important to establish the fact that several different kinds of evidence point in the same direction.

Two basic methods of attribute recognition and artifact classification are currently being used to improve the reliability of artifact analysis. One method involves the explicit definition and recording of each artifact's morphological attributes. The selection of these dimensions, such as weight, size, edge angles, etc., is a complex process in which the archeologist determines the attributes relevant to the particular hypotheses being tested from the numerous possibilities. Once attributes are selected and recorded, their covariance with other attribute values is calculated. After determining which attributes do, in fact, vary together in a nonrandom manner, the observed attribute values are statistically clustered into types that are empirically testable (Spaulding 1953; Sackett 1966; Movius, David, Bricker, and Clay 1968). Counts of these statistically derived types can be used as input for quantitative analysis and interpretation.

A second type of artifact analysis involves the recognition of attributes functionally related to artifact manufacture and use, such as flake scars, striations, or polish. Interpretation of these wear marks is based on experiments, laws of mechanics, and ethnographic analogy (Semenov 1964). Some of these traces can be discovered with the naked eye, but usually a microscope is necessary. This type of analysis is the most accurate method of determining the use of a tool because it does not involve as many inferential arguments as do types based on morphology alone. Division of the artifacts based on functional analysis can also be used as input for quantitative analysis and interpretation.

An effective artifact analysis integrates these two different types of classification into an ongoing reiterative procedure. When confronted with a large number of artifacts, the archeologist should first separate them into types based on traditional attribute combinations. One purpose of this procedure is to test, refine, alter, and possibly reject the initial categories. These types provide the initial structuring for both statistical analysis of the tool's morphology and microscopic

analysis of any evidence of wear or manufacture. Time and preservation permit the complete microscopic and morphological examination of only a portion of the total number of artifacts recovered. This
is an appropriate situation for probability sampling. In tool categories
with many pieces, the results of a relatively small sample approximates the parameters of the total population without examining
every piece (Redman 1973).

Although I recommend these procedures for artifact analysis,
there is not a "best" analytical scheme. Typologies should be
designed to solve particular problems and, therefore, the attributes
selected for measurement must be sensitive to meaningful variations
in the assemblage.

The above procedures are most directly designed to produce
information on the uses of artifacts, especially chipped stone and
other kinds of tools. There are other artifacts, such as pottery, where
an understanding of function is only one of a much wider range of
data that can be derived from the pieces. The examination of pottery
requires a different analytic framework but incorporates many of the
same principles as that of chipped stone.

Great control is often exercised during the fabrication of pottery,
and there are many ways in which a potter can alter the form or
design of pots. I suggest that a productive framework with which to
study pottery would maximize the variation that is recognized and
recorded. This procedure should be structured in a hierarchical
manner where comparisons can be made within each level of the
hierarchy, depending on the hypotheses being tested. Actually, this
system would be composed of a set matching the hierachies of categories with the potter's choices. Each hierarchy covers a major aspect
of the pot's construction, such as manufacture, form, or design. The
manufacturing classification would deal with fabric, temper, hard-
ness, firing temperature, and surface finish. The form classification
would start with major shapes, such as jars and bowls, then break
down into finer divisions of these classes and, finally, deal with
microvariations in rim form, bases, or other secondary elements of
the pot's morphology. Thus we would be able to investigate the form
at a general level that might directly reflect the vessel's uses, and then
we could concentrate on finer details that might be a stylistic reflection of different potters or of other organizational divisions.

The most complex hierarchy of classification would involve
design, especially if the pots are painted. In view of the many different design motifs, the classification could consist of a number of

different levels, depending on the complexity of the design and the preservation of the sherd. If the design were hatched lines, for example, the lowest level might be the line orientation within the hatched area. The next level of classification is the set of outline shapes that bound the hatching. Then, there is the manner in which these hatched areas are bound together into larger designs. The highest level of classification is the organization of the entire design as it appears on the pot. Starting with the same general ideal in mind, different potters probably would employ slightly different techniques at each level of the hierarchy in order to fill out the pot.

Another design factor that might more closely reflect the motor habits or equipment used is the metric aspects of the design, such as line width or frequency. This might be a completely unconsciously patterned variable but should reflect groups of potters (or even individuals).

The data gathered by these parallel hierarchical systems could be compared within different levels or proveniences of a single site, or between different sites, as a measure of communication or interaction. The relative amount of interaction and, hence, of exchange of ideas and techniques could be a result of wife exchange, trade, or warfare, for example. Different hierarchical levels could be compared, since they probably reflect different variables at work, some of which will be more sensitive measures than others to the factors in which one is interested.

As is true with all forms of classification, the major problem here is to associate the observed variation with the behavior that produced it. With these pottery designs, variations might be caused by differences in chronology, location, function, raw materials, conscious choice, implicit organization, and individual or group idiosyncracies. The archeologist's job is to determine and to justify the choice of variables being measured—if any—at each hierarchical level.

LOCATIONAL ANALYSIS: SETTLEMENT PATTERN STUDIES

The location and spatial arrangement of archeological remains is another primary data source . This includes the placement of individual or groups of artifacts, features and structures, and the location of the sites themselves. This type of spatial data provides important clues about the way people lived and organized their lives. More attention is being paid to the horizontal placement of artifacts within

archeological sites (Whallon 1973). Covariational patterning of artifacts between levels of Mousterian sites has been statistically analyzed
by Binford and Binford (1966). Stylistic associations of artifacts within
different rooms of specific structures have been investigated in detail
(Longacre 1970; Hill 1970). Locational analysis of artifacts is yielding
new insights into activities, residence patterns, and ancient social
organization. This type of research will continue to be exciting. It
promises to open new areas of archeological inquiry and to support
inferences that are already being made.

Another form of locational analysis being applied in many parts
of the world is the study of settlement patterns. Early studies of
archeological site distribution were made by L. Spier (1917) in the
New World and by R. Braidwood in the Old World (1937). This
approach to archeological data first came into its own with the publication of *Prehistoric Settlement Patterns in the New World* (Willey
1956). In the introduction to this work Willey says:

> In settlement, man inscribes upon the landscape certain modes of his
> existence. These settlement arrangements relate to the adjustments of man
> and culture to environment and to the organization of society in the
> broadest sense [1956:1].

Settlement pattern studies are a valuable source of data for
testing hypotheses on a wide range of topics. Successive configurations of communities can yield inferences that are relevant to various
topics concerning population, subsistence, sociopolitical systems,
trade, and warfare. There are three different levels of investigation
involving settlement patterns: those treating shape of individual
dwellings or structures, the layout of communities, and the spatial
relationship of one community to the others.

The shape and construction of unearthed buildings has long
been the subject of considerable study. Recently, these "architectural" studies have been undertaken in an attempt to seek generalizations about the types of structures encountered at large numbers
of sites and to relate their attributes to various elements of the
ancient society (Flannery 1972; Rappoport 1969). The relationship
between environment and house forms has been long recognized
and studied. Subsistence patterns and types of activities performed
also affect the shape and detail of houses. Family size, social organization, and conceptual patterning can be discovered through intensive investigation of the recovered material.

Community layout is affected by many of the same factors that determine the shape of buildings, although in different ways. The arrangement of structures in a settlement is directly affected by the local topography, other elements of the environmental situation, subsistence activities, the need for defense, and different aspects of organization (Cook and Heizer 1965; Frasier 1968; Mark P. Leone, Chapter 9 in this volume). Research has been conducted on the number of individuals per building in different areas and on the amount of floor space or community space utilized by each individual (Narrol 1962; LeBlanc 1971). Estimates must be checked against other variables and, in many diverse situations, before any generalizations can be accepted.

One type of settlement-pattern study that has recently gained widespread acceptance and that is yielding innovative results is the study of the spatial arrangement of communities across the landscape. This information is collected by surveying a region on foot, jeep, or by air. Archeological sites are located by surface indications, and their location, size, chronology, and other details are recorded. Questions can be answered on settlement size, distribution of sizes, the number of communities in each period, and the spatial arrangement of sites during each period. The work of geographers is a valuable source of analytical techniques in understanding distribution data on ancient settlement patterns. These researchers are concerned with problems of description, comparison, and process similar to those of archeologists. Geographers work with data in ways similar to that of archeologists, but from the present and historical periods. The settlement data that archeologists consider are density, agglomeration, scatter, extent, orientation, shape, and topographic location of prehistoric communities.

Many settlement-pattern models used by geographers are being applied productively to archeological data. One of these models— the principle of least cost—has been used to investigate settlement patterns in the southwestern United States (Fritz and Plog 1970; Gumerman 1971). The basic assumption is that settlements are located in such a way as to minimize the effort expended in dealing with the environment. Thus, necessities such as water, fuel, agricultural land, or collecting territory could be the prime determinants of site location. By recording the varying distances to these resources, the environmental zone, and the topographic situation of each site during successive periods in a region information is gained concerning the relative importance of these factors in determining settlement location in the respective periods. Directors of several expeditions have formed the Southwest Archeological Research Group (SARG) with the goal of answering the question "Why did people settle where they did?" (Gumerman 1971). Effort was made to standardize surveying techniques and to record equivalent categories of data. With this type of close communication, it may be possible for SARG to find more general regional patterns and to test patterns observed in one area against patterns discovered in another.

There are several methods for describing the nature of site distributions in a region. Plant ecologists Clark and Evans (1954) developed an index of clustering that utilizes the measurement of the distance to the nearest neighboring community for each site. The value of this coefficient varies from 0.0 (completely clustered) through 1.00 (random distribution) up to 2.15 (maximum dispersion). By calculating this measure for different periods in one area or for different regions, the researcher has a quantitative way to measure the differing agglomerative tendencies of settlements (Plog 1968a; Adams and Nissen 1972).

Another measure of site distribution involves covering the region with a rectangular grid and counting the number of sites within each grid square. If the sites are randomly distributed throughout the region, the patterning of sites per grid square will resemble a Poisson distribution—a mathematical representation that approximates a random distribution. The divergence of the observed values from the expected values gives a quantitative measure of the clustering or nonclustering (evenly dispersed) distribution of these communities (King 1969).

Calculations involving site distribution become more meaningful when combined with data on site size. The variation in average site size and the balance between large and small sites is very important to models of community organization. Many developmental processes involve population change, whereas others involve only the shifting of population from one type of community to another. By calculating community size, it is possible for an archeologist to determine whether there is more than one mode to the distribution of size. If there is, then it may represent a hierarchical system such as a village, town, and city. The hierarchy shown in settlement size may be the result of economic or political variables. Different approaches have been taken toward explaining these settlement hierarchies and the distribution of communities within a region.

One geographic model formulated by Christaller and refined by Losch is known as the central place theory (Haggett 1965; Berry 1967; and King 1969). This theory basically assumes that successively larger communities provide larger numbers of services for the surrounding smaller communities. Hence, larger central settlements should have larger hinterlands than smaller settlements. The second assumption of this theory is that, in locating settlements (or in the growth of older settlements), the inhabitants attempt to maximize the available resources. Farming settlements on an agriculturally homogeneous plain can provide for the best utilization of the land if they are arranged in a hexagonal lattice distribution. The most efficient location of larger settlements is in the center of hexagons of six villages with each large settlement serving six surrounding villages. If one knows the critical variables for site location and can assume certain uniformities in the physical situation, it is possible to construct the theoretical optimum distribution of villages and towns in a region. In reality, these ideal configurations are modified by other factors, such as limitations of transport, topography, localized natural resources, external influences, and the extent to which the prehistoric inhabitants recognized the potential of their surroundings. Actual settlement patterns discovered during a survey can be compared to the derived ideal models, and important ancient organizing factors can be inferred from the results of the comparison. The deviations of the observed patterns from the ideal will also yield valuable data on settlement interaction.

Combining data gathered on site size (hierarchy) and the spatial location of the sites, it is possible for one to discuss some settlements as central places. A central place is a community that provides certain services (or resources) not only for its own inhabitants but also for people from surrounding settlements who occupy the hinterland (Berry 1967). A modest-sized community can serve as a central place for a limited range of services and can serve a relatively small hinterland. Several of these limited central places could exist in one region, each specializing in a certain set of services or overlapping in the functions they provided. There also may be larger central places that provide a wider range of services and have larger hinterlands. Archeologically, one can begin to define the services provided by a central place by the types of activities occurring at the site that did not take place in the surrounding smaller sites. The smaller sites that were associated with their corresponding larger central place might be inferred from geographical and stylistic similarities. In dealing with proto-urban and urban situations, determination of these associations is one of the primary avenues of research leading to definitions of the nature and function of cities and civilizational networks.

SYSTEMS THEORY IN ARCHEOLOGY

Increasing numbers of archeologists are beginning to view their material in a systems framework. The interrelatedness of systems entities and the multivariate nature of cultural processes compel us to analyze and to interpret our data in a manner that reflects the assumptions of systems analysts. Instead of studying single settlements or viewing specific arrangements of artifacts as typifying all artifacts, systems archeologists investigate relationships beyond the bounds of individual sites in order to understand their variability. They analyze the material in a manner that emphasizes and delineates the maximum amount of variation and patterning present. The different patterns of artifacts and sites discerned reflect the sets of patterned activities that were participated in by the prehistoric inhabitants. It is a composite of these activities and their articulation that comprised the ongoing community and that is often referred to as "the culture."

The incorporation of an analytical systems framework shifts the emphasis from a primary concern with simple entities and a partitative view of culture to an investigation of complex relationships and variability. Various definitions and techniques for employing a systems framework have been developed by other scholars (especially by general-systems theorists). General-systems theorists seek a body of systematic theoretical contructs that integrates the general relationships in the empirical world (Boulding 1956). Insights into basic systems that have been derived from and tested on other bodies of data by general-systems theorists can be applied usefully to the archeologist's study of prehistoric cultural systems. The systems approach will enable archeologists to infer the full complexity of the interacting phenomena of cultural processes. This approach basically assumes that the great complexity of these systems and processes is systemically organized and potentially understandable.

For our purposes, a system is defined as a functioning set of elements that are interrelated so that a change in one affects the others. These elements (or variables) must be systematically articulated, and this articulation must be regulated in some manner. This regulation usually involves some form of steady-state feedback (homeostatic) mechanisms. By adjusting the organization of the elements in a system in response to stimuli from the outside environment, the homeostatic mechanism, through negative feedback, attempts to maintain the system as close to its previous state as possible. Systems often change their state in response to external stimuli. In these situations, a morphogenic mechanism regulates the change through positive and negative feedback. This addition of structure-changing and structure-elaborating features (to already-utilized structure-maintaining features) of inherently unstable systems makes systems theory relevant to the study of prehistoric cultures. There are many conditions under which a society reacts to minimize the effect of external stimuli and, therefore, to maintain its previous state (structure). In other situations, especially when the existing state is already unstable, the society may respond to external stimuli by changing its form significantly and by continuing in this altered form.

When defining a system, one must be careful not to confuse the state of the system with the system itself. A system is "a continuous, boundary-maintaining, variously related assemblage of parts," and it "is not to be confused with the structure or organization its components may take on at any particular time" (Buckley 1967:5). The criterion for a system classification should not be its structure at a particular time because this is a temporary condition. A system is an entity that exists over time. The unit of dynamic-processual analysis should be the systemic complex of goal-seeking, decision-making individuals and groups of individuals interacting through time.

Whenever an entity is investigated within a systemic framework, one must define it from two viewpoints. One way is to look at the entity itself to evaluate and recognize its basic properties. Another way (which is often overlooked) is to measure the entity in terms of its position within the system. System elements have values that are not inherent in themselves but that belong to them, depending on the way the elements function in an ongoing system. For example, if one is investigating a city in a complex society, one must approach the city in two ways: (1) considerable work must be done in the city to understand its properties and functions, and (2) the structure of the city can be partially understood in isolation, but a fuller understanding can be reached only by investigating its surrounding area and the relationships and central functions of the city to this area. The direction of this influence is certainly not just one way. Rural areas leave their imprint on the nature of the central cities, and this variable "folk" tradition differentiates many cities that might otherwise have developed in ways more similar to one another.

To describe a system, one must be able to describe its state (its structure at any particular time) in terms of attributes of its components and the nature of its relationships. This state can change in response to outside stimuli or to internal mechanisms with or without changing the structure of the system. Changes from one state to another can be described graphically by a vector describing the different values of relevant variables (Watson, LeBlanc, and Redman 1971). The line representing the various system changes is known as the trajectory of the system (path of the system through the different possible states). The accurate description of the various system states is an adequate description of what the system has been doing but it is not an explanation of the processes involved. The products (states) of an evolutionary or developmental sequence must not be confused with the processes that caused and governed that sequence. All too often archeologists describe a series of events and claim to have explained why these events occurred. However, even a systemic description is not per se an explanation.

According to Hill (1971), three factors are necessary to explain change within a systems framework: (1) the state and the functioning of a system prior to the change must be described in terms of its regulating mechanisms; (2) the extrasystemic (or internal stimuli) that promote change must be identified, and the reason why the regulating mechanisms failed to cope with these stimuli must be explained; and (3) it must be shown how new regulating mechanisms have been developed (selected) during the change that stabilizes the system in its new state. By describing the various aspects of change, the description of the process that caused the change is integrated with the changes in the system and is therefore explained.

There are several important contributions of the systems approach to archeological investigations. The broadest one is the emphasis on the great complexity of cultural processes and organization. Systems are complex until proved otherwise. The primary aspects of this complexity are the interrelatedness of elements in the system and the system's close relationship with its environment. The demands that this complexity places on archeological field investigations are clear. Data collection and analysis must be done in a manner that emphasizes the variability in the archeological record and provides a sample of the full range of variation. Single sites are not an adequate sample in a systems framework, and summaries about individual sites cannot be made from limited exposure of the site. Extensive investigations that study a representative sample of the entire population is necessary. Requirements for detail and broad coverage necessitate a sampling program to collect sufficiently reliable data within the constraints of limited time and money (Redman 1973).

The holistic nature of the systems approach allows the researcher to pursue the controlled investigation of his subject matter without requiring that he be able to hold certain variables constant (a difficult task when studying cultures). By studying what can be recognized of the structure and the responses of the system to various inputs, it is possible to infer the nature of the system. Expressing this structure in the form of a diagram (Watson, LeBlanc, and Redman 1971; Harary, Norman, and Cartwright 1965) forces the researcher to be explicit and precise about the way in which the various elements of the system interact and affect one another. If this representation is accurate, it is then possible to predict the way a system will react to various stimuli. The diagram also focuses research on aspects of the system that are least clear. This directs future research along more necessary lines.

Archeology is rapidly changing and developing. Many problems that have hindered archeological research are now being confronted, and diverse methods are being developed to overcome them. The problem of adequate classificatory and typological systems is as old as archeology itself, and this difficulty continues to be a major limiting factor in analysis and interpretation. As stated before, the classification of artifacts affects all later work and provides the perspective through which past behavior is investigated.

I have suggested that by combining current methods of statistical-morphological techniques with wear pattern and edge-use analysis, we can better understand the function of the tools being studied. After archeological objects have been properly categorized, the next major source of information is from locational analysis. The spatial patterns of artifacts and ancient communities reflect the activity sets of ancient peoples and the social organization of their communities. This information, although occassionally collected and interpreted in the past, has become a major focus of inquiry during the past 20 years. Settlement-pattern studies and the techniques of locational analysis have already yielded tentative solutions to problems that archeologists had not previously attempted to solve.

With the increase in the precision and coverage of archeological research, many investigators have sought better interpretive frameworks through which to understand their data. A systems-theory approach that emphasizes the interrelatedness and complexity of processes will be very useful. The greatest contribution of systems theory to archeological research is in the formulation of testable models of human behavior. The main purpose of a theoretical model is to help the researcher to select relevant variables and significant hypotheses from a large number of possibilities. This enables him to concentrate on specific problems that are conducive to solutions.

By combining efforts to improve data recognition, data manipulation, and interpretive frameworks, archeologists are confronted with new and more complex problems, and they are solving them with greater reliability and interest than before. Archeology, which began with an esoteric pursuit of prehistoric art that evolved into a full-scale study of prehistoric societies and their cultural evolution, today also contributes to the understanding of human behavior—past and present. Anthropological archeology is not merely art history, nor is it prehistory. Today's archeologist is a social scientist who studies human behavior and social organization by analyzing artifacts of past human activities.

2. ANALYTIC, SYNTHETIC, AND COMPARATIVE ARCHEOLOGY

IRVING ROUSE

Department of Anthropology
Yale University
New Haven, Connecticut

There are three main reasons for archeological research: (1) to learn the nature of the remains under study and the manner of their deposition, (2) to reconstruct the nature and development of the people who produced the remains, and (3) to discover the processes that affected the people's development. Each of these objectives requires a different research design—which I shall call the analytic, synthetic, and comparative strategies—and each leads to the accumulation of a different body of knowledge, which may correspondingly be called analytic, synthetic, and comparative archeology.

The purpose of this chapter is to differentiate the three strategies and their resulting bodies of knowledge and relate them to the other ways of dividing archeology that are discussed in this volume. Also I shall discuss the relevance of the three bodies of knowledge.

STRATEGY

First, let me clarify my usage of the term "strategy." It refers to the most logical way of achieving a research objective and contrasts with the most practicable research design, which I shall call "tactics"

(Rouse 1972: 27–29). In any particular instance, an archeologist may decide to conform to the strategy by proceeding in the most logical manner, or he may depart from it for various reasons. Parts of the strategy may already have been performed by other investigators, or the data needed to perform certain parts may not be available. Alternatively, researchers may not be interested in particular parts and may prefer to leave them to other archeologists who have more interest in them.

In other words, strategy refers to a theoretical model for the conduct of archeological research and tactics refers to the application of that model to a particular piece of research. Since the analytic, synthetic, and comparative strategies are theoretical models, they are subject to modification whenever a researcher moves from the level of strategy to the level of tactics. In planning any particular research project, the researcher has the option of choosing a purely analytic, synthetic, or comparative approach or of adopting tactics that combine two or more of these kinds of research.

This chapter is concerned only with the three strategies and their relevance. I shall not discuss their application to particular conditions of research, nor shall I attempt to evaluate their use, as other participants in the symposium have done, since this would require me to move from the level of strategy to the level of tactics.

ARCHEOLOGY

My usage of the term "archeology" also needs to be clarified, since it means different things to different people. Some authors apply the term to the results of archeological research, while others use it to refer to the methods of obtaining results. Thus, Willey's *Introduction to American Archaeology* (1966, 1971a) is a presentation of results, whereas Hole and Heizer's *Introduction to Prehistoric Archeology* (1969) summarizes methodology. Still others stress the individuals who do the research. For example, the "new" archeology consists of an ingroup of mostly young individuals who have differentiated themselves from the out group of individuals who practice the "old" archeology. Braidwood and Flannery liken the new archeology to a cult elsewhere in this volume (33–34, 47–53). The new archeology could also be considered as a product of the generation gap now prevalent in Western society.

In this chapter, "archeology" will be applied primarily to the results of archeological research, as opposed to the methods of research and the personnel involved. In my opinion, methods can be considered archeological only when they are successfully used to obtain results, and individuals qualify as archeologists only insofar as they contribute to the bodies of knowledge that we call archeology. For example, neither the stratigraphic nor the settlement approach is inherently archeological. The former was originally developed in geology and the latter in geography, and the two can be considered archeological only to the extent that they are used to draw conclusions from human remains. Similarly, an individual does not qualify as an archeologist simply because he has learned how to study stratigraphies or settlements; he must use these skills in such a way as to contribute to archeological knowledge.

My title, "Analytic, Synthetic, and Comparative Archeology," is to be read from this point of view. The three adjectives refer to the strategies for deriving knowledge from archeological remains, and the noun refers to the bodies of knowledge that result from use of the three strategies. If I had employed either methods or personnel as the primary basis for distinguishing different kinds of archeology, I would have arrived at very different divisions, as I shall attempt to show below.

ANALYTIC ARCHEOLOGY

The archeologist seeking to learn about remains as such will design his research to recover representative samples of the remains, will categorize them, and will describe them in site reports, museum exhibits, and lectures in order to impart his knowledge to other interested persons. In other words, he will treat the specimens he finds as his basic units of study and will analyze them individually or in groups—hence the phrase "analytic archeology."[1]

This type of archeology is sometimes dismissed as a purely descriptive enterprise. On the contrary, it requires a full set of interpretative procedures, although these have to be qualified as "primary," since they are only one step removed from the specimens under study.

Before excavating a site, for example, it is advisable to formulate hypotheses about the manner in which the site's deposits were laid down and about the changes since deposition, and to take these hypotheses into consideration in planning the excavation. In effect, the success of an excavation is a test of the hypotheses with which an archeologist has approached the deposits. For this reason, analytic archeologists have begun to study the processes of deposition and modification of remains.[2] Some new archeologists in particular are observing the deposition of remains at the present time (e.g., Longacre and Ayres 1968), and older archeologists have conducted experiments to determine what happens to remains after deposition (e.g., Jewell and Dimbleby 1966).

The new archeologists have also experimented in recent years with different kinds of sampling procedures in an effort to improve their knowledge of the nature of the remains (e.g., Redman and Watson 1970). They aim to make the samples of artifacts obtained from a site more representative of the totality of artifacts in that site.

Analytic archeology has often been considered unscientific because it does not deal with variables and therefore cannot use statistical procedures. In fact, the specimens are its variables[3] and they are now being treated statistically by means of the techniques of numerical taxonomy, as originally developed in biology (Clarke 1968). A large number of analytical techniques have also been adopted from the natural sciences, especially from chemistry and physics (e.g., Brothwell and Higgs 1969).

Academically, the relevance of analytic archeology rests on the information it supplies to other disciplines for use in the secondary and tertiary interpretation of archeological remains. From this standpoint, analytic archeology is no more relevant to anthropology than it is to the other disciplines that utilize knowledge of archeological remains, such as classics, history, Near Eastern studies, and history of art. Recognizing this, the Institute of Archaeology at the University of London has set up a Department of Archaeology to teach the analytic approach to students who do not wish to specialize in synthetic archeology within its Departments of Prehistory, Near Eastern Archaeology, Indian Archaeology, and so on. I know of no comparable program in the United States, although we at Yale are using the analytic approach as the core of an interdepartmental undergraduate major, in which we bring together the courses in archeology previously taught separately in the Departments of Anthropology, Classics, History of Art, and Near Eastern Languages and Literatures.[4] Also in this country, an Association for Field Archaeology is being formed to bring together all archeologists interested in field work and the primary interpretation of remains, regardless of their academic departments.

Both in Europe and the United States there are facilities for the development of new techniques to be used in accumulating analytic knowledge. The best known of these are the Research Laboratories for Archaeology and the History of Art at Oxford University and the Museum Applied Center for Archaeology at the University of Pennsylvania (e.g., Aitken 1961, and Michael and Ralph 1971).

In the profession of anthropology, analytical archeology is most closely related to ethnography. The two fields share a common interest in artifacts, past and present, and a common desire to conserve and make known the artifacts, as evidenced by the existence of joint museums of archeology and ethnography (Rouse 1972: 12–13).

Outside anthropology, the analytic approach is most closely related to the analytic subdivisions of the natural sciences (such as paleontology), with which it cooperates in our museums of natural history and in state surveys of natural resources. Archeological remains have come to be recognized as one of our natural resources, to be conserved like other parts of the environment. This is, of course, the basis for the development of salvage archeology since World War II, and it should ensure a steady demand for analytic archeologists, even though we have not developed formal programs for training them, as is done at the Institute of Archaeology in London.

On the other hand, the analytic approach has no relevance to the social sciences and is relevant to the humanities only insofar as the remains studied are art objects or the product of significant historical events. The student of the humanities can be expected to take an interest only in the outstanding structures and artifacts, not in ordinary remains.

Analytic archeology has always attracted popular interest, and this has been heightened by the increase in leisure time since World War II. The number of archeological monuments, museums, and associations of amateur archeologists continues to increase. They, too, require the services of professionals, who should be specially trained in analytic archeology.

SYNTHETIC ARCHEOLOGY

The synthetic archeologist focuses upon the people who produced the remains, instead of on the remains themselves. Peoples are his basic units of study. He uses the remains to learn all he can about them: who they were; when and where they lived; what cultures, social structures, languages, and morphologies they had; and how and why they developed their ethnic systems (Rouse 1972: 62–65). In other words, he extracts information from the artifacts with which to build up a picture of peoples, their lives and times—thus the phrase "synthetic archeology."

Synthetic archeology may be either prehistoric or historic, depending whether the peoples under study did little or no writing or have left adequate written records about themselves (Trigger 1968). In the former case, the synthesis must be based primarily on archeological evidence and in the latter case on documentary evidence, with the remains used only to fill in gaps in that evidence or to illustrate it. I shall concentrate on prehistory because of brevity and because it is my own specialty.

The fact that synthetic archeology is prehistoric does not mean that it is unscientific. Prehistoric archeologists work primarily with the methods and theories of the historical subdivisions of the natural sciences, such as historical geology and evolutionary biology. Like natural historians, prehistoric archeologists proceed inductively, by selecting a particular people for study, acquiring the pertinent knowledge about that people, synthesizing the knowledge (e.g., in the form of a chronology or a cultural subsystem) and, finally, considering the various hypotheses that might explain their syntheses in accordance with the principle of multiple working hypotheses (Chamberlain 1965).

In the final step of this procedure, the synthesizers shift from induction to deduction. They set up a series of alternative explanatory hypotheses, test them against the data—a procedure that usually requires more fieldwork in order to obtain data previously overlooked—and then select the hypothesis or hypotheses that best fit the data. Older archeologists like me have done this intuitively, but the new archeologists prefer to use formal testing procedures (e.g., Tuggle 1971). This is an improvement, except when the investigator limits himself to a single hypothesis instead of adopting the procedure of multiple working hypotheses. Archeologists who work with single hypotheses bias their tests by unconsciously selecting only the facts that "prove" the hypothesis of their choice.

Synthetic archeologists can and do use sampling procedures. However, these procedures must be based on the peoples and their activities—not on the sites and specimens per se—since the latter are not the basic units of synthetic research (e.g., Rouse 1952).

As Spaulding (1960) has pointed out, synthetic archeologists work with three sets of variables: the dimensions of space, time, and form. They can study variations in any or all of these dimensions, keeping any or all of them constant. In the past, synthetic archeologists have tended to study variations in the dimensions of space and time and to keep form constant, by distinguishing peoples and norms and tracing their distribution through space and time. It is to the credit of the new archeologist that they have also recognized the need to study variations in form, of peoples and their norms, and have called attention to the processes that must be used to explain such formal changes (e.g., Binford 1965).

This aspect of the new archeology is often called processual. Actually, there are two kinds of processual archaeology, one that uses processes to explain the functioning and development of particular peoples and one that focuses on the processes themselves, regardless of the peoples involved. These are the two sides of the schism discussed by Flannery in his chapter in this book (47–53), if I understand him correctly. Only the first side falls within the scope of synthetic archeology; the second is comparative archeology and will be discussed as such.

When I became an anthropologist 30 years ago, synthetic archeology was in the mainstream of our profession. Groups of people were the center of attention with prehistorically oriented archeologists studying people of the past and ethnologists studying people of the present; and each of us was known by the peoples he studied. Over the years, I have seen a gradual decline of interest in both prehistory and ethnology to the point where they are no longer at the center of the anthropological profession; their place has been taken by cultural, social, linguistic, and physical anthropology (Rouse 1972: 16–20). I suspect that this trend is to be correlated with the general decline of interest in history since World War II—especially among social scientists—and with the general tendency to concentrate on the beliefs of one's own ingroup at the expense of the principle of relativity, with its concern for the differences between groups of people, which preoccupied my generation. In addition, anthropology as a whole has shifted its orientation away from the natural sciences and towards the social sciences, with their emphasis on the deductive instead of the inductive approach.

Synthetic archeology has little appeal to those oriented toward the arts. Its appeal to the layman depends upon the ethnic group to which he belongs. For example, the prehistory of Europe has more relevance to white Americans than the prehistory of the United States, and the prehistory of Africa has more relevance to black

Americans, because the two groups have originated in Europe and Africa, respectively. The prehistory of the United States is directly relevant only to the American Indian.

Nevertheless, I believe that a case can be made for studying and teaching all local prehistory as a part of the prehistory and ethnohistory of the world as a whole. Our students need to acquire the perspectives in space and time that world prehistory and ethnohistory give, if only to counteract the tendency toward ethnocentrism and chauvinism that our educational system fosters by its traditional emphasis on the prehistory and history of western civilization.

COMPARATIVE ARCHEOLOGY

Instead of using archeological remains to study particular peoples, to learn their behavioral norms, and to explain the changes in norms the investigator may prefer to use the remains to study human behavior in general. He will select one particular aspect of behavior —whether it is culture or social structure—will formulate a hypothesis concerning its nature and development, and will test this hypothesis by applying it to archeological evidence. Hypotheses are, therefore, the basic units of study, taking the place of artifacts in analytic study and peoples in synthetic archeology; and the strategy is deductive rather than inductive.

This type of archeology is sometimes called "scientific" (e.g., Watson, LeBlanc, and Redman 1971). We have seen, however, that the first two types of archeology also fall within the generally accepted limits of science. To avoid confusion, we might call the third approach "explicitly scientific," as is done by several of the other contributors (e.g., Watson, LeBlanc, Redman 1971 and Longacre Chapter 22), but this would be ambiguous because the other two approaches are similarly explicit.

Alternatively, the third approach might be termed "experimental", because it utilizes the strategy of scientific experiments. However, this too would cause confusion. We have seen that analytic archeologists sometimes experiment with human remains on a primary level of interpretation, as in the case of the Overton earthwork cited above (Jewell and Dimbleby 1966). Synthesizers similarly experiment on a secondary level, for example, in order to determine the alternative ways in which a people may have produced its chipped flint artifacts (e.g., Crabtree 1966). We need a term that will apply only to a third level of experimentation, on which the archeologist formulates and tests a single, more general hypothesis.

The critical point about the third level is that its hypotheses are not framed in terms of changes in the remains themselves or in the behavioral norms peculiar to individual peoples and their cultures but in terms of behavioral variables that are cross-cultural and comparative. Therefore, I shall call the third approach "comparative archeology."

The comparative archeologist ignores variations along the dimensions of space and time, as these dimensions have been defined by Spaulding (1960). If the comparative archeologist were to take these two dimensions into consideration, he would be dealing with changes in the behavior of peoples living at successive points in space and time, and he would be doing synthetic research. Instead, he studies variations only along the third dimension, form, by formulating generally applicable variables, predicting the relationships among those variables, and testing the predictions by means of "case studies."

This raises a sampling problem. Social anthropologists who do comparative research are careful to select cases that illustrate typical form; and they try to choose cases that are randomly distributed along the dimensions of space and time (e.g., Murdock 1957). Insofar as I am aware, comparative archeologists have not yet faced up to this sampling problem.

The relationships that are predicted among the variables are usually statistical. Unless an investigator's hypothesis is derived from a universal law, he does not expect all his cases to conform to the prediction, since he cannot eliminate all extraneous factors (Spaulding 1968). Therefore, the results of comparative archeology are usually expressed in the form of probabilities, which may or may not be present in any particular situation. This is another major difference from synthetic archeology, where the aim is to learn what actually happened in a particular situation and why it happened there. As Trigger (1970) has put it, the conclusions of comparative archeology are nomothetic, whereas the conclusions of synthetic archeology are idiographic.

We have seen that analytic archeology may be said to operate on a primary level of interpretation and synthetic archeology on a secondary level of interpretation. Flannery (this volume, 47–53) argues that "processual archeology" is also on the secondary level. This is true of the synthetic side of Flannery's schism (where processes are used to explain particular instances of change) but not of the comparative side (which studies processes cross-culturally). To be sure, the comparative archeologist does formulate his own variables from the remains, without regard for the norms established through synthetic research, and is able to bypass the synthesizers' conclusions about variations in the dimensions of space and time. Nevertheless, the comparative archeologist must know whether or not his variables occurred together at the same points in time and space and within the same cultural, social, linguistic, and morphological systems. (He need know only the fact of co-occurrence, not the particular points in time and space and the particular systems involved.) He obtains such knowledge from historical syntheses, and to this extent the comparative approach may be said to constitute a tertiary level of interpretation, dependent not only on the results of the primary level of analytic interpretation but also on those of the secondary level of synthetic interpretation. Comparative interpretation is thus furthest removed from the remains with which all archeology must start.

As Watson, LeBlanc, and Redman (1971) have noted, synthetic and comparative archeology are complementary. Synthesizers furnish the case studies used by comparative archeologists in testing their hypotheses, and the comparative specialists provide hypotheses that the synthesizers can use to explain particular instances in accordance with the method of multiple working hypotheses.

The comparative approach has been around for some time. For example, it was used in the majority of the 1955 seminars of the Society for American Archaeology (Wauchope 1956). Nevertheless, the new archeologists have been the first to formalize it and to accord it independent status.

Comparative archeology derives much of its attractiveness from the fact that it is currently in the mainstream of anthropology as a whole. Indeed, it has often been called anthropological archeology (e.g., Binford 1962). Just as anthropologists who study the contemporary scene now prefer to call themselves cultural, social, linguistic, and physical anthropologists (instead of calling themselves ethnographers or ethnologists), many students of the past similarly prefer to call themselves paleoanthropologists, instead of archeologists or prehistorians (e.g., Freeman 1971).

The comparative approach is more relevant to the social sciences as a whole, with their emphasis on the experimental-science as opposed to the historical-science point of view. It is less relevant to the natural sciences, and especially to those subdivisions of the natural sciences that are analytic or synthetic. It has no relevance for the humanities and arouses little interest among laymen.

CONCLUSION

I have written this chapter from the point of view of an anthropologist who specializes in archeology. My comments about the three different kinds of archeology reflect my conception of the nature of anthropology. If I believed that anthropology is primarily a social science, I would have placed more emphasis on the comparative approach. If I considered it to be purely natural history, I would have been more insistent on the importance of the analytic and synthetic approaches. Actually, I view anthropology as a bridge between the social sciences, the natural sciences, and the humanities, and therefore I have tried to give equal weight to all three approaches.

NOTES

1. My usage of this phrase should not be confused with David Clarke's (1968). His "analytical archeology" also treats artifacts as the basic units of study, but in addition it uses the knowledge acquired through the analysis of artifacts for the study of general processes. Hence it combines the analytic and comparative strategies as they are defined here (Rouse 1970).
2. A similar development has taken place in paleontology, where the term "taphonomy" has been coined to refer to the study of the processes of deposition, preservation, and exposure of fossil bones (e.g., Dodson 1971).
3. I am indebted to Bruce Grove for pointing out this fact to me and thus stimulating me to think about the differences in variables among the three kinds of archeology.
4. William A. Longacre informs me that the University of Arizona offers a master's degree in analytic archeology.

3. ARCHEOLOGY: VIEW FROM SOUTHWESTERN ASIA

ROBERT J. BRAIDWOOD

The Oriental Institute and
The Department of Anthropology
The University of Chicago

The invitation to give the lecture from which the following chapter derives seemed to imply that I make an appraisal of where anthropologically oriented archeology stands today. My career has primarily developed in a penumbral area of anthropological archeology (as Robert Adams stated it, a few of us "have an uneasy foot in both camps, the humanities and the social sciences"). Therefore, I frankly admit that I cannot completely master the idiom of much of the "new" archeology[1] and that I am not a completely informed appraiser.

I shall discuss the state of archeology in Southwestern Asia, an area with which I have had fairly broad contact beginning 41 years ago. I leave to your judgment an assessment of how directly applicable the "new" archeology's more elegant research designs may now be to this area. I believe that the course of cultural evolution in the area is of such interest that it justifies the use of every method at the archeologist's disposal, as the raw data become more reliable and more readily available. Nowhere else in the world may we study cultural process and change with the assistance and control provided by written records for a period of more than 5000 years.

First, however let me comment briefly on the "new" archeology. As I understand it, *pure* "new" archeology views itself as an expression of a scientific revolution in the gathering and interpretation of evidence for the (essentially preliterate?) human past. In its own words, the new archeology's paradigm is nomothetic, not historic. Most of its literature has appeared within the past 10 years,[2] but Walter Taylor's 1948 study could doubtless qualify him as the movement's John the Baptist.

In fact, I wish a historian of religion would consider the rise of the "new" movement. It seems to have much of the eager, very earnest, humorless fervor of a new religious movement. There are minor prophets, there is at least one messiah, there is a band of disciples, and we can see a *deus ex machina* in the form of the IBM computer. The Pharisees and high priests of the old religion have been identified and sharply rebuked. There have been Pauline conversions and there is certainly a holy writ. But is there already a whiff of sectarianism, schism, and even revisionism? I should not be surprised if the Wenner-Gren Foundation is soon asked to fund a Council of Nicaea for "new" archeologists.

My own view of life (professional and otherwise) has always been one of cheerful agnosticism, of amused mistrust of promises of any one true road to salvation. It was my great fortune to have had a wide spectrum of inspiring teachers running from Leslie White to Henri Frankfort (a very wide spectrum indeed) with men such as Arthur Boak, Carl Guthe and Robert Redfield in the middle bands. This good fortune has continued, given the breadth of interests of my field and academic colleagues and students, in a career developed in a part of the world that reeks with history. I am interested in nomothetics, but I seem to want to see them in a historical context, if that makes sense. I also want a broad definition of both history and process supposing that good historians themselves have broad interests. I would gladly help to clear any blockages on the nomothetic road, even if I am not bound to think it is the only road to salvation. It is, however, fair to ask: How ready is Southwestern Asia for the extremes of the nomothetic approach? There seems to me adequate room and need for both the historic and the nomothetic approaches.

I now turn directly to Southwestern Asia. It has been suggested[3] that a "regional symbiosis" is conceivable for the area over much of its later prehistoric and historic ranges. Thus, the area in consideration would be a very large one. What is most conventionally taken to be Southwestern Asia totals nearly $2\frac{1}{4}$ million square miles. But—in the regional symbiotic sense—we may reasonably include both Egypt and the Aegean (with indeterminate portions of Southeastern Europe) as well as the lands of the Armenian, Azerbaijani, Georgian and a strip of the Turkmen republics, and Afghanistan. This area would easily be the areal equivalent of the continental United States (minus Alaska), while Lamberg-Karlovsky and others keep urging us eastward toward the Indus. When I speak of the Near East, I tend to think of so great an area. The environmental diversity of this vast area is also as considerable as is that of the United States. Furthermore, we have—so far—only intermittent clues as to the order of physiographic and environmental changes in response to almost 10,000 years of human manipulation of portions of the land by cultivation, deforestation and canal cutting, let alone by changes by natural agencies.

Although much has been done in the area in the name of archeology (by one definition or another!), I think that in Adams'[4] notion of a three-step progression of archeological investigation, only portions of the area are midway on the second step: that portion of the establishment of a time-space systematics. Very considerable portions of the whole area still call for the completion of the basic step: pure exploration. Proto-Elamite tablets in far eastern Iran and Ubaid pottery down the Persian Gulf coast are recent examples that our exploratory phase is not yet complete. In my opinion, at no one site (let alone at any cluster of adjacent contemporary sites) have such adequate exposures been made and such yields acquired to justify elegantly detailed processual studies (Adams' third step). But the fact that the area is not yet ready for such studies does not mean they will not or should not come. I stress again that the advantages for these studies consist of a very long range of assistance by written documents.

The Near East has always exerted a very strong "pull" on the peoples of the Western cultural tradition. The reasons for this attraction, of course, lie in Biblical and Greco-Roman accounts, either mythical or historical, to which subsequent "cradle of civilization" speculations came to be added. The popular mind (with the popular media bowing to it) of the West loves spectacular claims for Near Eastern earliness, richness, and grandness. Furthermore, in the history of ideas it is generally understandable that, up to now, scholarly attention to the cultural developments that took place in the Near East has come mainly from the humanities. The reason why modern anthropologically trained archeologists have tended to turn away from concern with these developments is a more complex issue and one we should honestly consider. Having committed ourselves to cultural relativism, are we then too embarrassed or too self-conscious to work comfortably within the framework of our own cultural tradition? Does the region's attraction for the Western mind (which we cannot define in purely rational terms) disarm us? As anthropologically oriented archeologists, we tend to be highly amused with what we take to be fumbling field efforts and restricted sense of problem-orientation of our humanistic colleagues. But then, it seems to me, we tend to turn to sites with less-complex inventories (usually preliterate, except in Mesoamerica, for example). We seem to assume we can only be nomoethetic by dealing with preliterate cultures, although our most explicit nomothetic studies also seem to utilize hypotheses drawn from a not-too-distant ethnohistory. Leo Oppenheim's[5] essay on Assyriology, in an explicitly anthropological journal, reminded us of a far more distant ethnohistorical vista for hypothesis making, but we seem either too embarrassed, too timid, or too frightened by the necessary preparation and dialogue with humanists to accept the challenge.

Admitting the ethnocentric (or "Westocentric") nature of the Near East's attraction but without adequately explaining it, I now turn to some of the more recent effects of this attraction. Since adequate and interesting accounts of archeology's early growth in the Near East are readily available,[6] we may let the blood-curdling ghosts of the nineteenth century antiquities-quarrying phase lie, except for a parenthetical mention of Nineveh because of some 1857 figures on size. In that year, Commander Felix Jones, R.N. surveyed the largest mound in the Nineveh complex—the Kuyunjik—for Sir Austin Henry Layard. Jones reckoned the mound to be 750 hectares (just under three square miles) in area—a height of over 30 meters— and figured that 1000 men digging 330 tons daily would clear the mound in 120 years. The Kuyunjik is indeed a large mound, as Near Eastern mounds go, but it is not the largest.

The archeological phase beginning after World War I was relatively less frantic than the phases of the nineteenth and the early twentieth century. The non-Turkish-speaking portions of the Ottoman Empire were split into separate states, most of these as British or French mandates. By the mid–1920s, the mandatory authorities had organized national museums, antiquities services, and laws for the regulation of archeological efforts (supplementing what already existed in Egypt and Turkey). Gertrude Bell, as the first Director General of Antiquities in Iraq, was instrumental in setting the model for these post-World War I antiquities services and laws. The laws set minimum staff requirements, gave a degree of protection from avaricious landowners, and required a half-and-half division of a season's yield (with "unique" objects also reserved for the national museum). However, for Egypt, Greece, and Turkey, the excesses of the earlier quarrying phase were too well-remembered and the export of antiquities was completely forbidden. The hot winds of nationalism have, since World War II, badly shredded the edges of the old laws of most of the ex-mandated states. Nevertheless, Egypt and Syria have recently made exceptions to the no-export rule for archeologists involved in their salvage programs, and divisions are still allowed in portions of Lebanon and in Iran and Israel.

What are the negative and positive factors that influence Near Eastern archeological research now and in the immediate future? I shall list these factors, beginning with the negative ones.

The old tradition of antiquities quarrying still complicates the honest professional's life. The various local authorities know these hairy stories only too well and have embroidered them with their own fantastic details—only too understandable in the present milieu of xenophobia. All antiquities *causes célèbres,* from the Hilprecht-Peters controversy to the Dorak affair and the Boston Museum's gold, hang heavily over our heads. The rise of the so-called primitive art market and the acquisition of illicitly acquired antiquities as good business investments or as gifts (with tax-dodging overtones) to museums only exacerbates the situation and contributes to the further destruction of sites and original contexts. Granted that the Near East is not the only region to suffer in this respect, we are nevertheless doubly cursed with the combination of the attraction the region exerts on the West and the fact that its antiquities (as Adams puts it) "pander to the prevailing mood of escapism". Hence the various local impositions of export restrictions are understandable on these as they well may be on more highly philosophical grounds.

The region's changing sociopolitical situation complicates things for us in other ways. Since the Near East has long been a scene of political instability and of Western manipulation of it, there remains much local resentment of attitudes typical of colonialistic superiority, even as these attitudes themselves begin to slacken. Furthermore, while I know of no modern colleagues, American or European, who use archeology as a cover for intelligence work (I cannot, of course, guarantee that there are none), the idea that every archeologist is a disguised spy is very real to many locals, official or otherwise. The result is a restriction on free-wandering surveys, on the availability of detailed maps and air photos, and the persistent gnawing feeling that whatever a field director (or his staff) says or does may prove disastrous. The official local image of the foreign archeologist (at its most generous) is of someone who stays quietly in one place and hires workmen to dig holes. Proposals to break out of this mold meet with suspicion. There may also remain, in the countryside particularly, strong traces of what we might call the Imam Ali Zadi effect:

... above all, as to the previous history of this city, God only knows the amount of dirt and confusion that the infidels may have eaten before the coming of the sword of Islam. It were unprofitable for us to inquire into it[7].

Of course, with the rise of regional nationalisms there is a trend away from the older traditional attitudes, but this is of no particular advantage to archeologists. Already, some of the national antiquities services have been shifted from ministries of education to ministries of "culture and tourism". Here, hopes for tourist dollars or marks, coupled with investigations favoring search for real or imaginary prestigious ancestors, may prevail. The tourist aspect may imply emphasis on elaborate on-site restorations and the filling of local museums. These implications, while again very understandable, could be a serious drain on the resources and valuable time of both foreign and local archeologists.

Naturally, archeological investigations in the Near East have various financially imposed restrictions. The cost of travel and staff maintenance is relatively high. This may be offset somewhat by relatively low labor costs, although the wise field director now resists the temptation to hire more locals than his limited staff can superintend knowing also that increased exposures mean increased yield to be processed. There is, especially, a lack of well-qualified nonacademic technical specialists to aid in processing (e.g., photographers, draftsmen, and preparators), both in the field and in home laboratories, largely, perhaps, because of lack of funds to provide them with respectable permanent careers. Where export restrictions are at all tight (now almost everywhere!), processing to the point of final descriptive manuscripts must be prepared in the field, and this implies the necessity of more staff time and adequate off-season living and laboratory quarters in the field. There is an obvious dilemma here for field staff who also have home teaching responsibilities. A field season's time-schedule must be tightly budgeted so that a staff's appetite for the fun of digging does not result in processing indigestion. With respect to these thoughts, it is very sobering to consider the relatively minuscule exposures and infinitesimal yields from sites whose names stand large in our literature. I select, as examples, two Prehistoric Project sites: only about 3% of the total area of surface indication of Çayönü has been exposed, while for Jarmo only about 1.5% of the approximate original site-size has been cleared—and neither site to the full depth of deposit in the total areas exposed. Many other well-known sites have far smaller ratios of present exposure to overall area, and we must ask whether such ratios make statistically significant bases for broad generalizations.

This consideration leads into the matter of prevailing blockages to understanding on a more scholarly level. While it is certainly doubtful that any one formula for methodological perfection will ever appear, field methods and record keeping techniques in the Near East (given understaffing and different national and philosophical emphases in goals) have tended to lag behind methods and techniques of some other areas. There is, furthermore, no dodging the issue that most Near Eastern excavation in the range of literate history has focused on monumental and aesthetic interests and has stressed the activities of political and sacred elites. For the literate range, clearance of villages or even of private house quarters in city sites is rare. Until World War II, sites were selected for excavation primarily on the basis of their identification (rightly or wrongly) with some ancient place name. The exceptions tended, naturally enough, to be prehistoric, such as Dorothy Garrod's early selection of a cave at Zarzi (which is simply a modern Kurdish village name). With the fashion for prehistoric digging following World War II, the trend away from site-name digging has increased. Another well remarked but persistent scholarly blockage is the lack of interdisciplinary dialogue (between archeologists of any intellectual complexion and philologists, between natural scientists and humanists, and now between "old" and "new" archeologists). For Americans especially, dialogue with foreign colleagues tends to be restricted along linguistic as well as philosophical lines, and the same obtains for some of the host countries but with political factors playing a more important role; for example, dialogue between Arab and Israeli colleagues. Finally, of course, there is the dead hand of unprocessed and unpublished materials (however insurmountable the various blockages to final publication may be, on grounds we have already noted), along with a lack of uniformity in what is considered desirable for full reporting and general methodology.

No matter how dreary all the foregoing negative aspects may sound, there are positive aspects for archeological research in Southwestern Asia. It is true that some of these aspects may only benefit culture-historical studies in their first impact; others promise more immediate ramifications for generalizing studies.

Although local responses to the destructive illicit antiquities operations have tended to be unimaginative shotgun blasts, overly repressive toward honest professionals but weakly applied on the local scene, several national museums have experimented with offering genuine duplicates from their own large collections for sale. In the period between World War I and World War II, this practice essentially destroyed illicit trading in Cyprus, setting an interesting example. I view the growth of successful fake manufacturing with impish delight. Most heartening is the position of most (unhappily not all) of the profession on the UNESCO antiquities declaration, the U.S.–Mexican agreement, Internal Revenue Service scrutiny of tax-exempt "gifts," and the strong resolutions of archeologically involved academic institutions and societies against receiving uncertified antiquities. There are, at least, polite noises of satisfaction regarding all this from the regulatory authorities in the Near East; hopefully they believe we are serious.

It would be completely unrealistic to think that the sociopolitical picture in the Near East is a cheerful one. Nevertheless, as the attitudes of foreign professionals shift away from colonial attitudes, and as more local professionals have training abroad and jointly with foreign expeditions, the basis for mutual understanding does grow. We keep our fingers very tightly crossed but, so far, no post-World War II foreign professional has been directly accused (rightly or wrongly) of using archeology as a cover for "dirty tricks" intelligence gathering. (There is speculation that the termination of a widely publicized search for Noah's ark—on the slopes of Mt. Ararat close to the U.S.S.R. frontier in Turkey—was, at least, partly because of its being a political embarrassment, but we can hardly credit such an excursion with having been professional.) There certainly have been positive effects from foreign participation in the various salvage efforts. An increase in the number of more problem-oriented joint expeditions could have even more positive effects. As a partner in such an effort, I can attest to the level of heartening warmth of welcome and interest that these partnerships stimulate on the local scene[8]. Another very positive step forward on the sociopolitical level could be more "applied archeology" efforts, such as those undertaken by Jacobsen and Adams for the Iraq Development Board and by Adams for the Kuzestan Development Service, in which modern development planners supported research, seeking information concerning successful agricultural-irrigation regimes of the past.[9]

Until the financial belt-tightening of the last several years, our needs for basic monetary support have been relatively well met, especially regarding the post-World War II fashion for prehistoric research in the Near East. In part, this doubtless reflects a general shift in archeological financing sources from the gifts of wealthy private individuals (now under sterner IRS controls) to fundings through foundations that are often publically endowed. This shift is not an American phenomenon alone; the French CNRS, the German Forschungsgemeinschaft, and the Dutch ZWO have played roles similar to that of our National Science Foundation, with the peer-refereeing of proposals that contributes to thoughtfully conceived field efforts. The traditional humanities-oriented efforts have had somewhat less favorable treatment. The effect of the Humanities Endowment Program on Near Eastern archeology by Americans is still new; although several expeditions have tapped this source, funding has so far remained relatively low. The Ford Foundation field traineeship program has been a great boon to us all, and the Wenner Gren Foundation has been a staunch friend. Public Law 480 funds, essentially available only for Egypt and Israel in regard to our area, have had relatively less positive effect on a fully problem-oriented chronological spectrum of activities, although significant additions to archeological knowledge have resulted from their use—especially in the prehistoric range. In Egypt, these funds have been primarily used for salvage. In Israel, these funds, coupled with amateur enthusiasm for digging in the Holy Land, have supported several large field schools.

It is on the side of long scholarly interest in this area (no matter how quaint some aspects of this interest may be) that Near Eastern archeology offers the most upon which to build positively. It was in Southwestern Asia that the very nature of the great layered mounds presented to Heinrich Schliemann a demonstration of the already known geological principle of stratigraphy, with successive inventories of artifacts as "type fossils." (That the stratification of such mounds does not always have layer-cake regularity and horizontality had to be learned later—the hard way.) Egypt was, of course, to remain an exception to stratigraphic digging; its impressive above-surface monuments and its tombs tended to lead archeologists in another direction. Nonetheless, Flinders Petrie made his basic exercise in the seriational technique (his "sequence dating system") in Egypt, although his visualization of the great value of potsherds as time and space indicators followed earlier work done at Tell el-Hesi in Palestine. There has been an early (if intermittent) attention to environmental studies; some overly generous students and colleagues claim I "pioneered" these studies, but these colleagues are poorly instructed. They should see the 19 magnificent volumes of the *Description de l'Egypte... publié par les ordres de Sa Majesté l'empereur Napoléon le Grand* (1809–1828) or examine the names and competences represented in Raphael Pumpelly's *Explorations in Turkestan* (the Anau report, 1908). The attraction which the Near East exerted on the west tended to make archeological observers of almost every foreign traveler, commercial agent, consul, missionary, railroad construction engineer, and map-maker—it is undoubtedly no accident that German expeditions came to work on choice sites strung along the route taken by surveyors for the planned Berlin-Baghdad railway. In fact, modern archeological surveyors have much earlier aids as well. Here speaks Assurnasirpal (ca. 800 B.C.):

> To the city of Hazazi, belonging to Lubarna [king] of the land of Hattina, I drew nigh. Gold, garments (of wool), linen garments I received. I passed on, I crossed the Aprê river and spent the night. From the Aprê I departed: to Kunulua, the royal city of Lubarna of Hattina I drew nigh. Before my terrible weapons and my furious battle array he became frightened... [after a long list of his rip-offs] ... I had mercy on him.[10]

Let this serve also as a reminder of that far longer range of written records (or ethnohistorical sources) than are available anywhere else in the world to complement the archeologist's task, whether he chooses to make this task historical or generalizing.

Perhaps partly for reasons of political prestige but certainly because of persistent scholarly interest, there have been some very long-range archeological involvements in the Near East. For example, the French have worked on or near Susa since 1897 and the Germans at Warka since 1912. J. H. Breasted had similar dreams for his Oriental Institute but the dreams faded considerably during the Great Depression. Such long involvements ideally provide continuity of scholarly effort, a splendid base for training young professionals, and the milieu for developing that combination of know-how, contacts, and temperament that is demanded for successful work in the host countries of the Near East. Finally, on the plus side, we might again note the growth of a corps of competent local professionals. This is especially heartening since it is madness to believe that foreigners could ever do the whole job. This underlines the high importance of the trend toward joint foreign-local field efforts (and suggests one reason for a badly felt need for the fellowship support to extend study opportunities abroad to the best local student trainees).

In conclusion, need we be concerned with the future of Near Eastern archeology? My answer would be an emphatic yes because the stakes—in terms of an increase in knowledge of a very important aspect of cultural evolution, both in a regionally historic and a generalizing sense—are very high indeed. At the same time, given the sociopolitical realities of the region, I would not think it moral for us to solicit students with promises of either old style fieldwork in romantic places or with opportunities to attempt field procedures so new that they arouse suspicions that more than archeology is at issue. My advice to students who seek me out is that while the stakes are very high, the betting odds on a field career are not guaranteed.

I would not, however, completely discourage students who yearn for the field and feel that familiar attraction of the Near East *if* they have the patient and tactful temperament demanded for successful joint field efforts. I fear that the opportunities for completely independent foreign field-programs will become fewer and fewer. Thus I am back on the theme that joint foreign and local field ventures, with heavy cooperative overtones in training (such as digging procedures, processing, and interpretation of data), are our best chance for increasing field-acquired evidence. It is completely unrealistic, in view of the prevailing mood of xenophobia and the vast amount of fieldwork yet to be done, that we foreigners even imagine that we can do the job alone (supposing we should, which I myself do not believe). But even our offers of cooperation in joint field programs may eventually be declined. An official of one of the American Near East colleges told me recently that because—for more than 100 years—they were successful in instilling the principles of rational independent thought in successive generations of students, the colleges now face the whirlwind of change and desire for local autonomy. The official was not completely sorry, of course; in a wry way the goal has been achieved. Even so, joint archeological ventures may be our only means of direct field dividends now, but they also serve as our hedge for the future in helping to enlarge the corps of competent local professionals.

An alternative route to the expansion of knowledge concerning the course of cultural evolution in the Near East—historical, generalizing, or both—would involve a turning away from fieldwork to the intensive study of already acquired materials (even if some such studies had to be done on materials in national museums abroad). I think not only of laboratory procedures, of course, but also of means whereby dialogue with our colleagues—especially historians and philologists, who control materials beyond our competences—could be increased. We Near Eastern archeologists have tended to remain primarily field-bound individualists simply to get ourselves beyond the phase of pure exploration to a level of time-space systematics. One consequence is that we suffer the blights of priority of site-discovery (suppose Çayönü or Mureybat had been the first early village site found instead of Jarmo). The vagaries of the record for space and time determinations (even with radiocarbon dating) bug us. I suggest that there is much we can do without excavation for some years; that we are not all bound to be excavators, and that Gordon Childe built a most useful career essentially without excavation. For example, we could respond to Colin Renfrew's interesting renewal of "La Mirage Orientale" theory without more digging.

I do not, however, imagine we can easily dissuade aspiring young archeologists from the fascination of digging. Let them, then, begin by learning the digger's craft in other regions, be fully prepared to tailor their procedures to the realities of the Near Eastern situation if digging opportunities do happily arise and, above all, learn all they can of the known history of the region from its remarkable bulk of source materials.

NOTES

1. I have often wondered whether this idiom itself is a fair part of our difficulty. Having developed an idiom and vocabulary of their own, the "new" archeologists obviously do not find the same usages in the writings of older archeologists. Hence, to the extent that older writings (whether generalizing, historical, or descriptive) are indeed consulted, there is an understandable lack of ease in communication. We "old" archeologists have the same difficulty in reverse. To the degree that we grit our teeth and attempt to translate many of the new writings, we often end with the exasperating conclusion that essentially the same ideas had been expressed long ago but in an earlier idiom. It now ruefully occurs to me how exasperating the idiom of my generation may well have been to the Frankforts and the Petries, for example.

    Charles Redman reminds me that, for example, an expressed concern with process is hardly new, and that I went on record in this matter almost 20 years ago, although it was another then graduate student, Robert McC. Adams, who prodded me to it. In 1953, I prepared the manuscript for the introduction for a new general entry, "Archaeology," in the *Encyclopaedia Britannica* (this new entry was first printed in 1956). Under a subheading "The Great Problems Approached by Archaeology," I had originally drafted five foci of historical problems, but Adams insisted that an additional general focus of problem might best be added. What we arrived at was:

Given the enormous time depth with which only archaeology is prepared to deal, what can we learn of the changing relation between man, society and culture on the one hand and environment on the other; what of the generalized cultural processes (diffusion, invention, acceptance, rejection, etc.) which, because of this time factor, can be examined in no other way? For the related set of problems within this general heading, it would not matter whether civilization proper ultimately had been achieved or not.

I only encountered the word "nomothetic" much later, and I still do not find it in *Webster's Seventh New Collegiate* (1967) or in *The American Heritage* (1969) dictionaries!

2. A general bibliography of the "new" archeology appears in Patty Jo Watson, Steven A. LeBlanc, and Charles L. Redman, *Explanation in Archeology: An Explicitly Scientific Approach*, Columbia University Press, New York, 1971. The term "new archeology" probably stems from an article by Joseph R. Caldwell, "The New American Archeology," *Science*, 129:303–307 (1959). There is interesting comment (by himself and others) on Bruce G. Trigger's historically oriented position in *Antiquity*, 45:130–134 (Tuggle 1971), while Glynn Isaac's measured assessment of the "new" archeology's position in prehistory appears in the same issue (pp. 123–129) and there is a thoughtful selection of reviews on David L. Clarke's book, *Analytical Archaeology* in the *Norwegian Archaeological Review*, 3: 4–34 (1970). Any fair appraisal of the position of the humanists must also include consideration of M. L. Finley's "Archaeology and History," *Daedalus*, 100:168–186 (1971).

3. In Robert J. Braidwood and Gordon R. Willey, "Conclusions and Afterthoughts," p. 355, in *id., Courses Toward Urban Life*, Viking Fund Publications in Anthropology, 32, Aldine, Chicago (1962). Sanders' earlier notion of "regional symbiosis" in Mesoamerica was suggested as being a useful concept for the Near East as well.

4. Robert McC. Adams, "Archeological Research Strategies: Past and Present," *Science*, 160:1187–1192 (1968). The present essay owes much to this thoughtful paper, also to the same author's "Trend and Tradition in Near Eastern Archaeology," *Proc. Am. Phil. Soc.*, 110:105–110 (1966).

5. A. Leo Oppenheim, "Assyriology—Why and How?" *Current Anthropology*, 1:409–423 (1960).

6. Glyn E. Daniel, *A Hundred Years of Archaeology*, Duckworth, London (1950) is generally useful, but Seton Lloyd's *Foundations in the Dust*, Oxford, London, 1947, and Svend A. Pallis, *The Antiquity of Iraq*, Munksgaard, Copenhagen, 1956, do more complete justice to the history of archeology in the greater Mesopotamian regions. John A. Wilson, *Signs and Wonders Upon Pharaoh*, University of Chicago Press, Chicago, 1964, covers Egyptian archeological history with knowledgeable affection, while various authors in James A. Sanders, ed., *Near Eastern Archaeology in the Twentieth Century* (Essays in Honor of Nelson Glueck), Doubleday, New York, 1970, and John A. Wilson, "A Century of Near Eastern Archeology and the Future" in William Ward, ed., The Role of the Phoenicians in the Interaction of Mediterranean *Civilizations*, American University Centennial Pub., Beirut, Lebanon, 1968, pp. 113–122, deal primarily with the Syro-Palestinian area and Biblical archeology. Although it appeared after this lecture was drafted, I note also Gary A. Wright, "Origins of Food Production in Southwestern Asia: A Survey of Ideas," *Current Anthropology* 12:447–477 (1971). Wright's treatment seems to me somewhat uneven and incomplete.

7. The complete text of the letter, to one of Layard's friends, from the Turkish judge Imam Ali Zade, is given on pages 565–566 of Austen H. Layard, *Discoveries Among the Ruins of Nineveh and Babylon...*, Harper & Brothers, New York, 1853.

8. Robert J. Braidwood, Halet Çambel, Charles L. Redman, and Patty Jo Watson, "Beginnings of Village-Farming Communities in Southeastern Turkey," *Proc. Nat. Acad. Sc. U.S.A.*, 68:1236–1240 (1971).

9. Thorkild Jacobsen and Robert M. Adams, "Salt and Silt in Ancient Mesopotamian Agriculture," *Science*, 128:1251–1258 (1958); Robert Adams, "Agriculture and Urban Life in Early Southwestern Iran," *Science*, 136:109–122 (1962), also *Land Behind Baghdad*, University of Chicago Press, Chicago, 1965.

10. See page 305 of James H. Breasted, *The Oriental Institute* (University of Chicago Survey, Vol. 12), University of Chicago Press, Chicago, 1933. We know the locations of Hattina (province of Hatay), of Hazazi (modern Azaz) and of the Aprê (modern Afrin) River. There are, however, two excavated candidates for Kunulua and perhaps one unexcavated one. How far did Assurnasirpal and his "furious battle array" go after spending the night and does he mean he reached Kunulua after only one day's march or after several?

4. ARCHEOLOGY WITH A CAPITAL "S"

KENT V. FLANNERY

Museum of Anthropology
University of Michigan
Ann Arbor, Michigan

I shall discuss the direction that archeology will take in the future. But as David Clarke (1968) has argued in *Analytical Archaeology*, it is difficult to understand any system without knowing its history and its trajectory. Other chapters in this volume (see Rouse and Braidwood) are concerned with American archeology's history and trajectory. However, I shall comment on the most recent history of the archeological system; we might be fooled by its direction unless we take a cold, hard look at the events of the last four or five years. Other chapters have commented on the directions archeology *ought* to take (see Fritz, Ford, Trigger, and Watson)—but things do not always go the way we would like them to. Let us examine some of the ways archeology has been going, and may *continue* to go, whether we like it or not.

Four years ago in *Scientific American* (Flannery 1967), I used Gordon R. Willey's *Introduction to American Archaeology* (Willey 1966) as a background for viewing what seemed to be the battle lines of New World prehistory. My description of the debate between archeologists interested mainly in "culture history" and those interested mainly in "cultural process" drew considerable fire. One colleague found my proposed methodology for the study of process to

47

be "ferocious dogmatism." Another rejected my dichotomy since it did not provide for eclectic men like himself, who "work with ideas drawn from anywhere in the wide intellectual world." Still another ventured that the debate between history and process was simply one of "different cognitive styles." If that is the case, the "process" cognitive style has won over a lot of adherents in the last four years. Now Patty Jo Watson, Steven LeBlanc, and Charles Redman have produced a new book devoted entirely to the rationale behind the study of prehistoric cultural process, which they call "explicitly scientific archaeology" (Watson, LeBlanc, and Redman 1971). This is the first book of its kind since Walter W. Taylor's *A Study of Archeology* (1948).

Because of this expanded interest in "processual archeology," I am supposed to be pleased with the way archeology has developed over the four years since my review of Willey. On the contrary, I feel somewhat like the male black widow spider who, having broken down the female black widow's resistance with great struggle and persuasion, suddenly realizes that his first date is not going to be all it was cracked up to be.

Briefly, I shall comment, here, on five interesting phenomena of the four years since my review and see if, by focusing on them, I can predict what will happen in the next four years. Some of these developments are discussed in earlier chapters of this volume (see Rouse and Braidwood). These phenomena trace the rocky path traveled by processual archeology since Lewis R. Binford gave it national exposure early in the 1960s. The process approach, sometimes pretentiously referred to as "the new archeology" and hailed in some quarters as a "theoretical revolution," has disenchanted many potential adherents because of the "hard sell" attitude of some of its practitioners. As Watson, LeBlanc, and Redman (1971) make clear, there has even been a great deal of confusion about what the new archeology is and a very inflated evaluation of what it has accomplished.

1. The first phenomenon, obviously, is the fact that the process approach has ridden a great crest of popularity, with all the dimensions of a fad. As Mark P. Leone (1971) stated in a recent review, "If anyone thinks a revolution did occur, these same must now think the revolution is over. Suddenly the new archeology is everybody's archeology. The rhetorical scene is quiet." But if, as it often seems, process archeology is

really the biggest thing since hula hoops, it is perhaps only because some people thought it would be even easier to operate.

2. But for every action there is an equal and opposite reaction. And so there has been a considerable "backlash" against the new archeology—and here is where we were fooled, because the backlash did not come from the old guard, who have been rather benevolent about the whole thing, but from two unexpected quarters. The first is a large group of young archeologists, many still in their twenties, who are harshly critical of process studies and militantly committed to purely inductive analyses of "real" data from traditionally conducted excavations; this group has been dubbed "the young fogeys" by one processual archeologist. The second group includes some of the original proponents of the new archeology—members of the first archeological generation ever to walk on water—who, once they had achieved some degree of national prominence (or tenure), forgot they had ever espoused processual studies and hastened to join the old guard on the pretext of "bridging the generation gap." In the idiom of the day, these are referred to simply as "cop-outs," and they include some of the very people whose earlier studies are frequently cited as good examples of process archeology.

3. Several prominent senior archeologists, drawing on the experience of their many years in the field, have presented "overviews" of the current archeological scene in which they attempt to reconcile all of the disparate opinions. They caution the new archeologists that their "general laws" must be "based on facts." Almost to a man, these senior archeologists argue that "processual archeology" cannot be carried out until *after* inductive archeology and culture history have been done; they do not view deductive models as *replacing* traditional analysis but, instead, as an additional step that is tacked on at the end. Watson, LeBlanc, and Redman (1971) counter this argument by pointing out that "inductive generalizations, that is, hypotheses inductively generated, give us certainty only about those cases of which we are already sure." (To which I add: the way data are collected to answer inductive questions of culture history may make it impossible to do processual studies later!)

4. Here is the fourth and, in some ways, the saddest point. In the last four or five years, considerable really bad "new archeology" has been published in journals or presented at meetings. Indeed, some pretentious statements have been made about archeological studies that are abominable by any criteria, not only the criteria of the processual archeologist. These bad examples only discourage potential students and add fuel to the arguments of the new archeology's critics, some of whom justifiably label it "the new alchemy." Unfortunately, I predict that this phenomenon will probably continue.

5. Finally, the fifth phenomenon—least mentioned, and yet perhaps the most theoretically significant—is that a schism was present in "process archeology" almost as soon as it appeared. Admittedly, it is a schism based not so much on ultimate goals—such as the discovery of order in the universe —as on the methodology for arriving at those goals. Nonetheless, it is significant that in the past 10 years there have developed at least two different approaches to the new archeology, which for convenience I will nickname the "law-and-order" and "Serutan" (or "Ex-Lax") approaches.

The law-and-order archeologists receive their nickname from the fact that they not only believe that Carl Hempel rose from the dead on the third day and ascended to heaven—where he sits at the right hand of Binford—but, to use their own words, "have made the formulation and testing of laws (their) goal." Thus they view the archeologist's major responsibility as developing the body of general laws necessary for a covering-law explanation. Using what Watson, LeBlanc, and Redman (1971) refer to as "if A, then B" assertions, the law-and-order archeologists attempt to discover the causes of cultural phenomena by accepting or rejecting hypotheses on the basis of statistical correlation. They share with the "Serutan" archeologists an interest in the use of such tests as chi-square, Pearson's r, and Fisher's exact test for showing relationships between variables or phenomena; they differ from the "Serutan" archeologists in that they frequently consider high statistical correlations to indicate that a general law has been demonstrated. Many of their procedures are patterned after the physical sciences, and their ultimate goal is to discover laws of human behavior that are analogous to the laws of thermodynamics. To this paradigm they have added an ethic:

archeology "must be made relevant to the problems of today's world."

This "Hempelian" approach has produced elegant results—at its best, as exemplified in the settlement pattern studies of U.C.L.A.'s Fred T. Plog (1968a) for example. At its worst, this approach has produced some of the worst archeology on record. In some cases, the statistics used have been so much more powerful than the raw data deserved, that one feels he is watching a grenade launcher being turned on a field mouse. In other cases, it seems that in order to discover a "natural law" in the allotted six weeks of his field season, the investigator was forced to attack a problem of the utmost trivia; this has produced a series of low-level generalizations that some critics have called "Mickey Mouse laws." These laws have even emerged from the lips of colleagues whom I regard as sane, serious, and competent men. For example, at a genuinely exciting seminar on the Bushmen I learned that "the size of a Bushman site is directly proportional to the number of houses on it." From a Southwestern colleague, I learned last year that "as the population of a site increases, the number of storage pits will go up." I am afraid that these "laws" will always elicit from me the response, "Leapin' lizards, Mr. Science!" (Or as my colleague, Robert Whallon, once said after reading one of these undeniable truths, "If this is the 'new archeology,' show me how to get back to the Renaissance.")

The "Serutan" archeologists pursue a systems-theory framework and derive their nickname from an inordinate interest in the "natural regulation" of systems. For them it seems that the law-and-order archeologists' version of Hempel—or at least, the way they apply it— is precisely the physical-science approach that von Bertalanffy rejected in the 1920s as being inadequate in dealing with biological phenomena. In fact, von Bertalanffy originally developed systems theories because the laws of physics and chemistry had failed to adequately describe or explain life processes and living systems, under which heading prehistoric populations must certainly fall. To be sure, the "Serutan" archeologists are interested in regularities and their explanation—but they have serious reservations about whether "laws" can be adequately tested by the statistical procedures used by their law-and-order colleagues. Watson, LeBlanc, and Redman point out, "some 'if A then B' assertions express deterministic or causal connections, while others reflect only contingent or accidental relations." Thus, high statistical correlations may reveal nothing whatsoever about causality. Indeed, Jay Forrester (1969) of M.I.T. has recently argued that when one is dealing with complex systems (which many prehistoric populations occupied), almost all phenomena that show a high correlation in time and space are likely to be *coincident symptoms* instead of cause and effect; this is because the ultimate causes for observed phenomena lie far back in time or in such a remote part of the system that they cannot be discovered by Fisher's exact test. Instead, these causes must be sought by simulation of long-term processes, as Forrester does in his urban studies. Only through this simulation can one experimentally alter variables in complex systems to see what their "causal" effects will be on later and distant parts of the system. To the "Serutan" archeologists, much of what their law-and-order colleagues do resembles the famous study of school children where shoe size showed a high positive correlation with vocabulary size. The correlation was real—since both variables were dependent on age—but did not reveal causality by any stretch of the imagination.

"Serutan" archeologists are not for chaos and against law. They recognize the existence of universal or nearly universal principles that govern a system's operation (principles such as positive and negative feedback, and the increase of information-processing institutions with systems of a higher order of complexity). But these archeologists are skeptical about the existence of an undiscovered set of "covering laws" that are specific to human behavior. Hence they are less concerned with a search for "laws of human behavior" than with a search for the ways human populations (in their own way) do the things that other living systems do. They tend to avoid "if A, then B" assertions because their systems orientation makes them skeptical of linear causality; they prefer feedback models in which causality is multivariate and mutual. In terms of scientific ethic, these archeologists are not particularly preoccupied with "making archeology relevant" because they feel we are still in a poor position to know what will be "relevant" in the year 2000. They are unconvinced that the new archeology will clean up our slums although, admittedly, it keeps a lot of young archeologists off the streets. However, to work only on things that seem relevant in 1971 might bypass useful experiments whose relevance is unrecognized at present.

Finally, the "Serutan" archeologists have earned as much well-deserved criticism as have their law-and-order colleagues. Among other things, in their zeal to apply systems models, the "Serutan" archeologists have tried to interpret everything as an example of population "self-regulation "—from prehistoric ritual cannibalism to dental mutilation and the use of arsenic-based paints.

Up to 1971, therefore, we have had at least two kinds of new archeology. One takes as its goal the definition of covering laws of human behavior, uses statistical correlations in an attempt to discover linear causality, and argues for relevance in the modern world. The other disbelieves in linear causality and specifically human covering laws, tries to discover the way human populations obey the general principles of systems by simulation instead of by correlation, and hopes that its work will be relevant in a future world. It is my prediction that the dialectic between these two approaches will continue for some years, that it will lead to some acrimonious debate, and that it may even lead to some flashes of better archeology. (Or, on the basis of my comments above, it might even give rise to a third approach, a kind of "irrelevant Renaissance archeology.")

Let me add, parenthetically, that some of my colleagues feel the two approaches are about to converge and, as evidence, they cite Fred Plog's recent attempts to combine law and order with simulation (Plog n.d.). One could, in fact, visualize a long-term simulation model (based on the principles of systems analysis) in which the linkages between variables (but not necessarily causality) were in fact determined by correlations done in the law-and-order style. I wish I could be more optimistic about such convergence, because I feel there is a good deal of mutual respect between the "Serutan" and "law-and-order" archeologists. After all, as much as the two approaches differ, and skeptical as they may be of each other's theoretical base, the two approaches are united in their efforts to make archeology explicitly scientific. While disagreeing on the nature of casuality, each respects the other for continuing this effort and for not "copping out" as soon as academic tenure had been achieved. At the root of this mutual respect is the fact that the "law-and-order" and "Serutan" archeologists are held together by a dream and a nightmare. The dream is their mutual vision of what archeology could become in the future, when it is science with a capital S. The nightmare is that the "young fogeys" will forever keep it the imprecise pseudoscience that it is today.

TWO

THE GOALS AND SCOPE
OF ARCHEOLOGY

The six chapters in this section discuss what some archeologists consider to be potentially realizable goals and why these goals should be pursued. Three different aspects of this problem are dealt with. In their chapters John M. Fritz and Richard I. Ford discuss the possible relevance and applicability of archeological research. Bruce G. Trigger and Patty Jo Watson's chapters deal with appropriate aims and approaches to research. And, Mark P. Leone and Bert Salwen discuss the potential scope of archeology expanded to include material not previously investigated. These contributions reflect a spectrum of ideas on the current intellectual foundations of archeology and what they should become.

John M. Fritz's article suggests that there is widespread dissatisfaction within the profession of archeology and that many within the field (and outside) consider it a technique that is important only to its own practitioners. Fritz claims that this is not true and outlines archeology's relationships and relevance to other disciplines and to the general public. He suggests that archeology is relevant to other disciplines, including branches of anthropology, when it yields data on questions of direct interest to them. It is also relevant to the

55

public in a number of important ways. In addition to the public's interest in the objects discovered and the origins of civilizations, archeologists have a special key to unlock the past. It is also possible that archeology can benefit man through the pursuit of scientific knowledge toward a better understanding of human behavior.

Richard I. Ford deals with the question of whether the results of archeology are actually applicable to contemporary problems. The application of the early archeological results toward understanding the antiquity and evolution of man is clear. Some of the recent uses of archeological knowledge involve environmental manipulation and land utilization. Archeology has been used by many groups in explicit and implicit ways to foster nationalism and general political goals. It accomplishes this through the formation of national images and tracing the origins of ethnic groups. The great public interest in archeologists' findings has also stimulated a large market for the illicit excavation and smuggling of archeological relics. The loss of these archeological treasures and their association with nationalistic feelings has caused many countries to take strong measures against legal and illegal excavations.

Bruce G. Trigger's article discusses the appropriate goals and approaches to be pursued by archeologists. His main concern is with archeologists' misunderstanding of the nature of historical inquiry. Trigger suggests that particular and general goals are integral elements of modern historical inquiry and that they should be incorporated into archeological research. He asserts that the most important goal of archeologists is the explanation of past events. Here the archeologist's contribution is unique and most realistically accomplished.

Patty Jo Watson deals with the debate over the appropriate goals and methods for archeological research. She attempts to determine whether there is a real difference between the processually oriented (or social scientific) approach and the approach of its most outspoken critics. Watson then defines nomothetic or processual archeology. After a review of scientific method, she pinpoints the two characteristics of the new archeology: (1) the emphasis on the completeness of the archeological record and the potential for learning a great deal about extinct cultures, and (2) the concern about the explicit use of the logic of science. She asserts that within this framework:

Archeological theory . . . consists of assumptions and lawlike generalizations about the physical aspects of archeological sites and the debris in, on, and about them left by past human groups, plus assumptions and generalizations about the relationships of that debris to the activities of those groups (p. 000).

She concludes her chapter with a consideration of whether archeologists can work together in spite of their theoretical schism. If limitations of funding and of other resources do not bring the different groups of archeologists into direct conflict, the diverse approaches to the archeological past can productively reinforce each other.

Mark P. Leone's chapter reviews the various goals and rationales that archeologists have for their own work. He analyzes the influences and forces that underlay popular support for archeology. Leone suggests that the American public receives an unrecognized product from archeology—an empirical substantiation of the national mythology. This takes two forms: the reconstruction and interpretation of historic and prehistoric sites (such as Williamsburg and Mesa Verde), and films made for television using archeology as a format for larger issues. These displays of the past require reinterpretation, most of which is derived from assumptions in our culture that use archeology as a substantiating medium.

Pointing out that archeologists are geared to studying technology, and that in American society technology is both problematic and poorly understood, Leone suggests that archeologists begin to examine the relationship between material culture and other cultural subsystems. Using nineteenth century Mormon techniques of town planning and fence construction, he shows how Mormons consciously manipulated space to facilitate ecological, social, and religious goals. It is then suggested that this kind of study of material culture be added to the archeological repertoire.

Bert Salwen's article discusses the conduct of archeology within the locus of an urban metropolis. He draws the important distinction between archeology *in* the city, which people are already practicing, and archeology *of* the city, which he recommends. In order to pursue this avenue of research, two fundamental assumptions about the scope of archeology must be reexamined. The temporal boundary of subjects that merit study must be extended to include anything occurring before the present. Any completed behavior can be studied by its remains. Moreover, one must accept the fact that all evidence of value to archeology is not necessarily buried. The spatial arrangement of remains of recent behavior can be used in archeological interpretations. Salwen suggests several projects that would help in training students, in testing archeological laws of distributions and change, and that would themselves be of interest because of their insights into the relationships between these spatial and technological patterns and the types of behavior that produced them.

The different views expressed in the articles in this section substantiate the turbulent period of evaluation that archeology is experiencing. There is concern and self-awareness about what one does and what one should be doing. In a period when disciplines are being asked to justify their existence, one must consider what makes archeology worthwhile. The goals appropriate for archeology and the methods that must be used to accomplish these goals are still matters of active debate. The articles in this section show a trend toward convergence on certain issues. Whatever the outcome of specific controversies, the discipline of archeology will be better off for having gone through this reexamination period.

Concurrent with the evaluation of goals and methods, there has been a broadening of the scope of materials that many archeologists feel should be studied. Initially, this involved sites of the historic time range, but now includes any remains of behavior that will yield insights into cultural patterning and cultural change.

5. RELEVANCE, ARCHEOLOGY, AND SUBSISTENCE THEORY

JOHN M. FRITZ

Anthropology Board of Studies
University of California
Santa Cruz, California

I believe that this volume reflects a long-standing dissatisfaction with archeology felt by many, both outside and inside the discipline. This dissatisfaction needs little documentation. One needs simply to recall statements made by Steward and Setzler (1938), Kluckhohn (1940), and Taylor (1948) and, more recently, by Spaulding (1953), Willey and Phillips (1958), Binford (1962), Fritz and Plog (1970), and Martin (1971). (For an explication of this dissatisfaction, see Binford 1968a.) The attitude of many thoughtful men outside the field may well be reflected in the view attributed to one college president that archeology was best taught in vocational training schools (Martin 1971:1). The view that archeology is primarily or "merely" a technique finds echoes in the discipline as well (Taylor 1948:42 and Spaulding 1968:38).

This dissatisfaction, of course, does not necessarily include dissatisfaction with the relevance of archeology. A perusal of pertinent literature disclosed few explicit references to the term "relevance." In a paper I wrote with Fred Plog, we suggest that an archeologist is obliged to justify the explanation which he chooses to test as being valuable uses of research time. In the long run, this obligation can be met only by taking as explanations to be tested problems which are relevant not only to archaeologists but to social science as a whole. Archaeologists claim to have a set of data which is of unique value in studying processes of long term change and development. Yet, we have rarely used data to do this. Given the freedom to choose explanations for testing, we have incurred the obligation to strive to be relevant. We suspect that unless archaeologists find ways to make their research increasingly relevant to the modern world, the modern world will find itself increasingly capable of getting along without archaeologists. [1970: 411-412].

Is this view representative of attitudes within the field? When it was first presented to professional archeologists (Plog 1968b), it struck an appreciative and approving chord in the audience. Many of the articles cited above suggest that archeology should establish a relationship with something outside itself. Thus, Spaulding (1953:590) criticizes the implicit view that "productivity is doing what makes archeologists happy." The view attacked by Spaulding has recently been stated explicity by Bayard (1969).

Many authors have suggested that a relation exists or should exist with anthropology (e.g., Taylor 1948; Thompson 1958; Binford 1962; Longacre 1964; Hill 1966; and Jennings 1968; 2-3). The oft-quoted passage from Willey and Phillips (1958:2)—"archeology is anthropology or it is nothing"—is not merely a description of institutional or academic affiliation. It expresses an additional relationship, one in which knowledge is derived from and added to anthropology more generally. Thus,

as archaeologists, with the entire span of culture history as our "laboratory," we cannot afford to keep our theoretical heads buried in the sand. We must shoulder our full share of responsibility within anthropology. Such a change could go far in advancing the field of archaeology specifically and would certainly advance the general field of anthropology. [Binford 1962: 224].

Others have implied or expressed the view that a relation should be established with social sciences or with natural—particularly evolutionary—sciences (Steward and Setzler 1938; Kluckhohn 1940; Willey and Phillips 1958:5-6; Steward 1955; Adams 1966a; Harris 1968; Spaulding 1968:38; Deetz 1970). Writing specifically with reference to archeological research, A. V. Kidder has suggested that "anthropology seeks to reconstruct the history of man, of his world, of his bodily structure, and of his mind, in order that there may be deduced from a study of the history, the basic laws which have governed in the past, and which therefore may be expected to control in the future, the destinies of the human race" [1926:2, quoted in Taylor 1948:47].

It is even possible to find attempts relating archeology to the modern world. For example, Leone has attempted to employ a hypothesis (1968b) to account for both prehistoric (1968a; 1968b) and contemporary (1968a; 1969) behavioral phenomena. Plog (1969) has, in effect, tested theories of contemporary modernization by analysis of prehistoric cultural transformations.

But if archeologists believe that archeology should be or is related to things outside itself, and if they are dissatisfied to the degree that such relationships are not established, does this mean that archeology is or should be relevant to these outside things? And if it does, what are or might be the specific natures of the relationships between these outside things and archeology? I shall deal with these questions below. I shall consider the meaning (or meanings) of the term "relevance" and the relevance between archeology and a variety of phenomena that lie outside it.

THE NATURE OF "RELEVANCE"

Before attempting to define relevant archeology it is essential to define the term, "relevance". In current usage the content of communications media—books, movies, lectures, and photographs—and even the media themselves [e.g., the television of McLuhan's Global Village (McLuhan 1964)] may be relevant. What individuals and institutions do may also be relevant or irrelevant.

Throughout this usage several constants are clear. First, as implied above, relevant means that a relationship is established between two or more phenomena. X is relevant to Y. But not all relations are relevant ones. A cloud cover is related to the rate of evaporation, for example, but we would not say that "the phenomenon—cloud cover—is relevant to evaporation." Second, the relation between the cloud cover and evaporation is one of implied causation. A cloud cover lowers the rate of evaporation. But in this and other cases, relevance is not a causal relation. Third, the relation is not reciprocal. That is, the fact that X is relevant to Y does not imply that Y is relevant to X in the same sense. Thus, a course on the history of ethnic groups in the United States might be relevant to a student from such a group but the student is not relevant to the course. Finally and most important, a relation is one in which the existence of some set of criteria for evaluating the relevance, irrelevance, or nonrelevance of something is implied. Two things may stand in relationship to one another. Without these criteria it would be impossible to know whether relevance was germane or whether the relation was relevant or irrelevant.

What are the natures of the phenomena standing in relation to one another and what are the criteria for relevant relations? Consultation of several dictionaries and reflection on current usages leads me to believe that these phenomena and criteria have changed markedly in the recent past. In *Webster's New International Dictionary* (Harris ed. 1918) relevance is defined as "bearing upon or properly applying to the case in hand; of a nature to afford evidence tending to prove or disprove the matter in issue . . . " [p.1801]. It is "applied particularly to what is said . . . [it] suggest[s] logical fitness, and . . . a *relevant* argument . . ." [p. 1611]. Here, what is relevant is a *statement*—some kind of oral or written idea or information. That to which this statement is relevant is an *issue* or *argument*. Thus, the criteria for relevance are *logical* ones. A statement is relevant to other statements in an argument if, according to the rules of logic or evidence, the first statement is linked with the others, and with them contributes to the proof or disproof of the whole argument and to the resolution of an issue. As such, the statement can be considered logically necessary for the truth of the argument.

This can be contrasted with the definition found in *Webster's New World Dictionary* (Friend and Guralnik, eds.), published in 1957. Here, relevance is defined as "bearing upon or relating to the matter in hand; pertinent; to the point; opposed to *irrelevant* . . . implies close logical relationship with, and importance to, the matter under consideration (*relevant* testimony) . . . " [p. 1228]. I suggest that the meaning has shifted in several subtle ways. First, the criteria for relevance have changed. The first definition connotes an explicit set of logical rules—such as those of symbolic logic—expressed as abstract formulas, according to which the pertinence of a particular statement can be determined. The second connotes not only this usage but also a usage that is "logical" in a more metaphorical sense (i.e., being connected or joined in some intelligible way). Thus, an idea would be relevant to a matter being examined if it were linked to other ideas having the same subject.

In addition, the criteria include an entirely new element: "importance." In the first definition there is no mention of importance. And when speaking of purely logical relations, it makes no sense to refer to importance. A statement is logically integral to an argument or it is not. Any statement is equally important in that it is necessary for the conclusion to be true. The importance of statements is not logical but *rhetorical*. An idea would be important if it had an impact on and had helped to convince an audience. If so, the desired outcome implicitly has shifted from logical truth to rhetorical effectiveness, that is, something is relevant if it convinces. This also supports the shift from logical in a narrow sense to logical, meaning "pertinence to a subject."

Second, the matter in hand has changed from an "issue" to a "consideration." Although it is true that the example—"*relevant* testimony"—employed in the latter definition implies the existence of an issue, the issue itself is not as vital. "Testimony" can provide information that (even though it is "relevant" to some matter) is not an integral part of an argument. Thus, the matter has shifted from one in which an explicit conflict exists to one in which the conflict is more implicit.

Implicity, the matter to which something is relevant has shifted not only to a "consideration" but also to the people involved in it. This follows from the criterion of rhetorical impact. Something is relevant if the audience to which it is communicated is convinced. In logic the audience is assumed to be constant, as is their response when an argument is logically correct. Judgment of relevance is made in terms of absolute standards developed in logic. In rhetoric, to decide whether something is relevant one must be concerned with the attributes of the audience. Since (as any debater knows) audiences vary in their attributes and responses, the importance of a particular idea must be judged in relation to a particular audience. If so, one can argue for the implicit relativity of criteria or, at least, the existence of several competing criteria, each held by different audiences.

Finally, there is an implied shift in the nature of that which is relevant. In logic the concern is chiefly with statements, their form, and their interrelationships but little with their content. A statement can "logically follow" even though its content is absurd. However, in rhetoric the content of statements (i.e., of ideas) is paramount and their logical forms and interrelations are relatively unimportant. It is content rather than form that has impact, particularly to audiences untutored in formal logic. In short, the latter definition implies (1) greater applicability of ideas, (2) the existence of implicitly instead of explicitly argumentive situations, (3) relation to an audience and to its particular criteria, and (4) the strength of conviction engendered in an audience.

All of these trends can be observed and more fully developed in contemporary usage. This is clear if we examine the statement "archeology is relevant." First, the statement makes no sense in relation to the first definition given above. Archeology is not a statement; it cannot be part of an argument; and its relevance cannot be judged in terms of formal logical criteria. In current usage, that to which archeology is relevant is audiences (or people). People ask archeology to be relevant, and they determine whether or not it is in terms of their particular and unique criteria.

That in archeology which is relevant to people is less obvious. It certainly includes knowledge. To say that the subject—the prehistory of North America—is relevant to some individual or group can only refer to the knowledge that archeologists have about the subject. Otherwise, some mystical or intuitive relation is implied. Actions, particularly when they themselves possess content, may also be relevant. One might say that archeological field methods are relevant in somewhat the same sense as the Living Theater. That is, the way that something is done may provide one kind of content that can be evaluated independently of another content.

Both knowledge and actions in these senses are not explicitly parts of conflicts or arguments. People are often surprised to learn that knowledge in a field like archeology is not a set of facts but a set of assertions and arguments, some (but not all) of which are related to things empirically observed. In the same sense, to be relevant does not imply "to be in dispute" or "at issue." Ethnic studies may be relevant and in dispute, but they are not in dispute *because* they are relevant.

The criteria for relevance in current usage are somewhat ambiguous. At their least sublimated, they appear to include visceral pleasure. Archeology is relevant because it is "interesting" or "fun". At another level, they include closeness or relation to one's past and present experience and self-awareness. Archeology would be relevant to the degree it touched on or was rooted in someone's experience and awareness. Thus, at this level, the prehistory of North

America might be very relevant to a North American Indian but irrelevant to an American black.

At another level the criteria include "betterment" or "improvement." This becomes apparent if one considers the strength of feeling against irrelevant things. In cases where something is uninteresting and unrelated to someone's experience *and* he is compelled to become involved with it, resentment is to be expected. But what if he is not compelled? Why not ignore the irrelevant? He may be resentful because it competes for and uses resources that otherwise might be put to relevant uses, and thus irrelevant things work a positive harm. Or it may simply do neither harm nor good where the feeling exists that it *should* do good. Relevant things not only are linked to the past and present conditions of individuals and groups but also may change their present state in a desirable direction by making it more intelligible, tolerable, or significant or by providing intellectual or other "tools" required to effect such changes. In this context it is useful to consider the etymology of the word "relevance." According to *Webster's* (Harris 1918:1801), it is derived from the Latin word meaning "raising" or "lifting up." In the first definition above, the statements raise an argument in the sense of supporting it. In current usage, the particular knowledge may raise people by being uplifting. Thus, it is possible to sympathize with those who believe archeology to be irrelevant. They are manifesting the Calvinistic precept with which many of us have been imbued: that what is, should be useful, and that it is a profligate waste of time and resources to do the useless and irrelevant.

In short, the criteria for relevance in contemporary usage include interest, relation to personally defined needs and experience, and psychological and perhaps physical betterment.

RELEVANT ARCHEOLOGY

How is archeology relevant? In what ways does it (if it does) satisfy the above criteria? Because these criteria were quite general, it is necessary to specify them so that they can be applied directly to archeology. But this leads us back to the problem "relevant to whom"? I assume that there is no universal standard against which the relevance of archeology can be evaluated. This, of course, does not imply that there is no such thing as relevance or that it cannot be defined. Instead, it implies that a variety of evaluative systems exist in terms under which the relevance of archeology can be determined. I will consider each of several such systems held by members of groups existing in the contemporary ideological environment of archeology. They are: professional archeology itself, professional anthropology, other academic disciplines and professional fields, and the common man.

Relevance to Archeology

How can archeology be relevant to itself? It can if it is not one but several things, each of which may be relevant. First, archeology is a group and an audience, men and women who consider themselves archeologists. Second, archeology is a discipline and process, a system of men, material, and ideas acting and interacting. Third, it is a body of knowledge that is held by archeologists and perhaps by others. Fourth, it is knowledge held by archeologists (and others) and applied to or integrated with other knowledge. In the analysis that follows I shall attempt to deal with only one kind of archeological knowledge: past subsistence systems. This is knowledge almost all archeologists employ or develop at one time or another and is a knowledge of the past that some feel to be most inherently credible (e.g., Hawkes 1954).

The *doing* of archeology and archeological knowledge are relevant to archeologists. Both are interesting, related to experience and needs, and contribute to our psychological and physical (economic) betterment. Our criteria are undoubtedly varied and crosscutting. For some people, opportunities to travel, to work out of doors, and to deal physically with physical things may make archeology relevant. For others, the organization and direction necessary for field and laboratory work—confronting and solving the physical, social, and psychological problems that normally arise in such work—may be important. The more abstract activities of classification, of discovering explanations for the archeological record, of attempting to confirm them, and of synthesizing them or relating them to knowledge of other fields may be most relevant for still others. The communication of archeological knowledge in books, articles, or teaching may also be relevant. These are highly personal criteria and their "mix" in various archeologists is varied. Yet in our own mythology we acknowledge the presence of central tendencies. There are groups of archeologists who prefer field work, being in a laboratory, dealing with the results of such work or, a very few, doing "meta-archeology."

Almost all the above criteria for relevance involve solving various kinds of puzzles: technical, organizational, and abstract. We create our own problems, solve them, and create new ones. Puzzle solving of these general kinds could be done in a variety of fields; for example, the army. But this lacks the unique content that makes archeology relevant to archeologists. One might suggest that archeologists deal with material objects. Indeed, some have defined archeology as the analysis of material objects (Clarke 1968). But since engineers also deal with material objects, this definition is not specific enough. Do archeologists deal with material objects produced in the past? Yes, but this does not distinguish us from paleontologists. Archeologists uniquely deal with material objects produced by other men in the past.

But even these criteria are not specific enough. Not all possible technical and abstract activities dealing with past artifacts are relevant to all archeologists. Not all archeologists value dynamite, bulldozers, or IBM cards. That is, for some, these objects are neither interesting, related to their experience, satisfying, nor of benefit to them as archeologists. Taking one narrowly defined part of archeological activity and problem solving, we can ask: What is the relevance of subsistence theory in archeology? I suggest that this knowledge (and others like it) has at least six kinds of relevance. First, it contributes to the justification for *doing* archeology. We do not value the excavation of artifacts for its own sake. Neither do we value the simple perception of these objects. We do attach a high positive value to the action of relating them to something else, that is, minimally to past human behavior in the broadest sense. Because we believe that many characteristics of the archeological record are potentially relatable to the operation of past subsistence systems (and we are quite able to do so in specific instances), subsistence theory facilitates our doing of valued archeology. Insofar as the performance of valued activities in archeology is a justification for accomplishing other activities (e.g., field work), subsistence theory facilitates this justification.

Second, this theory enables us to explain the archeological record. As has frequently been suggested (e.g., Spaulding 1960; Binford and Binford 1968:1–3), this is a major—some would say the primary—goal of archeology. Subsistence theory enables us to explain attributes of the archeological record by defining conditions that produced material phenomena in the past and that may have been transformed into the attributes observed in the present. The existence of fresh fish procurement might be cited to explain the occurrence of fish scales and fish hooks in a site, for example.

Third, subsistence theory enables us to know the past in particular instances. This is the reverse of explanation of the archeological record. Knowing the past is also a commonly expressed goal of archeology and includes the attempt to recover past "lifeways" (Binford 1968a; Freeman 1968). Subsistence theory, with other theories, enables us to use attributes of the archeological record as indicators of the operation of past subsistence systems. Thus, we may employ certain types of artifacts as indicators of characteristics of past seed processing or animal procurement.

Fourth, subsistence theory enables us to explain the past. This is not frequently an expressed goal in archeology although it is becoming so (Flannery 1967; Watson, LeBlanc, and Redman 1971). Explanation commonly includes the citation of some past phenomenon that was sufficient (or necessary and sufficient) to produce a subsequent past phenomena (Hempel and Oppenheim 1948; Fritz and Plog 1970; Watson, LeBlanc, and Redman 1971). Thus, an explanation of beans in the diet of prehistoric inhabitants of the Southwest might include reference to the nutritional requirements of the population and to the nutritional characteristics of beans and other components of their diet (Ford 1968).

Fifth, subsistence theory may be relevant because it enables us to explain our explanations, that is, to state why past subsistence phenomena were related in the ways we believe they are. Thus, it is one thing to suggest that hunting in a particular past subsistence system is explicable in part by the particular nutritional requirements of population. It is quite another to explain why this relation is true in such cases, that is, why it is a more general relation of which this is a particular instance.

In short, because these goals are valuable to us, that which helps us to accomplish them is very relevant. Subsistence theory is interesting, needed, and beneficial as it justifies and facilitates our work. And it is relevant not only in its use but also as its *development* becomes a valued goal in archeology. This is the tendency when we explain our explanations. It is a slight but significant shift in motivation to explore subsistence theory to explain or make intelligible the relation between past human and other events in a particular case and to do so for theoretical explication itself. This need not imply a loss of concern for the real world of the archeological record or for past human behavior. That would be foolhardy. However, it does imply a shift in the use of the archeological record to confirm hypotheses developed from subsistence theory. This tendency can be seen in the development of theory concerning the domestication of plants and animals, for instance (Braidwood 1960; Binford 1968b; Flannery 1969). In this case, then, subsistence theory is not relevant because it aids us in doing something else but because it is intrinsically valuable.

Relevance of Archeology to Anthropology

How is archeology relevant to other branches of anthropology? Archeology as a process may be relevant to other anthropologists if they consider it interesting or related to personal experience and needs. At this level, however, other anthropologists do not differ from other nonarcheologists. If the doing of archeology contributes to the achievement of the desired goals of other branches, it may be relevant. Archeology is relevant to evolutionary biological anthropology because its techniques recover fossil hominids and other data that may indicate the relation of biological and behavioral characteristics. To those anthropologists concerned with the present or recent past, archeological techniques are not relevant. They might even be irrelevant to the degree that they compete for scarce resources (e.g., grant money).

Although knowledge held by archeologists that is not related to other knowledge outside the discipline may be relevant to other anthropologists as particularly knowledgeable representatives of the "common man," it is reasonable to ask how relevant they might find it as *anthropologists*. The fact that a set of artifacts that we name "endscrapers" occurs in the archeological record at a particular point in space is probably irrelevant. The same can be said for the archeological knowledge of particular past events—both synchronic forms and diachronic relations. For example, how can maize cultivation or population movements (in partial response to climatic oscillations in the prehistoric Southwest) be relevant to the professional concerns or activities of other anthropologists? They might find it so if they teach courses or write texts surveying the knowledge of anthropology as a whole or if being a generalist (i.e., knowledgeable of all subdisciplines within anthropology) is their professional goal. For anthropologists with more narrowly defined interests (i.e., for most anthropologists) such knowledge must be nonrelevant or even irrelevant (see Soto and Szarek 1971). It is the "nothing" of Willey and Phillips (1968:2).

It is only when such knowledge is related to other knowledge (specifically, to knowledge held by other anthropologists) that it can be relevant to them. Archeological knowledge has been related to other anthropological knowledge by both archeologists and anthropologists. Some anthropologists have been interested in archeological theory, for instance, if only to point out its shortcomings (e.g., Heider 1967; Gould 1968; and Lee 1968). Some have found knowledge of the past relevant because their knowledge of the present may enlighten or contribute to the development of knowledge of the past (e.g., Lee and DeVore, eds. 1968; Levi-Strauss 1963). Other anthropologists have found archeological knowledge of particular past events relevant when they were antecedent to those that were the subject of their concern. This is particularly true of anthropologists concerned with the cultural history of an area, that is, the prehistoric events that produced characteristics of the ethnographic record observed at present. For example, Eggan (1950) has been concerned with prehistoric events in the Southwest that account for features of the social organization of the Western pueblos. However, it can be suggested that as culture history (or explanation of present sociocultural phenomena strictly by reference to prehistoric events) has become less and less the dominant concern of other anthropologists, archeological knowledge of this sort has become less relevant to anthropology. On the other hand, those anthropologists concerned with more general processes (particularly of long-term processes of social and cultural change) may discover in such culture-historical sequences, data that they may make relevant to their own research (e.g., Steward 1949).

Archeological knowledge of the past may also be relevant to those anthropologists who are concerned with events and processes that were contemporary with those events and processes with which archeologists normally deal. Thus, biological anthropologists may find information about past "style zones" (Binford 1965) relevant to their hypotheses about prehistoric racial distributions (e.g., Neumann 1952) or gene flow. Others may relate hominid mental and physical capacities to techniques used to produce and use tools, (e.g., Washburn and Lancaster 1968; Bordes 1971). Those who term themselves "paleoanthropologists" have attempted to relate such archeological and other anthropological knowledge.

Finally, anthropologists ultimately concerned with phenomena removed from the reference axes of time and space might find similar knowledge held by archeologists to be relevant. In this case the distinction is not one of area or period but of the data by which general structures or processes are observed. At several universities, courses in cultural ecology are being offered jointly by archeologists and ethnographers. I doubt that temporal and areal structures or variations of artifact forms or even of the past cultural and other events that produced them are relevant to these ethnographers. Instead, it is the theory that accounts for particular past subsistence processes, for example, and that applies or may be applied to present ones by the ethnographers.

Relevance of Archeology to Other Academic Disciplines and Professions

The case here is similar to archeology's relevance to anthropology. The doing of archeology is relevant to other disciplines if it recovers data that are related to their interests. For example, fossil pollen has been recovered by archeologists from sites in the Southwest and has been placed in time by archeological knowledge. This has furthered the work of botanists concerned with past plant communities and their changes and the work of those concerned with past climates and their changes (e.g., Martin 1963; Hevley 1964; Bohrer 1969). Archeology has also produced data for those concerned with past domestic plants. In a similar way archeology can be relevant to zoology, pedology, geology, geophysics, and other earth sciences. In short, archeological techniques are relevant to other disciplines if they produce data with which they are directly concerned. Archeological knowledge not directly related to the concerns of these disciplines is indirectly relevant if it provides information about these data that facilitates their analysis or interpretation.

Archeological techniques and unrelated knowledge are irrelevant to other disciplines. What possible relevance might knowledge of subsistence techniques used in the prehistoric Southwest (or knowledge of the archeological methods by which such information was obtained) have to a physicist, an astronomer, or a sociologist? Archeological knowledge and (indirectly) archeological techniques are relevant to other disciplines if they are related to their knowledge and interest. This relation can be of several kinds. First, archeological knowledge may not further the goals of the disciplines but may furnish information that is of interest to it. Methods of prehistoric metal working may interest metallurgists; or the design and construction of prehistoric structures may interest architects or structural engineers. Ancient crafts may be of interest to modern craftsmen or materials scientists, while past medical techniques may be of interest to contemporary doctors. Prehistoric agricultural techniques might interest present agricultural scientists or farmers. In these cases, archeology does not provide information that these fields did not already possess but does indicate how men confronted with similar problems dealt with them in the past. In this sense, archeology contributes information about the history of these fields.

In a similar set of cases, archeologists may describe phenomena in the past similar to those described by other scholars in the present but no further relation might be made. Thus, past prehistoric social systems might be interesting to a sociologist, although he makes no attempt to link them to those with which he deals. This is also the case with psychologists, geographers, and other behavioral scientists.

Second, archeological knowledge of specific past events may be related to the interests of a discipline if it forms part of the subject matter of the discipline and is added to it. This is particularly the case with history. In providing background for historical descriptions or analyses (or including them as integral parts of descriptions or analyses) a historian may find archeological knowledge quite relevant. This is commonly the case with archeology that deals with predecessors of contemporary Western civilization where the presumption is explicit or implicit: understanding the past aids understanding of its historical development into the present (e.g., McNeill 1963). In this sense historical archeology is quite relevant. However, art historians and historians of technology may find archeological knowledge of other times and places also relevant.

Third, archeological knowledge can be relevant to other disciplines if it concerns phenomena that are identical to those with which they deal. This is similar to the above in that the subject (e.g., technological systems) is identical. It differs in that here the absolute, temporal placement and relation of events is of no concern. If archeologists consider prehistoric events such as subsistence systems to be cases of more general phenomena (i.e., if they make scientific generalizations), and if these are the same phenomena that are the subject of another field, then archeological knowledge is relevant to that field. In some cases archeological knowledge of a class of human behavior may be related partly to more general behavior that cross-cuts the specific instance or class of behavior studied. Archeological knowledge of subsistence systems may be relevant to political scientists, that is, if the concern is with the conditions under which various forms of leadership obtain. Archeological knowledge might be relevant to sociology if the subject is of mutual interest, such as the behavior of small groups (for example, committees in the present and task groups in the past) or the relationship of small and large groups (for example, task groups and larger social units from which they derive). Archeology may be relevant to human biological or ethological sciences if the concern is with the biological basis for role behavior (for example, in the division of labor in a subsistence activity). Knowledge of subsistence systems as a whole may be relevant to other fields concerned with such phenomena. It is difficult to find a candidate for such a field in the behavioral sciences outside of anthropology. It is conceivable that environmental or ecological scientists more broadly might find archeology relevant to their concerns if human subsistence systems were shown to exemplify broader ecological structures or processes. Thus subsistence technologies or social patterns might be related to broader exploitative means in the animal kingdom.

Finally, archeology as a whole could be relevant to other disciplines if it were to constitute their subject matter in whole or in part. The history of archeology might be of interest to intellectual historians or to behavioral scientists concerned with the nature of science or scientific change. The interrelation of theory, technique, and data in archeology might be a fruitful historical or scientific subject, for example. Archeology might be relevant to the interests of the philosophy of science to the degree that philosophers found characteristics of the field illustrative of the propositions they argued; for example, the degree to which we differentiate and interrelate empiricals and theoreticals, or the reasoning processes we employ when we discover something. In the last example, at least, philosophy integrates with psychology.

While I have attempted to lay out several cases in which archeology might be relevant to other disciplines and fields, archeology is not now relevant to these fields in all these ways. Presently, archeology is most relevant as a technique for gathering raw data for other disciplines and as a means of providing knowledge about prior states of contemporary fields or prior events that have led to or are antecedent to contemporary events. It is least relevant now as a subject analyzed by other disciplines or as a set of problems and knowledge held in common by archeologists and members of other disciplines (who jointly attempt to generalize about human or general systems and processes).

Relevance of Archeology to the "Common Man"

Here I take it to be self-evident that the common man finds archeology relevant. Common men take our courses, watch our exploits on television, read about our work in popular journals (cf. Ascher 1960) and books (e.g., Ceram 1954; Bibby 1956), observe our excavations, form themselves into amateur archeological societies, and *do* archeology themselves. These men, women, and children do find archeology and its techniques relevant. The question is what in archeology is relevant to them and why.

In an analysis of 34 articles about archeology that appeared in *Life* between 1946 and 1955, Ascher (1960) found three that were wholly directed to descriptions of techniques and methods and mentions others in which techniques were an important theme. Archeological excavations in accessible areas are frequently visited by people who appear simply to watch archeologists in action. One is reminded of a group of men watching workmen through the windows of a fence surrounding an urban construction site. I know at least one archeological excavation that used a similar barrier to allow visitors visual (but not physical) access. In our technologically-centered culture there is perhaps no reason to ask why this is so. We provide the entertainment of spectator sports more widely and satisfy the interest in technological processes more narrowly. This might include the intellectual exercise of "learning the game" and the drama of observing the strength, endurance, precision, and technical proficiency of the "players".

Archeological techniques are interesting in themselves as are their immediate products. "Have you found any gold or arrowheads?" is a question with which many of us are familiar. "What was your most exciting (valuable, beautiful, ancient, or interesting) discovery?" is a common variant. The desired answer is not "The relation between two cultures on the basis of their pottery types" or "The high loading of three variables on factor 1." The act of discovery is partly relevant. Ascher notes several articles in which this forms a major theme (1960:402). It is worthy of note that in many cases the discoveries were not made by archeologists and that even when they were, the discoveries were unplanned and unsuspected. The vicarious experience of surprise, bewilderment, realization, excitement, and happiness is certainly relevant. But the drama of expectation is also set up: "If it happened to them, it could happen to me"; as well as the explanation for failure: "I wasn't lucky." At another level, it reinforces the common theme of individualism in American culture, that is, that one man is as good as the next, that being an expert does not mean that one is more successful in the things that matter, and that luck is not distributed with respect to Ph.Ds.

The product itself is partly relevant. The heavy use of superlatives in describing discoveries is noted by Ascher in conjunction with the theme "Firstest with the mostest" (1960:403). Archeological discoveries are interesting because they are rare, most valuable, beautiful, ancient, large, small, and so on. They are valuable because they are rare, exemplifying a basic assumption of economics, and as the heavy traffic in antiquities attests. In some cases archeological discoveries are interesting because they produce direct or indirect financial gain. However, the proportion of those who profit from the use of "archeological" techniques in making valuable discoveries is small in relation to those who profit vicariously. The beauty of objects discovered by archeologists is relevant to a smaller audience almost by definition. At one extreme, this includes art historians and critics trained to conceive such objects in terms of a system defining "the Beautiful." On the other hand, this includes those who simply consider them "pretty". The buyer of coffee table portfolios or museum reproductions falls somewhere in between.

Knowledge of the past not related by *archeologists* to other things is also relevant to the common man. For some, the prehistory of Arizona may be of interest in the same way that more recent periods are for some "history buffs." Becoming a lay expert may be sufficient motivation. The vicarious but safe experience of the drama implicit or explicit from archeological accounts of the invasions; the movements of people; the burning and looting of towns; the revolutionary transformations; the interplay of priests, rulers, and warrior castes; or simply the day-to-day exertions of living and of "man the hunter" are undoubtedly related to deeply felt needs. For others, the flow of past existences; the orderly unfolding of lives; and the preponderance of the predictable, the ordinary, or the romantic are equally (or more) important.

For such men and perhaps for us, the past is an empty stage to be filled with actors and actions dictated by our needs and desires. For individuals, the past provides escape (the term is admittedly superficial) and opportunity to produce good and evil and to create and thus control events we most desire or fear. In this sense the past is the extension of dreams and daydreams. For groups, the past may justify common behavior or release them from responsibility and guilt (e.g., human aggression, territoriality, Aryan expansionism [Daniel 1962]). Or the past may charter and validate the present. The archeology of the Holy Lands, of early Christian Rome, or of Mesoamerica are examples in which religious groups have sponsored work toward this goal.

The archeologist—what he is and what he does—is relevant in many of these same ways. A. V. Kidder (1949) has described two popular images of archeologists: the hairy-chested and hairy-chinned. The first is exemplified by Stewart Granger in his quest in *King Solomon's Mines*. He symbolizes the masculine, the physical, the conquest of physical objects (including women), and physical danger. The physical objects he finds are immediate, obvious, and valuable: treasures in gold or jewels. The hairy-chinned archeologist (an image distorted by present fashion) is exemplified by the epigrapher sequestered with long-forgotten inscriptions on ancient tombs or piles of musty books in a university museum. He symbolizes the feminine, the mental, the conquest of ideas, and the solution of riddles. He has little physical contact with the world and indeed is often incapable in it. The objects he finds are not valuable intrinsically but only insofar as they permit him to discover the past. These images are relevant at a level removed from that of knowledge of the past per se. It is the doing of archeology instead of the events of the past that potentially satisfies interests and needs. These images provide identification for those who wish to participate in and experience the actions of dealing with the past.

Another image of the archeologist can be suggested that, while it is less-obviously manifested, may partially underlie other images and account for some of the popular interest in archeologists and archeology. This image is the archeologist as intermediary between the worldly and the other worldly and between the quick and the dead. Briefly, I suggest that many representatives of the common man stand in awe of the past, thinking of it as remote and alien, filled with shadowy figures and events amplified by their ignorance. The past is often the playing ground of giants and gods and of powers beyond our comprehension. "Once upon a time . . . " is not followed by the mundane or the world of our experience. The popularity of Tolkien's works attests to the degree to which epics that relate the awe-inspiring events of the primordial past are still relevant to our needs and experience. The past is also the repository of the dead. But the dead do not lack potency. The dread of the graveyard is a common theme and is often intently felt in our culture. The curse of the pharaohs in popular literature or the vengeance of mummies in films indicate the power of the dead, particularly when disturbed by archeologists. How often are we asked whether we have found any skeletons. Even state agencies may put a premium on recovery of the dead in archeological salvage work.

If the past is the realm of the dead, the potentially powerful, the supernatural and the awesome, how must those who make the past their stock in trade be regarded? I suggest that they must also be held in awe, not only because they are most familiar with the past and have faculties not developed or possessed by other men, but also because they have the power to know and reveal the past. The power to deal with the past might be one separately gained or one gained by joining with the power in the past as did *Faustus*. Whatever the source, that there is a power and that it can be improperly used is indicated by the vengeance of the mummy's curse, a replaying of the ancient Greek theme of the wrath of the gods on those who attempt to know too much (hubris). To put it another way, one must be mad to dig the dead, but if not made so strong that the reasons for dreading them are suppressed. In fact, both are possible. It might also be noted that "seers" or those mediating between the normal world and the world of the gods are frequently blind, such as Teiresias in Sophocles' *Antigone*. The archeologist of Kidder's second image is also "blind" but in a metaphorical sense. He has eyes only for his work, and he is little able to perceive or deal with the real world. Hence, as Kidder notes, although he is achieving new insights into decipherment, his daughter must be rescued from savages by his handsome young assistant (Kidder 1949).

If this analysis is accepted, it is possible to suggest additional ways in which archeology is relevant to the common man. To watch archeological techniques is to watch the archeologist use his power to deal with the power of the past. To the uninitiated it must seem a mystical process, "mystical" not only in the sense of being "incompletely understood" or "dimly perceived" but also in the sense of "involving the unknown or mysterious." Thus, I have suggested elsewhere (1968) that some theories of knowledge in archeology can be related to those that are mystic in the strict sense (see also Northrup 1947). To watch archeology is to experience these powers, at least vicariously. To learn these techniques and employ them is to use this power directly. To learn about the past from archeologists is to be enlightened about the nature of another world. To the degree that knowledge yields control, knowledge of the past yields control over the past. It is as if new lights dispelled the dread of dark streets. Furthermore, the act of learning or becoming enlightened is itself exciting. In sum, archeological techniques and knowledge are relevant because they touch on matters related to those of ultimate concern. They satisfy the need to know, to experience, to control, and to be reassured about the "other world." Archeological *data* may be relevant in similar ways.

As archeologists, we are very concerned with things, and certainly the common man frequently seems to consider "things" to be the sole focus and the sum and substance of archeology. The philosopher Martin Heidegger has considered the nature of objects in an essay entitled "The Thing" (1971). It is not necessary to accept his underlying metaphysic in order to gain insight into the significance of things. He distinguishes between "objects" and "things". The former are perceived either when they occur before us or when we create their appearance in our minds. They exist only when these relations exist. A "thing" is independent of our observation or recreation. Its existence consists partly of its uses in the broadest possible sense and its contexts and partly of the web of conceptual links that we have established with it. This is not to say that things are essentially ideas in the platonic sense. They are simply not known as things unless they are conceived. Through or because of these linkages, we approach nearness with things and with the natural and supernatural worlds in which they are embedded. Heidegger is critical of science that knows things as objects conceived through its concepts rather than through concepts appropriate to their existence as things. I am reminded here of Redfield's dichotomy between the world view of High and Folk Cultures (1963), or between those of McLuhan's "sedentary specialists" and mobile hunter–gatherers (1964; see also White 1949:3).

As scientists we have learned to conceive the material world in terms of narrow and precisely defined ideas. The denotations of these concepts may have been developed at length and with great care so that no ambiguity remains. All of us agree on the definition of an "endscraper," a "metate," or a "St. Johns Polychrome Bowl." And some of the exciting work on the frontier of the field attempts to increase the rigor by which we define and observe our material subject (e.g., Wilmsen 1970b). This is an essential scientific activity, but it removes us from the rich connotations that these things may have had for us in the past and still may have for the common man. Thus, many archeologists state that the name of tool categories refer only to a formal clustering of attributes and not to their past uses (e.g., Jennings 1957; Clarke 1968). For us, "endscraper" refers to an object having a particular form, perhaps described by a set of numbers. For the contemplative, imaginative common man, this thing may crystallize images not only of its use in hide scraping, for instance, but also of the hunt that produced the hide, of the search for the raw material from which it was made, of its creator and creation, of the daily and spiritual life of its user and, perhaps, of his ultimate fate. The paintings by Z. Burian of Middle and Upper Paleolithic life in Europe (Howell 1968:131–135, 155–157) indicate the richness of detail that may be known from such things.

Because the past does not matter in the same way as the day-to-day world, the common man is free to extend such linkages indefinitely. Unless he is a novelist or poet, the act will not benefit him materially. But it will benefit him in other ways. These might include increasing nearness to an Ultimate as Heidegger suggests. Or they may include the exercise of imagination that cannot be channeled in other ways. And, as suggested previously, the expression of the content of the concepts may be beneficial in itself. Thus, archeological things may be relevant because through them we approach nearness to a world we do not experience in objective reality.

Turning to a different kind of relation, science in general and social science in particular have claimed to be relevant to the common man. A frequent defense of "big science" is that it produces technological or medical "fallout" that benefits everyone (e.g., the U.S. space program). Social scientists have suggested that their unique perspectives and knowledge help them to understand and solve problems of social dysfunction and conflict. If these claims are true, social sciences would certainly benefit the common man and, with sufficient proselytizing, most should recognize this relevance. If we assume that the claims are true, we can ask how archeological knowledge is or may be related to other knowledge of a scientific nature to benefit the common man. This assumes first that archeological knowledge unrelated to other knowledge cannot be relevant in this sense. Minimally it must be related to knowledge of the present, that is, where the common man dwells. Second, it assumes that archeological knowledge must be scientific. In one sense, this simply restates the first assumption: events of the past and present are not comparable unless they are both instances of more general events. (Hempel and Oppenheim 1948; Hempel 1966). Finally, it assumes that not all scientific knowledge is immediately or even potentially relevant. It is necessary to show that it is in the interest of (or beneficial to) man.

To ask if knowledge of this sort is relevant is not to ask whether knowledge of specific events—either past or present—is relevant. Instead, it is to ask whether theoretical knowledge is relevant. Subsistence theory held by archeologists is relevant if subsistence theory in general is relevant. This tends to direct inquiry away from the strict focus on archeology as we normally conceive of it and from the past. But this is also the implication of an explicitly scientific orientation in archeology. It can first be asked whether subsistence theory itself is relevant. It is if it helps to assure an adequate supply of food by contributing to the increased productivity or nutritional quality of food sources employed and to the development of new resources or more effective organizations of personnel and tools for the procurement (or processing) of resources. Archeologists cannot carry out such developments themselves but they could contribute to the confirmation of theory from which applied scientists might derive them. Subsistence theory might also be relevant if subsistence systems (or their components) were shown to be cases of more general sociocultural systems and processes, and if knowledge of the latter facilitated better understanding or design of contemporary, nonsubsistence systems.

Archeologists have frequently suggested that our discipline is unique in its potential to analyze long-term sociocultural stability and change. Theories of change could be tested by archeologists by demonstrating that past change is an instance of general processes. And these processes could also be shown to be manifest in the present, either in the operation of contemporary subsistence or other homologous systems. Such theory would afford understanding and a base for applied science. Perhaps more than any other system with which archeologists deal, subsistence systems involve the close articulation of technological, social, and natural environmental variables. They are also closely tied to demographic and other exterior social and cultural systems. Past changes might confirm the theory by which present changes in similar systems are explained, predicted, or created. Past changes ranging in impact from introduction of the bow and arrow or pottery to the agricultural revolution might be shown to be homologous to those resulting from the introduction of new harvesting machines to the "green revolution".

At another level, major contemporary problems are said to include undirected and poorly assimilated technological growth, environmental mismanagement, unchecked population growth, and social disintegration, (e.g., Mumford 1970; *The Progressive* 1970). Even the basic understanding of these processes and their interrelation would benefit and interest the common man by removing the anxiety of the unknown or little understood. But more important is theory that would enable engineers, applied scientists, and governmental managers to control or even direct such processes better. The similarity between these processes and subsistence systems is evident. The organizational and social effect of the introduction of the bow and arrow and of new industrial machinery might be cases of more general phenomena, for example. The possible parallelism of biotic destruction of the contemporary natural environment and of the extinction of the late Pleistocene extinction of North American megafauna has also been noted (Martin 1967; Butzer 1971: 503–512). However, few (if any) specific homologies have been sufficiently explicated or demonstrated to furnish a basis for either understanding or attempting solutions.

Of equal potential relevance and until now unaccomplished is the formulation of a plausible relation between subsystems of past subsistence systems and homologous contemporary subsystems of similar scale. The possible relevance of subsistence theory to theory of political organization (or of small groups) has been suggested above. It is even conceivable that psychological theory could be related to past subsistence systems (e.g., behavior under conditions of stress) if we could develop adequate means for observing such phenomena. A general theory of tool use tested partly against that of past subsistence systems might benefit contemporary skilled and unskilled workers.

In summary, archeology is of interest to, rooted in the experience of, and is beneficial to the common man in several respects. It provides puzzles to be solved, vicarious experience of the exotic and the adventurous, the hope of "striking it rich," and a form of contact with the "other world." Archeology is *potentially* relevant to the common man insofar as it develops and/or tests theories that afford understanding of contemporary systems or processes and from which solutions to contemporary problems can be derived. That archeology has not achieved this potential is not solely because of the disinterest of archeologists or incapacity of archeological knowledge. In some cases, theories of human behavior have not been explicated to the degree that archeological knowledge could be used to test and develop them. In some cases, theories have been developed, but the potential relation to behavioral phenomena of non-Western cultures is in question (e.g., economics). In other cases, either non-arch-eologists who know a theoretical system have lacked the archeolo-gical theory necessary to test it using past data, or archeologists with the necessary archeological theory have lacked sophisticated knowl-edge of the theoretical system. It may well be that if archeologists are to become relevant in this sense, they will have to learn and develop social scientific theory on their own.

CONCLUSION

In conclusion, I have attempted to define several ways archeology is or might be relevant and ways it has not been relevant. In so doing, I asked whether archeology is of interest to, rooted in the experience of, or beneficial to various audiences. This I take to be the contempo-rary meaning of relevance. The analysis has not attempted to be exhaustive. Other audiences might have been considered and other instances of relevance or irrelevance might have been defined. But the foregoing has shown that the question: "Is archeology relevant?" is not a simple one and that the answer cannot be a simple "yes" or "no". One is tempted to paraphrase Pope and say: "All that is, is relevant." This expresses an essential truth; that is, if archeology exists, it must be relevant to someone—if only to archeologists.

But if we are to take seriously the dissatisfaction outlined above, we will attempt to find relevant relations outside of ourselves. We are left with several possibilities. We can act as data gathers for other fields; we can provide entertainment and mystical fulfillment for the common man; we can contribute to the development and demon-stration of behavioral scientific theory, or we can direct our scientific efforts to theory that may benefit all men. The choice lies with archeologists. Many of us who have felt dissatisfaction with archeology have chosen to attempt one or both of the latter two. We do so, I think, with no certainty that we can attain or make substantial contributions to such theory in our generation. But we are certain that if we do not make an attempt we cannot justify our roles as archeologists.

6.   ARCHEOLOGY SERVING HUMANITY

RICHARD I. FORD

Museum of Anthropology
University of Michigan
Ann Arbor, Michigan

The last two digits of the code reflect the potential application of the results of the project.

Not Applicable 00
Health Related Sciences 01
Oceanography Related 02
Agricultural Sciences Related 03
Science Information Related 04
Water Resources Related 05
Etc.

From NSF Guide for Preparation of Proposals

There is admittedly little about archaeology that is immediately practical. Archaeological research does enrich present-day life through rediscovery of art motifs and other inventions of past times. It provides a healthy intellectual interest manifested in the archaeological National Monuments and Parks of the United States and in local archaeological societies.

Mirror for Man, Kluckhohn

I

Archeology champions time. With this there is little debate. The source of contention and, indeed, the challenge to archeology is the consequence of temporal sequences of events exposed by archeologists. To practitioners of prehistory a description of objects and events is ample (Hawkes 1968:255) and explanation need be no more than plausible inference. To other archeologists concerned with general processes operative in cultural systems, descriptions and observations of the past require explanation through testing, not intuition (Watson, LeBlanc, and Redman 1971). Each approach is characterized by its own accomplishments, and others outside the discipline will judge the universality of each approach for solving the problems humanity faces.

Applicability—not relevance—is prehistory's nemesis. Wedded to the events of the past and to a sequence of activities dimmed by the ages, prehistory has produced results of extreme importance to all men while, at the same time, its perspective of archeology as history has thwarted archeology from coping with a world changed by revolutionary ideas (including those it advanced more than a century ago).

Born in an era that acknowledged Archbishop Ussher's chronology and the authority of the Bible, prehistory as conducted by its fervent founders rocked the foundations of orthodoxy. Heresy it was. Untethered archeology, in concert with geology, rapidly unearthed the fossil antecedents of man, his association with extinct animals, and a paltry arsenal brazenly called tools.

Exploration discovered the primitive; and excavation unveiled the primordial. Together they redefined humanity. It was in the last century that prehistoric archeology made its most enduring contribution to mankind: all men evolved from common ancestry and share a nonbiological adaptation: culture. In the intervening years, prehistorians have, on one hand, propagated this theme and its variant: a knowledge of our past enriches the quality of our daily lives in ways written history cannot. On the other hand, despite its well-tested techniques (Trigger 1968) that still produce intriguing results, prehistory deviated and perverted its promising vision of human self awareness (Trigger 1970:36) by refocusing interest away from commonality to nationalism.

Nationalism and prehistory grew together in the same centuries with the latter the handmaiden more often than not. This relationship is not necessarily injurious, but at times the merits of nationalistic archeology are only vaguely distinguishable from the abuses of political archeology. From this perspective prehistory can be viewed as a continuum. At one end is a desire to reveal the archeological record with as much objectivity as science will permit (Rouse 1972). Midway on the scale is nationalistic archeology committed to investigating past events in one country or detailing the archeological past of a particular ethnic group. National interest and ethnic history are often coterminous. However, when explorations are fraught with xenophobic emotion, political archeology is unavoidable or, as Gjessing stated:

> In the twinkling of an eye, archaeology and political propoganda may get so tangled together that it may be extremely difficult, if not impossible, to unravel them [1963:264].

At the other extreme, then, political archeology seeks to find or feign evidence for a particular point of view and, more often than not, one previously disproven. Or it may simply ignore those aspects of the archeological record that contravene national myths.

Nationalistic archeology has dominated the history of archeology, and in many instances has provided a valuable service to a particular country while upholding high scientific standards. Certainly this archeology has characterized European prehistory epitomized by the highly regarded Ancient Peoples and Places series (published by Praeger, New York).

While prehistory plots the treks of ethnic groups in Europe, newly emergent nations in other continents rely on prehistory for other purposes. Israel employs archeology to justify her existence and to integrate immigrants whose recent histories and experiences have been widely divergent and often conflictory. Her coins, stamps, symbols, and language are drawn from ancient times and from Biblical times to recall historical continuity and to create a nation-state. Nations freed from colonialism have readily turned to archeology to help unite a potpourri of displaced (or badly divided) ethnic groups. In African countries an idyllic past blind to more recent ethnic rivalries is stressed with pride. Mexico preserves its Indian heritage within the cavernous halls of an outstanding national museum and at reconstructed archeological monuments, and other Latin American countries are rapidly following suit. In each instance the goal is to foster prehistory as an agent for the creation of national pride and for the perpetuation of national traditions.

Prehistorians working in the United States have also engaged in nationalistic archeology and have witnessed the application of their endeavors to nationalism. From its inception, prehistory has had, as a prime objective, the linking of archaeological sites with living Indian tribes, but only recently has this nationalistic archeology assumed any significance for the native American. With a resurgence of Indian nationalism, the efforts of archeologists have been valued in two distinct (although complementary) ways. The applicability of direct historical archeology reached fruition in the past two decades with the Indian Land Claims cases. At those hearings, archeologists testified that specific tribes occupied a particular area prior to and at the start of United States governmental authority. This straightforward interpretation was well served by historical archeology's "who, when, and where" questions. The same information now suffices more militant members of Indian communities to prevent excavation on former tribal territories. At another level, however, archeologists have shown a basic unity of Amerinds rooted in antiquity, justifying the "brotherhood of all Indians." As painful as it may be for those whose digs are disrupted, the results of prehistory are essential to Indian nationalists and are an important part of the Indians' proud cultural heritage.

Nevertheless, there are potential dangers for an unbiased understanding of native Americans' and other peoples' past inherent in the methodology of prehistory. By asserting intuitions as tested facts, or by assuming analogy with known forms describing past functions causes difficulties especially when they are conveyed to an unsuspecting public. A good example is found in the statements repeated several times a day by the Baptist guides who conduct tours of the partially excavated and protected Mississippian site popularly called the Ancient Buried City in Wickliffe, Kentucky. Here visitors are told that the double-necked bottles (called juice presses) were used by the Indians to make wine. There is no evidence that prehistoric Indians in the East made wine or any other alcoholic beverage. Furthermore, we do not even know that these vessels, despite their analogous shape, were used to press juice. Nevertheless, in a popular publication describing this and other sites, the author (King 1939:98) asserts the truthfulness of this statement, which is taught to unwary tourists, and directly contributes to a misrepresentation and possibly a degradation of prehistoric Indian culture. Obviously, this is a picayune example selected deliberately, but it is from such statements lacking scientific support that political archeology provides ammunition for demagoguery.

Governmental agencies have disregarded parts of the archeological record. Despite quality work by many archeologists employed by the Department of the Interior, the public is offered an interpretation of colonial and frontier life with archeological evidence marshaled to support great national myths: Anglo colonists, independent spirits, self-supportive families, and so on. The serenity and sterility of a reconstructed Jamestown disregards the town's boorish inhabitants and her economic outcasts. Which western mission depicts the harsh surroundings of the Indian neophytes, or which frontier outpost, now a national monument, shows the economic parasitism it exerted nationally? Dioramas and displays often omit the presence (no less the contribution) of other ethnic groups. Political archeology can be subtle, and one is prone to dismiss these misgivings as oversights. But for the non-Anglo visitor they are blatantly obvious.

The dangers of political archeology are patently clear. Two generations ago, archeologists' "facts" supported Aryan supremacy and subverted the classical foundations of Italy to benefit fascism. Today in Rhodesia, archeological ruins are once again the center of political machinations—this time to deny the black African his past. The careful and patient work of prehistorians in the twentieth century has dispelled the myths of foreign invaders and Hamite overlords by linking the builders of monumental ruins in southern Africa with living native descendants. Such scientific findings are unacceptable to the present government. A recent book by A. J. Bruwer, *Zimbabwe: Rhodesia's Ancient Greatness*, despite enormous evidence to the contrary, resurrects the outmoded view that Phoenicians created this masonry marvel. Reviewing this book, a vexed Brian Fagan noted:

> ... one cannot fail to be concerned at the effect which a book like this can have on public opinion about important archaeological sites ... The archaeologist's responsibility is to reconstruct history without regard to vested interest or racist thinking [Fagan 1970:322].

Archeologists Roger Summers and Peter Garlake followed this stricture and had to leave Rhodesia (Daniel 1971a:1).

Public interest in archeologists' findings is avid. By using the printed word, this interest is easily distorted for malicious political purposes. Yet, unknowingly and unintentionally, it can present a perspective of prehistory that leads to the destruction of archeology itself. By the very questions asked (Fritz, Chapter 5) and answers found in popular publications (Ascher 1960) and press releases, a fascinated public learns about one paradigm: prehistory. Each discovery produces a unique object and, with luck, anyone can find one. Archeologists feed this illusion by actively seeking rare objects and by stressing form over function. Sadly, this approach also has dire consequences for humanity by encouraging illicit digging and illegal trafficking in antiquities.

The magnitude of destruction caused by ransacking of sites is a result of prehistorians stressing the exotic and idiosyncratic nature of the archeological record. Armed with the unwitting testimony of archeologists—the acknowledged experts—the public has avariciously sought similar objects for vicarious pleasure and calculated investment. Each news article declaring that the "oldest" or a "previously unknown" artifact was discovered is answered by a new demand on the antiquity market.

The horrendous destruction of monuments in Cambodia, India, and Guatemala are frightening enough, but the demand for conspicuous facades or temple ornamentation—once the showpieces of collectors and museums—is abating somewhat in the face of international outrage, while smaller objects in clay, precious stone, and metal (often exempted from international importation agreements) are in greater demand than ever. The removal of monuments above ground left major portions of the archeological site intact; this is not the case in procuring smaller buried objects. To get these, tremendous damage ensues, rendering many sites totally destroyed and leaving artifacts without contextual assignment.

With site destruction comes governmental retaliation. I have already remarked that for many foreign countries antiquities are sources of national pride and ethnic integration. Outraged by the loss of this patrimony and unable to successfully affront the United States and Western European countries where the markets are, most countries are now taking retribution against the most vulnerable targets who represent these countries: professional archeologists. Permits are delayed or denied, excavations are curtailed, and analysis is restricted to inadequately equipped countries. Paradoxically, some of the most ardent crusaders against this destruction unintentionally support it through their own professional interests. Nor are public relations between the archeologist and the host country improved when eminent archeologists condone sloppy excavations practices and when the "legal" removal of national treasures during colonial regimes goes unquestioned (cf. Clark 1970:28–30). New laws are desperately needed to preserve archeological sites, but so is a shift by archeologists away from the chronologic interests of prehistory to a more comprehensive explanation of the past.

II

> Everything contributes to the belief that archaeology, this young and dynamic expression of the historical sciences can and should make a valid contribution to the defining of a new form of universal humanism, appropriate to the scientific age.
>
> *The Meaning of Archaeology*, Pallottino

The prehistorian's perspective delivered man to a place in eternity, presented nation–states (and ethnic groups) with a past, a future, and an identity, and led Kluckhohn (1961:42) to pen the pessimistic words that introduce this chapter. In the years since they were written (1948), the aims of archeology have changed; its practicality to today's problems is no longer questioned. More and more, archeologists are committed to discovering the dynamic processes affecting past man's life and his present situation. Explanation and understanding are given priority over places and events. Debate is shrill among anthropological archeologists, but their divorce from prehistory is affirmed.

Several recent publications (Binford 1968; Fritz and Plog 1970; Watson, LeBlanc, and Redman 1971) have delineated the logical structure of archeology as a behavioral science. Focusing on general problems leads to the formulation of more complicated hypotheses testable with methods that never characterized prehistory. These problems are not limited to describing episodes in the archeological record; instead, they are based on a presumed need to further our understanding of human behavior by recognizing universal processes operating in human evolution. This is the unique nature of archeology. By broadening its horizon, a revolution in archeological methodology quickly followed. It must be stressed, however, that new methods are developed or borrowed as appropriate components of sophisticated research designs to test proposals; the problem determines the techniques of excavation and analysis. These developments are in their second decade with the slow accumulation of results whose applicability to a humanity transcending national boundaries are only now beginning to be appreciated.

Prehistoric man's adaptations within his environment are acknowledged as a complexity of cause-and-effect processes. In some cases we can benefit from his management; in others we must avoid his mistakes. Taken together we are given general processes still needed for survival.

Wilmsen and Meyers' (1972) analysis of mercury in fish is a splendid example of the employment of borrowed technology used to understand the parameters of variables in the prehistoric man's habitat, which has immediate importance for human well-being. Knowledge of background levels of several potentially harmful trace elements in the environment is not known, and without archeology is almost unknowable in an already polluted and disrupted biosphere. Using the techniques of neutron activation analysis, Wilmsen and Meyers examined mercury levels in prehistoric fish bone from Michigan and Illinois and in desiccated flesh from coastal middens in Peru. Their results indicate that background levels of this element were higher in some seemingly pristine ecosystems than were once considered safe, and that in some environments mercury content in fish has not changed since prehistoric times. Archeological data provide much needed information for judging safe levels and actually questions the ceilings assumed by some ecologists.

The settlement and exploitation of marginal environments is of prime importance to many developing areas, but planners learn quite quickly that techniques operative in more favorable habitats are inapplicable in others. Much can be learned from prehistoric man's adaptive strategies in these regions. To date, deserts have yielded the most information with consequences of importance for most arid areas. For example, Evenari and his associates (Evenari, Shanan, and Tadmore 1971:95–119) observed in Israel that many parts of the Negev had supported substantial populations in ancient times. Their inquiries led to the establishment of a deductive model to test hypotheses related to water control and agricultural production. They demonstrated that utilization of rainfall runoff from large sections of land would produce a bounteous harvest. Through knowledge derived from archeological data, planners can now establish communities in the desert with an awareness of distinctive spatial patterns that will preserve ample land for comparable runoff control. Such knowledge will have further universal applicability as fossil water supplies diminish or become prohibitively costly.

Land use in the arid world has not always been so successful. Nevertheless, the mistakes made by former inhabitants and detectable through archeological techniques seeking answers to nontemporal, multifaceted questions alerts us to the operation of similar processes today. Archeological evidence provides a lesson in the consequences of mismanagement in the Diyala Basin of Iraq. Here Jacobsen and Adams (1958) exposed the disastrous cumulative effects of salinization from intensive irrigation and of sedimentation from large, overextended irrigation canals. In this example, archeological techniques can reveal the catastrophic effects of land abuse faster and at a lower cost than can contemporary experimentation or short-term observations of arid land agriculture.

While the significance of environmental monitoring by archeological means is becoming established and will continue to expand, other areas of archeological pursuit are affording methods and knowledge of general processes. Not unexpectedly, since ecological theory is important to archeology, information concerning population dynamics over time is now a primary pursuit of archeologists. Sociology yields correlations and history records trends, but archeology is the testing ground of the social consequences of long-term population fluctuations. So far, all the studies have employed statistically significant changes in variables of artifacts—especially ceramics—or in settlement patterns to discern the behavioral consequences of past population change. Parsons (1971) has examined changes in regional population configurations following the evolution of centralized administration in the Valley of Mexico. Population variables have a role in more orderly processes of growth as, tested by Plog (1969), with data from the Southwest. Leone (1968) also relied on material from this region to test the long-run implications of a changing subsistence economy for regional social interaction. Moving in the opposite direction, depopulation can cause familial disruption as Deetz (1965) has demonstrated. The role of population change in evolution is a source of debate. These examples show that current answers are too simplistic. In addition, reliance on archeological case studies would expose the social costs of various rates of population change prior to social experimentation.

At a more complex level, testing propositions concerning systems maintenance and change furthers our understanding of other global problems. With the archeological record as his laboratory, Flannery (1972) is modeling the evolutionary processes leading to the formation and administration of states. Although prime movers—warfare, irrigation, population growth, regional symbiosis, and social circumscription—have been proposed, they prove to be localized mechanisms through which other more general processes operate. Within a system, some low-level institutions may become elevated (promoted) to a higher level of administration. In this self-serving capacity, higher-level institutions (or bureaucrats) may circumvent lower-ranking personnel to regulate a variable directly. When these systemic rearrangements speed the processing and storage of information and lead to centralization, evolutionary advance has occurred. Yet the same processes can simplify a system rendering it incapable of buffering environmental perturbations. Conversely, checks and balances of regulatory institutions may be so interconnected at all levels that they are ineffectual at coping with changed selective forces. Archeological examples of hypercoherence (the previous process) leading to the destruction of regional systems are found in the Near East and the Mayan area, as Flannery demonstrates with settlement data and evidence for social alliances. Once again prehistory is contradicted by the revelation that it is more important to know the state of a system before the collapse of a state (historical event) is intelligible.

Flannery's model has obvious overtones for comprehending worldwide economic and political structuring. As formerly self-sustaining systems in the so-called primitive world are brought into plantation and extractive economies controlled by developed nations, the local regulatory mechanisms are removed and controls from the outside are imposed. No longer is the system self-regulated; no longer can it handle localized problems. The simplification of the ecosystem and the slow response of external administrators portend disaster for a dependent population. The processes of evolution (or is it advancement) are continuous, but at what cost? Having observed these processes many times in the past, archeology has an ominous answer.

Processual archeology is not oriented solely to the solution of particular social maladies. Whenever research is channeled into narrow lines of interest, even for human benefit, the potential for future developments is lost. This is what I see as a basic difficulty of prehistory; its inflexible methodology and restricted goals leave it with little to offer science or society. The procedural changes adopted by processual archeology initiate the garnering of previously ignored data and comprehension of past and present systems. Many contemporary, highly complex systems cannot be understood without knowing their structure at a simpler stage still to be unearthed. The consequences of systemic change and environmental alteration are now predictable with archeological evidence. The future will witness more proponents of this approach, tackling vistas never dreamed within the range of archeologists. The applicability of archeology is on the ascendancy; its serviceability to humanity is a byproduct of expanded basic research interests.

There are no cells of paleosocial workers. The double zero on the National Science Foundation (NSF) form can still be checked. But science has never been free from human interest and the needs of external constituencies. Archeologists serving nation-states have filled museums with relics from sites dug solely for the recovery of material objects. The chimera of pure science blinds many from the realization that research is always structured by forces outside the archeologist's control. Making archeology a more generalized science will remove some of the political constraints. Another hindrance to archeological progress is the indiscriminant publication of unverified hunches. Nomothetic science removes this albatross and escapes this aspect of prehistory's checkered past. It also solves behavioral questions with many spinoff benefits accruing for wide-ranging applications, and will return archeology (thus fulfilling Pallottino's wish [1968:332]) to the original consequence of prehistory: universal humanism.

7. THE FUTURE OF ARCHEOLOGY IS THE PAST

BRUCE G. TRIGGER

Department of Anthropology*
McGill University
Montreal, Canada

AIMS

This chapter aims to clarify and develop certain arguments originally presented by me in *Antiquity* (1970) concerning the role of so-called scientific and historical goals in prehistoric archeology. More generally, I wish to demonstrate that both idiographic, or particularizing (i.e., historical), and nomothetic, or generalizing, disciplines are vital components of a scientific study of human behavior. This kind of argument must involve some consideration of the role of idiographic and nomothetic approaches in the biological and physical sciences, although references to these will be limited to a few analogies.

The tendency to value generalizing disciplines more highly than historical ones can be traced at least as far back as Aristotle's argu-

* This chapter was written while I was the recipient of a Killam Award administered by the Canada Council. Participation in the symposium on "Archeology's Future," at which the first version of this paper was read, was sponsored by a grant from McGill University.

ments for rating poetry above history (since the former deals with more general problems than the latter). In recent years, however, the preference for nomothetic goals has become particularly strong in the social sciences. It is argued that progress toward science is made whenever variables are substituted for proper names—sites, artifact types, or cultures—and that whenever a researcher finds that a generalization holds for one period, region, or culture and not for another, his duty is to look for additional variables to explain the difference, instead of being content with merely citing it (Przeworski and Teune 1970). This has led certain archeologists to advocate that the principal goal of archeology should be to formulate and test hypotheses regarding social and cultural processes (Binford 1962) or, alternatively, that archeology should be viewed as constituting the basis of a nomothetic study of material culture (Clarke 1968:20–24).

Particularly in North America, this position has been reinforced by historical as well as institutional factors. Archeology and ethnology share a common interest in the American Indian and, at least until the recent development of ethnohistory, have been sharply distinguished from history, which concerns itself with the activities of European settlers. This is different from the study of European prehistory, which is viewed as a projection of history into the more remote past. Whereas European archeology has preserved its contacts with history as a discipline, and European archeologists have at least a working idea of what historians are doing, in North America history has become an alien discipline to most prehistoric archeologists. While not denying the value of the close links that exist between archeology and ethnology in North America, it is worth asking what has been lost through the absence of ties between archeology and history, and to what degree current arguments concerning the goals of archeology are merely an attempt to rationalize the unity of archeology and ethnology within the established discipline of anthropology.

ERRONEOUS VIEWS OF HISTORY

Among American archeologists, the estrangement of archeology from history has led to serious misconceptions about modern historical research, and indeed idiographic studies in general. One very common point of view is summarized in the following quotation from a recent issue of *Current Anthropology*:

The focus of interest is not only on the two traditional "goals" of archaeology—culture history and the reconstruction of past lifeways—but also on a third goal—the study of cultural process. That is, investigation now not only aims at chronology and description, but also attempts to *explain* under what conditions an adaptive shift . . . will occur [Wright 1971:449].

Far from expressing a novel position, this statement reflects the long-standing tendency of American archeologists to equate historical research with chronology and description (Taylor 1948:45; Willey and Phillips 1956:9). However, the quotation illustrates how easily a switch from description to nomothetic explanation can obscure the existence of a third type of study—one that has both idiographic and explanatory goals. Chronology and description are basic to both nomothetic and idiographic explanation but, by themselves, they do not constitute history. The goals of historical research are as explanatory as the goals of the nomothetic social sciences.

These misconceptions stem, in part, from a belief that century-old ideas about the nature of historical research are still accepted by most historians and also from undue emphasis being placed on minority opinions. The result is that historical research is not judged on the basis of its contemporary general trends. This is as serious as the corresponding error made by historians, that is, evaluating the significance of modern archeological research on the basis of research techniques of a generation or more ago (Elton 1969:23). The principal misconceptions that archeologists hold about the nature of history are:

1.   The principal aim of historians is to describe rather than to explain.

This view is based on the emphasis that historians, beginning with von Ranke, placed on facts as constituting the hard core of history. While this emphasis was itself a very healthy reaction against the opinionated and moralizing history of an earlier period, it has never, as E. H. Carr (1962) and others have pointed out, prevented historians from attempting to explain their facts. Now, historians generally recognize that pure description is an impossible goal, since even the historian's selection of facts is guided by his opinions concerning what is and what is not significant. As Carr (1962:84) has stated: "Every historical argument revolves round the question of the priority of causes." The significance of this point cannot be stressed too much. Historians agree that it is possible to be aware of facts about the past without attempting to explain them, but few would admit that it is possible to "know" or even to "describe" the past without also having attempted to explain it. The only difference between explanations is that some are based on explicit premises, while others remain largely implicit.

2. Historians depend on common sense to explain their data, unlike social scientists, who rely on testable theories of human behavior.

It is true that historians frequently rely on common sense when the bodies of theory needed to explain their data are not available. Furthermore, some historians pointedly decry the idea that more than common sense is needed to produce adequate historical explanations. In general, however, the recent tendency has been to replace this type of explanation with one based on solid bodies of social science theory. This has led to the emergence of social and economic history as vigorous subdisciplines, closely linked with sociology and economics. The influence of other generalizing social science disciplines, including psychology, has likewise been marked. Many historians are as convinced as nomothetic social scientists that human behavior is not random and, in order to explain their data, these historians are anxious to make use of the social sciences' current understanding of human behavior (Berkhofer 1969). In other words, good science is a necessary foundation for doing good history. Because of this, while history remains idiographic it is in no sense the antithesis of the social sciences, but instead establishes itself as a vital part of an overall science of human behavior.

3. Historians depend on a type of explanation that they claim is different from scientific explanation, while in fact no separate form of historical explanation exists (Spaulding 1968:35).

Scientific explanation generally means using the covering law model, that is, accounting for the occurrence of a particular event (E) by demonstrating that a specific set of determining conditions $(C_1, C_2 \ldots C_n)$ was present and that whenever these determining conditions are present, an event of that kind will take place (Hempel 1949: 459–460). Those who support this model consider explanations that do not conform with it to be false or incomplete and to fall short of scientific precision.

The problem of historical explanation deserves more careful consideration by archeologists than it has received so far. If historical explanation means either a separate body of theory pertaining specifically to the analysis of historical data, or assumptions about the nature of human behavior that are different from, or contrary to, those assumptions found in the generalizing social sciences, most historians would deny the existence of historical explanation. The explanations that historians give, insofar as they are reputable, must be scientific. Most historians agree that the explanations of human behavior that they use to interpret historical events and those formulated by social scientists ideally should be the same, since both are explaining the same thing. On the other hand, if historical explanation means that to explain historical data, special techniques are required that lie outside the normally accepted logical structure of covering law theory, then many historians and philosophers of science would agree that historical explanation does exist. Even more historians would maintain that in practice special modes of explanation are required, although they are uncertain of whether these modes are theoretically required.

IDIOGRAPHIC ASPECTS OF HISTORICAL INTERPRETATION

Problems of historical interpretation are of equal interest to prehistorians and historians. The aim of any idiographic discipline is to account for (i.e., to explain) specific events or situations. These events may be related to the development of geological formations, the paleontological evolution of particular species, or the course of human history (Kroeber 1952:63–78). The ideal in each case is to account for the particular development or event by isolating the determining conditions and showing how these were sufficient to cause it to take place. In a way, such an explanation is no different from a social anthropological explanation concerning, for example, the manner in which the introduction of steel axes among a people who previously had only stone ones affects their way of life. Almost invariably the explanation of such an event involves setting forth one or more testable generalizations about human behavior. Moreover, there is no formal difference between historical data and ethnological data gathered over time. Both involve complex situations that can be explained in terms of basic assumptions that, in turn, can be tested with other sets of data. Thus, it is not unreasonable to argue that the interpretation of historical, as well as ethnological, evidence should form a basis for significant generalizations about human behavior. This, in turn, supports the view that history is, or can be, a generalizing discipline like most of the social sciences. If there is a difference between history and the other social sciences, it is generally assumed that this is because historical data are less complete than are those that form the basis of other social sciences. Because of this, the historian tends to use already formulated laws, instead of formulating his own (Dray 1957:7).

Unfortunately, this particular interpretation is based on a false analogy, or, more precisely, on a false assessment of the nature of explanations offered by social scientists when they attempt to account for specific complex situations. For the most part, the claim that such studies are basically nomothetic is of limited validity. Generalizations may emerge from, or be tested by, such studies, but the situation being explained invariably contains many elements that are not covered in any way by the theoretical propositions being advanced. Insofar as these explanations of specific ethnographic situations claim to be adequate, they share far more in common with historical explanations than with nomothetic generalizations.

The resemblances between history and the generalizing social sciences also diminish when viewed in the broader contexts of these disciplines. In the generalizing social sciences, the principal emphasis is on the study of regularities and the formulation of explanations to account for them. Most observed regularities of human behavior are between a limited number of cultural variables, often only two. Ideally, relationships between such variables are studied in many specific cases of behavior, which occur in total contexts that frequently differ considerably from one another. It is assumed that given a sufficient variety of total contexts, the parameters of the variables being studied can be treated as "all things being equal." In this way, it is believed that valid relationships can be established between the variables being studied. Generally, however, because of the complexity and interrelatedness of human behavior, the result is the establishment of explanations to account for correlations that have a low to middle range of statistical significance. It is assumed that these middle-range generalizations can ultimately be subsumed under, and accounted for in terms of, broader generalizations about human behavior, or under headings such as individual behavior, social structure, or cultural process. At present, however, most higher level generalizations tend to be trivial, not generally accepted, or both. More important, the relationship of these higher level generalizations to middle level ones is generally obscure. From the point of view of explaining real situations, the main difference is that historians attempt to provide partial explanations for total situations, whereas social scientists with a nomothetic orientation aim to provide total explanations for selected aspects of these situations (cf. Kroeber 1952:63).

SYSTEMS THEORY

Recently, many archeologists have become concerned with the complexity of social systems and have sought to develop models to help them explain the variability that underlies these systems and the changes they undergo (Watson, LeBlanc, and Redman 1971:61–87). This has led to an increasing interest in applying the techniques, or at least the general ideas, of general systems theory to the explanation of archeological problems. This type of approach is interesting in the context of this discussion because it seems to approximate, on the one hand, the ideal of historical explanation and, on the other, the nomothetic goal of generalization. If the aim of the historian is to explain a specific situation or cultural transformation in its entirety, the explanation might be viewed ideally as taking the form of a complex system. It is inevitable, however, that the more complex a system becomes, the fewer examples of such a system are likely to be encountered. In principle, the systems designed by historians would be so complex that they would manifest themselves only once (see below). Yet, to be of cross-cultural significance, systems must be more general. It may be argued, of course, that systems constructed to explain specific situations will contain relationships of more general applicability and that various models, or parts of models, can be combined organically to provide more detailed explanations of specific circumstances than would otherwise be possible. However, it seems that, whatever the value of systems theory to prehistoric archeology or to the social sciences in general,* its application will

---

* In his recent review of D. L. Clarke's *Analytical Archaeology*, the mathematician William Steiger (1971) pointed out that except where a system's components, as well as their properties and linkages, are known in advance, or the analyst has the liberty to ask unlimited questions of those parts of the system that cannot be analyzed directly, the analytical value of systems theory may be very limited. Because of the nature of archeological data, these strictures may well apply to this discipline's contributions to generalizing types of analysis employing systems theory. If this is so, the most significant contributions of the latter approach to idiographic analysis may come, not through the nomothetically oriented analysis of archeological data, but through (a) the application of this approach in other generalizing social sciences and (b) the greater rigor with which the historian is led to formulate his explanations of specific events.

neither eliminate nor bridge the divergent tendencies of idiographic and nomothetic explanation. On the contrary, these opposing, but inextricably linked, modes of explanation will maintain the same dynamic tension within a systems theory approach as they have had within all other approaches.

EVOLUTIONISM

Anthropologists, including archeologists, who want to use a crude form of the covering law model to explain specific events are generally determinists. The basic assumption on which their explanations are based is that the totality of human behavior, or of cultural processes, is determined by a limited number of factors that constitute the core or substratum of a culture. This reduces the number of conditions that are required to be accounted for in order to explain a particular culture. Opinions differ concerning what factors, or how extensive a range of them, constitute the cultural core. In general, the theories predicating the minimum number of factors are those of the so-called unilineal or universal types (White 1959). By contrast, multilinear theories admit a larger range of basic types, mainly to take account of environmental variations (Steward 1955). Even with multilinear evolution, however, the number of cultural types requiring explanation is strictly limited.

The problem with all deterministic explanations of the evolutionary variety is that they tend to be overly general and trivial. By their very nature, they are unable to explain the total configurations of specific cultures; instead, they attempt to account for a limited number of features that a particular class of cultures may have in common. The broader the class of cultures being considered, the fewer are the features that they have in common and that need to be explained. All of these explanations suffer from the general weakness of candidate generalizations that ascend too far into generality and therefore lose their methodological interest. In Dray's (1957:29) words: "Their triviality lies in the fact that the farther the generalizing process is taken, the harder it becomes to conceive of anything which the truth of the law would rule out."

The reason for this is that social processes are complex, and the events they give rise to are even more so. In physics, the lawful explanation of a relatively few conditions accounts for any particular type of event, and these events tend to be repeated a vast number of times. In order to explain any event in the social sciences, it is necessary to account for many more conditions. This notion is implicit in the basic proposition that all elements of a cultural system are interrelated and that alterations in any one component will result in changes of varying degree in all features of the system and in their interrelationships. The number of variables is also considerably increased by the need to consider additional relationships between the natural and cultural systems, as well as biopsychological factors influencing human behavior. The complexity of the variables involved in concrete sociocultural relationships explains the often claimed uniqueness of historical events, which is the basis of much historiographic theorizing.

It may be argued that the limited nature of archeological data conforms better to a deterministic or evolutionary model than does purely historical data, because it automatically reduces the amount of detail to be explained. The assumption underlying this claim is that the segments of culture that are represented in the archeological record, particularly those that concern technological and economic patterns, are ones that constitute the core of a culture, whereas those areas that are more imperfectly represented are mainly random epiphenomena of minimal importance. While it may be argued, also along functionalist lines, that all aspects of human behavior in some way influence material culture, and are therefore available for study by the archeologist insofar as material culture is preserved in the archeological record, the fact remains that large domains of individual actions, oral culture, and belief systems are represented very imperfectly, or not at all in the archeological record. Nevertheless, if one accepts even a modified version of the functionalist view that all aspects of culture are in some way interrelated, then the more partial nature of archeological data does not signify that in reality the explanation of these data is necessarily any less complex than is the explanation of a contemporary situation.

Both archeologists and historians can also argue that the problems posed by the complexity of historical data can be minimized by concentrating on the features that classes of events have in common. It can be argued, for example, that all revolutions can be studied as examples of revolution and explained by accounting for the features that they have in common. Essentially, of course, this is what Steward (1955) has done in his so-called multilinear evolutionary approach, when he attempts to account for unilineal and composite bands, or early civilizations. It is, however, erroneous to identify this particular kind of generalizing as the only kind of explanation. Historians, while not denying the importance of features that events, such as revolutions, have in common, are more interested in explaining those features that are not common to all of them. They justify such an interest by pointing out that, in fact, each revolution is different from any other and that these differences are not less worthy of explanation than are the features common to revolutions.

THEORETICAL JUSTIFICATION OF PARTICULARIZING

The historians' position, as outlined above, could be dismissed as merely being an unscientific refusal to generalize. Some more conservative historians would accept this characterization and deny that their aim was to generalize or, indeed, that generalization was possible. This must be regarded, however, as being largely an antiquated opinion. The major proof that the explanation of an individual event, as it is attempted by historians, is a valid level of explanation lies in the fact that this level of specificity cannot be predicted from more general levels. It could be argued that the difference between individual events belonging to the same class (such as revolutions x, y, and z) is so small that these differences are of little or no theoretical interest. However, insofar as social scientists are concerned with explaining similarities and differences in human behavior, there is no obvious theoretical justification for such a position. It is possible for social scientists to make fairly accurate statistical predictions concerning complex phenomena, such as election results or national weekend accident rates, but these predictions are for the most part made, not on the basis of general theories, but on empirical evidence. Likewise, it is not possible to predict the specific features of one particular revolution from revolutions in general, and the armchair prehistorian, no matter how much general theory he knows, is unable to produce a detailed reconstruction of the course of human prehistory on the basis of what he knows about man at the present time. He is even less able, using theory alone, to rule out the possibility that alternative developments took place and thereby to demonstrate the accuracy of his reconstruction without making an appeal to outside evidence, in this case to the archeological record. The proof that even general trends, such as cultural evolution, as opposed to degeneration or cyclical developments, have been a major characteristic of human history does not rest on theory alone, but on external evidence of this sort. Predictions about human behavior tend to be either statistical or of a very high order of generality, but usually they cannot be used to reconstruct the past from a knowledge of the present alone. The inability to "predict" (i.e., retrodict) past events is of considerable theoretical significance. There is general agreement that the use of a theory to predict a specific event is merely another aspect of its use to explain that event (Dray 1957:2). It therefore becomes evident that existing theories of human behavior are inadequate to explain the past if explanation is used only in this sense. The question remains, however, of whether this is merely an indication of the immaturity of social science theory or a more permanent feature.

If complex situations involving human behavior tend to be unique, they evidently cannot be accounted for on an individual level by explaining the features that they have in common with other similar events. This does not, however, mean, as certain determinists and antiscientific historians suggest, that specific events cannot be accounted for in detail in terms of general laws. There is no scientific reason to believe that the most apparently trivial feature of an event is any more accidental or, in an ultimate sense, free or nondetermined than are the most significant regularities. Obviously, what is required is a different perspective on the mechanisms for explaining human behavior. An analogy with biology may be enlightening at this point. Just as each event in human history appears to be unique, so every genotype (with the exception of that of identical twins) is different from every other. The reason for this variation is the large variety of genes that can combine to give rise to any single genotype. Because of the number of genes involved, the chances of precisely the same combination coming together in any two individuals are vanishingly small. Nevertheless, in spite of this natural variation, processes of mutation, recombination, dominance, and selection have been formulated that explain what is happening to these genetic components. One can assume that variation in human behavior, that is, variation that makes each event unique, must be the product of many conditions, each subject to its own covering laws. These conditions are part of complex chains of causality that involve interaction between a wide variety of cultural subsystems, each with its own determining conditions. In the case of human behavior, the complexity of the situation is increased because more than one type of entity (equivalent to the gene) is involved and because the sociocultural system interacts with the natural one and with a series of factors that are part of man's biological nature. In specific situations, individual factors either reinforce or oppose one another, and by their combination shape the course of events. The involvement of factors derived from such a variety of systems in any specific historical event accounts, in large part, for the complex causality and hence uniqueness of such events.

INDETERMINACY IN EXPLAINING HISTORICAL EVENTS

In practice, the multiplicity of determining conditions that account for any one event means that historians usually lack sufficient theory to predict all the conditions required to explain it and therefore inadvertently they may be unaware of significant, and even key, elements in a particular situation. Second, social science explanations may be lacking for many elements known to be present, which means that their function remains uncertain. Because, as we have seen, the determining conditions of any particular event go well beyond the range of any one discipline and often beyond the range of the social sciences, the researcher rapidly reaches the point at which an attempt to account for the parameters in a specific situation becomes of trivial theoretical interest and transcends his ability to control the necessary data. Indeed, it is questionable whether a "total" explanation of an event can be given in the social sciences, in which at least some residual aspects of the events involved will not ultimately have to be accounted for in terms of chemistry and physics.

This situation has long been encountered in biology, where the understanding of process, as represented by the synthetic theory of evolution, is considerably more advanced than it is in the social sciences (Rouse 1964). Yet in biology it is generally recognized that it is impossible, on the basis of a knowledge of present life forms and of biological processes alone, to "predict" in detail the nature of species that are now extinct or the particular sequence of development that these species passed through. If this could be done, it would be also possible to "predict" with equal confidence the detailed "paleontological" record for future as well as past times. This deficiency does not result fully, or even in large part, from specific weaknesses in current biological theories of process. Instead, the situation arises because the parameters influencing the evolution of any species are extremely varied and difficult to control. To do this, not only would numerous biological variables have to be explained, but the biologist would have to have at his disposal detailed information about geological, climatic, and cosmological conditions in the past that exceeds anything that the disciplines dealing with these phenomena are able to provide. The possibility cannot be ruled out that someday enough will be known about process that the detailed prediction of the past and future will become possible in the biological and social sciences. Such a development would have to take place, however, within the framework of a unified general science, of a complexity unimaginable at this time. The prerequisite for prediction of this sort would be almost total, if not total, knowledge of process, which would mean that by the time it was possible, no further advances could be made in the nomothetic sciences.

"HOW POSSIBLY" EXPLANATIONS

If, given the state of knowledge existing in the social sciences now, or in the foreseeable future, it remains impossible to control for, or even to be certain of, the full range of conditions that are operative in any particular event, then it remains impossible to rule out the possibility that any event being predicted might turn out differently. Under these circumstances, the elucidation of historical events inevitably assumes the form of a "how possibly" rather than a "why necessarily" explanation (Dray 1957:158). As philosophers of history have pointed out, an important aspect of such explanations is having sufficient knowledge to see how x happened, rather than to be able to account for what made x happen. The latter implies that, given the explanatory conditions, it can be proved that nothing but x could have happened. An important characteristic of "how possibly" explanations is the reconstruction of a chain of events, accompanied by an effort to account for these events and their sequence. The explanations ideally should be based on well-established social science laws, but frequently common sense must be used as a filler because of the lack of such theory. The answers to many questions that arise as part of "how possibly" explanations take the form of additional data that eliminate one or more alternative possibilities (Dray 1957:156–169). The now venerable concept of archeological explanation taking the form of alternative possibilities may be viewed as a corollary of this theory (Chamberlain 1944). The same is true of the idea that archeological explanations represent approximations of truth that cannot be

proved and can only be disproved when shown not to explain the
data they were meant to cover.

Insofar as prehistoric archeology, like history, strives to explain
specific events, it becomes possible to define the special sense in
which it can be regarded as an experimental discipline. By experiments, we are not thinking of techniques for the controlled establishment of regularities, but rather of the testing of "how possibly"
reconstructions against new archeological evidence. By providing
new evidence about an event, or series of events, the archeological
record offers a test of the adequacy of the reconstruction, and also of
the interpretation, of the event. This is inevitable because, in
explaining the evidence, certain tentative hypotheses will have been
advanced concerning aspects of what happened not covered by the
archeological evidence that was originally available. Once more, this
is by no means a new view of archeological method. It is, however, a
view that fits very comfortably into a "how possibly" structure of
explanation, as opposed to a more rigid attempt to apply a covering
law model. This mode of explanation also attaches special significance to the archeological record. Instead of being seen as only
another source of data for generalizing about cultural processes, the
archeological record becomes by far the most important means by
which the prehistory of man may be reconstructed and explained. An
understanding of the past can be derived only by explaining the
evidence of the past as it has survived in the archeological record. If
archeological evidence can be used as a basis for generalizing about
the nature of culture, the reverse is not true—that generalizations
and a knowledge of present conditions alone can permit the reconstruction and study of the past. For this reason, it becomes both
expedient and reasonable to view the primary aim of archeology as
the explanation of the archeological record rather than the nature of
material culture.

A FINAL OBJECTION COUNTERED

It is frequently argued that certain generalizations about human
behavior can be based only on historical or archeological data
(Tuggle 1971:131). In particular, it is suggested that only these latter
disciplines may be able to produce the data concerning a variety of
slow, long-term processes about which general explanations should
be formulated and tested. A second argument draws attention to the

long periods of human development for which only archeology can provide behavioral data and argues that the use of such data to test general hypotheses is far from wasted effort. More specifically, it is argued that only archeological evidence can ever be used to test theories about the behavior of early hominids, which must certainly have been different from that of modern man.

I have no disagreement with the suggestion that archeological evidence can be used profitably to test theories about certain very significant categories of human behavior. I am convinced, however, that one of the weaknesses of much of the current theorizing in archeology can be traced to the tendency of some archeologists to treat their discipline as simply the "past tense of ethnology" or a kind of "paleoanthropology," instead of defining its goals in terms of the potentialities of its data and asking the kinds of questions with which the data of archeology are best equipped to deal.

I must confess that I share the traditional social anthropological view that long-term studies of the past are irrelevant for understanding the processes that underlie human behavior and that account for the functioning and changes that take place in all social systems, irrespective of age or degree of sociocultural complexity. Biologists are able to explain the paleontological record as the outcome, over long periods, of processes, such as mutation and natural selection, that are best studied as they occur at the present time. I believe that the same kind of uniformitarianism will apply in studies of human behavior and that ultimately archeologists should be able to explain the archeological record in terms of processes such as innovation, diffusion, and adaptation, which can be studied fully and completely in any contemporary society. I do not share the view of some social anthropologists that the past can only live in the present as myth and that therefore any objective understanding of the past is impossible. Nor do I wish to deny that the study of the past, either through written documents or the remains of material culture, can contribute to the formulation and testing of rules about human behavior. I would argue, however, that archeological evidence is a far more intractable source of information about many, if not all, areas of human behavior than are studies of contemporary man and that, since there are no generalizations about human behavior that one can expect to gain from archeological data that could not be gained far more efficiently from studies of contemporary societies, the use of archeological data for this purpose tends to be wasteful and inefficient. Explaining the behavior of early hominids must be viewed largely as an idiographic objective and, in any case, many more general principles are likely to be derived from the comparative study of living primates than from the analysis of archeological data. Future developments in archeology may prove my position to be wrong, but none of the developments in archeology to date appears to indicate that this will be the case.

SUMMARY

In light of the preceding discussion, it is possible to view prehistoric archeology as having four principal goals:

1. *To generalize about the nature of culture or human behavior.* It has not been my aim in this chapter to deny that archeological evidence can be used as a basis for generalizing, in the same manner as other data used by social scientists. However, in comparison with studies of living peoples, such evidence is more difficult to collect and the range of variables available for observations tends to be limited, as does the behavioral context of the data.

2. *To test existing theories.* The complexity of historical events (conceived of very broadly here) is such that the generalizations of the social sciences cannot be used to predict, or therefore to explain, the past without reference to archeological evidence. To explain the past, archeological evidence is essential. In spite of this, the explanation of these data requires the application of social science theory, particularly as derived from ethnology. Such explanations use theory and, in this sense, serve as a test of theory.

3. *To explore interconnections between existing bodies of theory.* From a theoretical point of view, the "how possibly" explanations of history and prehistory do more than merely test theory. By attempting to explain specific complex events, historical explanation facilitates the exploration of interconnections between bodies of theory associated with the various established nomothetic disciplines. This facilitates the discovery of unsuspected correlations requiring explanation and of interdisciplinary areas of considerable potential interest. This function, being a more particular property of prehistoric archeology than are the first two, may, in this sense, be regarded as a more important one.

4. *To explain the past.* If the social sciences possessed an almost total understanding of sociocultural process and were able to control for the effects of a sufficient number of parameters, it might be possible to predict the past or future on the basis of the present and to demonstrate that no other past or future was possible. Until such feats can be done, the study of prehistory must be essentially an explanation of the archeological record. Insofar as an understanding of past developments is an important aspect of understanding current variations in behavior and culture, such a study, while idiographic, is a vital part of a scientific study of man. Moreover, since the formulation and testing of generalizations about human behavior can be based on contemporary, as well as archeological, data, while the past can be explained only with the help of archeological data, the explanation of past events must be regarded as the most important goal of archeological research.

8. THE FUTURE OF ARCHEOLOGY IN ANTHROPOLOGY: CULTURE HISTORY AND SOCIAL SCIENCE

PATTY JO WATSON

Department of Anthropology
Washington University
St. Louis, Missouri

Four years ago Kent Flannery published a statement that defined the lines of theoretical debate in archeology as being drawn between those interested in culture history and those pursuing culture process (Flannery 1967). The culture process school, to use Flannery's terminology, is often identified with "new archeology" and thus is contrasted with "old archeology" or the culture history school. This raises the following questions: Is there a basic theoretical division within anthropological archeology? Is our future one of choosing up sides and fighting it out between old and new archeology, between culture historians and culture processualists, between archeology as history and archeology as science? During the last three years, reaction to new archeology (processual archeology, scientific archeology, systems archeology) has begun to appear in print. One way of assessing the nature and intensity of disagreement is to examine and discuss these printed statements.

Jacquetta Hawkes (1968) and Donn Bayard (1969) certainly agree that there is a dichotomy in archeological theory, and they are the most outspoken critics of what they take to be explicitly scientific archeology. Hawkes in particular believes that science and history are two quite different and antithetical pursuits, and that archeology cannot be a science but is a kind of history with the reconstruction of individual events in time as its aim.

However, as many others have argued (e.g., Hempel 1942; Brodbeck 1962; Schiffer 1971; R. Watson 1966, 1969; P. Watson, LeBlanc, and Redman 1971), there is no logical distinction between history and science, but only a difference in emphasis. Briefly outlined, the opposing view to that of Hawkes is that the empirical data of archeology, like any other body of empirical data, can be used or dealt with in a number of ways. Specifically, with respect to archeology, we can use our data in these ways.

1. To furnish collectors' items and museum objects.
2. To furnish documentation for the study of art history or the history of architecture.
3. To attain knowledge of sequences of events and chronologies in the absence of written documents (this is history *sensu stricto*, which Walter Taylor called "chronicle").
4. To help furnish data for much fuller historical studies (historiography, structural, or constructive history) with particularistic (idiographic) goals.
5. To furnish independent data that can be used to test hypotheses in order to confirm or disconfirm them as general laws about cultural processes (i.e., about the internal and external dynamics of human groups at one point in time or through time); this has to do with large-scale generalizing (nomothetic) goals; the general laws so confirmed provide us with an understanding of history (i.e., they are foundational in treating history as a science).

Hawkes apparently considers history and archeology to comprise number 3 essentially ("the final purposes [of archaeology] are historical; the reconstruction of individual events in time" [1968:255]. She expresses no clear ideas of what science is, except that it has to do with graphs, statistics, and esoteric hardware like proton magnetometers.

Most of the rest of Hawkes' general criticisms of new archeology and related developments are thoughtfully dealt with by Isaac (1971) and need not be further considered here.

Bayard (1969), like Hawkes, also believes archeology is not and cannot be a science. However, I refuse to accept, as he does, Onions' *Shorter Oxford Dictionary on Historical Principles* (1965) as the final authority on science and scientific method. In any case, the article may well be a hoax. The Spring 1971 issue of *Antiquity* reveals that Bayard, together with some of his colleagues at Otago University in New Zealand, have put together a logogenetic spoof of new archeology (Binclarke n.d.) that makes some much stronger critical points than the *American Antiquity* article. Even so, the major criticisms are of the jargon of new archeology rather than its logical structure.

Trigger (1970) is firm in his belief that prehistory must be predominantly idiographic (i.e., particularizing), instead of nomothetic (generalizing), but he does not deny the validity of a nomothetic approach to history. Quite the contrary, he takes some adherents of new archeology to task for not being aware of the nomothetic orientations of several practicing historians. Trigger's point is that it is inefficient to use the data of prehistory to aid in formulating and testing lawlike generalizations (general laws) about cultural process.

In some cases this is certainly true; however, it is also true that only by archeological means can we gain access to that immense reservoir of human behavioral data undocumented by written history. Contemporary and historically documented cultures represent a small fraction of the total universe of human societies, and the potential contribution is so great—if we can unlock this reservoir of behavioral data representing vast stretches of time and space in the human past—that we cannot afford to ignore it. Hence the direction much archeological work is now taking is toward trying to find the limits of valid behavioral interpretation based on detailed (usually computer-aided) associational analyses of the material remains of extinct human groups complemented by detailed, archeologically oriented ethnographic studies.

Kushner (1970) seems to be making two main criticisms of what he calls processual archeology:

1. The processualists rely much too heavily on a very limited kind of ecological approach and/or on a very limited aspect of a systems approach for their explanations.
2. The processualists do not consider the particular details of individual cultures, nor do they deal with individual human beings.

The first point is not really relevant to the present discussion, which concerns the questions: Is there a basic dichotomy between science and history? Must archeology choose one or the other? Hence I do not discuss it further here. The second point is very similar to Trigger's; Kushner, like Trigger, favors a particularistic emphasis and presumably would join Trigger in stressing the idiographic aspects of prehistoric archeology.

Allen and Richardson (1971) call attention to a potentially grave methodological problem for those adherents of the new archeology who are attempting to achieve greater sophistication in dealing with prehistoric social organization. Allen and Richardson's critique is potentially highly significant because archeologists cannot deal in a meaningful way with questions of social organization and culture process if they cannot use the archeological record to infer social organization. The question Allen and Richardson raise is this: How can archeologists (such as Longacre 1968 and Hill 1966) work with residence patterns and concepts of lineality when even ethnographers have trouble defining such concepts and/or identifying the patterns for any one living culture? The answer is that archeologists, potentially at any rate, can uncover the systematic arrangements of cultural debris that resulted from such patterned behavior as uxorilocality, for instance. Arguments by ethnologists and social anthropologists as to the reality of taxonomic units like Murdock's are not of immediate interest to archeologists; in practice, these concepts are one source of hypothetical explanations for archeological data.

In summary, the substantive criticisms of new archeology as represented by these publications are:

1. The Hawkes–Bayard position that prehistoric archeology cannot be a science.
2. The Trigger position (with Kushner concurring) that prehistoric archeology is or can be a science but, contrary to the opinions of new archeologists, must be primarily idiographic rather than nomothetic in emphasis (a consumer of laws rather than a producer of laws).

(In addition, Allen and Richardson, Hawkes, Bayard, and Kushner make several specific methodological criticisms of new archeology not dealt with in detail here because my concern in this chapter is with the most fundamental theoretical issues.)

Criticism 1 is discussed above: there is no *logical* reason why archeological data cannot be used scientifically, and therefore there is no *logical* reason why archeology cannot be a science.

With respect to criticism 2, both nomothetic and idiographic studies are necessary to a developed field of research. This is because the purpose of establishing general laws in nomothetically oriented studies is to enable explanation and prediction of the subject matter in question. And one cannot explain or predict without reference to the results of particularistic studies of concrete situations. Thus a developed field includes both emphases. But must we overtly stress one or the other emphasis?

Trigger says yes with respect to anthropological archeology: it must be an essentially *idiographic* discipline. Fritz and Plog say yes with respect to anthropological archeology; it must be an essentially *nomothetic* discipline. I say we need not and, indeed, cannot make such an overt choice in so far as the logic of the matter is concerned. As Schiffer notes (1971), the overall character of a field or discipline depends on the questions asked by the investigators at any one time. Early twentieth century archeology is characterized by particularistic interests, but during the past 10 years nomothetic interests have burgeoned. However, it would be extremely undesirable—even if it were possible—to choose one emphasis once and forever to dominate the entire field. The ideal situation is one in which both kinds of studies are explicitly carried out and in which maximum, sympathetic interaction occurs between particularists and generalists who understand each other's problems and respect each other's concerns and methods.

In view of many of the comments made by official and unofficial discussants at the symposium that instigated this volume, I believe it worthwhile to outline, in the interests of clarification, what I think nomothetically oriented (generalist) archeology is or might be.

First, some basic definitions are necessary. A law or lawlike generalization is a relationship between two or more variables or sets of variables. The relationship can be described by a statement having the following logical form: in circumstances of type C, if A (a phenomenon or complex of phenomena or an event or complex of events) occurs, then so does or will B (another phenomenon or complex of phenomena or another event or complex of events). A statement of this form that has been strongly confirmed by numerous or critical investigations is a lawlike generalization (or general law). A statement of this form that has not been tested and confirmed or disconfirmed is a hypothesis. The kind and degree of confirmation necessary to elevate the hypothesis to the status of a law or lawlike generalization is agreed upon, often implicitly, by the practitioners of the discipline in question.

Misunderstanding about the nature of general laws or lawlike generalizations often arises because some lawlike generalizations have highly specified circumstances and objects and thus apply only to a limited number of situations. An example is Worsaae's Law (Rowe 1962) that states that items associated in burials were in use at the same time: in C—excavation of a burial, if A—recovery of a number of pottery vessels and projectile points, then B—the vessels and points were in use at the same time in the society to which the defunct individual belonged. This law is a very useful one to the archeologist and is just as legitimate as other laws that apply to much more broadly defined circumstances and objects. Examples are Steno's Law (the law of superposition; see Hole and Heizer 1969: 16–17 or—probably the best known example from another field—the Law of Falling Bodies. The differences among these laws are in their content, not in their logical form. Highly specified laws are of the same logical form as those applicable to broadly defined circumstances and objects.

Explanation of any particular case or event consists of referring it to the relevant lawlike generalization or set of lawlike generalizations that show it to be a special instance of certain general relationships. This amounts to saying: given those circumstances (C) and this lawlike generalization or set of them (A), we would have expected that (B) to happen. So the structure of scientific explanations can also be written in shorthand as "in C, if A, then B."*

---

*It should be stressed that this framework does not prescribe monocausal explanations and laws. The circumstances C may be quite complex—temporally, spatially, and processually—and both A and B may stand for complexes of variables or laws in either a law statement or an explanation statement. See, for example, the article by Tuggle, Townsend, and Riley (1972:8) in which their diagrammatic rendering (following Meehan 1968) of a set of variables and their interrelations in a hypothetical systemic explanation can be summarized as "in C, if A then B":

$$\text{``} \begin{bmatrix} V_1 V_2 V_3 \ldots V_n \\ R_1 R_2 R_3 \ldots R_n \end{bmatrix} \mathbf{Z}\Phi \quad \text{''}$$

where V = Variable
R = Relationship (among the variables)
$\mathbf{Z}$ = "if . . . then. . . . "
Φ = " . . . any logical entailment of the system which may be deduced from the system through the application of rules of inference."

In other words, in circumstances C (such that variables 1 to n are present and exhibit relationships 1 to n), if A (variables 1 to n and relationships 1 to n operating in a closed system), then B[entailment(s) Φ].

In fact, on the page preceding the diagram (Tuggle, Townsend, and Riley 1972:7), Meehan is quoted as defining explanation in a Hempelian manner as follows. He sug-

A theory is a body of lawlike generalizations pertaining to the subject matter in question. In disciplines dealing with less complex aspects of reality—chemistry and physics for instance—sets of lawlike generalizations can be axiomatized so that some are presented as basic axioms from which the others can be deduced. However, theories that are unaxiomatized, or that cannot (yet) be axiomatized, can be perfectly respectable.

Archeological theory, then, would be and is a body of largely unaxiomatized, lawlike generalizations relevant to the subject matter of archeology: sites (site formation processes and stratigraphy, for example) and the ancient cultural debris found in, on, and about them. Under the immediate impetus of "new archeology," attention is being given to an explicit search for regularities (i.e., hypotheses to be tested) concerning the relationships between the cultural debris and the extinct society responsible for it. This behavioral data is then potentially available to persons seeking broader regularities about human societies existing anywhere or any time.

A question that always arises in this context is: What is new about new archeology, if anything? I think two points can be made in answer. The first is insistence by Taylor (1948) and Binford (1962) that a great deal of information about extinct cultures is preserved in the archeological remains and their microdistribution and associations. This emphasis reverses the stress formerly placed on the paucity and poverty of the archeological record. The eliciting of the distributional and associational information is made feasible by judicious and careful use of computer-aided statistical techniques; but any technique at all may be applied if the investigator knows how to use it and if it is appropriate to his problem.

The second point is the emphasis on the explicit use of the basic logic of science. This is to specify the propositions (hypothetical lawlike generalizations or hypothetical explanations referring to such generalizations) being tested, to make sure to get the appropriate data to test them (be it ceramic, lithic, or other), and then to evaluate

---

gests that explanation can validly be framed only in terms of change and he thus defines explanation as:

"a way of organizing human experience to show how or why events occur by linking those events to other events according to stipulated rules."

Or, in other words "in C (events of one sort), if A (the stipulated rules linking those events to other events), then D (other events)." Compare Hempel 1965:403-410; 297-330; and LeBlanc in this volume.

the status of each proposition (or hypothesis): Does it stand up or not? Is it confirmed or not?

I can now discuss archeological theory more specifically. The Binfords (1968), Schiffer (1971, 1972, and n.d.), R. Watson (1970), and P. Watson, LeBlanc, and Redman (1971:24–26) have stressed the twofold aspect of archeological theory. We must be able to interpret the remains per se in terms of stratigraphy, disturbed or undisturbed (in situ) situations, and so on. Here we have to do with the materials that make up an archeological site and their physical condition, especially the nature of deposition and of postdepositional events there.

We must be able to make valid inferences about the extinct society on the basis of the preserved material remains.

Archeological theory, then, consists of assumptions and lawlike generalizations about the physical aspects of archeological sites and the debris in, on, and about them left by past human groups, plus assumptions and lawlike generalizations about the relationships of that debris to the activities of those groups.

Explanation of the remains at any one site consists of relating the particular materials from that site to the assumptions and lawlike generalizations about sites and site formation processes in general and to our assumptions and lawlike generalizations about the ways human activities are reflected in archeologically recoverable debris.

There is a substantial body of generally agreed upon assumptions and generalizations for the first aspect of archeological theory, although there is certainly scope for further work. The second aspect is much less developed but is currently receiving more attention (Watson, LeBlanc, and Redman 1971:54–56).

I consider generalistic (or nomothetically oriented) archeology to be concerned with the status of those assumptions and generalizations that enable explanation of the archeological record at any one site or series of sites, and that enable interested persons to use archeological material as they might use historical data to suggest and test hypotheses about cultural processes. Hence, nomothetically oriented archeologists are concerned with particular sites and problems not for their intrinsic interest alone, but also for the contribution to general archeological or anthropological theory they make possible. As an example, consider Redman and Watson (1970): the specific results of the surface surveys at two Turkish prehistoric sites are highly relevant and important to the particular work undertaken at those sites, but are also a contribution to archeological theory (specifically to the first aspect of archeological theory as discussed above (p. 4).

As an example of particularistically oriented archeological work, see Watson et al. (1969). Our primary aim in this work is to describe and explain the prehistoric use of Salts Cave, paying little attention to generalizations reaching beyond this case (except for possible theoretical ramifications of the dietary remains).

As an example of nomothetically oriented archeology, see the work of Robert McC. Adams. His synthesis of earlier work, plus his own surveys and research (Adams 1956, 1965), can be viewed as testing Wittfogel's hydraulic hypothesis against the data from Mesopotamia. Adams found that the data do not support Wittfogel's hypothesis. Adams (1960, 1966a) inductively infers a series of alternative hypothetical lawlike generalizations that, if confirmed, would be at least partially explanatory of the development of early civilizations in Mesopotamia and Mesoamerica. Examples of the kinds of regularities he finds to be common to both developments are:

1. The effects of intensive agriculture combined with the effects of unequal access to vital resources.
2. Multiplicity of subsistence pursuits resulting in trade and the evolution of other redistributive mechanisms.

Both of these examples are trends having predictable results, and both could be tested in a third independent area; for example, that of the Shang dynasty in the Yellow River Valley of northern China. The Shang specialist with a strong particularistic interest in this aspect of ancient China may not have the slightest interest in searching for data from around the world at different times in order to test and help confirm generalizations about the origin and development of civilization as such. But his particularistic data about Shang development would be of considerable significance to a generalistic archeologist like Adams, who might be concerned with Shang origins as a test for the hypotheses formed on the basis of knowledge of Meso-potamian and Mesoamerican developments. The generalist cannot amass all the specific detail to test even one of the possible hypothetical regularities by his own field research but must rely on information furnished by various specialists. The specialists, however, cannot make sense of their data without referring to generalizations about cultural and social behavior of human groups in particular circumstances. Thus, as noted earlier, both nomothetically and particular-istically oriented studies are necessary to the advancing of knowledge in this—or any—field. It should also be stressed that both kinds of studies can be carried out in an explicitly hypothetico-deductive fashion. Of the examples referred to on pp. 120–121, the Turkish study

(Redman and Watson 1970) is explicitly hypothetico-deductive and nomothetic; the Salts Cave studies are predominantly particularistic and some of them are also explicitly hypothetico-deductive (Redman 1969).

I now return to my original point: the empirical data of the archeological record can be treated in an explicitly scientific manner by both nomotheticists and particularists and, in an ideal situation, both kinds of studies will be undertaken in an atmosphere of mutual respect.

There is, then, no logical reason to split the field into two contending camps labeled culture history and culture process, history and science, idiographic and nomothetic, old archeology and new archeology. Idiographic and nomothetic studies are both essential in building knowledge about any subject matter, including the prehistoric past. Once misunderstanding and confusion are removed, it should be clear that there is no *logical* conflict between the two, even though there is potential for conflict on *practical* grounds. There are three major sources for pragmatically based conflict:

1. Most researchers are trained in and feel comfortable with one approach or the other, but usually not with both. Thus, although the two are logically inseparable, they are often embodied in separate individuals who stress one or the other, so that there is a tendency for them to be treated as mutually exclusive in practice.

2. As we are all aware, digging, no matter how much data it brings to light, also destroys. Whatever data are not recorded during any excavation may be lost forever. Thus if the particularistic researcher does not record data relevant to the generalist (or vice versa), those data may be irretrievable. A special case of this general problem is salvage archeology, which is receiving considerable attention lately. Chenhall (1971) states that salvage archeology can and must proceed in a narrowly inductive way without reference to specific testable hypotheses. It is, of course, highly preferable and much more efficient nomothetically to be able to choose a site (or sites) freely to fit one's previously drawn-up research design. However, it is certainly possible to proceed in a more *post hoc*, but still overtly hypothetico-deductive fashion, and to generate interesting hypotheses that can be tested by excavation at previously designated sites menaced by roads, dams, and pipelines. In short, I think Chenhall is wrong in pre-

senting salvage archeology as necessarily particularistic and narrowly inductivistic. In fact, in the same issue of *American Antiquity* as Chenhall's note is an article by King (1971), in which he outlines a procedure that would enable salvage archeology in the North Coast ranges of California to be undertaken in a manner calculated to satisfy processualistic goals.

3. As competition becomes greater for less research money, we may be forced to draw more sharply lines that in affluent times could be left comfortably fuzzy. The result could be the nurturing of allegiances and animosities based on the practical fact noted above that although the field as a whole must include both approaches, individual researchers are either idiographically or nomothetically oriented but seldom combine the two approaches. For example, Hawkes objects strenuously to McBurney's statistics-laden *Haua Fteah* report because although, she says, it was heavily subsidized, the book costs 12 pounds, took 10 years of work by McBurney and his students, and is filled with charts and tables that Hawkes regards as ugly and inadequate representations of the material. "The archaeological purse, at least in this country, is not bottomless and extravagence in one direction must lead to deprivation in another" (Hawkes 1968:257). Even though others may find McBurney's report adequate, scientific, and beautiful, it is clear that Hawkes believes he used resources of money and labor that she could have put to much better use in the interests of what she takes to be proper archeology.

The Image of Limited Good threatens us all; in the competition for available research funds, lines will be drawn and names will be named, as Hawkes has done, not because logic dictates but because practical necessity impels.

What can be done to avert or ameliorate the conflict situation? Much of the difficulty stems from the fact that traditionally, at least, most researchers are wholeheartedly committed either to an idiographic or a nomothetic approach but not to both. This is, in many ways, an efficient division of labor but may have strong disadvantages as indicated in points 2 and 3 above. The disadvantages would be obviated if we all realize and agree upon the logical necessity for both kinds of research. This agreement must be combined with meaningful interchanges between individuals of different orienta-

tions and with the encouragement of students to develop both particularistic and generalistic research skills. The most important factor is
communication and interaction. It is a hopeful sign that so far we
have avoided the situation Harvey says prevails among geographers
of different theoretical persuasions: " ... the failure to indulge in
methodological debate which specifically considers the relationship
between the methodology of geography and scientific epistemology
in general, has led to the development of multiple methodological
frameworks within which specialist geographers pursue their own
interests in relative isolation" [Harvey 1969:66].

If, in contrast to such a situation, we can continue to be honest
and outspoken about our differences without coming to blows or
incurring lifelong enmity, then we are in a good position to work
toward a consensus on goals and methods for archeology.

9. ARCHEOLOGY AS THE SCIENCE OF TECHNOLOGY: MORMON TOWN PLANS AND FENCES

MARK P. LEONE

Department of Anthropology
Princeton University
Princeton, New Jersey

For as long as archeology has been practiced, archeologists have been concerned with what the discipline is about. That is probably as it should be and, when compared with similar preoccupations in other disciplines, is not unusual. Whether long-standing concern with rationales is a uniquely American phenomenon is unclear, but not at all unclear is that American archeologists have long been making public statements devoted to what makes them do what they do. Wissler, Taylor, Binford and almost every practitioner who has seriously lifted a spade has felt compelled to explain why he did so. The explanations occasionally are personal and idiosyncratic. More common is the usual explanation about wanting to know what the prehistoric past was all about. But in general, as Taylor showed in 1948 and as Binford demonstrated in 1968, there are really two or three basic aims that unify the whole of the archeological subfield.

The first is history: culture history, culture-historical reconstruction, reconstruction of past lifeways, putting the flesh on the bones of the past, or discovering the Indian behind the artifact. This goal of archeology deals with unique, particular, nonrepetitive events. It is history; it aims to do history. Dealing with this aim, Taylor distinguished between mere chronicle and social history (or functional history). The distinction issues from the observed discrepancy between announced archeological goals and archeological results. The former is what archeologists can be observed to do and is chronicle; the latter—functional history—is an unrealized aim. This was Taylor's judgment and, as of 1948, there was no gainsaying him.

Two and a half decades later we are presented with several widely celebrated efforts at social or cultural history. They are not called that, to be sure. The new archeology has given us consistent efforts to understand the social and economic organization of several extinct societies. That they are completely novel and innovative is beyond reasonable questioning at this late date. These studies (Binford, Deetz, Flannery, Hill, Longacre, and Whallon, for example) are based on the now widely understood effort to link archeological contributions to anthropological theory, especially materialist evolutionary theory. The studies have not been assessed yet as a coherent body of contributions using the explicit goals that they themselves set out to achieve. Preliminary judgments offered in *New Perspectives in Archeology* (Binford and Binford, 1968b:343–361) indicate happiness with the potential transformation archeology is capable of, but some doubt about whether it can ever really be achieved. Two questions are posed by the commentators in *New Perspectives*. The first is traditional and wonders whether archeologists will ever discover what questions cultural anthropologists think are significant. The second is a bit more implicit and wonders whether, because of the muteness of its data, archeology is not permanently condemned to subordinate status in anthropology. This second question asks whether any of the primary models for comprehending cultural phenomena can spring from prehistoric data. This question has its traditional answers. To answer it, we should ask whether any recent pieces of archeological research contribute new models to the domain of social organization. For instance, do we now know more about the general patterning of either the subsistence activities or the kinship systems of hunting-gathering or agricultural peoples? We may. On the other hand, we may simply have a bigger fund of data and problems than before. A clear answer to this question is not yet in hand. To see if recent archeological work is really contributing in a primary way to cultural anthropology, we might choose to ask whether or not the models used by archeologists are assessed as valid after being subjected to testing on the prehistoric record. That this question has no unambiguous answer is an index to the irrelevance of testing in the research design of most archeologists.

The second aim of anthropological archeology is harder to put into words. The ringing phrase of the 1960s is "culture process." The goal is a knowledge of the systematic ways in which cultures fit their subsystems together and how such articulated variables shift or change over time. Through the use of the strategy of cultural ecology, this goal of archeology is aimed at establishing the principles of cultural evolution. Some excellent examples of scholarship are addressed to this aim. Adams (1966a), Binford (1968b), Flannery (1965), Murra (1968), and others have attempted to isolate the processes behind uniform sets of cultural events. In many ways these are the most recent and widely known contributions of archeology to its parent discipline. It is important, nonetheless, to see that every one transgresses—really overcomes—the chief boundary around prehistoric archeology. Researchers are not content to borrow bits and pieces of the present and, by analogy, apply them to the past; they borrow a model whole-hog out of the living (historic) present. In the work of Adams and Murra, both possess long chains of written records for the very periods with which they are concerned. Both are as deeply immersed in the written records of the periods surrounding the events they are trying to explain as they are with the archeology of the problem. They are, in fact, doing a form of historical archeology (Schuyler 1970). Binford and Flannery have used models from demography and plant genetics and applied them to the origins of domestication. While it is an exaggeration to say that those disciplines are the only sources of their respective inspiration, it is also an error to suppose that they picked up a model one place and plunked it down at another. The living ethnography of the Middle East, of hunters and gathers, of pastoral nomads, and of Inca ethnohistory played an important role in formulating their models. Furthermore, the models were modified to fit prehistoric data. Leaving such qualifications aside for a moment, these archeologists, in borrowing models, borrow the processes that link together a set of factors. They utilize in their own analysis a system (a set of understood interconnections) that is the product of an investigation that took place in the present. The present here may even be the ethnohistoric record, as is the case with Murra but, nonetheless, it is the present in the sense that it is living or was recorded while it was living. Such models are then fitted on the past and the goodness of fit is an index to their success as models.

Some assessment is needed about the scale of the contribution made by efforts at studying culture process. That cannot be done with any sophistication here. It may just be too early to do so anywhere. A few observations can be made without prejudice, however. Such contributions are rare. They are rare because few archeologists comprehend the rationale of culture process and still fewer attempt to actualize it. They are also rare because to make such a contribution demands that the prehistoric data be tied to documents, or that the archeologist must become familiar enough with another discipline to borrow from it in reasonably sophisticated ways. In sum, it is the muteness inherent in prehistoric data. When processualist-oriented archeologists are successful, it is because they keyed into models that could be adjusted to fit the data they had in hand for their particular problem. In principle, this need not limit an archeologist. But, in fact, few archeologists deal comfortably with living or historic models, and few can take time to discover what other disciplines can contribute to their own range of problems. Where does this leave us?

There is a sense of incompleteness in archeology. It may have always been there, but there is little doubt about its heightened presence at the moment. A reading of the present temper of our subdiscipline shows a growing (but undirected and unrealized) promise and a temper tied (in ways that should be specified better than has been done here) to the predicament related above. Thus, of the two goals of archeology, the first—history, even social history—today leaves people with genuine doubts about its ultimate validity. The second—studies of cultural evolution—has seen well over a decade's worth of attempts with relatively few results and some staggering conceptual problems.

When archeologists talk about their own field, they are myopic. After all, how do you obtain any kind of objective perspective on yourself—especially when you have never been trained to do ethnographic fieldwork, let alone intellectual history? Most people who have done the history of archeology have generally been so unconscious that they have built their schemes around the public statements archeologists made or, doing some fieldwork, they have contrasted different periods of research with an eye to the different kinds of empirical results produced. None has systematically contrasted the public pronouncements with the published results. But, more to the point, rarely has a historian of archeology stepped aside to ask what are the patterns in American culture of which archeology is a product. Every anthropologist, on the other hand, makes it a point in his professional teaching career to reveal to students that they are the products of culture, that they, like all people, are molded by culture to behave the way they do, and that they behave neither randomly nor through the exercise of free will Inevitably our subdiscipline is the product of and is subject to the same forces that we as individuals are. As Glyn Daniel (1962) has shown, archeology is the product of a set of larger events: processes that are tied to the Industrial Revolution and half a dozen associated events. If we assume that archeology was not created by mistake, then I think we must assume that there are some systematic reasons for its present activities. In the absence of an intellectual history of archeology, it is appropriate to ask not what archeologists say to themselves or to the public but, instead, what does the public do with archeology? What does a nation that spends millions of dollars annually on archeology get out of that investment? The answer to these questions could show us that there is more to archeology than the two aims discussed. It is just too naïve to suppose that the return on the investment really takes the form of monographs, journal articles, and professional conventions. Even classroom teaching is not a sufficient return.

What the public gets out of archeology is archeology's third major, but unrecognized, rationale: the empirical substantiation of national mythology. Such a hypothesis deserves more careful scrutiny than it is possible to give here where it serves as a foil for a larger issue. There are two clusters of evidence that serve to illustrate some of the uses to which archeology is being put. The first is exemplified by the reconstruction colonial Williamsburg, the Mormon reconstruction of Nauvoo, and the Canadian reconstruction of the colonial French fortress of Louisbourg. Subsets of this genre are the great and popular archeological national parks of the southwestern United States, typified by Mesa Verde. The genre is the three-dimensional reconstruction of past lifeways.

There isn't a soul who needs colonial Williamsburg identified for him. The role of archeology in providing the endless accuracies that are said to be represented there is primary. Archeology provides a level of credibility or probability—in short, believability—for all the uses Williamsburg was to be put (Cotter 1970).

The Mormon restoration of Nauvoo will be, as one journalist put it, the "Williamsburg of the West." Nauvoo, a city of 12,000–15,000 people in 1845 (then the largest city in Illinois), had been founded some 12 years earlier by the Mormons after they had been run out of

Missouri. The Mormons completely abandoned the city in 1846–1847 after the death of their prophet at the hands of a mob in 1844. Nauvoo partly fell into ruins and partly was sacked by anti-Mormons; it was in a state not unlike Williamsburg before reconstruction was begun. The Mormons are spending a large amount of money to restore parts of Nauvoo. They are quite explicit about the potential usefulness of this reconstruction as a center for demonstrating their own history for the purpose of making converts. The excavation of Nauvoo is in the hands of competent archeologists and there is no doubt that the effort at literal accuracy in recreating what the place looked like will be as fastidious as Williamsburg.

The same kind of instantaneous national monument (or monument to national culture) has been put together with the rebuilding of the royal French fortress at Louisbourg. This is an ongoing project as those at Williamsburg and Nauvoo and, because the installations are so massive, it will require decades to complete. This, of course, has the advantage of allowing the site to reflect the change that interpretations undergo. Dozens of archeologists have been employed by the central Canadian government in the primary work needed to insure authenticity.

What are these sites all about and why do they rely as heavily as they seem to on archeological techniques? All of the three-dimensional reconstructions that archeology is responsible for are sets (or microenvironments). They are the literally reconstructed lifeway of an extinct epoch. The crucial factor is that you, the visitor, the living native from another culture, walk through the set and bring life to it with your own imagination, aided by the many sights, sounds, smells, feels, signs, labels, talks by local folk in eighteenth-century costumes, and your own textbook knowledge of American history. As visitor, you take all this folklore and all this symbol mongering and imagine yourself to be the native of Williamsburg or Mesa Verde and, as the anthropologist would say, attempt to get inside the heads of the original natives. And because the data are relatively mute and the colonial stones do not speak distinctly, they are then more easily made to give the messages of those who do the reconstructing. Modern America rebuilt Williamsburg: modern America and not the eighteenth century is the source of the message derived from Williamsburg. The tourist does not really become immersed in the real eighteenth century at all; he is spared the shock of the filth, degradation, and misery common to that era, and is led into a fake eighteenth century, a creation of the twentieth. While in this altered frame of mind he is faced with messages—the reinforcement of standard modern American values like those surrounding the myths of our own origin as a nation—that come out of today, not two centuries ago.

The archeologically based set—the recreated stage—provides the empirical environment for the tourist to transport himself physically and mentally out of the immediate present. In that environment the tourist is told certain things. They may be things pertaining to the eighteenth century or to the way the twentieth century handles the eighteenth. At any rate, they are communicated with unusual effectiveness because of the environmental niche of extraordinary reality in which they are set. Because most of the original context of meaning surrounding the artifacts is gone, such extraordinary reality is far more easily produced by using archeological materials. Meanings are notoriously difficult to recreate and recapture and, as a result, a new set of meanings—more accurately, a reinterpreted set of meanings—is readily imposed on the artifacts themselves. The meanings and interpretations that the visitor picks up are those created by administrators and technicians. Archeologists usually play a small role in constructing these meanings and sometimes, because of their ability to read the archeological record, they are in disagreement with the official version. For any disagreement to exist, the archeological record has to be somewhat less than mute. I think we can admit that it is. But because it is so often difficult to read and because the reading is so often anemic, the record is more easily molded and distorted (or simply fleshed out) by official interpreters.

A caution is necessary: because what goes on in the minds of the visitors at an archeological site is essentially a mystery and has never been the subject of ethnography, much of the above is hypothetical. But if any part of the argument seems plausible, then surely we should make every effort to get that ethnography done.

The messages communicated by sites like Williamsburg, Nauvoo, Mesa Verde, and the hundreds of national, state, and private parks that use archeological materials are difficult to establish without doing the ethnography of specific sites. There is nothing mysterious about what they have to say; I think the sites should be seen as being straightforward in their goals. Listen to the guides, read the signs, and the messages are clear. As Voltaire has pointed out, "History is the lie commonly agreed on." Agreeing with the interpretation—his meaning of a lie—is implied by visiting the site. But the site (the environment) is especially effective because it is up to you, the visitor, to reach the message yourself by wandering through the setting, picking out in empirical detail how something you are looking at strikes you. History may be the commonly agreed-on lie but, for that common agreement to be sustained and realized in individuals, they must see it for themselves. They must decipher it for themselves, live in history, first-hand. This can be done by using artifacts that have no meaning in themselves apart from their archeological context, no meaning that will contradict the one imposed on them by those responsible for the "authenticity" of the hundreds of colonial Williamsburgs throughout this country.

The ability of Americans to manage the past is probably not unique, but the extensive use to which we put the past may be. We certainly do not comprehend what happens to us as we are submerged in environments composed by prehistoric and historic archeologists and the "interpreters" who reassemble the fragmentary archeological record. We have no real idea that this use of archeology educates (not just in the usual sense) and reinforces values we are not always consciously aware of. In that sense, either as archeologists or as citizens, we are not aware that the ideas we propagate are those of our culture. Nor, as Marx has said that, "The ruling ideas are the ideas of the ruling class." As scientists we need to be more aware of what we have been doing, who our masters are, and whom we serve. We can properly be accused of being acolytes and prostitutes to our culture; so we will remain until we see our third role as archeologists clearly and consciously.

We need to be aware that Mesa Verde and Williamsburg use archeology for the same purpose, and that those two sites substantiate bits of our national mythology. There is absolutely nothing wrong with that in principle; however, you may agree or disagree with the factuality of the particular bit of mythology in any one case. But we should realize that all of these hundreds of sites are merely an example of how our culture manipulates history. Cultures have a set of techniques at their disposal to reconstruct history. We provide living fairy tales for every man—ourselves included—to participate in, not as spectators but as creators.

The uses of archeology I have been suggesting are not exhausted by the movie-set dioramas just described. There are also films. They are the second cluster of evidence for archeology's third role. Of the films, usually first produced as television programs based on prehistoric data, two come to mind. One is the CBS program on Stonehenge as an astronomical calculator, *The Mystery of Stonehenge*. The other is the equally well-known *Dr. Leakey and the Dawn of Man*.

Both of these hour-long television programs, shown in prime evening time, used prehistoric archeology as their basic data. One has to assume that there is something inherent in these topics for them to be exposed by sponsors to millions of Americans. I think the inherent interest of the data is clear enough and need not be argued over. Here, too, basically mute data are being interpreted within the framework of powerful ideas used in the service of living national cultures. Stonehenge is turned from a scene of romantic and misplaced Druids into a massive computer invented by people living in a place directly ancestral to us. Stonehenge is putative Anglo-Saxon glory. It competes, we are urged to suppose, with the material from the eastern Mediterranean and Near East that for so long has been proclaimed the root of civilization.

I do not think the surface theme of *Dr. Leakey and the Dawn of Man* will lead us away from the central idea behind that film. The message is: everything changes and can be expected to continue changing because everything has always changed. After all, it is through evolution, or change, that we have come to occupy the present position of eminence we enjoy, and it might safely be reasoned that evolution is the key to the future well-being of us all, might it not? Here, in another medium, is archeology and its data serving goals and ideas of which it is largely unaware. Thus the empirical base for human evolution falls into those ideas that belong today to the ruling elite (at least that part of it represented by northeast-coast television people and sponsors).

Certainly there is nothing wrong with this last use of archeology. Indeed, none of the uses to which our subdiscipline is put seems objectively unworthy. Archeology in the service of national goals hardly merits condemnation; in fact, it merits some celebration. We would, I think, be a good deal happier with our own work if we appreciated the high degree to which we did serve. What is unfortunate, however, is that archeology as a subdiscipline is quite unaware of this last function. Its role in national myth substantiation is, it seems to me, quite inoffensive, but what is not inoffensive is the archeologists' unawareness of this function. A distinction should be made between one of the uses of our discipline and the obligation its members have to participate in that use. Because substantiation is an end to which archeology is put does not mean we, as archeologists, must participate in it. Until we become aware that there is an activity we have the option of choosing or avoiding, we cannot even make the choice.

One of the early standard lessons one learns in archeology is the relative muteness of archeological data. That relativity is often assumed to be a function of the distance of the data from the present. The farther artifacts are removed from the present or from historical sources, the harder it is to figure out the function of the artifacts and, consequently, anything about the culture that produced them. Recently archeologists have started with the reverse assumption: since an artifact is the product of a total cultural system, it is likely to present evidence about the perishable parts of the systems that created it (Binford 1962). The logic of that assumption cannot be denied. The positive effect it has had on the higher quality of archeological analyses is there for the whole discipline to see.

However, one point common to all archeology, new and more traditional (despite internal theoretical differences on the relative muteness of artifacts), is that all investigators assume that the job of archeology is to deal with the past and to extrapolate from the artifacts to the subsystems that created them. Almost every archeologist is concerned with the subsystems (usually the subsistence system) as they are reflected in the patterns of artifacts. The general assumption is that some subsystem, or factors found in several subsystems, are responsible in a positive, causal sense for the artifacts we dig up. The subsystems created and patterned artifacts as we see the remains in the archeological record. The artifacts are regarded as indices to the systems of primary subsistence and exchange, of social relations, and of beliefs that brought them into existence. However, the artifacts and pieces of technology are, in some sense, determined in form and distribution by other systems including the social and ideological structures.

Have we as archeologists, and especially those of us interested in aspects of prehistoric social organization, allowed ourselves to fall into the error of idealism? We assume that since other systems created the system of patterned artifacts, those systems become recoverable through the artifacts. The error is not in attempting to recover extinct systems. But there is something incorrect for professed materialists—all new archeologists and many more traditional ones—to use as a primary assumption the supposition that other systems, which are theoretically derivative, determine the system of technology. It is a perversion of materialism to have as our primary concern the use of artifacts to show how they reflect other parts of an extinct or historic system. Instead, we might consider asking how the system of artifacts, the primary and undestroyed system of technology, caused or determined the other systems to take shape. What is there about the system of technology that either facilitated or determined parts of the social or belief systems?

We have understood for some time the relationship between tool use and the development of the brain in human, biological evolution. We have understood for an even longer time the relationship between the use of machines in factories and forms of economic and social organization. Industrial sociology has contributed considerable knowledge to our understanding the relationship between using large, powerful, repetitive machines and assembly lines and the psychic and social problems they produce. Many sociologists have shown how the determinitive powers of technological devices—from cars to buildings—are used to influence our behavior. More recently, we have begun to be aware of the impact of all forms of media on us. All of this is so much sophisticated technological determinism and materialism, and it has told us important and remarkable things, things the Greeks did not see and things we never saw before at all.

Although it is argued that archeology should concern itself with the relationship between technology and the rest of culture, it should also be pointed out that there is a discipline already doing just that. Historians of technology have devoted themselves to understanding technology in the context of culture: the Society for the History of Technology has published *Technology and Culture* since 1960. Then is the job of understanding already done? Not exactly. Historians of technology have been concerned with several central themes: the relationship of technology to science, engineering, and art; the nature of invention; and "how things are done and made" (Daniels 1970). This latter phrase is what most essays on the history of technology are about. This group of historical scholars has done critical work and considers itself allied to historical archeology, as can be seen in articles that appear in *Technology and Culture*. There is much to praise in the accomplishments of historians of technology but, for obvious reasons, I am more interested in the shortcomings.

Labeling themselves "antiquarians of technology" (Daniels 1970: 2), the historians of technology have discovered that they are rarely concerned with technology as a social phenomenon. They usually deal with complex machines of the sort produced by the more recent phases of the Industrial Revolution. They are, as historians, concerned with the particular, not with the comparative nor with the general. They are not cross-cultural nor, as historians, are they concerned with applying the goals of science to the study of technology.

As a consequence, they have left most technology, including simple machines, outside their domain and thus have deprived themselves of the temporal laboratory in which change could be examined. As technological determinists, most historians of technology have considered technology in and of itself, divorced from social and ideological concerns. They deal with the skyscraper in terms of structural steel and the revolving door; they are not concerned with the effects that such buildings have on culture. The historians of technology are uninterested in generalizing and are quite restricted in time. Furthermore, they have little training in handling social and cultural variables: the causal relationship between technology and the rest of culture does not really interest them.

Considering the state of the history of technology and the unconscious state of archeology, neither discipline is concerned with how technology affects culture and how technology is manipulated by culture. These two concerns would seem to be appropriate domains for archeology. We have seen the way archeology is tied to the present. Not only are all of its models derived from the present but, more to the point here, one of archeology's major roles is a function of how it is used in the present. Should not archeology then study how it is used, how its data (i.e., material culture) are used by the present, and how material culture, when used, affects the culture doing the using? Archeology could profitably study both the manipulation of material culture (why and how we do what we do with technology) and the manipulating that technology does on the rest of culture.

Archeology is a product of the present; it is used by the present. Of course, it has other, better recognized uses, too. We should then study how material culture works in the present. "In other words archeology *already* has more to do with the present than the past (cf. Fontana 1968), so why not *also move on a scholarly level* to catch up with what has already happened to the function of the field and *study* technology in the present as well" [Schuyler, personal communication]. Archeologists would automatically contribute several dimensions to the work of the historians of technology. We would add a comparative and, hence, a more formally scientific approach; we would vastly increase the temporal depth of the field and; most important, we would be studying technology within the matrix of culture.

If such welding of archeology's potential and the activity of historians of technology is plausible, then an example of how it might be done is in order. The example is drawn from my own work with Mormons and Mormon technology in Arizona and utilizes Mormon town plans and fences. In this space it is only possible to illustrate some of the points an archeological analysis of material culture might cover.

In 1847 the first 10,000 Mormon settlers reached the area of Great Salt Lake in the Great Basin. They entered an area that had been passed through and over by people going to California and Oregon. Utah was sampled and rejected: the few attempts to explore and settle it found it a semiarid waste supporting what were considered to be poverty-stricken Utes, Paiutes, Shoshones, and other Great Basin groups. The Mormons, as everyone knows, settled the Great Basin successfully—so successfully, in fact, that by the early 1870s the valleys of central Utah were overpopulated. It was then that areas of the Great Basin peripheral to Utah were purposefully colonized by the Mormons. One such area was the drainage of the middle and upper Little Colorado River in eastern and central Arizona. A southern, semiarid extension of the Colorado Plateau, the Little Colorado offers a more severe version of the environmental zones into which Mormons brought and perfected a technology.

The Little Colorado River had not been occupied by an extensive population since long-term prehistoric settlement ended in the fourteenth century of the present era. Since then the only Indians were small groups of Western Apaches wandering in from their home area to the west of the Little Colorado and occasional Navajos and Hopis passing through from their home areas to the north. There were some dispersed Anglos and more dispersed Mexicans. Into this environment moved Mormon colonists. The Mormons understood the harshness of the environment and they understood how marginal it was for farming. Mormon settlement pattern, broadly conceived, is directly related to the success of Mormon culture in settling this semiarid region. The pieces of technology articulated the religious culture with the environment with which it had to cope. The settlement plan was the conscious product of religion. The plan for laying out a town, called the Plat of the City of Zion, was drawn up by the Prophet Joseph Smith and came to have a status not unlike revelation. The settlement pattern determined some of the relations Mormons had with each other. It is those relations that helped form the basis for Mormon adaptive success. They saw their problem as setting up the kind of social and religious systems that would allow them to extract a living from harsh circumstances. This was done through the use of several pieces of technology, and those to be illustrated are the devices used to parcel out space. The way in which Mormons set up villages, farm sites, and house plans is closely tied to what they knew their social and religious systems would accomplish.

Some of the reasons for living in villages come directly from the Church leadership:

> In all cases in making new settlements the Saints should be advised to gather together in villages, as has been our custom from the time of our earliest settlement in these mountain valleys. The advantages of this plan, instead of carelessly scattering out over a wide extent of country, are many and obvious to all who have a desire to serve the Lord. By this means the people can retain their ecclesiastical organizations, have regular meetings of the quorums of the priesthood and establish and maintain Sunday schools, Improvement Associations, and Relief Societies. They can also cooperate for the good of all in financial and secular matters, in making ditches (for irrigation), fencing fields, building bridges, and other necessary improvements. Further than this they are a mutual protection and strength against horse and cattle thieves, land jumpers, etc., and against hostile Indians, should there be any, while their compact organization gives them many advantages of social and civil character which might be lost, misapplied or fritted away by spreading out so thinly that intercommunication is difficult, dangerous, inconvenient, or expensive [Fox 1932:93].

This letter from the Church First Presidency to the Freemont Stake in Utah specifies village life as opposed to scattered homesteading. It also specifies the effects of living in a village cluster. All forms of cooperation are facilitated. Farming, irrigation, exchange of essential scarce goods, schooling, worship, government, and Mormon endogamy were all facilitated through the village plan. But there is the reverse, too, of which the Mormons were well-aware. If proximity meant cooperation, it also meant a means to insure homogeneous behavior. Proximity allowed the continual contact that all village members were to have with each other. Such a system allowed public and neighborly sanctions to operate with greatest effectiveness. Although there was a hierarchy and a system of ecclesiastical courts, neither of these was the chief instrument for keeping social order; proximity was.

Initially Mormons were to be completely communal, sharing all property and living in common quarters. That failed during the Prophet Joseph's lifetime and failed again on the frontiers of Utah when it was tried a second time in the 1870s and 1880s. By holding all property in common, wealth was to be equalized. All were to have an equal amount, according to need. Equality in all earthly things was the stated goal of the Prophet's plan. When, after the sharing of one-tenth of one's annual increase was substituted for complete sharing of property, some means had to be found to guarantee that the resources available were evenly distributed. In an agrarian community, this was largely a matter of parceling out land. When a town was surveyed and plots were laid out,

Every family was to receive a building lot in the city. In addition the farmers were to receive an allotment of land outside the city. The mechanic was to receive the necessary tools and materials for his trade, the teachers, writers, musicians were to have a home site and a license or appointment to serve the community according to their respective abilities. The town residents, of course, would participate in the production of the farmers through regular commercial channels or through the redistribution of the storehouse [Spencer 1937:103].

Furthermore, farming plots as well as house lots in the village "were distributed in the following manner: by ballot, each lot having been numbered previous ... each man's name (who was) applying for a lot formed a ticket, which tickets were thrown together in a hat and shaken up together, then drawn out one by one ... the first name drawn took the first lot ... " [Ricks 1964:60]. Drawing land parcels by lot (distribution therefore being based on chance) guaranteed equal access to all land. Since land was usually sectioned according to quality, a man would be allotted proportionate shares of good and less good land. All of these niceties of distribution could only be realized if the land itself were subdivided before parceling out in a way that predetermined equality. That guarantee was provided by the Plat of the City of Zion.

The Plat was originally conceived by the Prophet Joseph in 1833, but it underwent several modifications as the Mormons moved west. The modifications were mainly in the size of the city. The key determinative feature was the equal size of all plots in the city. Furthermore, there was to be only one house to a plot. " ... the city (was to) be laid out in ten-acre squares, each divided into eight lots, ten by twenty rods; that streets be eight rods wide, and that houses be built one to a lot in the middle, as a precaution against fire, and twenty feet back from the line, to leave ample space for the planting of flower gardens" [Fox 1932:41].

In addition to the equal size of all lots in a town, the Plat, which was a grid, guaranteed equal access to irrigation water. The canals flowed down the streets on the side. A grid made water dispersal efficient by packing farm land in the village close, and choosing lots by chance meant that water rights could not provide a basis for social inequality. Land and water, the two key sources of wealth for farmers in a semidesert, were distributed in equal amounts based on chance. Chance, when applied to land and water, could guarantee equal distribution only because a preexisting grid with equal divisions and equal access to water had subdivided those resources in the first place. The grid with equal-size rectangles was a piece of technology that enabled the principle of equality to be realized in land and water distribution. This, together with distribution based on chance—a practice deduced from the ideological notion of equality—made economic equality a reality. There is nothing inherent in a grid except its equal subdivisions that links it to equality in land access. But that trait, combined with the ideological goal of equality and the social device of drawing by lot for rights to land, did promote equality.

It was obvious to the leaders of the Mormon population, as to most other nineteenth-century utopian planners, that the way the physical environment was managed had direct effects on behavior. They believed that there were direct, causative effects. We, I think, are ready to accept the fact that at least there were enabling (or facilitating) effects. With a systematic view of mutual cause, it makes sense that a basic relationship should exist between technology and all subsystems. In the Mormon case, the strongest illustration of this relationship exists in the designs Joseph Smith did not choose for his people's city. He had several alternatives open to him in terms of the traditional ways frontier towns were designed (Reps 1969). In view of his decision to put his people in a town, as opposed to scattering them over the countryside in homesteads, the town could simply have been allowed to grow around some central intersection of one or two planned streets, the pattern closest to the early New England heritage Joseph Smith knew. Boston and the other cities of New England had only a planned main street or two and the city or town defined itself from these streets. That may have been the most natural and the easiest way to set up a new settlement. Main-street towns were a common frontier alternative: one long, central axis along which the principal buildings were erected with homes and secondary buildings scattered in a planless way behind this facade. This sort of town was located along a regional trade artery or crossroads. The utopian planners, on the other hand, offered several types of town plans. The star or circle plan focused on a central place and radiated all streets and lots out from that point. This graduates land in two ways. Lots are inherently unequal in size and are graduated more precisely from the central point. The star or circle could be transformed into a grid with ranked sets of concentric blocks spreading out from the center. Such blocks were of unequal size, and distance from the center was especially emphasized. This type of grid could vary street width and block size, thereby segregating neighbors and neighborhoods from each other. Grids may well be the logical way to set up instant towns on any frontier, but their properties vary widely and can be geared to accomplishing varied social purposes. The grid of Manhattan was geared maximally for land speculation (Reps 1969: 194–203). Long, narrow blocks, in contrast to a grid of equal-sized squares, hold more houses, waste less central space, force houses close to each other, and allow less freedom expressed in terms of unbuilt land.

Joseph Smith did not choose a grid with equal-sized squares by chance. The fact that he understood the physical properties of a technological device for subdividing space, as did all other utopian planners, is indisputable. Indisputable, too, is the fact that the piece of technology he chose facilitated and helped to realize the social and religious goals he was after. There is a nonarbitrary connection between equal-sized pieces of space available to farmers and egalitarianism. A lot of things have to be held equal for this to be true—such as quality of land—but one would never think the reverse to be true: that unequal distribution of land of equal quality would produce economic equality.

The Prophet Joseph built another guarantee of equality into the Plat of the City of Zion. The city was made up of large square blocks with wide streets between. Each block was subdivided into equal-size, rectangular house lots. To create the subdivision, an axis was drawn down the middle of the block. At right angles to this property line were drawn four or five other lines that divided up the block into smaller, equal rectangles. A house was to be centered in each rectangle facing the street. With such a setup, houses would be back-to-back facing in opposite directions. No houses would face out to the streets on two sides of the block. If every block were divided the same way, half the streets in the town would automatically be side streets, devoid of houses and inferior to the others. Furthermore, if every block were divided the same way, the front of every house would look into the front of every other house, optimizing visual contact but minimizing privacy. To correct both of these flaws, Joseph Smith alternated the central axis on every other block in the city. This reversed the direction of house lots in every other block.* It meant that every street had people facing it in equal numbers. It also meant that nobody looked into anybody else's front yard. It made all streets equal and simultaneously heightened the level of privacy.

Mormon settlers paid close attention to the allotment of land in a uniform way in a community. They paid equally close (but less conscious) attention to the layout of the house lot in a town. Mormons built an identifiable type of house all over the Great Basin and set up the large space around the house in a characteristic way. In addition to the house, the most noticeable artifact was the fence. There are a set of distinctive pieces of technology that set off a Mormon town from all others in the desert West. In addition to its grid settlement pattern are its broad streets lined with trees giving the town the appearance of an oasis, its two-story gabled brick and wood houses, its hay lifts or cranes pointing heavenward like so many mechanical steeples, and its fences. There are several types of fences. By far, the most common fences in a town are standard, average, picket fences. Outside the town in the fields, barbed wire strung between posts was typical. But there are remnants of fences made by fitting broken tree and shrub limbs against each other; these are called rip-rap fences. Wire and branches were not used in the town, however; there, picket fences predominated. Between the town and the fields, rows of lombardy poplars were planted. These stand like walls between the residential and farming areas and are one of the characteristic traits of all Great Basin Mormon towns. They, too, are a kind of fence.

Mormons built fences throughout the nineteenth century and, today, they continue to build fences, walls, partitions, and other separators. Historians have suggested that this is a carryover of the New England heritage Mormons brought with them across the Great Plains. That is probably true but does not tell us why, under such stressful conditions, Mormons continued and still continue to put up fences. They left other things behind, like the New England settlement pattern, so why should they drag fences 2000 miles out of one environment into a completely different one? And, even more curiously, why should they continue to build them today?

Like any artifact, especially one for which we have the historic context, we can make fences tell us about the rest of the culture—in

* I am grateful to Hanno Weber for pointing out the implications of this innovation.

this case Mormon culture. As will become clear, that is not a dull business. But in addition to being the passive product of Mormon culture, fences are also a causative agent. When dealing with an object (a piece of technology) one needs to know what the forces are that bring it into being, what causes it to be, what the object causes in its own right. I would like to make that analytical distinction to get at the difference between reconstructing a historical context—the usual business of prehistoric and historic archeology—and doing an analysis of the determinative characteristics of technology. The second half of the distinction asks what using fences does to Mormon culture, as opposed to asking what can we learn about Mormon culture from their fences. The latter question is not significant, because you can learn more about almost any aspect of Mormon culture by sitting down in a library and reading about it. But no library has the answer to the question: What did Mormon fences enable Mormons to do? Even the Mormons do not have the whole answer.

Every house (indeed every building in a Mormon town, and every Mormon house in a Gentile town) had a fence around it. They still do. In the nineteenth century, picket fences were used. Picket fences were used around gardens and lawns and continue to be used in those contexts now throughout the Little Colorado River area. Wire and brush were used in the pastures outside the towns. Larger fields were surrounded not by fences but by hedgerows and rows of trees, including poplars. There was, in other words, a nonrandom pattern of fence use. The kind of fence used was decided by what was kept in or, as the case will show, what was kept out.

While the Little Colorado region as a whole contains a fair range of environmental variation in terms of flora and fauna, no one site contains such a range. The zones are very spread out and cannot be encompassed by any one farm, let alone something the size of a Mormon farm. Nonetheless, the Mormon settler operating under the ideal of self-sufficiency attempted to control a whole set of ranges of plants and animals in his allotted area. He had to keep horses and dairy cattle, and sheep and goats; he had to keep a supply of poultry for eggs and meat, an extensive kitchen garden, and an orchard. That is not very different from the standard American farmer, except that it had to be done on a single piece of land, in a town, and in an area that was a semidesert. The Mormon farmer had to reproduce in one fair-sized plot the varied environments that guaranteed the success of all the diverse living things he needed for survival. But he had a plot where not one of them lived naturally. He not only had to reproduce in his farm yard the niches available to him in the Great Basin, he had to create niches that did not exist for a thousand miles around. Once that was done, he then had to keep the competition between occupants of different niches apart. Browsers had to be kept out of the orchards and gardens, sheep and goats separate from horses and cattle, and natural predators from everything domesticated.

Fences created the boundaries between all the niches. In addition to the scarcity of water, which fences did not alleviate, one of the critical environmental hazards to plant life in central and northern Arizona is windblown soil particles. In this area very strong winds blow day and night from January to May. That is bad enough, but when, starting in the late 1880s, overgrazing removed the ground cover, the wind lifted the soil and sand grains and carried them away in large quantities. Because the particles picked up are naturally smaller than those that are larger and heavier, they fell between the larger soil particles when they were redeposited on the ground. The fine wind-borne sand seals the ground where it falls, with the result that air and water cannot penetrate down to plant roots, and seeds cannot break the seal to reach the surface. The amount of sand deposited in a five to six month season of wind storms would be enough to lower the capacity of a field. Picket fences, hedgerows, and rows of trees serve as windbreaks to protect the crops from the destructive capacity of the wind itself and to filter out the sand before it lands on cultivated areas. Picket fences, hedgerows, and rows of trees function the way snow fences do along highways. A solid wall of fencing could not withstand the velocity of the wind, yet enough of the force is broken by closely placed slats to protect whatever is on the other side, in addition to filtering out the wind-borne material. Hence, there are picket fences around crop-growing areas, along with hedgerows and tree lines. These were used as opposed to wire fences and tree limbs, which were cheaper and protected areas used for domestic animals.

Fences are an ecological necessity for any agrarian regime in the plateau country of Arizona. They separate competitive niches from each other and protect all artificially created niches from the universally destructive wind. The ecological functions of fences could be further specified, considering this region, but I think their primary role as a piece of enabling technology is established.

The determinative or causal aspects of technology are not limited to the subsistence system. We should assume that it is possible to show how aspects of social and ideological organization are influenced by technology, that is, how technology operates to shape these aspects. Here, too, Mormon fences serve quite well. Although streets and irrigation ditches separated blocks in a town from each other, fences provided the visible distinction between individual property holdings. They did this within a town and in the fields and ranges surrounding the town. The essential insight into the social functions of a fence is the tired but accurate line from Robert Frost: good fences make good neighbors. In a town where the social structure was based on equal property and close cooperation, and where order was maintained through everybody knowing everybody else's business, fences drew the literal line between closeness and privacy. Land was subdivided and allotted to guarantee equality, but town life among people who were supposed to be economic equals still had to solve the problem of privacy. The Mormons put people more closely together than any other Anglo group in the West but separated them by using fences. Just as the barnyard containing the many competitors necessary for life could only exist using fencing, so the propinquity of town life could only work by providing a degree of distance within the essential closeness. The neighborliness that expressed itself in watchfulness had a natural limit set to it. The spatial closeness that enabled cooperation and survival also needed fences, hedgerows, and trees to prevent the other kind of closeness that destroyed privacy and caused friction.

Fences, like house decorations, also were used to express status and, later, wealth differences. This seems to be a less important function. But the number of gates in a fence, like the number of doors in a house, indicated the number of wives in a man's household and hence his status. The Church maintained elaborate rules about the equivalent treatment due to a man's plural wives. If they were not given separate houses, they were to have separate and equal apartments in the same house. Separate meant, among other things, separate gates in the fencing. These have served as examples of how technological items served to accomplish some social tasks. Since the technological items also helped to shape parts of Mormon ideology, the following view of Mormon beliefs is appropriately considered.

The religious reasoning was as follows: God's elect, in these latter days, exist because they please God. The Lord suffers them to exist because they continue to please him. In all millenial movements the imminent Second Coming of Christ meant that a group, for whom he was explicitly to come, was to prepare the way for that coming. The preparation of that way was in the hands of those specially chosen by God for the task. The task was enormously difficult because it was two-sided. The earth had to be changed and prepared for its redemption by God's more recent elect. But the very process of preparation was a demonstration by his elect that they themselves were worthy of the Second Coming. For Mormons, the kingdom that was to be the theater for the Second Coming was founded in the 1820s when God directed his latter-day prophet—Joseph—to set up a church that was to be the major instrument insuring the apt preparing of the earth for Christ's early reappearance.

The process of redeeming the earth was carried out by an agrarian people and, as a result, or perhaps by design, actually involved making the earth bloom. When the Mormons reached the desert West, the redemption of the earth was to involve making the desert bloom like a rose. Just as the desert of the original Zion was made green under the ministration of God's elect, so the new Zion, also in a desert, was to be subject to an identical process. The original beauty of God's creation and the Garden of Eden was to be reestablished. A semblance of the divine was to be called back into existence. While the language was metaphorical, the redemption process involved the substantial reification of the metaphors. The land of the saints really was going to bloom and, by God, it did. And it bloomed because they used fences.

Picket fences, barbed-wire fences, hedgerows, lines of brush, and lines of trees were all fences. The saints also used other equipment to make agriculture in the desert work and some of it was even more important, such as irrigation. But without the repertory of fences and the way they were used, settlement would not have worked. The act of fence building was and remains part of the necessary landscaping of a house and farm; in fact, both living informants and statements from nineteenth-century journals say that a fence is an inherent part of the house itself. A building is not complete until it has a fence around it, holding it down. But the act of fence-building itself is not what was most crucial. What was crucial is what fence building allows a Mormon to accomplish. Building fences allows Mormons to do things. The ecological and subsistence accomplishments dependent on fences are clear; so are the social benefits. However, when a Mormon raises a garden or a lawn behind a fence, he has shown that he has subdued a piece of the earth and made a bit of the desert bloom. He has helped redeem the earth. Growing a garden or a lawn is a challenge that he has met. He has made something more beautiful, more orderly, and more refreshing; something neater, cleaner, and more desirable. He has created a semblance of the divine. By managing, manipulating, and grooming the earth, he has imitated God and proven that he is worthy: he is a saint. A Mormon who creates something green has shown his inner state. In this context, fences are valuable because of what they preserve behind them. What they preserve in addition to a subsistence base is a man's right to a place in the Kingdom of God. One local Mormon summed it up: "The state of a man's yard is the state of his religion." In this way, the enabling role of a system of technology operating within the sphere of religion is somewhat clearer. In a complementary way, it is also possible to see how something like fences, which have no obvious iconographic value, become religious artifacts.

Mormon fences, insofar as they are artifacts arranged in regular, predictable patterns surrounding the living spaces of the people, have a final dynamic and, if you will, determinative role. The whole living space of agrarian Mormons and of Mormons today in towns throughout the Great Basin is parceled out by fences. The Mormon's physical world is divided or compartmentalized by interior walled spaces, yards full of fences, and gridded towns with gridded fields. This is the cultural environment the Mormon was and is born into and raised in. He knows it all his life and it is reasonable to assume it has an effect on him: a cognitive effect. Such an environment is the product of ecological constraints but also is an explicit statement of some part of the religious system we have seen above. This environment is a result of the way Mormons have had to think about their world and of what the Mormon idea-system was and has become. If fences are a piece of enabling (even determinative) technology, then it is reasonable to suppose that the technology enables them to think in certain ways, as well as to grow crops in certain ways. As a result, this system of technology should have cognitive consequences. It ought to affect the way they think. The question is no sooner asked than answered, at least tentatively. One of the standard observations made about Mormons is that they see no contradictions between the literalism of their doctrine and a scientific world view. That Mormons have established a huge educational network and have produced many excellent scholars while supporting belief in a literal reading of the Bible, a belief in continual revelation and an imminent Second Coming, has puzzled more than one observer. That the problem of blacks is not a social or civil problem for them but a religious one only, illustrates the distinctions current Mormons make between levels of reality. And that most outside witnesses see contradictions where Mormons see harmony hardly needs to be emphasized. How then, at a general level, can one have literal religion and rather full participation in modern science? This puts the problem of compartmentalization in current context, but it was just as much a problem in the nineteenth century.

Mormons have lived by the Little Colorado for a century. They are still building fences. The materials are different now: cinderblocks, chain link fences with and without aluminum slats woven into them, and prefabricated wooden fences that are almost walls. Their yards are still subdivided very finely by using smaller, lower fences; plants; flowers; trees; vines; stones; and even prehistoric artifacts. The farmyards are now flower gardens. The manifest subsistence explanation for the fences has disappeared. It is still necessary to keep out the wind and wind-blown sand in order for anything to grow. And it is still crucial to demarcate the visibly redeemed land of the Saints from the rest. Furthermore, especially in towns where Mormons are not in a majority, Mormons draw a clear line between themselves and the others. If we look at the changes in fence use among Mormons in this one place in Arizona over 100 years, we see that the materials with which fences are constructed have completely changed, and we find that the barnyard ecology that required intricate fencing has completely disappeared and does not survive in the many present subdivisions of gardens. We also find a more immediate need to separate their pieces of Zion from the Gentile world and this sometimes requires walls instead of fences. Despite these changes in the material and distribution of these artifacts, we can see what no prehistorian could know and what no historian of technology would ask about: despite overwhelming changes in Mormon culture, there is an unchanged relationship between a key set of artifacts and a set of religious symbols. Fences still keep the same things in and keep the same things out. They keep out very literal things like wind and sand. They also keep out and keep separate less literal but no less powerful things like the Gentile world and internal categories that do not mix. Consequently, now, as in the nineteenth century, fences do the same things for Mormons, and Mormons do the same things with fences. The fences enable them to redeem the earth and manipulate and act out the categories used to deal with the world. Despite changes in form, there have been few changes in function.

Fences and their use, the way Mormons divide up the space that immediately surrounds them, are the concrete representations of the

Mormons' many separate categories. Fences—and the compartments they create—reify and reinforce the noncomparable divisions Mormons (and Mormonism) use to understand the world. In this way, Mormons live in their categories. It is not just that Mormons and their religion created settlements and spatial subdivisions and made life work; Mormonism could not exist without the spatial representations and technological devices that allowed its population to exist. Here we see that mental processes are as much a product of the use of tools, as the way that the tools are used is a product of mental rules. And, as a result, we also see the incomplete understanding we have of the role of technology and an area that archeologists may choose to give some thought to as well.

All of these data on Mormon town plans and fences demonstrate how thoroughly technology is embedded in the subsistence, social, and ideological systems of culture. Since this chapter has dealt with Mormon cultural subsystems (and the influence of technology on them), the shifting locus of cause can be more clearly seen. We can, for one thing, be sure that technology really did and does cause Mormons to do some things, and we can be just as sure that Mormons manipulated technology to accomplish some ideological principles. Cause works both ways, and by considering plural contexts we can assign it a locus, albeit a shifting one.

By taking technological determinism seriously, we can see the effect of artifacts on culture. We do more than "read" Mormon culture from their use of fences, which is what even the most sophisticated prehistoric archeologists do in principle. Instead, we can begin to straighten out the determinative characteristics of technology.

Nothing has been said here about town plans and fences that is necessarily true outside of Mormonism. A comparative, generalizing study has not been done. Such an approach is clearly within the scope of this type of archeology, although it is not within the scope of this chapter. There is a good literature within architecture (Reps 1969; Evans 1971a, 1971b) on the function of town plans, walls, and fences. There is also a superb literature on the technology used to divide space by other utopian groups in the nineteenth century. The work ranges very widely from analyses of Jeremy Bentham's panopticon (Evans 1971a) to the panopticon's American derivative, the domestic octagon (Creese 1946) to the relationship between the American Shakers, famed for their furniture, and their precept: "Hands to work and hearts to God" (Andrews and Andrews 1966).

Further, as archeologists we already have a supporting competence in settlement pattern studies. That, with the concerns outlined in this chapter, constitutes a new problem with new data. Will we choose it?

ACKNOWLEDGMENTS

The comments and suggestions of friends and colleagues have been very helpful in developing the ideas in this chapter. I thank Steve Barnett, David Crabb, Vincent Crapanzano, Hildred Geertz, Gilbert Kushner, Mary Miller, Peter Nowicki, Sherry Ortner, Peter Seitel, Martin Silverman, and Hanno Weber. I am particularly indebted to Robert Schuyler for clarifying several points regarding historic archeology and its relationship to the rest of the field. Conversations with Richard Swiderski clarified many of the arguments on technology and behavior, and editing by Jeanette Mirsky has made the chapter significantly better.

10. ARCHEOLOGY IN MEGALOPOLIS*

BERT SALWEN

Department of Anthropology
New York University
New York, New York

A useful distinction has been made between archeology *in* the city and the archeology *of* the city. Americanists (including those of us in the New York City area) have, up until now, concentrated almost exclusively on the former: the frustrating attempt to snatch scraps of information about prehistoric aboriginal cultural systems from the path of advancing urban sprawl. Generally, the depth of frustration seems to be directly proportional to the size of the city; in New York it is monumental!

In an attempt to make archeological life bearable in such an environment, nine professional archeologists working for seven institutions in Long Island, New York City, and eastern New Jersey got together in 1968 to form a self-help organization—the Metropolitan Area Archaeological Survey—which has since grown in membership to 15 archeologists working for 12 institutions, and is now legitimatized as a nonprofit corporation under the laws of New York State.

* This chapter is a greatly expanded revision of a paper with the same title presented at the annual meeting of the Society for American Archaeology, Mexico City, May 1970, as part of a symposium entitled "The Crisis of Urban Archaeology."

MAAS has been extremely useful in many ways. It has served as a clearing house for scientific information on local archeology: initiating a site register, a bibliographic file, and a catalog of specimen materials from the area in the local museums. In some cases, it has made possible cooperative fieldwork by more than one institution at the same site; for example, New York University, Columbia, and the City College of New York worked together at a Staten Island site in the spring of 1970, and Lehman College and Jersey City State College are returning to this same site in 1972. MAAS is playing a growing role as the spokesman for the professional archeologist in relationships with local governmental agencies and is now officially consulted by New York City's Parks Department before the Department grants permission for excavations on its properties. The organization is beginning to work with other groups on regional salvage problems and in the fight for statewide legislation. Finally, and very importantly, it has helped to keep relationships between professionals and the growing numbers of amateurs in the area on an almost pleasant level; MAAS members give lectures and classes for amateurs, and members of recognized amateur groups are usually welcomed on professionally excavated sites.

In the past three years, the work of MAAS members has produced a few short papers on local prehistoric archeology (Salwen 1968; Williams 1968; Rutsch 1968, 1970a; Deustua 1969; Horwitz 1971) and we expect that continuing work will increase the flow of publications. But, all in all, it must be admitted that much of the activity of MAAS has been a desperate attempt to keep up with the forces of destruction through salvage excavation and political efforts to protect the few prehistoric sites that are still intact. While it is true that the situation is not this bad throughout the area—there is still a lot of good work to be done in localities somewhat farther from the urban center—it sometimes seems as though the chief function of MAAS is to help us find out more quickly about the destruction after it occurs.

During these years, I have become convinced that part of the problem stems from an inherent theoretical weakness in the concept behind the formation of MAAS. It was formed to help us do archeology *in* the city—really, in spite of the city—and, at least up until now, we have rarely taken the urban situation itself (as a source of either data or inspiration) into account in our work. In other words, we have not yet begun to take advantage of the theoretical possibilities inherent in the more rewarding concept of archeology *of* the city.

Since metropolitan New York is completely a product of the historic period, this must mean, in our case, a concern for historical archeology.

Very little historical archeology has ever been done in the New York area. Some of the historic Indian villages were "explored" and briefly and impressionistically reported by workers like Bolton (1920) in the first quarter of this century. A few Revolutionary War forts have been tested, most frequently by nonprofessionals. There are at least two "historic reconstructions": one at Richmondtown on Staten Island and another at Bethpage, Long Island; both groups of buildings assembled with minimal archeological consultation.

Current activities in this field include the South Street Seaport project, an ambitious attempt to accurately resurrect a nineteenth century port area in lower Manhattan, and Project Weeksville, a much more limited nonprofessional exploration of a pre-Civil War free Negro community in an urban renewal area in Brooklyn (Fleming 1971). In the Black Reservation in Morris County, New Jersey, Edward Rutsch of Fairleigh–Dickinson University is engaged in a long-term study of an eighteenth century industrial "plantation." He is particularly interested in the light that this early "industrial park" can throw on later steam–age urban industrial complexes (Rutsch 1970b). Rutsch has also been involved in excavations at the eighteenth century Beverwyck Manor and at the Jockey Hollow National Historic Site (Rutsch 1972), both also in Morris County.

Paul Huey, of the New York State Historic Trust, was recently able to devote a day or two to the testing of the Uris Building excavation at the tip of Manhattan Island, near the South Street Seaport area. He recorded an archeological column over 30 feet deep, spanning the history of the city from the days of its earliest Dutch settlement almost to the present. Huey has also used early maps and records to document the changing shoreline of this part of New York (Huey 1970). He reports that the Dutch colonists created slips (or short canals) along their waterfront in sharp contrast to the pier (or wharf) construction that was typical of the shorefronts of English colonial cities like Boston and Philadelphia.

Robert Schuyler of the City College of New York is conducting a summer field-school at the site of an early nineteenth to early twentieth century settlement in the Rossville area of Staten Island, some of it only recently razed to make way for an express highway. "Using historical, archaeological, and ethnographic data as sources, a culture history of the area is planned that will especially focus on critical periods of culture change, such as the end of the 19th century" (Schuyler 1972:12).

These beginnings by Rutsch, Huey, and Schuyler hint at the rich possibilities for urban archeology in New York—both historical/evolutionary studies of the development of the city and structural/functional studies of the relationships between this giant product of human behavior and the sociocultural configurations that produced and were modified by it. There are, of course, other examples from other North American cities, and there will undoubtedly be a great deal more work of this more or less traditional nature in the immediate future, in New York and elsewhere.

But, along with the new possibilities, this additional emphasis on urban archeology will inevitably bring new problems of definition and role. Two questions, in particular, seem worthy of discussion.

1. Once we cross the line from prehistory to history, where should we draw a new temporal boundary? If a nineteenth century seaport is legitimate subject matter, is not a 1930 Hooverville . . . or, for that matter, the site of last week's "confrontation" also legitimate? In fact, it might be argued that a site becomes the proper domain of the anthropological archeologist as soon as the behavior stops and as soon as the actors leave the scene!

2. As we get closer to the present, more of our raw data tends to be above ground. Structures are still standing, sometimes with original contents still more or less in place. There are maps, plans, photographs, and documentary records. Is the study of this kind of subject matter still archeology? Some, like Foley, feel strongly that "the archaeologist must dig for his data" (1968:67). But "industrial archeologists" use precisely these kinds of uninterred data (e.g., Hudson 1966; Pannell 1966). Dalibard, a Canadian archaeologist, recently suggested that architectural recording should be considered "above-ground archaeology" (1970:15). Dethlefsen and Deetz, whose work with New England colonial cemeteries has been widely approved as an interesting example of the "new" archeology, even suggest that we can learn more about culture change from the above-ground tombstones than from the graves they identify (Dethlefsen and Deetz 1967:40).

Obviously the field situation at an above-ground site is not the traditional one. But the analytical problems are the same—they involve the search for correlations between regular patterns of socio-cultural behavior and the material products of that behavior—and these sites may yield exactly that kind of data that anthropological archeologists are most interested in today. It appears to be necessary to expand the limits of our subject matter.

(After making this suggestion in 1970, I discovered that I had arrived—independently and at about the same time—at precisely the spot reached by Deetz when he rejected the concept of " . . . the archaeologist as an anthropologist who digs" and suggested, instead, that "A coherent and unified body of subject matter entirely appro-priate to the archaeologist is the study of the material aspects of cul-ture in their behavioral context, regardless of provenience" [Deetz 1970:123]. I agree wholeheartedly with Deetz's further development of this theme.)

Along these lines, I shall discuss some specific subjects for inves-tigation that might fall within the scope of a more broadly defined archeology, and suggest how such studies can contribute to the growing field of urban anthropology. Two of these are currently being investigated in pilot projects sponsored by the New York Uni-versity Department of Anthropology and can, therefore, be presented more concretely and in more detail.

SOUP-CAN TYPES AND ATTRIBUTES

Quantitative distributional studies of ceramic traits are a standard source of archeological information about behavior patterns. Similar studies of the distribution of types and varieties of shoes in shoe stores, doorknobs on classroom doors, or soup cans on supermarket shelves might prove equally enlightening. Might one expect to find, for example, an inverse relationship between the number of chicken noodle and chicken rice cans, and might this ratio turn out to be related in some way to the ethnic composition of the neighborhood in which the particular store is located?

To test this general approach, we chose two supermarkets belonging to the same chain, but located in different parts of Man-hattan, one in the more prosperous portion of Greenwich Village, the other in a mixed lower- to middle-class neighborhood on the Upper West Side. After examining displays of different kinds of foods, we decided that soup cans did indeed provide a reasonably easily controlled subject matter with relatively few distinctive attri-butes that clearly clustered to form easily recognizable types. On the

assumption that soup sales in each store would be patterned in ways
related to sociocultural factors in the respective geographic localities
and, furthermore, that soup displays on the store shelves would have
some patterned relationship to sales (we would not expect, for
example, to find the bulk of the display space devoted to items that
move very slowly), we mapped the shelves in the soup sections of
both stores, noting distribution of our soup-can types as determined
by the attributes of brand name, soup variety, can size, and price.

We have just begun to process the data collected in this way, but
it is already quite clear that the pattern in each store is distinctively
different from the pattern in the other. The Greenwich Village outlet
displays a much greater proportion of what we have called "luxury"
soups (snapping turtle, Vichyssoise, and clam bisque, often packaged
to be served without adding water) while there are almost none of
these in the West Side store. The West Side store, on the other hand,
displays a selection of the larger "family size" cans while there are
none of these on display in the other store; the West Side store also
offers a larger selection of Progresso brand soups, which are presumably consumed primarily by Spanish-speaking customers. We have
not yet tabulated the chicken soup data.

This first field trial has been extremely encouraging. It has clearly
indicated some of the variables that we can profitably watch for in
future tests, and it has also alerted us to some problems. For example,
the West Side store is located in a very "uneven" neighborhood;
class and ethnic composition changes radically from block to block,
making it difficult to determine which particular groups, if any,
patronize this store. We have also discovered that the soup displays
seem to vary to some extent over the course of the week. We must
perfect our sampling techniques.

We are now framing concrete hypotheses about the relationships
between soup can type frequencies and sociocultural dimensions
such as income range, family size, and ethnic composition, and are
preparing to collect a somewhat larger sample, using four stores
belonging to two different chains. Two (more homogeneous but
contrasting) neighborhoods have been selected, and in each of these
we will gather data from one store belonging to each of the chains.
We have also started to gather independent data about the sociocultural characteristics of each neighborhood, which we can compare
with our "archeological" conclusions.

In ongoing cultures (unlike conventional archeological sites)
there are many other ways to learn about sociocultural dimensions,

but this approach may prove to be a convenient and quite sensitive index for the cultural anthropologist interested in quickly evaluating a particular neighborhood situation. Of course, one need not count actual soup cans. The same information is available in the form of sales records.

PATTERNS OF APARTMENT (OR ROOM) UTILIZATION

Any large U.S. city contains many public housing projects, usually consisting of only a few basic building shapes (each high-rise building containing dozens of apartments with identical floor plans). The archeologist who has developed techniques for the study of prehistoric house patterns might be able to gain new information about ongoing sociocultural behavior through study of differences in the use of identical spaces by families of differing cultural and /or economic backgrounds.

In testing this approach, the NYU study group has sidestepped, for the moment at least, some of the problems involved in a frontal attack on an occupied New York City housing project and, instead, has chosen to study the arrangement of furniture and other artifacts in university dormitory rooms. The general assumption, of course, is that furniture layout and use of space in particular rooms will be related in patterned ways to sociocultural attributes (statuses and personality types) of the occupants of these rooms.

A former hotel, converted by NYU into a dormitory, has been chosen for the initial test. Thirteen of the 15 floors in this building are used for student housing. Each floor contains 17 rectangular rooms, each room housing two students. All rooms are more or less similar in layout: a door on the corridor wall, a large window in the opposite wall, and the other two walls without major features. The longer dimension of the rectangle usually runs from the door wall to the window wall. All the furniture is movable (an important consideration in choosing this particular building) and may be rearranged at will by room occupants. Each room is equipped with two single beds, two dressers, two bookcases, two desks, two desk chairs, and two more comfortable chairs. Students may bring in other pieces of furniture if they wish to.

Our basic procedure is quite simple in concept, although sometimes unexpectedly complicated in application. Working with dittoed room plans prepared in advance from building floor-plans, one team of investigators has been mapping room arrangements, noting floor and wall treatment, level of lighting, and similar important but more elusive traits, as well as the locations of the major pieces of furniture. A second team, working independently, has been questioning room occupants, collecting information about family background, academic status, and (cautiously) relationships with roommate. We are particularly interested in determining if the present occupants of the room have rearranged the furnishings since they moved in and, if so, for what reasons.

As with the soup-can project, we are still in the early stages of data collecting, and only the most preliminary analytical work has been done, but, in this case also, clear patterns seem to be emerging. If rooms can be classified into valid types on the basis of layout of contents, this will probably be accomplished by concentrating on those attributes that measure the placement of bed, desk, and dresser in relation to walls. So far, most rooms (over 50%) fall into a "split" arrangement type: one bed, desk, and dresser against one side wall, and the other set of similar items against the other side wall, thus effectively dividing the room into two more or less equal "use zones," each including approximately half of the window and door walls. A less-frequent subtype of the "split" arrangement again uses furniture placement to divide the room into two "use zones" of equal area but, in these cases, the division is along the other axis, resulting in the creation of a "corridor" zone and a "window" zone, each side wall being divided between the two zones.

A third group of rooms (about 15% of the total) have been tentatively classified as exhibiting "shared" arrangements. These vary in details of furniture placement, but all share a key characteristic: it is impossible to isolate a major areal zone that is the exclusive locus of either set of furniture. For example, both beds may be placed close together, with a small table between them, while desks are back-to-back in another part of the room.

We have developed some very tentative hypotheses concerning the behavioral correlates of these different arrangement types, some of these involving concepts such as "territoriality" and "cooperation," but it is probably wisest to stop the discussion at this point for the time being; the questionnaire portion of the project has not yet caught up with the room maps. We also realize that a larger sample and additional analysis may produce other, quite different, patterns that have not as yet been recognized.

BROWNSTONE HOUSE TYPES

Manhattan contains thousands of three- and four-story structures known locally as "brownstones." Many of these were built a hundred or more years ago as single-family homes. Later, many were converted into three- or four-family structures and, still later, into "multiple-occupancy" buildings containing even smaller apartments housing many more people. At each stage of modification, the floor plan of the New York brownstone tends to be strikingly like the floor plans of all of the others. It would not be too difficult to create a developmental typology into which most of them would fit. It should also be possible, with somewhat more effort, to find correlations between house type and behavior. The occupants of the original (Stage I?) brownstone were, in most cases, properly polite upper- and upper middle-class New Yorkers. At what stage do the crowded occupants of the modified house begin to throw their garbage out of the window?

As noted above, there are other ways of learning about ongoing behavior, but a survey of brownstone house types in a block under ethnographic investigation might well provide unexpected information or, at very least, new checks on data obtained in old ways.

VANDALISM

Classical archeologists are familiar with the destruction of public buildings and the defacement of statues of gods and kings that almost invariably followed the conquest of one ancient state by another. School authorities are equally familiar with the tendency of school children to toss rocks through the windows of the schools that they attend. There is a popular belief that the "willful and malicious" destruction of both public and private property is on the increase in American cities. Whether or not this is the case, it is certainly true that examples of vandalism are a frequently visible part of the urban setting. If my basic thesis is correct, these evidences of destruction should be patterned, and study of these patterns should provide insights into aspects of behavior and the values that lie behind the behavior.

We have not yet attempted to test this approach in a controlled manner, but some unstructured observations suggest to us that such a test would prove profitable. We have noted, for example, that New York's street corner phone booths—both phones and booths—are subjected to ferocious attack, although the mailboxes that stand next to them are never harmed. As noted above, school windows and other school properties seem to be more frequently attacked than most other structures. Are some kinds of stores more subject to defacement than others? A systematic survey of a few carefully sampled blocks or neighborhoods might reveal clear patterns of vandalism—"artifactual" patterns—which could then be related to the ideologies and behaviors that instigated and created them.

COMMUNITY PATTERNING

Ever since the publication of Willey's Viru Valley study (Willey 1953), many archeologists have focused on the prehistoric "settlement" as the precise point at which to seek articulations between behavior and the products of that behavior as preserved in the archeological record (see, for example, the many papers in Willey 1956 and Chang 1968.

In addition, archeologists, as well as other anthropologists, sociologists, psychologists, city planners, and geographers, have attempted, in a variety of ways, to specify correlations between settlement morphology and various patterns of living in extant communities, both urban and nonurban.

To list just some of these approaches: Naroll (1962) used a crosscultural sample to demonstrate correlations between enclosed floor space and settlement population, while Cook and Heizer (1965, 1968) used ethnographic data from California to derive relationships between population and settlement size; Robbins (1966) and Whiting and Ayres (1968) employed ethnographic materials to study possible relationships between house shapes and arrangements and other sociocultural dimensions; Chang (1958) used a crosscultural sample of neolithic settlements to support hypotheses concerning relationships between community patterns and forms of kinship organization; Leone (1972) investigated relationships between Mormon town layouts and aspects of Mormon ideology; sociologists of the so-called Chicago school proposed an ecological model to explain regular patterns of urban growth (Park, Burgess, and McKenzie 1925); Milgram (1970), a psychologist, is concerned with patterned responses of city dwellers to the urban environment and has employed, among other techniques, the construction of "cognitive maps" of cities; Lynch (1960), a city planner, is developing techniques for mapping the "image" of the city that is shared by its inhabitants.

Arensberg and Kimball state: "For every American regional (sub) culture that we can distinguish in American society and civilization, a particular form of community is to be found" (Arensberg and Kimball 1965:115). They illustrate this thesis by describing the New England town, with its white church and town hall on the village common; the Southern county, dominated by the courthouse in the center of the square in the county seat; and other settlement forms; and persuasivly link these physical forms with the sociocultural structure and history of each community.

I am not prepared to contribute new theoretical insights about this relatively well-explored subject, but I would like to point out that the search for meaningful correlations of the kinds that are the overall subject of this paper has been unusually successful in this particular area, and I suggest that further explorations in these directions merit vigorous support.

On the level of broad crosscultural comparison, it might prove rewarding to apply techniques such as those used on house types by Whiting and Ayres to whole settlements, working from the large corpus of maps and aerial photos that are already available (see, for example, Fraser 1968, Hardoy 1968, and Reps 1969). It would be overly mechanistic to expect clear one-to-one correlations; I am sure that it is my own bias that makes the Shavante village, with its circle of equal sized houses surrounding an empty plaza (Fraser 1968: illustration 73), look so economically "reciprocal," in the terminology of Polanyi, Arensberg, and Pearson (1957); while the Natchez town, with the great chief's house "larger and higher than the rest, placed on a somewhat elevated spot . . ." (Charlevoix, quoted in Swanton 1911: 59) seems to reflect "redistributive" economic arrangements. Nevertheless, it appears certain that this kind of research will reveal crosscultural regularities that will be both significant and useful.

At the other extreme, concentrated studies of the relationships among details of settlement form and local cultural and natural environmental factors should be equally rewarding. One example: Kimball, in a study of a "fringe" community in Monroe County, Michigan, records the fact that city people, moving into the surrounding open country, settled first in areas with poorer, lighter, sandier soils, because these areas were more quickly farmed out and offered for sale at relatively low prices (Arensberg and Kimball 1965:144). Soil maps and other sources of microenvironmental data should help toward the anthropological understanding of changing urban morphology.

The examples discussed above were chosen, in most cases, because we have given them more than passing thought, or have actually begun to work with them in field test situations. There are, of course, innumerable other possibilities. The changing physical layout of the factory is intimately connected with changes in the socioeconomic system that produces it. The formal attributes of classrooms affect student participation, and there are demonstrable connections between physical setting, social custom, legal regulations, and patterns of drinking behavior in Canadian beer parlors (Sommer 1969). Even processes of destruction and disorganization of cultural materials are patterned and amenable to systematic analysis, as has been demonstrated by studies in an Ithaca, New York, automobile junk yard and a Mexican Indian village (Ascher 1968). The elusive definition of the city itself (or of the even more elusive "communities" that it is reputed to contain) may be newly and, possibly, more successfully approached through the study of the complex material patterns that both reflect and channel the patterns of movement of its inhabitants.

All investigations of this nature must share one central assumption: regular, repeated patterns of sociocultural behavior leave "impressions" in time and space; it is the job of the anthropological archeologist to discover and interpret these impressions, no matter when or where they occur.

Although it is evident from the brief survey presented above that this kind of urban archeology has already attracted the interest of a respectable number of archeologists, there are undoubtedly others who view it with mixed feelings. It is tempting to try to win the interest of these skeptics by pointing out some fringe benefits. The projects described above can sometimes be carried out during the academic year, in urban settings, and with the aid of students who learn basic techniques of data collecting and analysis in the process. Furthermore, by permitting the simultaneous collection of data about behavior and the products of that behavior, they appear to offer opportunities for the formulation and testing of general hypotheses about the relationships between behavior and its products that can then become, at least tentatively, "laws" for use with prehistoric materials. But it must be clearly stated that these studies are not merely "teaching exercises," nor need they be justified as aids to the prehistorian.

Neither are they simply a return to the old-fashioned study of material culture that lost popularity among ethnologists many years ago. The old material culture studies were hampered by a constricting theoretical orientation. When they were not purely descriptive, they almost always tended to be simplistically distributional or evolutionary. Today's anthropological archeologists are working within a developing theoretical framework and with the aid of a set of analytical techniques (including computer data processing) that were not available to their predecessors. A renewed, sophisticated, social anthropologically oriented interest in the material products of ongoing behavior may be enormously productive today.

There may also be those who consider this to be a legitimate field of study for the city planner, the architectural historian, or even the market analyst, but not for the archeologist. Certainly, workers in other disciplines are becoming interested in problems involving the relationships between aspects of human behavior and the environments in which these aspects occur. The spokesmen for "environmental psychology . . . the study of human behavior in relation to the man-ordered and -defined environment" (Proshansky, Ittelson, and Rivlin 1970:5), for example, would consider many of the studies discussed in this paper to be safely within the limits of their quite broadly defined new field. It is also true that this kind of urban research must almost always involve interdisciplinary cooperation, but this is equally applicable to all of the most fruitful areas of modern archeological research.

Anthropology, as a whole, is concentrating more and more on complex cultures in general and on the urban situation in particular. Anthropological archeologists have developed, in other contexts, techniques for both recording and analyzing data that could, with relatively little modification, be applied to the study of urban phenomena, past and present. It would appear almost inevitable that more archeologists will test the possibilities of this new field under whatever label seems most appropriate. If they do not, someone else will do the work—and we will miss all the fun.

THREE

METHODOLOGICAL FRONTIERS

If the proposed goals of archeology are to be achieved, and the precision and reliability of the results are to increase, there must also be improvements in the methods of archeological research. The assumptions used and the methods employed by archeologists must be attuned to the goals and subject matter of the discipline. Fundamental concepts concerning artifact deposition and interpretation must be reexamined, as done in the articles by Michael B. Schiffer and William L. Rathje, and Fred T. Plog. The detailed intellectual process of analysis and interpretation must be clearly understood, as discussed in the article by Steven A. LeBlanc. New approaches and models should be developed and employed as demonstrated by Leonard Williams, David Hurst Thomas, and Robert Bettinger, and by Ezra Zubrow. By explicitly questioning and then improving underlying definitions, methods of reasoning, and techniques employed, archeologists can attain some of their proposed goals.

Michael B. Schiffer and William L. Rathje rigorously examine the most fundamental archeological problem: the relationship between the operation of past cultural systems and the location and interpretation of the data that remains. They consider it necessary to explicitly outline the physical and cultural processes that have led to the present state of the archeological record. Noncultural transformations of the materials remains, such as their deposition and erosion, are called *n*-transforms. Cultural formation processes, such as organizational patterns or activity locations, are referred to as *c*-transforms. If one can accurately describe the transforms that the archeological remains experienced, then it is possible to plan one's investigations more efficiently. Experimental and ethnographic studies should be utilized to provide a more thorough understanding of the exact nature of various kinds of transforms.

Fred T. Plog addresses his chapter to another fundamental aspect of archeological inquiry: its temporal base. He uses the term "diachronic anthropology" to refer to the study of temporal variability in human behavior and products. Plog considers archeology's potential area of greatest contribution to be investigations of variability through time and of changes occurring over long periods. If this is taken to be a major goal of research, then the methods of data collection and analysis must be adjusted to maximize sensitivity to temporal changes. The normal practice of working with time periods of relatively long duration is counterproductive in this framework. The investigator's rationale for using broad chronological periods usually is based on an imprecise knowledge of the exact age of the cultural deposit. Plog suggests that this imprecision is not overcome by using broad chronological periods that are excessively imprecise, but is overcome by attempting to be as exact as possible with the chronological attribution of recovered data. He then suggests three interpretive models that are appropriate to his view of diachronic anthropology: systemic models, adaptive models, and dynamic equilibrium models.

In his article, Steven A. LeBlanc discusses two widely held misconceptions about important steps in archeological reasoning. He asserts that data used in forming hypothesis can also be used as a test of the hypothesis. Although at a certain level this seems to be circular reasoning, LeBlanc demonstrates that it is logically sound and, in some cases, necessary. The second point involves whether there really is a logical difference between archeologists who "test general laws" and those who "use a systems model". LeBlanc shows there is no fundamental difference, but the complexity of hypotheses and the nature of assumed relationships may vary.

The article by Leonard Williams, David Hurst Thomas, and Robert Bettinger considers the proper testing of hypotheses and the operationalization of intuitive concepts. An attempt is made to quantify intuitive concepts held about the environmental variables crucial to the location of settlements in a region. In order to accomplish this, a polythetic definition of environmental requirements is formulated from data collected during previous field work. Use of a polythetic definition, means that only a predetermined number of the possible characteristics must be present to have a positive result. This is a useful and realistic framework of definition and prediction for dealing with some archeological materials. The testing of the suggested polythetic definition was carried out in a rigorous fashion and accurately predicted the location of sites in 95% of the situations.

Ezra Zubrow's chapter deals with the question of adequacy and prediction in archeological models. He begins by outlining the relationships between models, data, and theory. The main goal of testing archeological models is to evaluate the viability of the theory behind the model in light of the society being investigated. An effective method of measuring the relative adequacy of competing models is by means of a simulation analysis. Empirical data consistent with each alternate simulation model is generated and can be compared with the archeological remains. In this way it is possible to differentiate between alternate interpretations in an objective and quantifiable manner.

This section covers a broad range of problems concerning archeological methods and reasoning. Methodological developments can be considered in two major categories as reflected by these arti cles. First, there is significant attention being paid to an evaluation of some of the basic assumptions about the nature of archeological data and the best means to understand it. Second, there is tendency to improve the precision and broaden the scope of archeological analysis and investigations by refining current techniques and incorporating techniques developed in other disciplines. Both of these trends are healthy and will be most effective if the methods employed are designed to be appropriate to the material being investigated, sensitive to the questions being asked, and attuned to the assumptions being made and the interpretive framework used by the investigator.

11. EFFICIENT EXPLOITATION OF THE ARCHEOLOGICAL RECORD: PENETRATING PROBLEMS

MICHAEL B. SCHIFFER AND WILLIAM L. RATHJE

Department of Anthropology
University of Arizona
Tucson, Arizona

If you had asked a man in the sixteenth century how an archeological site was created, he would probably have told you that it was the work of the devil, giants, or catastrophe. During the past four centuries archeology has developed into a discipline concerned with using the material remains in sites to answer questions about the processes of long-term cultural change. Although the archeological record presents unique opportunities for examining cultural change, it also presents unique difficulties for the archeologist who must retrieve data to answer his questions. As a result, archeologists have had to grapple with the sophisticated processes of site formation and replace devils, witches, and catastrophe with principles that make the archeological record understandable for their purposes.

The beginning of any archeological study is a specification of the data that must be retrieved in order to reconstruct a behavioral or organizational aspect of a past cultural system, and the expected location of those data in the archeological record. The ability to build a bridge between the operation of a past cultural system and the location and interpretation of data in the archeological record depends on developing and systematically applying the principles from two areas of archeological theory. The first area, noncultural formation process concepts (Schiffer 1972), or *n-transforms* (i.e., bone decays in acid soil), allows the archeologist to explain and predict the interactions through time between a culturally deposited assemblage and the specific environmental conditions in which it was deposited. The second area, cultural formation process concepts (Schiffer 1972), or *c-transforms* (i.e., relating remains in a hunting kill site to those in a village, the larger the animal the fewer of its bones will be removed from the kill site and discarded at the village [Daly 1969]), explains the spatial, quantitative, and associational attributes of archeological materials as a function of the depositional behavior of the cultural system that produced them. The use of both concept sets allows the archeologist to mediate between the archeological context—the present—and the systemic context—the past behavioral system—of the materials under investigation. These two concept domains are specifically archeological (cf. Willey and McGimsey 1954). They are utilized to minimize the time-labor-cost variables in archeological information retrieval and to form the basis for interpretation of data.

To be exploited efficiently *c-transforms* and *n-transforms* should be accessible for discussion and testing. Although all archeologists implicitly use these concept sets to construct research designs and to make interpretations, these concepts are not consistently or explicitly recorded in archeological reports. Even one of the most widely used principles of both cultural and noncultural deposition made its way slowly into the explicit conceptual repertoire of archeology. Hole and Heizer (1969:17) trace the principle of stratigraphic superposition to Nicolaus Steno in 1669. Archeologists, however, did not consistently make use of this important law until the last 70 or 80 years. Sensitivity to an explicit use of both *c-transforms* and *n-transforms* would provide feedback on the testing and modification of these concepts, which is implicit in any archeological excavation. Archeologists must be able to profit from the mistakes and insights of their colleagues.

N-TRANSFORMS

Although systematization of *n*-transforms is unevenly developed, this area of archeological theory, drawing on the physical sciences, has achieved a level of moderately sophisticated explanation and prediction. When an archeologist seeks a certain kind of data for a problem, he is able to limit environmental situations of likely occurrence to a manageable number. For example, in seeking the origins of domestication in Mesoamerica, Richard MacNeish deduced likely locations of plant preservation from his knowledge of n-transforms. Reasoning that organic materials will be preserved under conditions that inhibit the growth of soil bacteria, and that this condition will obtain in continually dry deposits, he excavated dry caves in the Tamaulipas, Chiapas, and Tehuacan areas of Mesoamerica. The success of his predictions is amply documented (MacNeish 1964; MacNeish and Peterson 1962; and Byers 1967a, 1967b). At the well known site of Star Carr, J. G. D. Clark faced the problem of where to excavate with the greatest probability of recovering perishable materials. Based on Clark's knowledge of n-transforms he decided "the indications were that by excavating on the lakeward side, where the alluvial deposits were likely to be waterlogged, [he]would find skeletal material in a good state of preservation as well as indications of wood and vegetation. And so it was to prove" (Clark 1972:3).

Other useful noncultural formation processes have been discovered by chance. For example, in 1962 Frank Hole declared that "plant remains were scarce at Ali Kosh" (Hole 1962:125), an early farming village in the Near East. Later, seeds were noticed while cleaning an ashy radiocarbon sample. This discovery caused the excavators to reexamine their assumptions about the noncultural formation processes that operated to produce the site. Assuming that seeds would be found in similar situations, a water separation technique was applied to extract carbonized plant material from ash. This change in technique resulted in the recovery of tens of thousands of seeds useful in documenting the processes of evolutionary change in domesticated cereals (Hole, Flannery, and Neely 1969).

Generally, archeologists become well acquainted with the conditions of preservation operating in the environments where they work most often. These conditions are tied implicitly to a set of individually internalized n-transforms that render the usual conditions of preservation and site morphology predictable and understandable. Because these principles are largely implicit, rarely is a second thought accorded to ordinary conditions of preservation. Only exceptional cases, such as a man fully preserved in a bog for 2000 years (Glob 1971), or 1200-year-old temple murals in the humid Guatemalan rain forest (Ruppert, Thompson, and Proskouriakoff 1955), elicit conscious efforts at explanation. What should be pointed out is that the pedestrian occurrences and the anomalous cases or "freaks" are all explained by use of the same body of usually implicit archeological laws—n-transforms.

The failure to consistently utilize these principles in prediction and in preparation for fieldwork is evidenced by those excavators who "go into the field without any thought of possible conservation problems [and] with no equipment to deal with those that may arise" (Dowman 1970:55). Dowman (1970) has argued persuasively that before starting excavation archeologists must predict what sorts of artifacts are likely to be found and in what condition they are likely to be discovered, so that appropriate preparation can be made for their recovery and preservation. By examining, systematizing, and testing n-transforms, archeologists can construct efficient research designs for data retrieval and make adequate preparations for preservation of those remains located in excavation.

Investigations at the Joint Site, a 36-room Pueblo III ruin in east-central Arizona (Hanson and Schiffer n.d.), provide a good example of how n-transforms can be tested by excavation and employed in research designs. In an attempt to retrieve a representative sample of major artifact classes and locate subsurface features, a sampling design was applied to the nonarchitectural areas of the site. Excavation units were selected on the basis of a stratified random sample. Sampling strata were defined by major variations in the density of surface lithic and ceramic materials. The hypothesis to be tested was that material densities and/or distributions on the surface of the site closely reflect material densities and/or distributions below the surface.

Excavation of the Joint Site demonstrated that this hypothesis was false, and led to the construction of principles that could have been used to structure a better excavation design. Sample pits excavated in areas of high surface material density often proved to be sterile. The excavators discovered that there was no direct correspondence between surface and subsurface material distributions, even at this single component site. The results of this test should not have been as surprising as they were. Assuming constant patterns of cultural deposition, variations in the noncultural processes that act on a site, or portions of a site, can generate surface variability that may be misleading as a guide to excavation.

At the Joint Site n-transforms could have been applied to patterns of surface material distribution to provide a better basis for excavation decisions than undigested surface counts. For example, after excavation the investigators abduced the principle that:

When noncultural deposition of some material occurs on a site of cultural deposition, the most recent surface will not directly reflect the nature of the underlying remains. Holding other variables constant, standing walls will act as a barrier, piling up loose windblown materials over an area proportional to the size of the wall. Thus, by a tall wall, there is likely to be little correspondence between surface and subsurface material culture remains [adapted from Hanson and Schiffer n.d.].

The areas of the site adjacent to the room blocks have a consistently low density of surface materials. Knowing that some rooms have standing walls to the height of 1.5 meters, one can conclude that there is no basis for assuming that the subsurface materials also occur in low density. In fact, several midden areas were encountered below the aeolian sand adjacent to the room blocks.

Another principle abduced from the Joint Site excavation is certainly known to archeologists:

Holding other variables constant, when wind and water act on a site having an elevation gradient, some materials will be transported downhill away from their locations of cultural deposition [adapted from Hanson and Schiffer n.d.].

This n-transform leads directly to the implication that under the above conditions materials in downhill areas will have a low probability of correctly indicating subsurface cultural remains at the same location; however, a high density of such materials may indicate the uphill presence of subsurface cultural remains. Had the excavators applied this principle at the Joint Site, surface materials of high density downhill from the room block would have led to the hypothesis that a midden or refuse area of some sort was to be found below the sand deposit near the pueblo walls. Testing this hypothesis would have resulted in the rapid discovery of several refuse areas.

The Joint Site example and the results of studies by Redman and Watson (1970) and Binford and others (1970) suggest that the explicit use of n-transforms can lead to verifiable predictions about the nature of subsurface material distributions. Excavation sampling designs based on surface distributions alone are wasteful of information that archeologists and physical scientists have worked hard to obtain. Sampling designs, for optimal efficiency in data recovery, should be modified to take into account the noncultural processes that have operated to form what is today observable as a site.

The use of n-transforms not only allows archeologists to locate data of interest, but also can be applied to data interpretation. For example, using smoke-stained walls and data on wind patterns, Sir

Arthur Evans was able to date the month (March) during which several places on Crete were destroyed by fire (Hole and Heizer 1969:91). Wooley (1953:25) dated the length of occupation of Tell esh Sheikh at 350 years based on assumptions about the weathering of mud-brick houses and the number of construction phases that were represented in his excavations.

Not only can n-transforms be derived from the excavation of sites, but they may also be the objective of experimental studies undertaken in artificially constructed situations (Kim 1966; Brothwell and Spearman 1963; and Gordon 1953). Although n-transforms are not used to the extent possible, because of their base in the physical sciences, they will have strong predictive power when properly systematized and tested (Dowman 1970).

C-TRANSFORMS

In order to take full advantage of the predictive utility of n-transforms, they must be integrated with an understanding of cultural deposition behavior and where cultural deposition is likely to occur in an environment. Although all archeologists invent and employ c-transforms, they do so implicitly. Through long familiarity with an area most archeologists make generalizations about the nature of cultural deposition. From these generalizations, they derive predictions about the probable locations and contents of different kinds of deposits.

One need not search far to uncover examples of how c-transform predictions are useful for efficient information retrieval. In planning excavations at Tell esh Sheikh, Sir Leonard Woolley used intuitive c-transforms to good advantage. He wished to amass as much pottery in a stratified sequence as possible. To do this he employed area-specific c-transforms:

Houses would give us a stratified sequence, which is essential, but on the other hand houses are sometimes so cleanly swept [in the Near East] that there is little left in them to show of what the sequence consisted; nowhere would pot-sherds be so abundant as in the village rubbish heap [Woolley 1953:25].

Predictions about the location of middens were made by employing the principle that people dump garbage downwind from their habitations (Woolley 1953:25).

Although a search of the literature, and to a certain extent introductory texts, will produce hundreds of examples of possible laws of cultural deposition, few of them have been tested. The danger in not testing these principles comes not only from misapplications, but from an overgeneralization of these concepts and their use in a premature form. For example, Southwesternists have generalized that middens often occur to the south and east of Pueblos. This is not a processual statement, it is only an empirical generalization, and one easily falsified. At the Joint Site, middens and burials were encountered north and west of the room blocks as well as to the south and east (Hanson and Schiffer n.d.). This argues strongly for the extrication, systematization, and testing of the implicit c-transforms that archeologists now use to make predictions about cultural deposition.

Another example concerns the locations where large quantities of ancient Greek antiquities are to be found. During the latter part of the nineteenth century, excavations were conducted in classical Greek sites in search of art objects—pottery, glass, jewelry, and sculpture. Many excavators who concentrated their efforts in mainland Greek sites were not excessively rewarded for their efforts. This failure is a direct consequence of deductions based on incorrect assumptions about the cultural processes responsible for forming the Greek archeological record. Greek sites have been systematically looted or scavenged by the Romans, Byzantines, Turks, Germans, British, and French. Many of these materials were transported by sea, and were therefore highly concentrated in boats. Knowing this, it can be deduced that shipwrecks in the Mediterranean, and especially off the Greek coast, would provide a fruitful field for investigation. In fact, underwater archeologists have retrieved more specimens of classical Greek art from shipwrecks than have been uncovered through excavation (Wolf Rackl 1968:22).

Most of the shipwrecks were found by accident. The careful employment of n-transforms and c-transforms promises more efficient site location in the future. In a recent article Bascom (1971) outlined the potential data retrievable from the Mediterranean Sea floor and argued for a systematic attempt at research. This argument gains potency through his explicit use of n-transforms (for example, wooden hulls are likely to be preserved in deep water where there are minimal currents, low temperatures, and protective silts) and c-transforms (constructed from "statistics that are based on knowledge of the ancient ports and population centers, the kinds of cargoes and location of trade routes, and the nature of old ships and the way they were sailed" [Bascom 1971:264]). Clearly, expectations about how a particular cultural system produced archeological remains, and assumptions about cultural activities subsequent to the original deposition of materials, have crucial effects on the efficient selection of research designs, site choice, and excavation locations within sites.

Not only do cultural formation process concepts play an important role in designing data retrieval, but they also function to bolster interpretations about the past. Statements purporting to describe any aspect of a past cultural system—whether states, variables, properties, or specific behaviors—depend on usually implicit assumptions about the way particular data sets become a part of the archeological record. For example, in a highly creative application of general systems theory principles, Kent V. Flannery (1968) described the past operation of scheduling and procurement subsystems among the early "incipient cultivators" of the Southwest Highlands of Mexico. His model is based on a series of unstated but necessary assumptions about cultural deposition. For example, if the percentage of deer bones found at sites imperfectly reflects the actual number of deer killed or the age-sex distributions of those killed, erroneous statements about hunting behavior and subsystem structuring could result. If maguey hearts from dying plants were brought back to the cave sites and young maguey were generally roasted, consumed, and excreted closer to the site of procurement, then subsystem operation would be considerably different from the highly equilibrated picture that Flannery presents. Different assumptions about cultural deposition could have led to the conclusion that domestication occurred in response to overexploitation of maguey and deer. This is not to suggest that Flannery's assumptions about cultural deposition are unreasonable. They are probably well founded, but the extent to which they are sound depends on the validity of the laws of cultural deposition that he has employed implicitly to justify his subsystem reconstructions.

Another example of the crucial, but usually unspecified role of c-transforms, is to be found in the reconstructions by Longacre (1970) and Hill (1970) of postmarital residence patterns. Their inferences are based in part on the nonrandom distribution of Snowflake Black-on-White ceramic design elements within pueblo rooms at the sites of Carter Ranch and Broken K Pueblo. Longacre and Hill, in their reports, make explicit several basic assumptions: (1) that women made the pottery, (2) that mothers taught their daughters how to make pottery, and (3) if (1) and (2) hold in an uxorilocal system, then design elements on pots will form nonrandom distributions coincident with uxorilocal residence units. Although these are important (explicit) assumptions, the whole study stands or falls on a much more basic assumption concerning cultural deposition of pottery at the sites: most of the pottery in pueblo rooms was broken and discarded or abandoned in the uxorilocal residence unit of manufacture.

Several investigators have recently been attracted to the problem area of cultural deposition among living groups. Karl Heider, an ethnographer, has suggested that archeologists begin to study the contexts of use and discard of cultural materials in ongoing systems (1967). His paper provides some examples of cultural deposition from the Dugum Dani of New Guinea that might not normally come to the attention of many archeologists. For example, the Dugum Dani frequently move their compounds and reuse the spaces for sweet potato gardens that disrupt the archeological record of the previous huts.

In another study, Foster (1960) investigated the factors affecting the life expectancy of various kinds of domestic pottery in Tzintzuntzan, a peasant village in Mexico. He discovered that basic strength, function, patterns of use, causes of breakage, and costs were all related to the life-expectancy of utilitarian pottery. Knowledge of these factors is important in explaining the variations in use-life among archeologically discovered elements (also cf. David and Hennig 1972).

Papers written by interested ethnographers can and should function to alert archeologists to the variability in extant patterns of cultural deposition. But such ethnographic case studies are insufficient to provide archeologists with useful c-transforms. General, culturally nonspecific hypotheses must be formulated and tested in the context of ethnographic investigations.

Studies of cultural deposition in ethnographic situations are being undertaken increasingly by archeologists themselves. Stanislawsky (1969) has studied recycling of pottery among the modern Hopi; and although his study has not produced any lawlike statements to date, the potential is certainly present. Nicholas David (1971) has worked among the Fulani of Cameroon to discover whether or not an archeologist would be able to reconstruct household composition from the remains of material structures. One interesting aspect of his study presents the useful concept of "devolutionary cycle" of structures, whereby the successive states in the decay of structures are related to changing functions (David 1971:119).

Lewis R. Binford (1973) has been conducting ethnoarcheological studies among the Nunamiut Eskimo, and a preliminary presentation of results contains many explicit c-transforms derived from the observation of cultural deposition. A major discovery to date is that of "curate behavior." Binford found that artifacts that are expensive to procure or produce are transported from site to site in anticipation of future use and that the ultimate location of discard of these artifacts may bear only a vague relationship to their many locations of use. On the other hand, relatively useless by products of activity performance, such as debitage or butchering waste, were observed to closely reflect locations of activity performance. As a result of curate behavior, items of importance in ongoing cultural systems may appear only infrequently in the archeological record if their use-life is relatively long (cf. Jennings 1957; Schiffer 1972:163).

Studies such as those mentioned above must be undertaken in many different cultural contexts in order (1) to produce a body of useful principles for explaining archeological remains, (2) to provide information about the operation of past cultural systems, and above all, (3) to aid in the design of efficient means of information retrieval. Long neglected questions have begun to be examined in the domain of c-transforms: causes for variation in use-life expectancies of different cultural elements, associations of materials produced by differential refuse storage and transport systems (Schiffer 1972), conditions under which recycling will occur, the effects of site abandonment processes (Ascher 1968), and numerous others. Such studies will lead to a body of archeological laws useful for prediction, explanation, and facilitating sound excavation decisions. More and more c-transforms will be published and available as archeologists become increasingly aware of the sensitivity of the link between cultural formation process concepts and the nature of extinct cultural systems.

CONCLUSION

Archeologists have been looking for specific types of data, whether gold cups or stone tools, for well over 100 years. However, except for a few shortcuts (proton magnetometers, miniaturized periscope cameras, infrared photography, aerial photography, etc.) to the location of a few types of data, little consistent effort has been allocated to developing the principles necessary to define the best areas from which to retrieve data. Each archeologist must often devise and apply his own assumptions about cultural and noncultural formation processes. He rarely makes consistent reports about his assumptions or his results, especially if the latter are negative. The only sources containing an appreciable quantity of explicit concepts are introductory textbooks like Hole and Heizer (1969), Fagan (1972), Clark (1957), and Rouse (1972). But even in these works the concepts presented remain unsystematized and untested assumptions.

The efficient location of archeological data relevant to a particular problem is made possible, in part, by use of two sets of archeological concepts—n-transforms and c-transforms. The first set specifies the interaction of cultural materials with the noncultural properties of the environment. These concepts permit the archeologist to predict the structure and content of a subsurface site. The second set of principles, c-transforms, are derived from the study of the processes by which cultural systems discard or abandon constituent materials. These concepts allow the prediction of specific locations, quantities, and associations of archeological data. When used together, n-transforms and c-transforms provide relevant information for determining efficient choices among excavation locations based on an investigator's problems. In addition, assumptions about how these processes operated to produce materials under examination underlie all uses of archeological context data.

To minimize retrieval costs and to free models of archeologically derived systems from untested assumptions, n-transforms and c-transforms must be organized into a base of genuinely predictive archeological laws that are systematically defined and tested. The set of past excavation reports and the results of all future excavations provide archeologists with a data bank for developing and testing generalizations about the processes responsible for forming the archeological record.

When the cultural and noncultural formation processes discovered since the sixteenth century are integrated into a systematized and tested body of archeological principles, then and only then, will archeologists be able to make efficient use of the archeological record to answer their questions about the past.

12. DIACHRONIC ANTHROPOLOGY

FRED T. PLOG

Department of Anthropology
State University of New York
Binghamton, New York

I use the term *diachronic anthropology* to refer to the study of temporal variability in human behavior and the products of that behavior. Diachronic anthropology may be contrasted with *synchronic anthropology*, the study of spatial variability in human behavior and its products. Thus, diachronic anthropology refers primarily to a data base—cultural and behavioral variability in time. It is not currently possible to refer to a set of models and theories appropriate to doing diachronic anthropology, and this situation is in part what has motivated me to write this chapter. I do not believe that diachronic anthropology is a more worthwhile activity than synchronic anthropology, nor do I wish to imply that a single investigator must do either synchronic anthropology or diachronic anthropology, but not both. I will consider, however, some problems that arise when clear distinctions are not made between synchronic and diachronic studies and synchronic and diachronic models and theories.

The last decades have seen a very rapid growth in the number of practicing archeologists. With this growth have come some serious questions concerning the appropriate goals and responsibilities of archeologists. Twenty years ago, Spaulding warned against an archeology in which "the only purpose of archaeology is to make archaeologists happy" (1953:590). More recently, David Clarke in his comprehensive review of the state of the discipline characterized archeology as "an undisciplined empirical discipline" (1968:xiii). Of late, this search for goals has been represented in the desires of some, usually younger, archeologists for "relevance" in prehistory. Yet, there is still considerable disagreement on the part of archeologists as to what their discipline is and/or should be about, as the diverse statements of purpose in this volume will make clear.

I do not intend to call for a simple dogmatic phrase that all archeologists can recite in characterizing the discipline. Diversity and disagreement are useful and necessary. But I agree with Clarke that extant diversity is greater than one would expect among a group of cooperating scholars. And I wonder if some more consideration of the nature of our data and what we can and cannot do with it would not produce significantly more agreement and a concomitant increase in our ability to participate in and contribute to each other's research. In any case, I will use this chapter to give my own answers to questions concerning what archeology is and/or should be about.

Many archeologists are content to see this discipline as the science of the artifact. Certainly, a science of material culture including prehistoric artifacts is a fundamental component of a science of archeology. Artifacts are our empirical data base, and without offering explanations for their formal variation in time and space we can proceed little further. But many archeologists, myself included, cannot limit their concern with the past to material culture. We are interested in archeology as a social science and, therefore, in the inferences concerning cultural systems and behavior in the past that can be made from and with artifacts, and in deriving explanations for prehistoric sociocultural phenomena. In this regard, archeology is a science that uses artifacts in explicating and explaining prehistoric behavior and cultural processes.

Such a definition raises a fundamental question: If a scholar is interested in behavior and cultural processes, why would he not choose to work with these topics using the far richer sociocultural record of the present rather than the limited and elusive record of the prehistoric past? One might initially answer this question by pointing to an intrinsic interest in the past. While such a response justifies an interest in prehistory, it does not justify a claim to a primary commitment to the study of sociocultural processes, if it is admitted that such processes are more readily observed in modern data. Some archeologists would go further and argue that there may be sociocultural phenomena represented in the record of the past that do not occur in the modern record. While this proposition is very likely a valid one, it is hardly the kind of statement on which one could base a career. It implies a commitment to the unique and unusual, the kind of commitment for which anthropologists are already infamous. Current knowledge does not suggest that the range of sociocultural phenomena in the archeological record differs greatly from that represented in the ethnographic record. Certain stages of cultural evolution, hunting-gathering bands, for example, may be better represented in the archeological record, but a significant question remains as to whether the nature of such groups cannot be better understood using ethnographic and ethnoarcheological approaches to modern data.

The justification for a science of past sociocultural phenomena that I find most appealing focuses on change in time. By and large, it is difficult and even impossible to study sociocultural change using modern data. Adequate event records that describe sequences of change cover longer periods of time than most ethnographers spend in the field. These periods are sometimes longer than the lifetime of a scholar. But, such event records or sequences are the everyday concern of the archeologist. I believe that the most significant contributions archeologists can offer to their fellow social scientists are answers to our many questions about the whys and wherefores of behavioral and cultural change.

Unfortunately, the archeologist's ability to understand and explain sociocultural change is poorly developed at this moment in the history of our discipline. We have spent much less time than our sociocultural colleagues in creating models and theories of change. We have been content to borrow their models and theories, and often without thinking about how these might be modified to offer greater insight into our own data. This borrowing would not constitute a problem were it not for the fact that most sociocultural investigations concern synchronic phenomena. Even the patterns of change with which sociocultural anthropologists work are more frequently inferred than observed. Patterns of temporal variability are inferred from patterns of variation in space. One should not *infer* a data base when that same data base can be *observed* elsewhere. Archeologists can observe sociocultural changes. Social scientists, by and large, must infer them. To the extent that archeologists wish to identify their archeological goals with goals of the social sciences, the study of change is a topic where we might make significant contributions.

INFERRING TEMPORAL PATTERNS FROM SPATIAL ONES

Let us explore the ideas of the preceding paragraph in some detail. After all, there are sociocultural anthropologists who call themselves evolutionists, and evolutionism is concerned with change. This I do not deny. But I believe that evolutionists are primarily interested in processes of change in time as a vehicle for explaining similarities and differences between existing societies, that is spatial variability. And to the extent that they use sequences of change, these are typically inferred from patterns of spatial variation. Are such inferences legitimate? Not for the study of change. The following example illustrates the reasons for my negative response to this question.

A number of social scientists working with evolutionary problems have used scaling techniques in inferring temporal patterns from spatial ones. Scaling techniques begin with the observation that a number of societies at discrete spatial loci differentially possess attributes that are seen by an investigator to have evolutionary import. Figure 1 shows a simple example of this observational strategy. Three societies, A, B, and C, are observed. The investigator records the presence or absence of three attributes, 1, 2, and 3. He finds that society A possesses attribute 1, society B possesses 1 and 2, and society C, 1, 2, and 3. Using evolutionary assumptions, he argues that society C is further along some evolutionary trajectory than B, and that B is further along the same trajectory than A. Similarly, he argues that trait 1 is a "functional prerequisite" for 2, and that 1 and 2 are functional prerequisites for 3. If the investigator is a unilineal

Societies

A	B	C		
		X	3	A t t r i
	X	X	2	b u
X	X	X	1	t e s

Fig. 1.   A scale of three societies and three attributes.

evolutionist, he will argue that at some earlier point, society C had only attributes 1 and 2 and at a still earlier point, only attribute 1. If he is a multilineal evolutionist, he will argue that societies in general evolve in a fashion similar to this model, although a given society may skip a stage.

How valid is this chain of arguments? Without observing the evolution of society C and other societies like it, we do not know. But we can gain some idea of the magnitude of the problem by asking a slightly different question: What is the probability that society C went through a sequence of change that corresponds to the scaled relationships among A, B, and C? To answer this question, we will assume that we are observing society C at t_3, and wish to know what it looked like at two preceding points in time, t_2, and t_1. In looking at C's developmental trajectory over time, I employ a simple and a complex model. In the simple model, we will be concerned with the question of whether the *number of attributes* that C possesses at each time interval corresponds to the prediction of the scale. In the complex model, we will be concerned with the question of whether the *specific attributes* that C possesses correspond to the prediction derived from the scale.

Beginning with the simple model, how many different sequences of change involving three attributes over three time intervals are there that result in the outcome $C = 3$ at t_3? The answer to this question is shown in Figure 2. There are 16 sequences of change over three time periods that have the outcome $C = 3$, and only one of these corresponds to the inferred pattern. Thus, the intrinsic or logical probability that the inferred sequence corresponds to a real temporal pattern is .063.

Turning to the complex model, how many different sequences of change involving different attributes are there that result in C possessing all three attributes at t_3? There are 64 such sequences, and the intrinsic or logical probability that the inferred sequence is the real one is .016.

Finally, we can add to our calculations the number of ways that the outcomes $B = 2$ and $A = 1$ might have developed. There are 16 or 64 possibilities for each society, corresponding to the simple and complex models, respectively. For the entire problem, there are 4096 sequences of change that result in the outcome $A = 1$, $B = 2$, $C = 3$ for the simple model and 262,144 such sequences for the more complex model. The probability that the scale model corresponds to reality is very slight.

```
                X                           X
                X               X           X
        —   X   X               X   —   X
        
                X                           X
                X               X           X
        —   —   X               X   X   X
        
                X                           X
            X   X               X   X   X
        —   X   X               X   X   X
        
            X   X                   X   X
            X   X               X   X   X
        —   X   X               X   X   X
        
                X                   X       X
                X                   X       X
        X   —   X               X   —   X
        
                X               X           X
                X               X           X
        X   X   X               X   X   X
        
                X               X           X
            X   X               X   X   X
        X   X   X               X   X   X
        
            X   X                   X   X   X
            X   X                   X   X   X
        X   X   X               X   X   X

        t¹   t²   t³              t¹   t²   t³
```

Fig. 2.   Sixteen sequences of change that have the outcome $C = 3$ at t^3.

The usual response to such exercises made by the proponents of scaling is to point out that they are based on the assumption that human behavior is random, and we know it is not random. Indeed, we know that human behavior is not random. But that does not provide us with any justification for assuming that human behavior follows only a single pattern. Certainly, the probability that some of the logically possible sequences of change will actually occur is close to zero. But this is no reason for throwing out all the other potential sequences. What does explaining change mean if not showing why one sequence of events occurs instead of some near or equiprobable alternatives? It is precisely in defining the real probabilities of alternative sequences or trajectories rather than their intrinsic or logical probabilities, in showing why some sequences are more probable than others, and in explaining why a given sequence occurs in a given situation, that models, theories, and explanations of change will be created.

The scalar model is a fly paper model of change: it assumes that societies acquire but don't maintain or lose characteristics. This assumption is as gross a violation of our intuitive notion of reality as the assumption that human behavior is random. Let me add an important qualification. When our interest is principally in synchronic phenomena, it may be economical to use inferences about temporal sequences instead of inferring them. The probability of a sequence such as that shown in Figure 1 is sufficiently high that it provides an acceptable model. But, when diachronic variability is our concern, the exclusive use of such models amounts to assuming one's data base rather than observing it and at least flirting with assuming one's conclusions.

Many of these same problems exist in other techniques that ethnographers have used in studying change. Some ethnographers study a population and then return 10 or 20 years later to do a restudy. They focus on the changes that have occurred in the intervening years. This kind of study is of course a legitimate study of change. But it is a poor research strategy. The investigator usually assumes a linear relationship between observations at the two points in time. If dependence on agriculture has increased, the increase is inferred to have had the shape of a straight line. Unfortunately, while two points provide a minimal definition for a straight line, they do not necessarily define a straight line. Lines of many different shapes could connect the two points; dependence on agriculture could have varied significantly rather than increasing regularly.

Archeologists, too, are involved in the game of inferring temporal patterns from spatial ones. Our greatest use of this strategy has been in trying to understand patterns of diffusion. While age-area hypotheses are no longer magically invoked, there is still a significant explicit and implicit use of assumptions like this one in our studies. When we find that a trait is more abundant or more varied at a locus and increasingly less abundant or varied as we move away from the

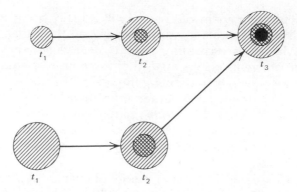

Fig. 3. Two alternative patterns for changes in the distribution of an innovation over time.

locus, we infer that the item was invented or at least initially appeared at this locus. Our reconstruction of events in time is similar to path A in Figure 3. Needless to say, there are many other event sequences that could produce the same pattern. One of them is shown in path B of the figure. Here an innovation achieves an initially widespread distribution over an area and is then adopted or developed at loci where it proves adaptive. A pattern such as this one probably underlies the anomaly of pottery types that are present as "trade" types before they become indigenous to any locality. Different kinds of innovations have different diffusionary patterns. And this variability is worth explaining. But we will never even observe, much less explain, this variability as long as we believe that diffusion has one characteristic pattern, that spatial patterns can easily be converted into temporal ones. Again, I do not wish to imply that rampant diffusionism is a part of modern archeology, only that we are still using and suffering from some subtle assumptions from diffusionary paradigms.

The point of this extensive discussion is simple: in order to understand processes of change, it is necessary to observe changes. The archeological record is an excellent source of such observations. However, we have generally failed to make use of that record in ways and for reasons that I consider below.

CHRONOLOGIES

The effect of our predominantly synchronic discipline on the way we think about time is most evident in our use of chronologies. A number of archeologists have observed that typologies are increasingly less useful for the kinds of problems we are investigating (e.g., Adams 1966a). Yet, it is clearly the case that the chronology remains one of our most fundamental conceptual tools. It is the model that most archeologists employ in describing changes over time, the model we use in thinking about these changes, and most important, the model we use in thinking about time. We visualize time as a sequence of periods, stages, or phases. We talk as if everyday events were very much the same during one of these periods and changed as the periods changed. Archeologists have probably spent more time in attempting to infer and describe the lifeways associated with a given stage than in accounting for changes from stage to stage.

Undoubtedly, this occurs because chronologies cause us to think of time as a series of successive units rather than as a continuous flow. (Many other disciplines have had to overcome this difficulty before they began to make progress in understanding their topic phenomena, e.g., the invention of calculus in physics.) In so doing, chronologies direct our attention away from sociocultural change and prevent us from making optimal use of the diachronic potential of our data base. Let us see why and how.

In the best of all possible worlds, it would be possible to construct a chronology by specifying a series of temporally ordered periods, each with a unique artifactual definition. Thus, period 1 would be defined by the presence of artifacts a–e, period 2 by the presence of artifacts f–k, and period 3 by the presence of artifacts l–p. But, this is not the best of all possible worlds. We all know that the pattern of artifactual variation is complex and overlapping. (In short, artifactual change is continuous rather than categorical.) Figure 4 more closely approximates the way in which we think about reality. Artifacts a, b, and c are most abundant during period 1, and d, e, and f during period 2. There is considerable overlap, but we try to construct the period boundaries so that this overlap is minimized. Variability within periods should be minimal, and between periods maximal.

This strategy provides the best distinctions between successive periods of time. However, it minimizes the probability that we will understand and explain changes. The presence of a stage or period boundary suggests that some artifacts are being replaced by others that serve the same or different purposes. (Artifact as used here refers to settlements and settlements patterns as well as to technological items and ecofacts.) But what happens to this period of change in a chronology? Either it falls half in one period and half in the other, or it is represented only as the line that bounds the two periods. If an

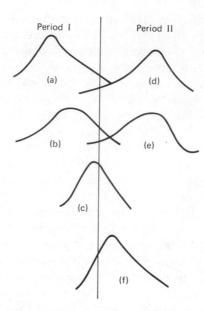

Fig. 4.   Patterns of artifactual change and period boundaries.

investigator is interested in change, this period is clearly the critical one. However, a chronology directs our attention away from rather than toward that period.

One attempt to solve this problem has involved the creation of chronologies that focus on the progress of a particular pattern of change. Thus, one finds dichotomies—incipient X, developed X—and trichotomies—incipient X, developing X, established X—that seem to speak to questions of change. But surely we hope to be able to say more about change than: it starts to happen, then it is happening, then it has happened. We are interested in the dynamic interaction of environmental and sociocultural phenomena that produces the changes we are observing.

If we are to conceive of change in time as involving dynamic interaction patterns, we must measure our variables and attributes and make our observations in a dynamic fashion. The changes that we observe in the archeological record can be represented as time traces or trajectories. Artifactual change, demographic change, organizational change, change in subsistence strategies, and stylistic change can all be represented in this way, and sometimes are. If we were to use these trajectories as a primary mechanism for dealing with temporal variabilities rather than by lumping them creating a series of polythetically defined time units, we would be employing an operational procedure that has a greater potential for elucidating patterns of change. We would have a set of data that describe the dynamics of change.

SERIATION: MISSING THE DIACHRONIC POINT

It will undoubtedly have occurred to some readers that archeologists do sometimes describe their data by creating time traces. The use of seriation techniques involves creating a continuous record of artifactual variation over time. (I will not address the question of whether such seriations are based on stylistic or functional definitions of artifact types. The distinction between style and function is never a clear one. Moreover, most type definitions that I have read are a mixture of stylistic and functional attributes.) A seriogram such as the one in Figure 5 is a record of the adoption of technological innovations over time. It explicates variability in the adoption process. But, the archeologist's use of the seriation model is a synchronic one. We seriate in order to date the archeological units from which the artifacts were taken, whether they are levels or sites. We could use seriation to generate a data base from which we would work in

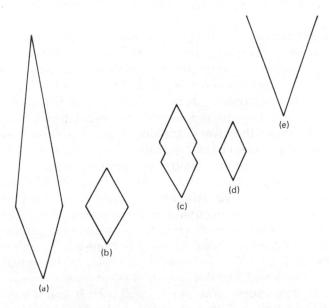

Fig. 5. A seriogram.

attempting to explain variability in the way that human populations adopt innovations. Some of the types in Figure 5 were adopted very rapidly, others very slowly. Some of them became abundant, others never did. Some decline in use very rapidly, others slowly. One could easily use these data in studying variability in the adoption of innovations, but we do not. We use the pattern to date sites.

None of the preceding discussion attempts to question the basic "battleship" configuration of the adoption process. Deetz (Deetz and Dethlefsen 1966) and others have demonstrated that this configuration is a typical one. But any innovation, if it is adopted at all, will have a beginning, a point of peak abundance, and an end. However, the specific shape of such curves varies considerably as Deetz's own data indicate. For engraved funeral stones, we may not be interested in constructing explanations. But the whole range of material data that archeologists use can be treated in this fashion and used in characterizing a data base for which and from which explanations of changes in subsistence, organization, activity structure, and so on, can be derived. Seriation is a good diachronic tool. But we have failed to realize its diachronic potential and have emphasized synchronic applications.

FACTS AND ASSUMPTIONS IN THE DEMOGRAPHIC RECORD

In some ways, our commitment to a synchronic viewpoint is so thorough that synchronic assumptions take on the character of facts while diachronic assumptions are treated as they should be, as assumptions. This problem is nowhere more evident than in archeologist's constructions of demographic records. At least in the Southwest, many archeologists have constructed records of population change over time for the regions they were studying. Having defined a series of time periods, the archeologist calculates the number of sites occupied during the phase or the number of rooms on the sites.

When a demographic record is constructed in this fashion, the archeologist is making two assumptions, one about the probability that particular sites were occupied at successive points in time and the other about patterns of site growth. Every archeologist knows the difficulty of establishing with precision the dates of a site's occupation no matter what kind of chemical, isotopic, or artifactual dating technique is employed. For this reason, it seems "safe" to place a site in a phase or stage, some time period, and treat it as if it were occupied during that period. This feeling is a misleading one. There is no safety in trying to overcome precision by becoming less precise or by not trying to be precise. One overcomes imprecision by being as precise as possible. Almost every archeologist could identify a point when he thinks a site was most probably occupied. Having done so, he can also define a series of points extending into the past and the future (vis à vis the point of greatest probability) when the probabilities of occupation are decreased. When we treat a site as if it had been occupied throughout a time period, we are arguing that the probabilities that the site was inhabited are equal at all points in time during that period. Any crude approximation of a probability distribution will be more sensitive to archeological reality than this one. But the former treatment is more consistent with our synchronic way of approaching time.

This problem is compounded when we are dealing with sites that have definable dwelling units. To treat the site as if it were occupied throughout a phase is to treat it as if all rooms were built in a day, occupied continuously, and abandoned in a day. No one really believes that sites grow and decline in this fashion. There are good data within archeology and elsewhere concerning village growth patterns. We would be creating a more precise record of demographic change if we used the knowledge about village growth patterns in counting the number of rooms occupied at the successive points in time for which we are making observations. But the use of a model of village growth somehow seems like an assumption that is different from the assumption of synchrony. I have performed enough experiments with the construction of demographic curves to know that different assumptions about the probability of occupation and different assumptions about village growth patterns can and frequently do result in very different population growth curves. It is absolutely necessary that we learn which assumptions are most appropriate to our data. But as long as we continue to use a seemingly simpler synchronic assumption even when it contradicts information we have in hand, we will surely fail to use the diachronic potential of our data, and may well build for ourselves a very misleading set of prehistoric "facts."

THE DIACHRONIC MILLENNIUM

I have heard and read anthropologists who refer to diachronic studies as if they would immediately clarify all issues of sociocultural causality. They seem to believe that if we had diachronic data it would be clear that sociocultural event *A* characteristically occurred before *B*, which in turn always preceded *C*. My interest in a greater emphasis on diachronic studies is not based on such arguments. It is my experience that patterns of variability in time have no less complex a relationship to each other than patterns in space. Fluctuations rather than steady and ordered increases are the rule. And all of our discussions of feedback mechanisms, thresholds, and tolerance limits should lead us to believe that we are unlikely to find simple $A \rightarrow B \rightarrow C$ chains of causality. Cultural phenomena deserve to be studied diachronically, but beginning this effort in no way implies an immediate solution to all or even some of anthropologists' outstanding questions.

DIRECTIONS AND APPROACHES

I have argued that archeology's strong point as a social science is a data base that permits the *observation* of temporal variation in behavior and in cultural processes. I have also argued that as a result of relying too heavily on models invented by sociocultural anthropologists for organizing and explaining spatial or synchronic variability, we have failed to develop a set of tools that aids us in realizing the diachronic potential of our data. I have not called for ignoring all archeological research done prior to this point, nor have I waved diachronic anthropology as a magic wand. I have simply said that the temporal dimension of variability in our data deserves greater attention, that we lack the tools for meaningful consideration of these data at present, and that we should work to develop such tools.

It would be desirable to end this chapter with a discussion of models and theories appropriate to diachronic anthropology. However, any such models and theories that I might offer at this point would be grossly oversimplified and would prove to be overly influenced by synchronic considerations. I am, however, involved in two projects that attempt to come to grips with some of the issues raised here, the Chevelon Archeological Research Project and the Northeast Arizona Development Project. The Chevelon Archeological Research Project is a study of the prehistoric record of the Chevelon drainage, an area of about 900 square miles, southeast of Winslow, Arizona. The archeological record of this region covers a period of at least 10,000 years. Most of the important technological and organizational innovations that occurred in the prehistoric Southwest occurred in this region. The Northeast Arizona Development Project studies the evolution of about 50 modern communities in that region. These communities were founded about 100 years ago. Some were Mormon communities that were agricultural, polygynous, and communalistic. Others were founded by Spanish sheepherders and Anglo ranchers and traders. Over the last century, all of the communities have undergone significant technoeconomic and organizational changes.

Our approach to these data places a heavy emphasis on the construction of a continuous record of variation over time, with chronologies receiving correspondingly less attention. Our attempt is to explain variability in the adoption of technoeconomic and organizational variations in both the prehistoric and modern records. Explanations for variability in the adoption of innovations are sought by considering the origin and nature of the innovations and the context in which innovations are introduced.

1. *Origins.* The term "adoption" has been used in referring to the events involved in a population beginning to use an innovation precisely because this term implies no particular origin for the innovation. Nevertheless, it is important to determine whether innovations that were diffused into a given region show a different pattern of adoption from those that were invented there.

2. *Nature of the innovations.* Gross categories of innovations may prove to require very different explanatory models. Stylistic innovations may be adopted differently from functional ones. Technoeconomic innovations may as a group show very different patterns of adoption from organizational ones. Tools that are very basic to a production process may show different patterns of adoption than secondary tools.

3. *The context in which innovations are adopted.* This topic is the most important one: what kinds of situational variables describe contexts in which innovations are characteristically adopted and what variables describe situations in which they are not? Are innovations more likely to be adopted when population is increasing, decreasing, or remaining constant? Are innovations more likely to be adopted in specialized work structures than in more generalized ones? How are environmental changes related to patterns of adoption? Does the level or stability of resource acquisition affect the pattern

of adoption? How does the extent of social integration effect adoption?

All of these are, of course, very general topics and questions, and our work is aimed at far more specific behavioral and sociocultural variables. Three models of change have been basic to the projects: a systemic model, an adaptive model, and a model of dynamic equilibrium.

The systemic model is by far the most synchronically oriented of the three. A system is understood to mean a series of groups (families, communities, lineages, etc.) exchanging goods, services, and information with each other in such a way that a change in one component of the system is likely to produce changes in the others. A "thermostatic" notion of a system is less appropriate to this model than an "exchange" or "alliance" notion. Human groups exchange things and ideas with each other. These exchanges are regulated by institutionalized ideas and behaviors. Regulators are themselves sensitive to a variety of different environmental and sociocultural variables. If these variables can be identified, then the investigator knows what changes in the system environment are likely to produce changes in the system.

Systems are always changing. But some of these changes are homeostatic, that is, they act to maintain a given set of relationships in the system. Other changes are morphogenetic, they act to replace an existing system with a new and different one. As long as the critical environmental variables that affect system regulators vary within established tolerance limits, the system will be in a homeostatic state. But if these variables exceed tolerance limits, a morphogenetic state is the likely outcome. The synchronic bias of this model should be clear. There is little potential for dealing with changes in terms of alternating system states. Nevertheless systemic models have proved useful in the social sciences, and an understanding of change that can be described in terms of these models seems desirable.

Systemic models also place a heavy emphasis on the normal or usual events that characterize a system's operation. Social scientists have been aware for some time that marginal or atypical institutions, events, and behaviors are crucial in periods of change. For this reason, we have found it useful to deal with models that focus on behavioral variability and the process of adaptation in a population. Adaptive models focus on processes of variety and selection.

Anthropologists have tended to focus their attention on normal behavior in a population. Yet we all know that within populations, within communities, behavior varies. Different individuals follow different strategies in acquiring social and natural resources. Strategies are combinations of two or more acts all of which result in the acquisition of the same natural or social resource. One might speak, for example, of subsistence acquisition strategies. Within a given population, one might find that different mixes of hunting-gathering and agriculture are practiced by different communities. Within communities, different individuals practice different mixes of the two strategies. Archeological evidence for such strategies may be found from examining the tools used in productive processes as well as from faunal and floral remains, ecofacts.

Adaptive models seek to explicate the interaction between new and different strategies that are continually generated in a population and the selective pressures that limit the effectiveness of those strategies. As long as environmental variables or selective pressures vary within definable limits, the changes in behavior that are observed will reflect either the deletion of strategies that are unsuccessful in acquiring needed natural or social resources, or the adoption of more successful strategies by individuals practicing less successful ones. Institutional changes within communities will reflect these same trends. Significant changes in environmental variables that exceed tolerance limits making formerly productive strategies unproductive, are likely to produce shifts in strategies. Normal strategies may no longer be productive. Strategies that were marginally productive in the old environment may be optimally productive in the new one.

Adaptive models have proven particularly useful in working with the archeological record. We have found, for example, that locations that are used for small, limited activity sites at one point in time, may become the locus of large settlements, given a significant change in social or natural environmental variables. Similarly, changes in processes of tool manufacture and tool use tend to fit such a model very well. Basin, trough, and slab metates, for example, coexist on sites in the Southwest for long periods of time, but the specific form of metate that is important changes, and this change is understandable in terms of adaptive models.

Dynamic equilibrium models deal with changes in sociocultural phenomena in the most general terms. Variables that measure the size and performance of human sociocultural systems—population, specialization of activities, extent and effectiveness of integration, resource production—have frequently proven to have very high correlations with each other. Moreover, such variables have proved to be good predictors of the adoption or nonadoption of innovations at the community level. And they are sufficiently general that they can be defined in almost any archeological or ethnographic situation.

If one can create temporal records of changes in each of these variables, it is possible to ask how a change in one variable affects the others. Do population increases, for example, have regular and describable effects on specialization, integration, or productivity? And if so, why? Is it possible to show that a dynamic equilibrium between these variables is maintained over time, and if so, what is the nature of this equilibrium?

All of these models have been discussed very briefly. In order to be used, each must be defined in a way that is appropriate to a given research effort and that is as specific as possible. I have described the models only to provide an idea of the directions in which the Chevelon Archeological Research Project and the Northeast Arizona Development Project are moving in the search for explanations of variability in behavior and in cultural processes along a temporal dimension.

13. TWO POINTS OF LOGIC CONCERNING DATA , HYPOTHESES, GENERAL LAWS, AND SYSTEMS *

STEVEN A. LEBLANC

Department of Anthropology
Wichita State University,
Wichita, Kansas

There seems to exist among archeologists some unclarity about the nature of scientific explanation. This situation does not necessarily affect an archeologist's ability to do good scientific research, but it does confuse the discussion of several basic issues and leads to statements whose implications are probably not intended by their makers. However, if we are going to ask others to consider seriously our efforts to derive and test propositions explicitly, we must not only perform these tests properly but we also must describe correctly the reasoning involved in this process. For this reason, two points of logic are discussed below.

THE USE OF PREVIOUSLY COLLECTED DATA IN HYPOTHESIS DERIVATION AND TESTING

A principal tenet of the "new" or scientific archeology is that hypotheses must be explicitly tested. This first requires a definition of

* This chapter has benefited greatly from my discussions with Richard A. Watson, who also composed the footnotes.

the hypothesis (*H*) and then a deduction from the hypothesis of a series of implications (*I*'s). The hypothesis is then tested for conformation by checking to see if its implications conform with empirical data. This hypothetico-deductive procedure has recently been gaining acceptance among archeologists. In particular, several contributors to *Reconstructing Prehistoric Pueblo Societies* (Longacre 1970) follow this procedure in some detail. However, many archeologists—including some of these contributors—misconstrue the logic underlying the relationships among hypotheses, implications, and testing. Basically, these researchers incorrectly suggest that data used to derive a hypothesis may not be legitimately used to test that hypothesis.

To show that this claim is not always true, I discuss three propositions.

1. The logic of hypothesis testing is atemporal; therefore, the *order* of data collecting, deduction of test implications for hypotheses, and testing is irrelevant to the validity of the reasoning involved.* This is shown below.

2. Implications from any hypothesis are deduced from the hypothesis, usually in combination with previously confirmed lawlike generalizations; no hypothesis is in any way logically dependent on actual data (either collected or potentially collectable) even though it may, in fact, have been derived from or confirmed by a set of actual data. That is, the implications themselves are logical entities logically deduced— whatever the facts may be. These implications are as hypothetical (and general) as the hypothesis from which they are deduced, and the validity of their deduction is a logical matter. Only their empirical truth depends on the data. (Testing a hypothesis is a matter of checking the truth of its implications.) The same hypothesis can be derived from data or fabricated; it makes no difference in determining its logical implications or whether it is true. This also is discussed below in detail.

3. Data itself has no memory. Its use has no effect on it. Data used to derive a hypothesis is not so contaminated that it cannot thereafter be used to test the hypothesis. Testing is

---

* However, there is a tremendous *practical* difference in the order of data collecting and hypotheses formulation (Watson, LeBlanc, and Redman 1971:16).

not always a matter of using new data but also a matter of looking at old data from a new or different point of view. This should be obvious, but the charge that testing always leads to circular reasoning is refuted below.

To demonstrate these propositions, the nature of hypothesis confirmation must be examined. Given an H, the strength of its confirmation depends on three factors: (1) the number of I's that can be shown to be empirically true; (2) the independence of the true I's (the greater their independence one from another, the stronger the confirmation of H); and (3) the logical completeness of the I's (the greater the probability that all possible I's have been deduced and found to be true, the stronger the confirmation of H).

Clearly these rules do not lead to the automatic acceptance of any particular H. In fact, many of the great debates in science have involved differences of opinion about whether one or more of these criteria have been met.

As a simple example of the application of these principles, let us hypothesize that all hunters and gatherers are patrilocal. In this case, the I's are easily deduced. Every hunting-gathering group should meet the definition of patrilocality so that the I's are that Group A and Group B are patrilocal, as are every known group. Assume that 20 such groups are checked and found to be patrilocal. Twenty instances of a true I thus go toward confirming H. How well is H confirmed in general? It depends, of course, on which 20 groups were examined. If they were all from Australia and belonged to the same linguistic group, the H would not be sufficiently confirmed because the groups are not independent enough from one another. If 20 hunting-gathering groups shown to be patrilocal were drawn from each linguistic group in Australia and similarly from every other continent, the confirmation of H would be much more convincing.

In this case, the demonstration that H holds also for groups known only archeologically would increase the number of true and independent examples of I. Moreover, if one could ultimately show that the I's of H are true for all known living groups (and all known historical groups), then we must accept H. When all possible I's of H are shown to be true, then we must accept H because there is no possibility of disconfirming it. In fact, this seldom happens and is usually empirically impossible to accomplish. We usually accept an H to be confirmed long before all its I's are shown to be true.

There is no discussion of hypothesis disconfirmation here. Logically, if one *I* from *H* is shown to be false, then *H* is disconfirmed and one must reject *H*. In practice, this is not necessarily true. This is partly because the *H* is a logical model, and no scientist claims that any logical model fits the world *exactly*. Logically, even though one false *I* disconfirms an *H*, the number of false *I*'s required for an *H* to be revised or rejected is strictly a practical matter. However, this problem is not the main one being discussed. It is enough to say that all the *H*'s presented are logically susceptible to disconfirmation (i.e., they are really testable). A disconfirmed *H* might be revised, but if it were rejected then a new *H* would be made and the test procedure repeated.

One point needs to be made: a panel of scientists or philosophers could gather at any stage in the investigation described above and be given an *H* and collected data. They could then report on the validity of the *H*. They do not need to know anything about the order of the data collected or about the derivation of *H* to make their decision.

Clearly, before proposing most *H*'s in anthropology, some information has been examined. Suppose one had examined the 20 Australian groups, had proposed an *H*, and then used these 20 cases to test the *H*? Is this a valid test of *H*? This is *logically* a valid procedure but it would be a very poor practical test of *H*. The test is not weak because the data were collected first but because the true *I*'s are few and not independent of one another. If a researcher gathered data on 200 groups, derived *H*, and then used this data to test *H*, *H* would be more convincing but still poorly confirmed if the 200 groups were not independent of one another. The test would be just as poor even if *H* had been created and then tested by checking the 20 or the 200 groups. The point is that the test weakness is not a matter of whether the *H* was derived from the data but of how the data fulfills the criteria for confirming *H*. Whether the data is independent of the derivation of *H* is not important; but whether the true *I*'s (the same data) are independent of one another *is* important in determining whether the data provide weak or strong confirmation for *H*.

However, there appears to be an intuitive inadequacy about the above procedure. It appears that if the primary data collected are used first to derive and test *H*, and *H* will always be confirmed. But this is not true. For almost any *H* derived in this manner, the possible *I*'s that could be found to test the *H* would require data far beyond that available when *H* was first formulated. Even if the data seem to confirm the *H*, as shown in the above example, this confirmation is often very weak. That is, the primary error in using the data to test *H* (from which *H* is derived) is not that these data cannot be used legitimately but that they are invariably insufficient.

Usually, *I*'s going beyond the original data are deducible, and thus must be tested before any *H* can be confirmed for an initial set of data. Again, this is *not* because we cannot use the original set of data as *part* of the confirmation of *H* but because to test any *H* we must deduce all possible *I*'s and check the truth of as many as possible. Thus, we follow the same procedure and produce the same *I*'s regardless of when, how, or from what data *H* is derived. Usually, if the data gathered prior to the formulation of an *H* verify an *I* deduced from that *H*, this is not sufficient to confirm *H*. This would be true of the *I* in question even if the data verifying it had been collected after *H* was created.

The crucial point is that *all* *I*'s must be considered in testing *H*, and none may be disregarded; this is true because *H* is confirmed logically. If an *I* can be validly deduced from *H*, it must be shown to be empirically true if *H* is to be confirmed. The deducibility of *I*'s is logical and not a temporal matter. Implications may be deduced from an *H* now or in the year 2000. If correctly deducible, implications remain the same now and in 2000 whether the data are collected in the 1800s or in 2001. Their truth is another (empirical not logical) matter.

Let us illustrate this argument by an extreme example. One could proceed on a purely inductive basis (with no *H*'s) to collect all possible data (this could not be done in practice) on all hunting-gathering groups. Suppose this data show all groups to be patrilocal. Would it be possible to test *H* if the data for all *I*'s had been gathered prior to the discovery of *H*? Certainly it would; *H* would clearly be confirmed. In this instance, *H* is logically identical with an inductive generalization based on all of the data. In such an instance, this generalization might not ever have been called an "hypothesis." Logically, however, it means the same thing, and that is the point.

If we throw out data collected prior to *H* derivation, another equally absurd situation could arise. Two workers might collect different data leading to the same *H*. It might then be claimed that to confirm *H*, each worker must show his *I*'s to be true in a manner different from the *I*'s of the other worker, since each worker had arrived at *H* with different data in hand. Furthermore, it might also be claimed that a third worker who formulated *H* without data *could* use the total set of I's. Again the solution is obvious; all three workers can and must check the truth of all I's deducible from H. The third individual would need to collect data on all the I's just as the other two would; but since the other two already had some of these data, they need not regather them.

I do not think that any of the archeologists who have suggested ignoring previously collected data would actually do so when presenting a final case for the acceptance of a lawlike generalization. What researchers are worried about is the possibility of their tests being found circular. While circularity does exist when data used to derive an H are also used to test it, these data form a necessary part of the test. Such data is seldom (and seldom taken to be) sufficient to confirm the H and, finally, it certainly cannot be excluded from test data.

GENERAL LAWS AND SYSTEMS THEORY

Flannery, in another chapter of this book, suggests that there is a major division within the "new" archeology. He views this difference to be between those who are intent on deriving and testing general laws "comparable to those of thermodynamics" and those who are interested in understanding cultures as total systems. Flannery discusses the practical differences in what these archeologists do and *not* the logical differences in their positions. Is there any logical difference between these approaches?

This problem is much more critical to the framework of processual archeology than the first point of logic discussed above. Although it is difficult to assess what systemic archeologists really do (because of a lack of published examples), some tentative opinions appear valid.

I argue that there is no logical difference between the procedure of deriving and testing hypothetical laws and the procedure of explaining cultures as systems. Both procedures must result in identical patterns of hypothesis derivation and testing, although an important addition from systems theory is that the systemic approach should result in the production of systems models. These models consist of a series of interrelated H's, traditionally called theories.*

---

* A model or theory that consists of a set or system of H's can be written in the form of $c(complex)H$. Because a cH has the logical characteristics of an H, anything said of a particular H can be said of a system model (or theory).

The theories do result in increased power to test H's, but again the difference is one of degree and not of kind.

Let us use an hypothetical example to clarify these points. An archeologist might propose an H of social overhead as follows: The amount of resources used by a group for social purposes increases faster than the population growth of that group. That is, if the population doubles, the resources used for social purposes will more than double. This hypothesis is called $H_{overhead}$. An archeologist might then go to the American Southwest and deduce a series of implications (I's) applicable to a particular culture (C) and then check the truth of these I's. If the I's are found to be true, he has confirmed a lawlike generalization. However, $H_{overhead}$ as originally stated has not been confirmed; instead, it has merely been shown to be true for one case. This can be observed in Table 1.

Notice that H_1 can be confirmed when H cannot. Clearly, the subordinate hypotheses could be confirmed for some but not all cultures. However, if for every culture examined the H for that particular culture is confirmed, then $H_{overhead}$ is confirmed. As explained above, both the number of cultures examined and the independence of these cultures from one another are important in testing $H_{overhead}$.

The test of H_1 may be more complex than appears in the Table 1. In particular, some of the I's for H_1 may be stated as lawlike generalizations. H_1 would be supported if the following lawlike generalization were confirmed: as the size of the pueblo increases a greater proportion of stone is used in constructing kivas. Thus, the confirmation of H_1 may be supported by the confirmation of another lawlike generalization, H_{stone}. And so on.

TABLE 1. RELATIONSHIP OF A PRIMARY HYPOTHESIS (H) TO THE IMPLICATIONS (I) EXPRESSED AS SUBORDINATE HYPOTHESES DEDUCED FROM (H) FOR PARTICULAR CULTURES (C) AND TO THE IMPLICATIONS OF THE SUBORDINATE HYPOTHESES FOR THESE CULTURES

$H_{overhead}$ social overhead occurs in all cultures.

$I_{overhead}$ (a series of I's) deduced from $H_{overhead}$ for all cultures:

    (1) $H_{overhead}$ holds for C_1, that is, social overhead occurs in C_1.

        $I_{1overhead}$ (a series of I's) deduced from $H_{1overhead}$ for C_1.

    (2) $H_{2overhead}$ holds for C_2, that is, social overhead occurs in C_2.

        $I_{2overhead}$ (a series of I's) deduced from $H_{2overhead}$ for C_2.

    . . . .

    (n) $H_{n\,overhead}$ holds for C_n, that is, social overhead occurs in C_n.

        $I_{n\,overhead}$ (a series of I's) deduced from $H_{n\,overhead}$ for C_n.

This last point is very important. Confirmed lawlike statements of regularity, by themselves, may appear to be trivial or obvious as H_{stone} might. However, when these possibly trivial generalizations are confirmed, they can be used to confirm more interesting generalizations such as H_1. It is entirely possible that H_1 may appear to be only slightly interesting; however, a series of H's, (each confirmed for a different culture) may confirm an H that is of substantial interest, such as $H_{overhead}$. It is probably wise to reserve the label "general law" for hypotheses of higher levels of abstraction; the logically identical $H_1 \ldots H_n$'s are usually merely steppingstones to the derivation or confirmation of the more general H. A goal of social science—and of scientific archeology—is the derivation, testing, and confirmation of hypotheses of the scope of $H_{overhead}$.

But we must be cautious. If we criticize the demonstration of the presence or absence of patterns of regularity in order to test H's (such as H_{stone}) as being trivial, this is ultimately equivalent to regrading $H_{overhead}$ as trivial. Clearly, in the early stages of the derivation and testing of hypotheses that may be confirmed as significant general laws, many superficially trivial H's (or generalizations describing patterns of regularity) will need to be tested and confirmed; we must keep in mind their role in the overall process that engages us. On the other hand, it is of limited interest to study such H's as H_{stone} for their own sake. Thus, although it is incorrect to criticize confirmed generalizations merely because they are trivial in some sense, it is acceptable to require a demonstration of their logical importance in the search for "significant" laws.

The above discussion deals with the derivation and testing of lawlike generalizations or hypotheses in traditional terms. However, the basic assumption in searching for general laws of this type is that the effects of other variables (or boundary conditions) on the phenomena being studied are (1) insignificant; (2) they are or can be held constant; or (3) they can be averaged out. This assumption appears to be true for the phenomena of physics and chemistry, but when parts of more complex systems such as those in biology or anthropology are examined, this assumption may no longer be true. It might not be possible to ignore or control other aspects or parts of these systems when examining the relationships among selected parts of the entire system. For this reason, it is suggested that the laws of the form "If A, then B" (similar to $H_{overhead}$) do not appear to be adequate to explain the workings of biological or other complex systems, and that such systems must be described and understood in their entirety. However, choosing to study a system as a whole does not require us to change the logic of our analysis. It appears that we perform the same pattern of H testing as described previously with two modifications: (1) the procedure will, by necessity, become very complex, and (2) we are capable of constructing models or theories that give us increased power to test our hypotheses.

For example, assume we have a system that can be broken down into three subsystems—A, B, and C—with the following relationships:

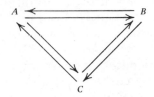

Here, a change in subsystem A affects every other subsystem that, in turn, reaffects A, and so on. If the nature of these interactions and the initial states of B and C is known, then for each change in A the outcome of the system as a whole can be predicted. In other words, to understand the system, one needs to be able to describe the nature of the process represented by each arrow in the diagram. However, any arrow can also be described as a series of "If A, then B" statements. These may be relatively simple, such as: if the population increases in a particular cultural system, then the amount of firewood needed increases proportionally. On the other hand, these statements may become extremely complex, and one may find a different relationship of B to A for each different value of A.

Finally, a system is described by a series of lawlike generalizations particular to that system and not necessarily of universal validity. These generalizations are of the same logical form as that of H_1 in the preceding example. These "laws" are no more the goal of the systems analyst than H_1 is the goal of the previous researcher. The ultimate goal of the systems analyst is a series of laws about groups of systems (see Hempel 1959).

Although there is no difference in the logical form of the H's in systems-theory analysis, nor in the nature of its ultimate goal (compared with other means of formulating and testing H's), there is a difference in the manner of testing these H's. A systemic analysis can provide a very powerful means of generating I's and testing H's. If we understand the relationships $A \rightarrow B$ and $B \rightarrow C$, then we can make generalizations about the joint outcome of B and C, given a change in A. That is, we can deduce I's that would not be produced from generalizations of A and B or B and C alone. The implications resulting from joining several generalizations are often greater than the sum of the individual implications. We check the truth of these I's as described above. If we show that a particular I deduced from an interconnected series of H's is true, then this is a particularly powerful confirmation of these H's. Furthermore, in a systemic analysis the disconfirmation of an I implies that we have not identified a relationship (represented by an arrow) existing in the system. Thus, a disconfirmation in a systemic analysis can lead to new insights about the system in a way that the disconfirmation of the H in simpler cases does not.

The similarities and differences between the two methods of analysis can be shown by constructing another hypothetical lawlike generalization (or H): all cultural systems are adaptive, that is, they respond to change in order to bring the system to optimum output, given the inputs. This hypothesis (adaptation) is more or less confirmed by the number of cultural systems shown to fit it and by the independence in space and time of these systems (Table 2).

In detail, $H_{adaptation}$ states: for each possible change in any component of a culture there is (1) a set of "If x, then y" statements describing how the first change affects all other components, and how the newly changed components affect each other, and (2) this set of "If x, then y" statements will result in greater output than any other possible combination of "If x then y" statements.

Thus the I_1's for any culture are all the possible changes in that culture. These changes can be tested by examining the relevant "If x then y" statements that are, in fact, a series of already confirmed H's.

Observe that Table 2 is exactly the same form as Table 1 for $H_{overhead}$.

TABLE 2. RELATIONSHIP OF THE PRIMARY HYPOTHESIS TO THE IMPLICATIONS
FOR A SYSTEMIC HYPOTHESIS

$H_{adaptation}$: all cultures are adaptive, that is, optimizing.
I (a series of I's) deduced from $H_{adaptation}$ for all cultures:
   (1) $H_{1 adaptation}$ holds for C_1, that is, adaptive behavior occurs in culture C_1.
     $I_{1 adaptation}$ (a series of I's) deduced from $H_{1 adaptation}$ for C_1.
   $\vdots$
   (n) $H_{n\,adaptation}$ holds for C_n, that is, adaptive behavior occurs in culture C_n.
     $I_{n\,adaptation}$ (a series of I's) deduced from $H_{n\,adaptation}$ for C_n.

The testing of $H_{adaptation}$ is directly analogous to the testing of $H_{overhead}$. Beginning with a particular system, each lesser hypothesis must be tested (as was done for H_{stone}). That is, each relevant "If x, then y" statement relating the components (the ABC's) of the system must be hypothesized and tested. Then, the systems hypothesis (i.e., the statement of the systemic relations of the lesser hypotheses) must be tested to see whether it holds true for all changes in the whole system. Finally, $H_{adaptation}$ is tested to see whether it holds true for all systems examined. If all of these tests have positive results, $H_{adaptation}$ is thus far confirmed.

Although the logic behind the testing of $H_{overhead}$ and $H_{adaptation}$ is identical, the complexity of the testing is not. It is very difficult to test all of the generalizations necessary for a complete description of a cultural system, and even more difficult to derive higher generalizations about the systemic interrelationships of the lesser generalizations that can also be tested.

General laws, such as the law of social overhead, may be confirmed for cultures, or they may be confirmed for cultural systems, such as the law of adaptation. In these cases, the laws have the same general logical form. The significant differences are (1) that more exciting and profound laws will result from generalizations about systems than about parts of these systems, and (2) that generalizations are much harder to derive, test, and confirm for systems than for parts of systems.

In arguing for the logical equivalence of lawlike generalizations and systemic generalizations—from their derivation to their testing—I emphasize hypothesis testing. Alternatively, these two frames of reference can be considered as means of explaining phenomena. This suggests that *explanations* based on lawlike generalizations are not logically different from explanations based on the results of systemic analysis. Tuggle, Townsend, and Riley (1972) suggest that there is a difference. Their argument appears to be based largely on Meehan's (1968) work. He presents a detailed argument for the inadequacy of deductive-nomothetic (or covering law) explanation and for its difference from systemic or processual explanation.

Meehan considers several aspects of explanation critical to this problem. One is that covering-law explanations can be objectively tested for being true or false but not for being "adequate." To use Meehan's example, one can explain the white color of a European swan by reference to the covering law stating "all European swans are white." Alternatively, one can refer to the genetic law that says "the offspring of two white swans will be white." If both laws are true, both explanations are true. However, Meehan says that neither explanation really explains *why* the swans are white, as would an evolutionist explanation. Evolutionists would appeal to the law of evolution and to a law stating the adaptive advantage of white coat-color under European conditions. Thus, it can be true that an explanation can be "correct" but not adequate for particular purposes. Although Meehan's point is relevant to the question of what determines the "adequacy" of an explanation, it does not establish any pertinent difference between covering-law (deductive-nomothetic) explanation and systemic explanation.

None of the explanations is systemic in the above example. However, the genetic law could be put in a systemic framework. The fertilized egg could be defined as a system. It could then be shown that the combination of the initial state (genes) and the environment during the growth period would result in a white adult. While this explanation would be true, it would not be an evolutionary answer. Conversely, the Darwinian explanation might appeal to systemic analysis in treating the adaptability of coat color, but it would also have to appeal to the nonsystemically framed covering-law of the theory of evolution. Although it is true that systemic (or processual) explanations are more likely to be "adequate" than nonprocessual explanations in answering the question "Why?", this is not inherent in the systemic frame of explanation.* The point cannot be made too strongly that science has presented us with a great number of explanations that are not obviously systemic, many of which are adequate (i.e., useful) in various contexts. Thus, while the question of determining the adequacy of any explanation is important and must be answered, the fact that systemic laws are sometimes adequate in contexts in which nonsystemic laws are not does not establish a pertinent logical difference between them. The adequacy of an explanation is not an internal characteristic; it is an external, contextual characteristic depending, in many cases, on the scientist's needs, interests, and intelligence.

The basic error that Tuggle et al. and Meehan make is that they do not realize that Meehan's systemic analysis is designed to result in a model, and that the derived model is not generally different in

---

* It is doubtful that any scientific explanation—systemic or otherwise—can be adequate in answering the question "Why?" if one demands—as Meehan seems to—more than a lawlike description of what takes place. Science *is* logically different from theology.

logical form from many complex covering laws or interrelated sets of covering laws. By Meehan's own definition, "A system consists of a set of variables (V_1, V_2, V_3... V_n) and a set of rules that define the interactions among those variables (R_1, R_2, R_3, ... R_n," (Meehan 1968: 50). Clearly these R's are nothing more than an expression of a covering law, whether it be a formula such as $F=ma$ or the statement that "The amount of resources used for social purposes by a group increases faster than the population of that group." This is exactly the point I make above with the example of the law of adaptation. Meehan's systemic explanation is a model compounded of a set of laws and, as such, it allows for a more powerful explanation than any single lawlike generalization encompassed by it. The extremely important difference between these forms of explanation is not logical, but results mainly from the high degree of comprehension of the information in and the complexity of systemic explanation.

Let us assume that community size is very large in A.D. 1200 in the American Southwest. Either one of two hypothetical covering laws might be used to explain this large size: (1) matrilocality results in large communities, and (2) warfare results in large communities. If it could be shown that these cultures were matrilocal and were engaging in warfare, there might be no reason for choosing between these explanations. If this were all that were archeologically known about these cultures, these explanations would be equivalently adequate or inadequate. But if we know that community size increased dramatically from A.D. 700 to A.D. 1200, we would surely appeal to one of two other hypothetical laws: (1) if communities shift from patrilocality to matrilocality, they tend to increase in size, and (2) if communities begin intensive warfare, they increase in size. In this case we would need to demonstrate either: (1) patrilocality at A.D. 700 and matrilocality at A.D. 1200, or (2) no warfare at A.D. 700 and widespread warfare at A.D. 1200. If both series of events were shown to have taken place, either or both explanations would be adequate.

In this expansion of the example I assume that there is a marked increase in the available data. Originally, I assumed that we knew only the community size, residence rules, and warfare patterns in A.D. 1200. The second pair of explanations also requires, knowledge of community size, of residence patterns, and of warfare at A.D. 700.

However, it is possible to refine these explanations or even to rule one out. With a systemic explanation we could show which of the two factors (if not a third) contributed—and in what degree—to increased community size. To do this systemic analysis, we would need still more information than is given to show that the second two laws fit the particular situation.

For example, if we know that there was a shift from patrilocality to matrilocality at A.D. 800 and that warfare began at A.D. 900, then a systemic explanation could be formulated in terms of an initial residence rule change leading to increased community size. This community size led to increased warfare so that by A.D. 1200 both changes had been effected. Thus, we could describe the relationships among all the variables. This description would be possible only because more data are used here than in the preceding explanations. In fact, the explanations are not comparable in detail. With the original data, no systemic explanation is possible, and it is meaningless to say, with such limited data, that a processual description would give a more adequate explanation than a restricted covering-law description would in the original context. With the introduction of the additional information on the order of residence change and warfare patterns, the first explanation becomes entirely inadequate, not because it is not systemic or processual but because it does not account for all the known data. That is, the less we actually know of a situation, the broader or weaker the available explanatory laws will be. The more we know, the more adequate (i.e., more complete) or more systemic our explanations will be.

To show that there is no pertinent logical difference between these two types of explanations, we can review the logic of the systemic explanation shown above: (1) there is a shift away from patrilocality toward matrilocality; (2) this shift leads to increased village size which (3) then leads to incipient warfare; (4) both of these trends are reinforced by feedback until (5) large matrilocal communities and endemic warfare are found at A.D. 1200. Is this outline an adequate explanation? No. Why does (2) follow from (1) or (3) from (2)? If the above explanation is accepted as adequate, it is because of intuition. The nature of this procedure has been discussed amply (Binford 1968c; Watson et al. 1971:26ff; and Hempel 1942).

The essence of the argument is that mere description is not a sufficient explanation. Describing the relationship (R) among several variables does not explain the final state of a system. For the above example, consider V_1 to represent community size and V_2 to represent the matrilocal residence rule (possibly measurable in percentages of female offspring living with a female parent). For the Southwestern example, R_1 would have the form $V_1 = kV_2$, or the statement that "Community size increases as matrilocality increases." This statement is not an explanation, but is simply a description. We can explain the increased community size only if it already has been demonstrated that the relationship $V_1 = kV_2$ is true for all situations of this type. Then we can explain the particular case under the confirmed general law. Merely to write an equation that represents the observed situation does not explain it. If it did, science would consist of writing down (in mathematical form or otherwise) descriptions of all particular situations. Obviously, explanations depend on lawlike generalizations usually drawn from descriptions of many particular situations and always confirmed by reference to particular descriptions. Here, adequacy is taken to be a matter of the completeness of the lawlike explanation for covering particular situations; mere descriptions of particular situations are never adequate as explanations.

What form must the explanation take in the Southwestern example? (1) The initial tendency toward matrilocality must be explained in terms of the increased importance of women. Although we have not been given the data, we would need to explain its derivation under some general law underlying the conditions of A.D. 700–800. (2) We explain the increases in village size only by appealing to a law similar to the one given earlier (e.g., "Matrilocality results in increased village size"). (3) Similarly, we need to have a law relating village size increases to warfare in order to explain the third process. Finally, the positive feedback cycles resulting in the final state at A.D. 1200 are, in fact, explicable if they can be shown to fit general-systems-theory laws concerning feedback. It must be demonstrated that, under the given conditions, the cycles would be amplifying and not decaying in order to explain the final state.

Therefore, the systemic or processual argument must subsume particulars under at least four general laws to provide an adequate explanation for the Southwestern example. This is the same point I made above. When systemic explanations are more adequate than an explanation making reference to a single covering law, it is not because the systemic explanations are logically different from the single covering law in any pertinent way, but because the explanations cover far more data than the single covering law and involve the use of many covering laws in an integrated way, giving a complete explanation of the situation.

In conclusion, there is often an advantage to formulating H's within a systemic framework even though there is no basic logical difference between the systems approach and the hypothetico deductive approach. On the other hand, we should not discredit the role of nonsystemic generalizations in scientific explanation. In biology—the discipline that first produced the need for a systems approach—generalizations that have been made are not about biological systems but, instead, are concerned with small subunits of total systems. This suggests that much can be learned from a nonsystemic approach and that the complexity of the most interesting systems makes their total analysis tremendously difficult. We must balance the use of the two approaches as required by our questions and resources, while operating with each approach in the same framework of explicit hypothesis formulation and testing.

14. NOTIONS TO NUMBERS: GREAT BASIN SETTLEMENTS AS POLYTHETIC SETS

LEONARD WILLIAMS

Department of Anthropology
University of California
Davis, California

DAVID HURST THOMAS

American Museum of Natural History
New York, New York

ROBERT BETTINGER

Department of Anthropology
University of California
Riverside, California

This chapter addresses two theoretical issues confronting modern American archeology: proper testing of hypothesis and operationalization of intuitive concepts. Based on earlier computer simulation models *(BASIN I)* and fieldwork in central Nevada, the authors derived hypotheses (integrated into the overall Reese River Subsistence-Settlement System) regarding winter village placement. Given the proper set of environmental conditions, we felt that we could successfully predict presence/absence of archeological sites, a hypothesis that required testing by independent data. But to conduct

further field investigation, such intuitive concepts had to be quantified where possible. The relevant environmental variables were then
defined into measurable quantities and these diverse criteria then
welded into a single *polythetic definition*. In this manner, whenever
at least five of the seven quantitative propositions were satisfied in
nature, a site was predicted to occur. Subsequent fieldwork indicated
the polythetic predictors to be accurate in approximately 95% of all
cases in this area.

Change from a qualitative to a quantitative approach is characteristic of
the development of any branch of science. As some understanding is
achieved of the broader aspects of phenomena, interest naturally turns to the
finer detail of structure or behavior, in which the observable differences are
smaller and can only be appreciated in terms of measurement [Greig-Smith
1964:ix].

In examining the literature of modern archeology, one cannot
fail to notice the conscious and explicit trend toward rigorous quantification. While this is surely a laudable and in fact imperative bias, we
feel that many quantitative studies tend to overstate their point; too
often these products of numerical research are presented as something "brand-new," without traditional precedent. This approach
ignores the many purely intuitive and qualitative constructs that serve
archeology quite admirably—without objectivity. Much of the controversy between the traditionalist and the so-called new archeologist
regards the proper role of intuition in archeological methods and
theory. In the extreme, both positions fall far short of the mark. As
we increase our knowledge of the past, we must continually refine
and polish our definitions, a necessity due in part to the increasing
importance of the computer. As Pelto (1971) has stressed, computers
permit little room for ambiguity since machines take the worker at
his word. In the rush to quantification, however, some have inadvertently lost sight of the true role of measurement in archeology.
Instead of being an end in itself, quantification must always satisfy a
nonquantitative need in pragmatic, problem-oriented research.
Although a few quantitative techniques, such as factor analysis, can
boast of being truly "new" (to archeology) and without analogic
precursors, most methods of quantification have their epistemological ancestry in traditional archeological theory. We reject the adage
seemingly implied in some recent studies: "If you can't measure it,
you don't understand it." In fact, too often one gets the uncomfort-
able feeling that some recent papers can *measure* the phenomenon

—often to several decimal places—but true understanding seems curiously lacking.

Our position is thus a middle-of-the-road stance, stressing that quantification in moderation is a logical and necessary step in the advancement of all sciences. Sometimes the early progress of a discipline can be gauged by its ascendency above the simple nominal (typological) level. And yet we cannot deny the overall utility and validity of what Phillips (1958) has called *feel*. As in *all* science, some of archeology's most significant breakthroughs come as the direct result of feel, through intuitive insight gained only from intimate familiarity with the primary data. Often such insights can be objectively framed as hypotheses and immediately tested; the recent success of archeological research in the American Southwest is largely the result of applying the quantitative approach to intuitive concepts. Hill's (1968) analysis of pueblo room patterning, for example, while providing an excellent model for archeological scholarship, did not produce startling results. Everyone familiar with the data already knew (intuitively) that the large rooms with hearths, mealing bins, and food remains were probably areas of habitation and that the deep, round features with the slab benches were the prehistoric analogs of kivas. The import of Hill's work is clearly not in providing us with penetrating new insights into Southwestern prehistory, but rather with the systematization and testing of notions that veteran archeologists have held implicitly for decades.

Although some of archeology's traditional techniques—such as seriation and dendrochronology—are relatively easy to quantify, the more diaphanous concepts have proven recalcitrant. The *type concept*, for example, plays a pivotal role in all archeological procedure, yet no investigator, to our knowledge, has succeeded in a truly objective treatment of typology. It is interesting that archeology's most sophisticated and quantitative analyses must still begin with an initial intuitive typology of artifacts, for example, Binford and Binford (1966), Longacre (1970), Hill (1970). This is not to belittle the work of these scholars—clearly this is the best set of treatments yet available —but rather to underscore the intuitive and subjective foundations of much of current archeological thought.

In exploring this topic further, we shall focus on a single aspect of modern archeology, the study of subsistence-settlement patterning. Despite the substantive progress in this area, most settlement studies remain at an intuitive, gut-level of analysis, for example, Willey (1956), Struever (1968a). While intuitive assessment is sufficient for discussing a single ecosystem, large-scale comparisons and broad ecological studies are severely hampered by this lack of comparability and replicability. This chapter attempts, in a preliminary way, to add a measure of rigor to the analysis of prehistoric settlements.

THE NATURE OF POLYTHETIC ENTITIES

In his recent book *Analytical Archaeology* (1968), David L. Clarke repeatedly stressed that archeological entities are best analyzed within a polythetic framework. While agreeing with Clarke's position, we wish to consider the polythetic concept a bit further, in part to provide the proper background for our own research and also because we feel that the full import of polythetic description may have been somewhat obscured in Clarke's comprehensive monograph.

The biologist Morton Beckner (1959) outlined the basis of monothetic and polythetic entities in his book *The Biological Way of Thought*. Although Beckner originally coined the terms "monotypic" and "polytypic," Sneath (1962) suggested that since "polytypic" already has an established meaning in biology, that Beckner's concepts, while perfectly valid, should be renamed *monothetic* and *polythetic* ("mono" means one; "poly," many; and "thetos," arrangement). In the following discussion, we have substituted Sneath's terms into Beckner's original exposition.

A monothetic criterion is one in which a set of propositions is considered both *necessary* and *sufficient* for group membership. Consider the following statement: all mammals have body hair, bear live offspring, and suckle their young. The assumption is that any creature satisfying these three criteria will be a mammal; furthermore, any individual without all three will *not* be a member of the class Mammalia. Following this reasoning, it is said that Clarence Darrow "established" that his opponent, William Jennings Bryan was not a mammal, since Bryan had never born offspring, had obviously never suckled his young, and was in fact quite bald.

It seems that nascent sciences often rely rather heavily on such definitions, while research remains concerned with finding gross divisions in long continua; monothetic statements are still frequent in preliminary archeological investigations:

The cylinder jar with slab-shaped tripod legs is diagnostic of Teotihuacan III.
All kivas have a *sipapu*.

In each case, a set of propositions is both necessary for membership in the class and sufficient for assigning an unidentified specimen to the previously designated category: all structures with a *sipapu* are kivas; no structure without a *sipapu* is a kiva.

Such all-embracing criteria are popular among some scientists—and despised by undergraduate students—because of the felicity with which new specimens may be classified, once one memorizes the rules. Yet as knowledge increases, these classifications invariably become oversimplistic: some kivas are found lacking a *sipapu* and Teotihuacan-like cylinder jars appear in Guatemala. The fault is not with the defining characteristics, for any such rigid set will eventually prove inaccurate, but rather with the monothetic approach to classification per se—the real world usually refuses to operate in a rigid, one-to-one fashion.

Beckner's remedy for this situation is the recommendation that the scientist explicitly recognize a more realistic mode of analysis, the polythetic framework. In Beckner's terminology, the classificatory problem is one of defining a group K in terms of a set G, comprised of the properties $f_1, f_2, \ldots f_n$; to consider K as a valid polythetic class, two basic properties must be satisfied:

1. Each individual must possess a large number of the f-properties in G.
2. Each f in G must be possessed by a large number of the individuals.

In addition, Beckner stipulated that for a class to be considered *fully polythetic*, no f in G is possessed by every individual in the aggregate. This definition is little more than a rigorous approach to the definition of intuitively valid categories, since no single criterion will adequately separate the given class—that is, exceptions are anticipated. Polythetic definition avoids the necessity for arbitrary delimitation of the K, non-K border since the polythetic sets are operational categories, adequately justified if only on the grounds of scientific economy. A de facto construct, the polythetic definition always allows for later redefinition in monothetic terms, should future research justify the more expeditious boundaries, such as all atoms have nuclei. We can thus define groups as *operationally* polythetic while recognizing that the entities may one day be proven as ultimately monothetic.

It must be stressed that the monothetic-polythetic dichotomy is not necessarily a division between good and bad, for each arrangement has its function in scientific research. Monothetic divisions are most useful in "classification from above," the sorting of specimens into progressively finer groupings. Excavators operate in this fashion by separating the grimy archeological specimens into rough field categories such as bone, sherds, chipped stones, ocher, and debitage. One experiences little difficulty in applying monothetic definitions at this point: all pottery sherds are expected to be made of clay and to be extremely hard or brittle. Monothetic divisions are also useful in classifying unknown artifacts into preexisting groups (identification): operational "keys" are becoming more important in the classification of archeological artifacts (see Thomas 1970 for an example of an operational dichotomous key for identifying projectile points).

Polythetic groupings on the other hand offer the archeologist his best hope in quantifying intuitive feel. Archeological typology has never been bound by rigid adherence to specific rules, and archeologists are usually unable to agree on even a preliminary definition of *type*. The higher levels of classification suffer from this same problem, for although intuitive units usually seem to work in practice, scientific procedure requires that such categories be more efficiently defined and made repeatable between different investigators where possible.

To illustrate this point, let us consider the synthetic concept of the *Desert culture*, one of archeology's more prolific integrative concepts. As more data becomes available, however, it becomes clear that the Desert culture in its present form has nearly outlived its usefulness as a conceptual device. With Great Basin research largely beyond the typological level, the rubric of the Desert culture too often obscures rather than clarifies. Nevertheless, there remains that elusive essence, that flavor, that distinguishes Great Basin adaptations from those of nearby California, the Plateau, and the earlier Southwest. Why is it so difficult to put one's finger on precisely what makes the Desert culture distinctive? The problem is not in the subject matter, we feel, but rather in the theoretical framework in which the concept has been approached.

We shall argue that the Desert culture is a perfect example of a polythetic concept operating in archeology. In examining this question, let us use an indirect proof, assuming the opposite and demonstrating that this assumption leads us to an absurdity. The Desert culture has been variously defined by trait lists, such as that offered by Jennings:

cave and overhang locations for settlement, bark or grass beds, seasonal gathering, intensive exploitation of resources, small seed harvesting and special cooking techniques, basketry (twining predominant), netting and matting, fur cloth, tumpline, sandals (moccasins rare), atlatl, pointed hardwood dart shafts, varied (relatively small) projectile points, preferential use of glassy textured stone, flat milling stone and mano, a high percentage of crude scraper and chopper tools, digging stick, firedrill and hearth, bunt points, wooden clubs, horn-shaft wrenches, tubular pipes, use of olivella and other shells, vegetable quids [1964:154].

This list, while not exhaustive, is sufficient to give the flavor of a Desert culture existence. In considering the Danger Cave assemblages, Jennings further synthesized this trait list into two basic components: "The twin hall marks [sic] of the Desert culture were the basket and the flat milling stone" (Jennings 1957:7). *Webster's Seventh New Collegiate Dictionary* defines *hallmark* as "a distinguishing characteristic, trait, or feature." If we assume that the Desert culture is monothetic, then these hallmarks must be both necessary and sufficient criteria of the concept. That is, the hallmarks must be present at all Desert culture sites and not present at any non-Desert culture sites. We know, of course, that both traits are quite frequent outside the Desert West, but let us restrict our gaze to the Desert West for the moment. Lovelock Cave, for example, is considered by Jennings (1964:153, 164) as a typical Desert culture site and as such, Lovelock can be expected to contain the hallmarks of the Desert culture. Yet in their report on the early excavations in Lovelock Cave, Loud and Harrington (1929:106) reported that out of hundreds of artifacts recovered, only two pieces of grinding stones were found—and those were both fragments of mortars, not flat milling stones! How can Lovelock Cave be said to represent the Desert culture if one of the two hallmarks is lacking? By our monothetic definition Lovelock Cave is not of the Desert culture, yet any archeologist familiar with the material would doubtless place Lovelock squarely in what Jennings' called the Desert culture. The fault lies neither with the site nor with Jennings' definition, for he surely never intended his "hallmarks" as ironclad rules. The fault is to consider the Desert culture as monothetic. It is not.

We can thus see—if only through the process of elimination—that the Desert culture and many other archeological units have yet to establish any concrete examples of how such definitions will really help the practicing field archeologist. The rest of this chapter will demonstrate how the explicit use of a polythetic framework has aided us in clarifying the prehistoric settlement pattern relationships in the Reese River Valley of the central Great Basin.

THE REESE RIVER ECOLOGICAL PROJECT

The Reese River Ecological Project functions as a continuing program of paleoanthropology in the central Great Basin. The first phase of research was designed to test two hypotheses:

1. Julian Steward's (1938) theory of protohistoric patterns for the Great Basin Shoshoneans.
2. The applicability of this theory to the prehistoric periods of the same region.

Steward's excellent ethnographic data was translated into a computer simulation model (*BASIN I*) that generated over 100 quantitative propositions from the Steward theory (discussed in Thomas 1971, 1972). In 1969 and 1970 field crews from the University of California (Davis) and the University of Nevada conducted a regional random sample of the Reese River Valley, gathering data relevant to the *BASIN I* predictions. The results of this phase of investigation seem to have adequately confirmed Steward's work at the protohistoric level and now permit archeologists to tentatively extend the Steward model from the historic period back to about 2500 B.C. in the Reese River area. In addition to testing Steward's theory, the field work generated new data that were synthesized into a new and more comprehensive theory describing the *Reese River Subsistence-Settlement System*.

The Reese River Subsistence-Settlement System is defined for the Medithermal *Period* at the Reese River *Locality* . . . [and] is characterized by two types of settlements. The *Shoreline Settlement* consists of a series of sites located on a permanent water source within a lower sagebrush-grass lifezone . . . [and consisting] of massive linear scatters of artifacts, generally parallel to the flowing source of water. No consistent locus of habitation was re-occupied; apparently campsites were situated near scattered caches of seeds. . . . The *Piñon Ecotone* Settlement corresponds to Steward's winter village sites . . . [which] were located in stands of piñon and juniper trees, often on long, low ridges which fingered onto the valley floor . . . the precise locus of winter habitation varied from year to year; this fluctuating locus can perhaps be planned up to three years in advance . . . it is suggested that about five families lived on each ridge-top, but there might be several such ridge-top villages within a one mile radius . . . the Reese River system is really based upon a dual central base pattern, since habitation alternated between the two settlement types, depending upon the seasonal available resources . . . this adaptation, as "on the fence" compromise between wand-dering and sedentary life, seems to provide the flexibility required for success in a situation such as the central Great Basin [Thomas 1973].

These habitation camps are complemented by a series of task-specific groupings, discussed by Thomas (1971).

ANOTHER LOOP IN THE CYCLE

The preceding operations can be viewed most profitably as the initial round in a generalized *scientific cycle* (Kemeny 1959):

LOOP I

  i. FACTS: Steward's ethnographic field work
                                     (1935, 1936)
                                       |
                                 INDUCTION
                                    ↓
  ii. THEORY: Steward's theory of Great Basin
                                    settlement patterns
                                       |
                                   DEDUCTION
                                    ↓
 iii. PREDICTIONS: The BASIN I computer simulation
                                         model
                                    |
                                  VERIFICATION
                                    ↓
  iv. FACTS: Reese River archeological field
                                    work (1969, 1970)

This initial cycle verified Steward's hypothesis and also produced a new set of untested facts, systematized into the Reese River Subsistence-Settlement System. As Kemeny has pointed out:

> These facts form a fourth stage for the old theory as well as the first stage of the new theory. Since we expect that Science consists of an endless chain of progress, we may expect this cyclical process to continue indefinitely [Kemeny 1959:86].

The second round of the specific cycle requires a different research design and additional fieldwork in order to test the new theory.

LOOP II

i. FACTS: Reese River archeological field
                                                work (1969, 1970)
                                                        |
                                                  INDUCTION
                                                        ↓
ii. THEORY: The Reese River Subsistence-Settlement
                                                    System
                                                        |
                                                  DEDUCTION
                                                        ↓
iii. PREDICTIONS: Specific site locations in the
                                                Reese River area
                                                        |
                                                 VERIFICATION
                                                        ↓
iv. FACTS: Additional, independent field work
                                                    (1971)

It is in this logical framework that we approached the 1971 field season at Reese River. Since economic necessities limited us to a single field session, we were forced to test only part of the total subsistence-settlement hypothesis. We elected to concentrate our resources on a quantitative test of the *Piñon Ecotone Settlement*. These sites are the prehistoric analog to the classic Shoshonean winter villages and seem to provide the mainstay in prehistoric settlement patterns.

OPERATIONAL AND POLYTHETIC DEFINITIONS

At the outset, we were faced with a situation common to many field archeologists—after years of working in an area, we gained an intuitive feeling of where unknown sites "ought to be." Given an archeologically unexplored area within the general region, we felt secure—perhaps arrogantly so—that our cumulative experience enabled us to predict where most of the sites would occur. In planning to test this intuition, we conferred with Julian Steward, experienced in both ethnographic and archeological research in the area:

In my own fieldwork I made it a point to go over the root areas and the camping areas with my informant. It was commonly possible to verify the location of campsites and winter settlements by the presence of artifacts, particularly pottery which I believe implies some stability.... May I venture a couple of suggestions about the prehistoric settlement patterns ... it would be most profitable to ascertain the specific factors determining winter settlement locations and then explore such places to see whether they were indeed utilized. I have always regretted that I did not have the time to do this to a much greater extent but what little I was able to do, I invariably found signs of occupation where the critical factors came together. These are reasonable access to pinenuts, a piñon-juniper belt which supplied firewood and preferably a stream for water or else higher altitudes where snow could be obtained [Julian Steward, personal communication 1971].

Steward's feeling coincided with our own, that specific factors determined the winter village locality and where the factors co-occurred in nature, one could expect to find an archeological site.

The task then became one of *operationalizing* such variables into quantities directly observable in the field. We reviewed our previous survey data and found several common denominators that were present at most piñon ecotone settlements. The sites usually were located on long ridges that extended far onto the valley floor, although several sites were situated on gentle saddles between low piñon-covered knolls. Although access to the sites was often steep, the habitation areas themselves were generally quite flat and smooth. The winter sites were located in the low foothills, not far from the modern piñon-juniper ecotone, and finally, the sites generally had relatively easy access to either springs or flowing streams. As is true of many hunter-gatherer stations, however, the foragers preferred to camp a discreet distance from the water source. Unlike many modern campers, the Shoshoneans and their ancestors realized that in order to see and hunt game animals, they had to avoid the watering areas as much as possible. Experience told us that the piñon ecotone settlements consistently clustered about these resource areas.

The first critical decision is to agree on what precisely constitutes a "site." In an ideal sense, we could have rigorously defined a site as a "scatter of prehistoric cultural debris that extends over a discernible extent (at least x square meters) and consists of a density of at least y cultural items per square meter." In practice, however, we lacked the quantitative survey data necessary for a serviceable definition of a site, so we elected to rely on our experience to tell us when we encountered a site in the field. We feel that this procedure, while haphazard and subject to later refinement, in no way hampered our work. We neglected no archeological sites in the area and, furthermore, we feel that any qualified visiting archeologist would be equally capable of locating these same sites in practice.

To some, our procedure may sound contradictory and perhaps even self-defeating. We have on the one hand called for precise definition of settlement patterns and then opted for a subjective assessment of our basic unit, the site. The first defense of this position was a pragmatic one, since we lacked suitable data to reach a workable definition prior to the 1971 season of field work. Yet there is another, more powerful justification for this position. Our acknowledged intent is to operationalize the definition of variables that condition Great Basin settlement patterns, that is, we wish to connect our intuitions to some measurable reality, as we felt it necessary to ensure that other investigators could test our hypothesis independently, and that our measurements were replicable. In dealing with operationism, one must continually balance empirical rigor against pragmatic necessity, for to demand precision in all definitions will lead one into the trap of an infinite regress, in which one's previous definition must be redefined continually. In practice, science simply accepts certain preliminary definitions as basic; mathematics, for example, considers certain premises that are accepted perforce—the "line," a "point," "the point lies on the line" and so forth—and these units become the foundation for a rigorous superstructure. We suggest a similar procedure for archeological entities; although we could define "site," we would still leave "cultural debris" and "cultural items" undefined. These terms could also be rigorously demarcated, but more undefined terms would arise until one is finally forced to accept some concept as given. Rather than chase the infinite regress, we have elected to simply accept "site" as our given and proceed from there (for further discussion of operationism in archeology, see Thomas 1970). Perhaps David Hull has summarized our position most succinctly in his parable about early date farmers:

> To increase their yield they began to weed out the "sterile" trees. For a while they were successful until the last sterile male tree was cut down. Then all the other trees stopped producing. Theoretical terms are like the male tree. They are not completely operational, but they are necessary for the progress of science. Operationism is fruitful only when it is not total [Hull 1968:448].

With this hurdle of site definition suitably considered, we are free to operationally define the seven critical variables for site location:

f_1 The locus should be on a *ridge* or a *saddle*.

f_2 The ground should be *relatively flat*.
"relatively flat" $\leqslant 5\%$ slope

f_3 The locus should be in the *low foothills*.
"low foothills" $\leqslant$ 250 meters above the valley floor.

f_4 The locus should be within the modern piñon-juniper lifezone.

f_5 The locus should be *near* the extant piñon-juniper ecotone.
"near" $\leqslant$ 1000 meters

f_6 The locus should be *near* a semipermanent water source.
"near" $\leqslant$ 1000 meters

f_7 The locus should be *some minimal distance* from this source.
"some minimal distance" $\leqslant$ 100 meters

These figures are estimated from previous surveys and in a couple of cases, from our past field experience, without benefit of previous measurements. We have implied a few undefined terms such as *length, height, ridge, saddle,* and *ecotone*; we propose that each of these terms be accepted as given in the same sense as *site*.

To this point we have a set of partitive *f*-variables, operationally defined yet unrelated holistically. One could combine the seven variables into an inclusive definition of all potential piñon ecotone areas by simply requiring that all seven variables measure positively for all sites—yet this situation would suffer from all of the woes inherent in monothetic definition. We prefer to consider archeological sites as *operationally polythetic*, assuming no *sine qua non* variables. Accordingly, we define a *potential habitation locus*.

Group *K* (the set of all potential piñon ecotone habitation loci in the upper Reese River Valley) is defined in terms of a set *G* of properties $f_1, f_2 \ldots f_7$ such that:

1. Each locus possesses a large ($n \geqslant 5$) number of the properties in *G*.
2. Each *f*-variable in *G* is possessed by large numbers of these loci.

Additionally, for the potential loci to be considered *fully polythetic*:

3. No *f* in *G* is possessed by every locus in the aggregation.

We have chosen the *five out of seven* as an arbitrary starting point, subject to verification and refinement by later field work.

In effect, this definition established two discrete populations. We have the population of all piñon-gathering sites in the Reese River Valley, which are defined by our intuitive notion of "site." The polythetic definition sets out a second population, the population of all potential habitation loci in the same area, defined by a polythetic combination of strictly topographic variables. The field work is designed to establish whether the population defined by cultural criteria is in fact isomorphic with the population defined by natural variables. That is, we wished to find whether the potential loci are acceptable predictors of archeological sites, and vice versa.

SURVEY RESULTS

To test the hypothesis of piñon ecotone locations, a 12-mile strip on the western slope of the Toiyabe Mountains was selected for intensive site survey (see Figure 1); this same area has been included in the stratified random sampling of previous years (see Thomas 1969). Since hypothesis testing (verification) always necessitates data *independent* from those involved in the hypothesis formation (induction), the 13 randomly selected 500 square meter tracks were excluded from the 1971 survey. Thus no sites involved in forming the theory of Reese River settlement patterns were included in the sample selected to test this theory.*

* Elsewhere in this volume, Professor Spaulding has disputed our stricture regarding independence of data used in hypothesis testing. This section of our paper is specifically addressed toward *statistical* hypothesis testing. It seems that Spaulding confuses LeBlanc's discussion of the logical structure of scientific explanation (chapter 13) with the specifics of statistical inference. Statistical inference is but a very specialized aspect of scientific explanation, and nowhere can we find a discussion of statistical hypothesis testing in LeBlanc's paper. We were making the simple point that when an investigator develops a *statistical hypothesis* on the basis of relationships observed in a set of data, he would be foolish to turn around and validate the hypothesis by "testing for statistical independence" on the same relationships in the same data. Let us hasten to add that there is nothing intrinsically wrong with formulating statistical hypotheses after examining the data, so long as these hypotheses are *tested on other* data. But when statistical hypotheses are "tested" on the same data that spawned them, a spurious impression of validity results, and the computed level of significance bears almost no relationship to the true value. We do not argue against the use of a *posteriori* statistical hypotheses, because rigorous a *priori* hypotheses are often hard to come by in archeology. But we do object to the improper use of statistical inference in archeology which results in unwarranted confidence in our (untested) hypotheses.

Spaulding also charges that our hypothesis "would have been forever unverifiable if it had happened that it was formulated after all of the Reese River sites had been inspected, a pretty pickle indeed." Apparently Spaulding uses an unusual definition of hypothesis. Spaulding suggests that had we first inspected *all* of the Reese River sites and *then* stated our "hypothesis", we would find ourselves in a logical pickle, since no independent data would be left for testing; our hypothesis would be "forever unverifiable." We see no pickle at all. Had we found *all* of the Reese River sites and then proceeded to frame a statement of our results, we would not be in-

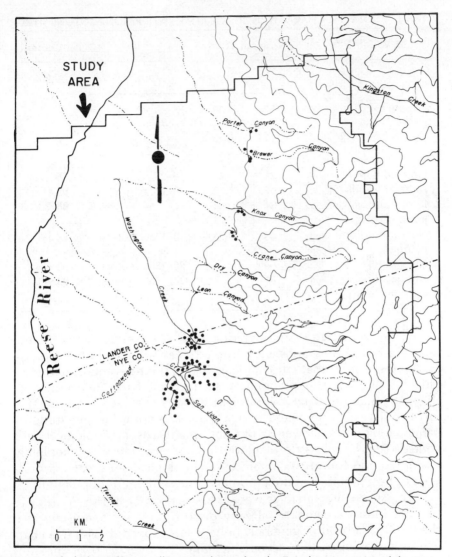

Fig. 1. Black dots indicate village sites located in the Toiyabe Mountains of the Reese River Valley, about 30 miles south of Austin, Nevada (see Thomas 1972 for details).

volved with hypothesis testing at all—we would be stating a *fact*. Hypotheses generalize from sample statistics to unknown population parameters, and hypotheses must be tested. Parameters, on the other hand, are invariant phenomena (facts) which describe the characteristics of the existing population. Facts are not tested, as Spaulding seems to imply.

TABLE 1. NOMINAL CHARACTERISTICS OF REESE RIVER PIÑON ECOTONE SITES

Variable	Nominal Totals			Agreement
	Ridge	Saddle	Other	96.9%
f_1 Topography	52	11	2	
	Yes (+)	No (−)	Range	
f_2 Ground flat?	24	41	0–20%	36.9%
f_3 In low foothills?	62	3	0-322 meters	95.4%
f_4 In modern piñon-juniper zone?	64	1	—	98.5%
f_5 Near piñon-juniper ectone?	60	5	0–1400 meters	92.3%
f_6 Near water?	59	6	20–1500 meters	90.8%
f_7 Site not directly on water source?	61	4	20–1500 meters	93.9%

As an initial step, stereographic pairs of United States Forest Service aerial photographs were studied in an attempt to find potential site loci—areas that satisfy at least five of the relevant topographic variables (the f_i). This preliminary scan enabled the field crews to efficiently plan the daily trek prior to survey of the area on foot. The survey itself was completed by teams of archeologists and students participating in the University of California (Davis) archeological field course. The 12-mile strip of piñon-juniper ecotone was completely examined and found to contain 65 archeological sites, each considered to be a member of the piñon ecotone settlement population.

The seven site variables were measured on each site in order to test the intuitive estimates already discussed. Table 1 indicates that the nominal attributes generally behaved as expected, with five characteristics falling within acceptable limits in over 90% of the sites measured. Variable f_6, the expectation that loci should be within 1000 meters of a semipermanent water source, agree with the expectation only about 77% of the time. Since no sites were over 1500 meters from water, this variable was perhaps too restrictive and a better estimate would probably be 1200 meters. The most inaccurate variable of all was f_2, the expectation that sites should be on ground with a slope no steeper than 5%. The 65 sample sites ranged from absolutely flat (0% slope) to a steep 20% slope; only about 35% of the sample sites proved as flat as expected. In previous fieldwork at Reese River, we never actually measured slope, so in considering the polythetic definition of site patterns, we had to guess at the operational figure of 5%, an estimate that was obviously too conservative. For future field work, the more suitable figure of 10% could be adopted.

Table 2 presents the tabulated findings of the metric expressions of these variables. The sample of 65 sites were analyzed to provide an estimate of the population parameter of all Reese River piñon sites—the 95% confidence limits. The figures for percentage of slope confirm that the f_2 variable limit should be changed to $\leqslant 10\%$.

Yet the operational definition and testing of site parameters was only the first part of this field experiment, for we were also concerned with the *holistic* definition of site locations. This aspect of the fieldwork considered two hypotheses:

1. Null Hypothesis (H_0): Sites occur on potential loci with only random frequency.
2. Alternative Hypothesis (H_1): Sites occur on potential loci with a greater than random frequency in this case, defined as greater than the .05 level of statistical significance.

To test these competing propositions, field crews not only had to locate all archeological sites within the test region, but additionally, all potential loci of habitation had to be found and recorded. That is, in the 12-mile survey area, every time at least five of the f-variables were satisfied, the locus was recorded as an area of potential habitation, whether or not cultural material was present.

TABLE 2. METRIC CHARACTERISTICS OF REESE RIVER PIÑON SITES

Variable	n	$\overline{X}$	S.D.	95% Confidence Interval
Percent slope	65	8.4%	4.2%	± 1.0%
Distance to ecotone	65	520.9 meters	357.1 meters	±86.8 meters
Distance to valley floor	65	94.7 meters	63.5 meters	±15.4 meters
Distance to water source	65	451.4 meters	354.7 meters	±86.2 meters

The survey results of holistic site definition are summarized in the following contingency table:

Archeological Sites

		Present (+)	Absent (−)
Potential Loci	(+)	63	11
	(−)	2	∞

TABLE 3.

Of the 65 sites located, all but 2 were located on areas considered potential loci, areas that satisfied at least five of the seven critical environmental variables. The survey located only 11 potential loci that lacked archeological sites.

Obviously the polythetic definition is a highly successful predictor of site locations in this area; 97% of the sites are on potential loci. Additionally, 85% of the potential loci contained sites, accuracy that we feel is exceptional for most treatments of archeological survey material.

Yet simple percentages provide no measure of statistical probability of success, no statement of how often such results can be expected to occur through simple chance. Significance of contingency table results is usually assessed by the chi-square test of independence (Siegel 1956:104). In this case, however, we cannot use the chi-square since the d box in Table 3 is undefined. Most association or correlation indices, such as Pearson's r, the phi coefficient, and Yule's Q consider common absence, the case in which both variables are negative or absent. In our experiment, we failed to derive a workable method of measuring the number of times sites did not appear where they should have; we lack significant information content in the d cell. To consider this factor, one would have to define a *minimal locus* as an arbitrary areal limit. Defining the spatial limit of sites is not difficult; one merely determines the extent of cultural debris. But the case of common absence requires the definition of an entirely synthetic unit, such as a 10- or 100- or 1000-meter grid. Consider the case of a steep hillside, an area that is predicted to not contain debris from the piñon ecotone sites (although it could perhaps contain lithic debris from task-specific activities such as hunting, root gathering, etc). If the habitation debris is absent from the hillside, how many times should we count this success? If the hillside itself is a natural unit, the case receives one count. But one could just as easily consider the hillside as a series of 25 discrete microtopographic features, each of them lacking cultural material. It should be clear that the d box could easily be inflated to infinity, invalidating any contingency statistic.

In order to properly assess the statistical probability of our results, we analyzed the data by the binomial theorem. Let us define the probability of finding a site at any given locus as p and the probability of not finding a site as q; p and q must sum to 1 since they are both mutually exclusive and exhaustive. The expected value of finding a site at any given locus is equal to

$$p = \frac{a_1}{a_2}$$

where a_1 = the total area occupied by archeological sites and a_2 = the total area surveyed. Unfortunately time did not permit the accurate measurement of a_1, so it is necessary to estimate the quantity. We feel that the value of $p = .01$ is a conservative and realistic estimate. The null hypothesis can now be refined to a point estimate.

$$H_0 : p = .01$$
$$H_1 : p .> .01$$

The alternative hypothesis—that archeological sites should occur on areas of potential habitation with a greater than average frequency—is directional and hence one-tailed. The significance of our results can be computed by the z test of a binomial proportion (see Snedecor and Cochran 1967:211–213).

$$z = \frac{(|\hat{p} - p| - 1/2 \, n)}{\sqrt{pq / n}}$$

where p and q are the expected probabilities and $\hat{p}$ is the observed value of a success (site corresponding to locus). The resulting z is 77.64, an astronomically high value, significant at much greater than the .001 level. These results permit us to reject the null hypothesis of no association and conclude that the polythetic definition of potential loci is a significant predictor of piñon village location. A similar case for the probability of a site at any given locus shows $z = 52.85$, again a highly significant outcome.

In addition to verifying the predictions of site location, data collected in the 1971 survey constitute further, and perhaps more refined, support for Steward's theory of Great Basin settlement and subsistence patterns and the *BASIN I* computer simulation of this same system (Thomas 1972). This is based on three assumptions. First, as a basic premise we hold that site locations are affected in no small way by such considerations as the season of occupation, size of the occupying population, and the types of activities carried out at those locations. Individually, each of these and other variables probably exerts some demands in the logistics of site location. Second, no one of these variables by itself is sufficient to determine site location. This follows from earlier statements concerning the value of polythetic set criteria, and is evidenced by the fact that "winter-site" definition in the Reese River Valley is fully polythetic (see below). Third, in spite of the fact that single locational criterion would not significantly restrict the spacial distributions of sites (e.g., the piñon-juniper lifezone comprises a vast portion of the Reese River Valley), combinations of two or more mildly restrictive criteria quickly reduce the number of possible locations that will fit the specified criteria. *If*, as we believe, site locations are sensitive to seasonality and resource procurement systems—among other things—and *if* combinations of several locational criteria (in this case five out of seven, delimit areas that are relatively small in comparison to the area denoted by any single criterion, *then* it follows that sites of a given type (here, type is defined on the basis of comparable social groups, season of occupation, and range of activities) should reveal a consistent polythetic set of locational criteria. On the other hand, shifts in subsistence, social units, or seasonality should be accompanied by concomitant—but not necessarily simple or direct changes in the polythetic set of locational criteria. The sites located in the Reese River Valley in 1971 did indeed display a consistent set of polythetic locational criteria even though they represented over 4000 years of occupation. This then can be taken as confirmation that these sites were all of a single type, described by Steward (1938) as "winter camps" and that the subsistence and settlement system described by Steward (1938) and modeled by Thomas (1972) can successfully account for the character and distribution of archeological materials deposited during this portion of the year.

SUMMARY

This experiment was designed to satisfy two purposes. The first was to provide an objective and independent test of part of the hypothesis of Reese River Subsistence-Settlement Systems that, it will be remembered, was the direct outcome of a previous test of Steward's theory. We wish to underscore the *cyclical* nature of such hypothesis testing, since every test produces a host of new hypotheses, which in turn must be verified. We feel that the results of the 1971 field season provided more than acceptable confirmation of the theory regarding the location of piñon ecotone settlements, and constitute additional support for Steward's discussion of settlement and subsistence in the Great Basin. It remains to test the rest of the propositions of the Reese River Subsistence-Settlement Systems, and finally, these results and new data must be synthesized into a new, more comprehensive hypothesis, subject again to verification. In theory at least, the inductive-deductive interplay should continue indefinitely.

Our second objective lay on a more generalized level, since the polythetic set has been shown to actually perform a valuable service in primary archeological contexts. In fact, without considering the sites in such polythetic fashion, we should have been unable to synthesize the partitive *f*-variables into a single holistic index of potential site location. As we have already pointed out site definition is *fully* polythetic, since no *f*-variable was common to any of the 65 sites; we could not have chosen any monothetic criteria for none exists. Although Clarke (1968) has discussed the *logic* of polythetic sets and archeological entities, we feel that for the Reese River Valley at least, we have demonstrated the significant *utility* of the concept. Furthermore, the concept and application of polythetic procedures probably offers the archeologist his greatest hope in objectifying that elusive yet viable notion of *feel*.

In presenting the polythetic predictors of winter village sites, we harbor no illusions about having supplied a statement of absolute causality; we do not claim, for example, that the coincidence of at least five out of seven critical topographic variables *caused* archeological sites to be constructed on that spot. Absolute causality is a difficult matter indeed. A detailed discussion would be superficial at best, if not somewhat overbold at this point. Let us admit for clarity that we raise no cavil in applying the terms cause and effect to this or any similar archeological analysis so long as it is clearly understood in the Humean sense to imply no more and no less than *A* is always followed in a statistical sense by *B*. In the case at hand, *A*, the presence of a potential locus of habitation is a 97% efficient predictor—the cause if you wish—of *B*, the presence of an archeological site. To push causality further is to fall into the anthropomorphic trap of attempting to model behavioral laws in our own human image.

We also wish to disclaim any flirtation with passing off our settlement pattern predictors as anything like overt "ethnoecology"; in fact, we feel rather strongly that this research has very little to do with the prehistoric mind—no concious mental templates or percepta are implied. The cognitive correlates of prehistoric settlement behavior remain a mystery. These data can perhaps be compared most closely to the results of the explicit etic ethnographic school, described by Pelto (1971). We can envision the case in which inhabitants of these ecotone sites—were they still alive—claim that such villages were moved due to purely ceremonial or religious circumstances, for example, death of a relative, omens of misfortune, or shamanistic visions. Yet as archeologists, we can be little concerned with emic causes, since these mentalistic configurations perished with the informants; students of archeology are free to deal exclusively with existential on-the-ground behavior of this and other past ecosystems. We feel that through a solid ecological approach to settlement pattern studies, the archeologist can produce etic data compatible with that obtained among living human societies.

ACKNOWLEDGMENTS

For most archeological field research programs, certain basic requirements will never change regardless of the trend toward sophisticated problem solving and methods of analysis. The notion of field work will continue to conjure up a certain feeling of romance and excitement no matter how experienced the field worker. However, upon completion of each archeological field season one thing always rings true: the work was hard and expensive. It is fitting at this point to extend our thanks to the various individuals, institutions, and students who provided the guidance, support, and labor necessary for a successful 1971 field season.

The 1971 field season was carried out under the auspices of the Department of Anthropology, University of California, Davis, California. We wish to acknowledge M. A. Baumhoff, D. L. True, and W.

G. Davis of that department for their encouragement, interest, and cooperation concerning the Reese River Ecological Project in general and the 1971 University of California (Davis) Summer Field Course in particular.

We wish to acknowledge Julian H. Steward for his rigorous field work, which served as the framework for a series of hypotheses regarding winter village placement in the Reese River Valley area, and for his endorsement of the project.

For the countless blisters and sore feet encountered in the field, we acknowledge the students of the 1971 University of California (Davis) Summer Field Class.

We wish to thank the following people for their comments and suggestions in the final preparation of this manuscript: M. A. Baumhoff, James O'Connell, Jerry Moles, Rick Casteel, and Brian Hatoff.

The 1971 phase of the Reese River Ecological Project was supported by the National Science Foundation Traineeship and the Chancellor's Patent Fund (University of California, Davis), which we gratefully acknowledge.

Finally, to Liz Williams and Trudy Thomas go our deepest thanks and appreciation. Trudy served full time in the field from the very beginning of the Reese River Ecological Project in 1969. Liz, although serving only for brief periods during the three years, assumed the unenviable task of remaining at home and working. Their enthusiasm for the project and willingness to "carry their share of the load," made the project performance an easier task.

This chapter is Contribution Number 11 of the Reese River Ecological Project.

15. ADEQUACY CRITERIA AND PREDICTION IN ARCHEOLOGICAL MODELS *

EZRA ZUBROW

Department of Anthropology
Stanford University
Stanford, California

This chapter examines the general question of adequacy and prediction in archeological models. It shows that prediction is not always sufficiently powerful to allow one to make a choice between alternative models. Furthermore, it suggests that at least six criteria should be used in conjunction to make such choices. In order to organize the data from a complex subject into a coherent chapter, I discuss briefly (a) the historical background to archeological formalization, (b) the relationships of theory, models, and data, (c) types and archeological examples of models, (d) the potential confusion between generated data and real data, (e) nonpredictive and predictive adequacy, (f) the archeological testing of a theory, and (g) evaluation and the inadequacy of prediction.

THE HISTORICAL BACKGROUND TO ARCHEOLOGICAL FORMALIZATION

Archeology is a discipline in the process of developing theory. This is not a new process. The multiple chronologies, reconstructions, and

* Paper prepared for the American Anthropological Association Meetings, November 1971, New York City.

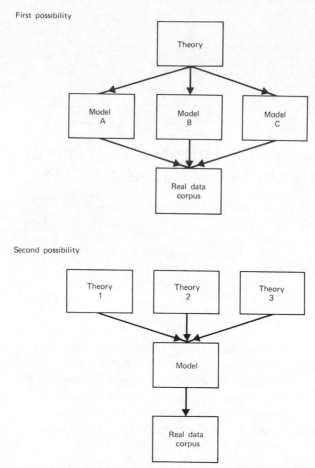

Fig. 1.   The possible relationships between theory, models, and data.

interpretations of time-space systematics have been an informal test
of theories in the widest sense of the term "theory." Taylor (1948)
and later Binford (1968a) have pointed out the shortcomings of
informal theory construction and testing as well as particular examples of logical inconsistency. During the last decade, this criticism has
elicited a series of studies that emphasize more explicit theoretical
formulations and more explicit testing procedures (Binford, 1968a;
Fritz and Plog, 1970). This has been complemented by a change in
focus from time-space systematics to questions of cultural process
(Binford 1968a; Flannery 1968b; and Zubrow 1971a).

THE RELATIONSHIPS OF THEORY, MODELS, AND DATA

Science aims not only to describe events, but to explain events. Explanations are achieved by testing theories and, thus, several methods for testing theory have been developed. First, hypotheses may be deduced from the theory and tested on data. Second, hypotheses may be induced from the data, tested on independent data, and then examined for their relationships to existing theory. Third, the theory may be modeled and the results generated from the

Third possibility

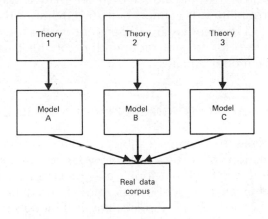

Fourth possibility

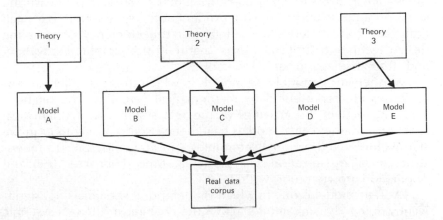

model compared to the real data. These three possibilities should not be considered exhaustive nor mutually exclusive.

When modeling is used, a serious methodological problem arises. How does one choose between alternative models that partially predict the real data? Before discussing this question, it is necessary to examine the four possible relationships of theory, models, and data. The first relationship is one theory that has multiple alternative models to explain a set of data. The second is having multiple theories that may be represented by a single model. The third relationship is multiple theories that purport to explain the same process, each theory being separately modeled. The fourth is multiple theories, at least one of which may be modeled in alternative ways. Figure 1 shows these possibilities. It is important to remember that in all the above possibilities the models are dependent on the theory, which is epistemologically prior to and independent of the particular phenomena that the model explains.

TYPES AND ARCHEOLOGICAL EXAMPLES OF MODELS

Models themselves are a complex subject. I define a model as an artificial representation of reality. Many types of models may be included under this definition. Models may be classified into physical models or mathematical models, static models or dynamic models, and deterministic or stochastic models. Physical models represent the real system's components by physical measures. Thus, physical attributes such as stress on an airplane wing may be studied by measuring stress on a model airplane wing. An archeological example is a small artificially constructed site used to test the efficiency of sampling design technique, artificial versus "natural" stratigraphic excavation, and alternative classification techniques.

Mathematical models are models in which the real system and its attributes are represented by mathematical variables. The relationships that reflect the activities of the real system are mathematical functions. Mathematical models have been used not only to examine star evolution and national economies, but archeologically to reconstruct social organization at a particular time (Longacre 1968) and population growth (Zubrow 1971a).

A static model is one in which the temporal variable is not significant, while a dynamic model allows the changes in the real systemic attributes to be a function of time. Sophisticated static models have brought major innovations to the sciences, such as the Watson-Crick-Wilkins famous double helix that modeled the chemical construction of DNA and revolutionized the field of genetics. Museums, perhaps the largest archeological users of static models, bring dioramas and exhibits together to represent cultures to the public. Dynamic models, whether simple electric trains or complex models of modern urban dynamics (Forrester 1969) allow the examination of processual change. Traditionally, archeologists have implicitly used a neo-evolutionary model to explain the developmental sequence of increasing cultural innovation and complexity. More recently, formalized dynamic models have begun to be used by archeologists, as represented by Deetz's Arikara study (1965), which examines the changes in social organization through time.

Models are deterministic if the outcome of any activity can be described and the precise history of the system may be traced. In deterministic models, no variables are random, or based on probability—classic examples are Zipf's gravity model of migration, Bohr's model of an atom, and the numerous models derived from Newtonian mechanics. Stochastic models have one or more random or probability-based variables. The variables may enter the model randomly or take on values determined by a random or probability-based process. In short, stochastic models have at least one functional relationship dependent on probability distributions.

An archeological example of a deterministic model is Deetz's "Doppler Model," which shows that the seriation frequency trends will be altered if there has been selection of successive sites running towards, away from, or obliquely to, the original direction of the diffusion of the element being seriated (Deetz and Dethlefsen 1965). Examples of stochastic models such as modern models of the atom derived from quantum mechanics are less common than the other types. Stochastic archeological models are just beginning to be developed. Later in this chapter an archeological example of a stochastic model will be discussed.

THE POTENTIAL CONFUSION BETWEEN GENERATED DATA AND REAL DATA

One area of model testing that often causes unnecessary confusion is the distinction between generated data and real data. This confusion is usually found when there are multiple models hierarchically

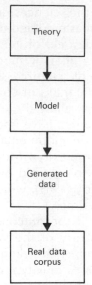

Fig. 2.   The relationship between generated data and the real data corpus.

arranged or where the models are highly abstract and are tested against abstract data. Some, but not all, types of models will generate data. Two cases are generative grammars and simulation models. For example, complex models of language will generate the structures for strings of sounds that are potentially meaningful sentences. In the same way, simulation models of population growth will generate data about age-cohorts or community size. The generated data should be kept distinct from the real data (see Figure 2). Thus, in the above examples, no one would confuse the potential sentence structures generated by the model with the real sentences or the generated age-cohorts with the real age-cohorts.

NONPREDICTIVE AND PREDICTIVE ADEQUACY

Adequacy and prediction have been the subject of much anthropological discussion. Ethnoscientists and generative grammarians use nonpredictive adequacy criteria to evaluate their theories and models while archeologists and physical anthropologists have used prediction.

What is adequacy? Adequacy refers to whether or not an explanation is sufficient. Ethnoscientists claim that a set of rules that generate the categories of a domain or a componential analysis, which is a description of a domain, are adequate when they allow the analyst to use the categories in a manner acceptable to a native. Generative grammarians use a similar but slightly different criterion to determine explanatory sufficiency. If a theory or a model generates data that corresponds to a native's intuition about grammaticalness it is considered adequate. Chomsky justifies using the native's intuition as a test of a particular grammar that is an explanatory model derived from a linguistic theory:

It is sometimes claimed that operational tests for degree of grammaticalness and the like can guarantee both objectivity and significance for the theory of grammar, but this is a misconception. If an operational measure for grammaticalness were devised, we would have to test it by determining how well it accords with the linguistic intuition of native speakers. . . . There is no sense in which the operational test is "prior" to the theory, or conversely. Optimally, we would like to have both, and we would like them to converge, but they must for significance converge on the linguistic intuition of the native speaker [Chomsky 1962].

Generalizing then, both ethnoscientists and generative grammarians have rejected prediction in favor of using a criterion of adequacy that compares the generated data not with the corpus of behavioral data, but with an independent evaluation procedure. Figure 3 illustrates the above types of adequacy criteria.

Most other social scientists agree that prediction is a necessary component of explanation. However, prediction is not an equivalent of explanation. Modifying Rescher (1970), an explanation that contains predictions should as a minimum not only rule out most alternative theories, it should establish its theory as more credible than its negation. A prediction, on the other hand, need only show that the theory is more credible than any alternative theory.

To the layman, prediction is a temporally based concept. It means to foretell on the basis of observation, experience, or scientific reason. Usually, prediction is the application of a theory or model to future events, arguing that if principles hold and conditions are fulfilled, the expected event will follow. However, prediction does not have to be future oriented. Instead, it is temporally relative to the analysis and not the data. Thus, few archeologists object to using a model based on modern data, predicting into the past, and then

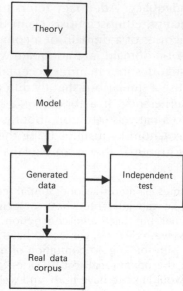

Fig. 3.   Predictive and a type of non-predictive adequacy.

examining the archeological data to validate the prediction. This is sometimes called ethnographic analogy. The substantive limitations of this type of prediction have been examined by Longacre and Ayres (1968) in their study of an Apache wickiup.

Prediction, then, is the expectations that are derived from a theory, hypothesis, or model. When there are models that generate data, the expectations are that the generated data will correspond with the real data corpus. In other words, in this case the generated data are the predictions for, initially, they are more credible than other sets of expectations. Figure 4 illustrates this type of predictive adequacy.

THE ARCHEOLOGICAL TESTING OF A THEORY

I have suggested a theory of population growth within a region with differentiated resources (Zubrow 1969, 1971a, 1971b). This theory analyzes carrying capacity as a dynamic equilibrium system and is a specific case of general equilibrium and systems theory. Essentially, the theory begins by suggesting that population growth in a particular resource zone is limited by the carrying capacity of that zone.

When an initial population reaches the limits defined by the carrying capacity, a homeostatic equilibrium exists. It is homeostatic in that there is a tendency toward the maintenance of a state of balance between opposite forces or processes that result in a diminishing net change or a stable constant. It is dynamic in that the point at which the state of balance exists may change over time and space.

The theory was expanded and examined both across time and space. Initially, it was tested on native (Pueblo) and nonnative population data within New Mexico between A.D. 1580–1960. It was shown that prior to reaching the equilibrium point, native and nonnative population growth was not limited by factors influencing the local resources. Later, the equilibrium point was reached and even surpassed, so that a disequilibrium resulted with population being greater than local resources. Under these conditions of increasing population surplus, it was shown that factors limiting the resource curves were also increasingly limiting native population. What allowed the disequilibrium to be maintained was that a large part of the nonnative population was being supported by external resources being imported into the region (i.e., from outside of the universe being analyzed). This was concluded to be a positive but somewhat limited test of the theory.

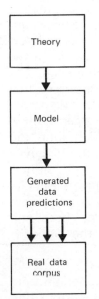

Fig. 4.   Prediction.

In order to test the theory a second time, a new set of data was obtained in a different geographic area and in a different series of temporal periods. The real data corpus consisted of approximately 320 sites in the Hay Hollow Valley in Arizona. All of these sites have been surveyed and some of them have been excavated. They span a time period of approximately 4500 years (3000 B.C. to A.D. 1425). From the theory in its expanded form four hypotheses were derived:

1. The development of population in marginal resource zones is a function of optimal zone exploitation.
2. Population aggregation is a function of population excess disequilibrium.
3. Spatial aggregation is a function of population excess disequilibrium.
4. Residential area is a function of population excess disequilibrium.

Predictions were made on the basis of these hypotheses. All four were tested positively by comparing these predictions to the real data corpus.

In order to operationalize the theory, a simulation model was developed. The model is actually a simulation system written in FORTRAN EXTENDED that replicates the processes of the theory in a computer. The system consists of four components: a population growth function, a population resource check, a settlement locator, and a longevity function. The population growth function determines, at different birth, death, and migration rates, how much the population of a settlement grows through a given time span. The population resource check defines the amount of resources that exist, and how much of the usable resources can be used at a particular level of technology, and checks the population size against these limiting values. The settlement locator determines which zone and where in each zone new settlements will exist. Finally, the longevity function determines how long each settlement will exist for nonresource reasons discussed above. Thus, a population in a particular settlement may become extinct for two reasons: (1) for resource reasons that will be calculated in the population resource check, and (2) for nonresource reasons that will be calculated in the longevity function.

At the most simplistic level the four components fit together in the following way. The population growth component operates until the population resource check component shows that the population is too large for a single settlement as defined by the settlement threshold. It then checks to see whether or not this population is too large for the resource zone. If it is not, the settlement locator locates a new settlement in the same zone as the original settlement and populates it with the excess population. If the total population is too large for the zone, the population resource check component calculates the best zone for the excess population and the settlement locator locates the site within that zone. Finally, the longevity function is called into play. If it causes a population to become extinct at a particular time, it resets the population growth function, the population check, and the settlement locator so that the settlement no longer exists. When usable resources diminish, the four components act in reverse to minimize the loss.

Actually, the systemic simulation model is more complex for three reasons. First, when there are multiple settlements growing in multiple zones and being checked against multiple resource levels, the number of possible variations and optimizations increases extensively, if not geometrically. Second, the population growth component and the population resource check component are defined by multiple equations and are not just single relationships. Third, the settlement locator and the longevity function components are both testing three alternative methods of determining the settlement location and two alternative methods of determining settlement longevity.

EVALUATION AND THE INADEQUACY OF PREDICTION

Before evaluating the various models that I have developed, I shall briefly show how the various hypotheses, predictions, and models are integrated in one research design that tests a theory. Two sets of hypotheses were derived from the theory. One set was tested on the New Mexican ethnohistoric data; one set was tested on prehistoric data. A general simulation model was also derived from the model. Since the longevity component and the settlement locator have interchangeable alternatives, at the component level there are actually six possible ways to construct the model. One may use each of the three settlement locators with either longevity alternatives. However, at a lower level of abstraction there are an infinite number of birth, death, and migration rates in the population growth component.

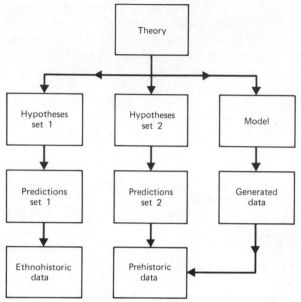

Fig. 5.   Research design for carrying capacity as a dynamic equilibrium system.

Each time you use a new combination, you get a new set of generated data.

In any case, each of the models at the component level was
tested with combinations of birth, death, and migration rates. The
resulting generated data were compared to the real prehistoric data.
In addition, the generated data were compared to a set of predictions
derived directly from the theory. This whole research design is illustrated concisely in Figure 5.

The method of evaluating the theory of the models is to show
the degree of confirmation between the generated data and the real
data.

The generated data from the models confirm the prediction
made from the theory. In order to see this confirmation compare
Figures 6a–6h, which represent the models generated data with
Figure 6i, which is the prediction from the theory. There is also a
degree of confirmation between the various sets of generated data
from the models and the real data (Figure 6j). It is clear that the
curves follow the same general shape of zonal population growth
and that they are in the same general order of zonal growth. How-

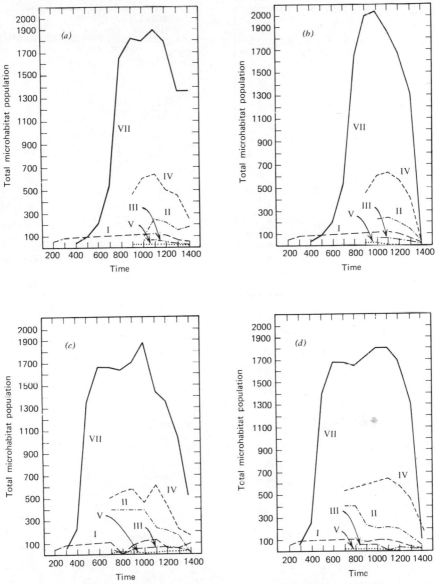

Fig. 6 a-h. The generated data (size of population per microhabitat per time period) from eight simulations in which the birth rates, death rates, migration velocity, and longevity alternatives have been varied. Each line on the graph represents a different microhabitat.

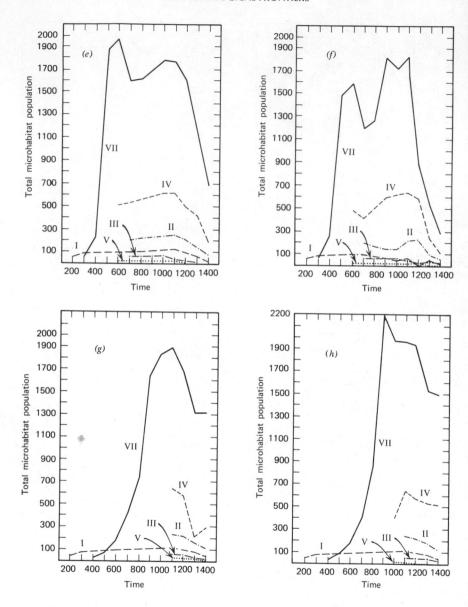

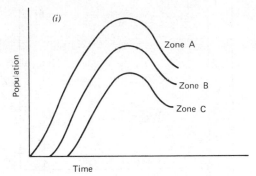

Fig. 6i.   The theoretical predictions derived directly from the model.

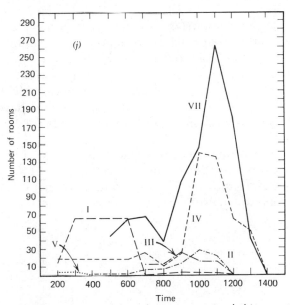

Fig. 6j.   The real data corpus, in number of rooms per microhabitat per time period.

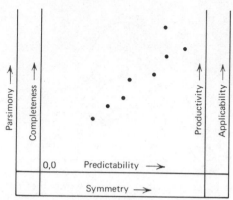

Fig. 7. Models uniquely ranked by the six criteria.

ever, what is far more important for this discussion is that within this general confirmation there is a high degree of variability. Particular models predict better than others for particular time periods and particular resource zones. Under these types of conditions is it actually possible to evaluate the alternative models solely on the basis of prediction? The answer is no because one would have to refine the criteria to specify evaluation with regard to a particular zone or a particular time.

Does this mean that one must reject predictive adequacy as do the ethnoscientists and generative grammarians? Once again, the answer is no. Before moving to independent criteria, it is possible to use other formal explanatory criteria to show sufficiency.

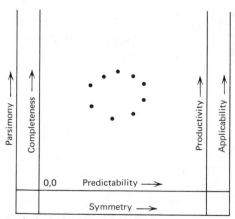

Fig. 8. Models nonsimilarly ranked by the six criteria.

These criteria include parsimony, completeness, symmetry, productivity, applicability, as well as prediction. Ideally, the six criteria could be used in conjunction with each other. Examining one extreme, a group of alternative models might be uniquely ranked by the six criteria so that one alternative model is clearly the best (see Figure 7). Examining the other extreme, the alternative models might not be ranked similarly on each criteria (see Figure 8). Thus the model that is most parsimonious might be least predictive. In these circumstances, the model with the best overall ranking criteria should be given different weights and applied hierarchically. Needless to say, there is a continuum between the extremes.

This chapter has examined the following:

1. The relationships between theory, models, generated data, and real data.
2. The types of models with archeological examples.
3. Nonpredictive and predictive adequacy.
4. The testing of a theory of carrying capacity as a dynamic equilibrium on ethnohistoric and archeological data.

It concludes that predictive adequacy criteria are not always sufficient to allow one to make a choice between alternative models.

FOUR

RESTRUCTURING THE ORGANIZATION OF ARCHEOLOGY

The contributors to this section and most other archeologists agree that there has been a rapid increase in the complexity of many aspects of archeology, and that the performance of archeologists has not fully adjusted to this transformation nor kept pace with theoretical and technical advances. The incorporation of specialists from other disciplines and the increasing specialization within archeological analysis require the abandonment of the traditional concept of a single researcher running all aspects of a project. At the same time new techniques of measurement, identification, and analysis have been introduced. Each of these techniques needs specialized personnel to utilize them and new types of institutions to support them. Concurrent with these developments are advances in archeological theory that require new varieties and quantities of data. The potential of these advances is unrealized within the present form of archeological organization. The three major aspects of archeological organization that need restructuring are covered by the chapters in this section. First, the organization of the archeological field expedition must be broadened to include specialists and sufficient personnel to gather adequate data for current theoretical requirements and complex models. Second, the institutions sponsoring research must reorganize in order to support the necessary specialists and draw in sufficient financial backing to fund the expanded scope of research. Third, the training of students, and ultimate educational goals must be reconsidered in terms of the future professional roles created by the above-mentioned organizational changes and made more responsive to the aspirations and abilities of the students themselves.

James A. Brown and Stuart Struever are concerned with the widening gap between ideas and performance in archeology. They see cultural ecology as the most useful interpretive framework, and emphasize man-culture-environment relationships in their research. This approach requires the collaboration of natural scientists to furnish biophysical data on the environment and on the subsistence resources utilized by the prehistoric society. They propose the formation of a new type of "archeological institute" to facilitate multidisciplinary research such as their own. To provide a broad financial basis for an operation of this sort Brown, Struever, and others have formed the Foundation for Illinois Archeology, which solicits funds from a number of sources, both public and private. Their purpose is to create at their site an entire research center including numerous laboratories. This enables the analysis to be an integral part of the field work. In this way it is possible to have preliminary results redirect future investigations. Also, with the specialists on hand necessary decisions can be made in a truly collaborative manner.

Together with these suggestions on necessary personnel, Brown and Struever outline some principles of their investigations. Initially a decision must be made as to whether the research is going to use a problem-optimizing strategy or a site-optimizing strategy. The research itself is structured in a stepwise analytical and observational procedure. This promotes an efficient data flow system and facilitates ongoing analysis of the expedition's progress.

Walter W. Taylor agrees with Brown and Struever that requirements of research have vastly proliferated and resources have failed to keep pace. There are two aspects to the increasing complexity. First, archeologists are attempting to "wring dry" their data in order to learn as much as possible from the available evidence. Second, the multidisciplinary team is increasingly accepted as the only suitable approach to ecologically oriented research. Taylor sees the necessity for two new types of organizations to facilitate research. Some form of archeological institute or clearinghouse should be created to act as a middle-man for the variety of specialists and natural scientists who could be consulted by archeologists for individual research projects. To attack problems of common interest, organizations such as the Southwest Anthropological Research Group should be formed. This is a group of expedition directors that address part of their research effort to a common question and collect data in a compatible format so that the members' results are comparable. These two organizational developments would economize on the resources currently available to archeologists. Taylor goes on to say that if archeology is to reach its potential, then more resources must be brought in and this would be facilitated by modernizing our image and improving communications with financial administrators.

George J. Gumerman's article also is concerned with the more effective use of available resources. He points out that at least in the United States, there is more money in salvage archeology than in the usual form of research. Unfortunately, most salvage work is done without problem orientation, and he suggests that it is little more than "stamp collecting." Gumerman asserts that this is not necessary and problem orientation can be incorporated into most salvage work. Many salvage projects have sufficient warning time so that the award of the contract can be based on which group develops the most promising program of research, instead of giving the contract to one or more groups in the hope that they will come up with something. Salvage operations that must be carried out with little or no warning cannot easily be put into a problem-oriented framework. Nevertheless, efforts can be made to make their results more generally applicable and of interest to a broader audience.

Frank Hole's article discusses the goals of archeology, the manner in which these goals are achieved, and their relevance to the kinds of talents and training necessary for future archeologists. As the methods and organization of archeological research change, so must the training that archeologists receive. Archeology is a complicated undertaking that requires diverse skills. To be a successful field excavator one must have a highly developed sensory system. In addition to well-developed sensory perception, the excavator must be able to integrate sensory data, and be capable of recognizing three-dimensional patterns as they are unearthed. Students should be trained and tested in physical perception. Not every student has the requisite skills and may not have the inclination to develop them. With the increasing complexity and specialization of archeological work it should no longer be expected that every student will eventually be able to run his own dig, but, rather, many students could be channeled into other necessary aspects of archeological research.

Richard B. Woodbury expands on this theme of restructuring student training. He asserts that the current explosion in methods is a challenge to the financial basis and organization of archeological research. Rarely are students trained for a specialty within archeology. Currently the Ph.D. seems to be the only fully acceptable degree for the professional archeologist. Woodbury suggests that there should be two educational routes for the students to pursue. One would be the already established Ph.D. in anthropology. The other would be a new degree, perhaps a masters degree or the equivalent, in a specialty within archeological research. This would prepare the technicians needed by expeditions and would offer an accredited outlet for those who chose not to be university professors. This dual opportunity would be more responsive to the needs of archeology in the future and would provide realistic opportunities for many of today's students.

16. THE ORGANIZATION OF ARCHEOLOGICAL RESEARCH: AN ILLINOIS EXAMPLE

JAMES A. BROWN AND STUART STRUEVER

Department of Anthropology
Northwestern University
Evanston, Illinois

If there is anything that can be said to characterize archeology today, it is the widening gap between its ability to state new and important problems and its capacity to actually perform the research to solve these problems. This discrepancy between ideas and performance is aggravated by the lack of response to the problem by the institutions that perform archeology—universities and museums. They are not prepared to assemble the funds, equipment, facilities, and expertise necessary to conduct long-term multidisciplinary archeology. In addition, the collective experience among archeologists in executing large-scale research strategies is small.

This lack of experience, moreover, has led to uncertainty and even some misunderstanding about large-scale research strategies in archeology, since those with the most experience have usually not taken the time to describe explicitly their methods of performing the strategies.

These developments are best understood in the context of new demands placed on archeological research.

A central theme of modern archeology is the study of prehistoric cultural ecology—the idea that the history of culture is best understood in terms of the complex interdependence of human biological, physical environmental, and cultural systems. The history of any one of these three systems is intimately tied to gradual or abrupt changes in the other two. Therefore, cultural process can be abstracted from the archeological record by understanding the stable or changing reciprocal relationships between culture, the human organism, and their environments.

This proposition has important implications, both for archeological programs in universities and for the entire structure of performing archeological research.

First, to understand cultural-biological-environmental relationships in prehistory requires a greater diversity of expertise than is embodied in any single academic discipline at present and most certainly in the future. We know of no more persuasive argument for a multidisciplinary program in archeology than the proposition that this discipline's capacity to contribute to human knowledge is closely tied to its ability to understand complex man-culture-environment relationships, an understanding that archeology alone cannot achieve.

The biophysical environment has been intensively studied for at least a century and a half. A number of disciplines in the biological and physical sciences, organized in a hierarchy of scale and specificity, are an outgrowth of this interest. Today, geomorphologists, sedimentologists, and pedologists study the history of land forms and soils, together with the processes by which they developed and changed. Hydrographers have a similar interest in water and its history. With this information, and a firm grasp of meteorological processes, paleoclimatologists attempt to reconstruct a history of climates. Botanists and palynologists, the former working with macroscale and the latter with microscale plant remains, are also concerned with the history of climates. Both are concerned with the adaptive interdependence of plant species and of plants and other aspects of the physical environment; out of this has grown the study of plant ecology with its focus on plant communities and the processes responsible for them.

Zoologists are concerned with another part of the biological aspect of environment: animals. Again, attention is directed to describing multispecies animal populations and to delineating the adaptive processes that account for change and stability in these populations.

Ecologists attempt to integrate this information into a complex web of interdependent plant and animal populations. Whatever integrative role ecologists play in understanding the biological aspect of environment, geographers play for the physical aspect.

All of these environmental systems—land forms, soil, water, climate, plants, and animals—became extinct with the prehistoric cultures and the human animals whose relationships to them we are attempting to understand. And therefore, "paleoenvironmental reconstruction" becomes an integral part of archeology whenever archeology is concerned with comprehending the relationship of culture and biological man to these environments.

To achieve an understanding of extinct environments requires the collaboration of the various specialists on land, plants, and animals as discussed above. Collectively, however, these paleoenvironmentalists must work with the archeologist, since it is only possible to devise an appropriate strategy for discovering culture-environment relationships through a mutual definition of the problem and a mutual identification of the relevant variables. It is for this reason that students of archeology must have a grounding in the natural sciences. Students concerned with the history of human adaptation, as reconstructable from the archeological record, must appreciate the potentialities and limitations of the paleoenvironmental record for aiding or restricting this study. This requires that they listen to and, moreover, work with the natural scientists involved.

Against this background, the development of a new form of institution—the archeological institute—takes on special relevance.

THE NEED FOR A NEW FORM OF ARCHEOLOGICAL INSTITUTION

Today archeology is undertaken in two kinds of institutions—universities and museums. The primary responsibility of the university is teaching, while the primary responsibility of the museum is public communication: both conduct archeological research as a secondary activity related to their primary objective. A university's resources are dispersed through a wide range of undergraduate and professional teaching programs. A museum commits its major resources to exhibit development and the curating of collections.

Thus, one of the major requirements of the New Archeology is the development of a new form of institution—the archeological institute. Unlike the university or the museum, the institute would be structured specifically to organize and conduct large-scale, long-term archeological research programs that would involve the integration of numerous specialists in the physical, biological, and social sciences. These specialists, with the aid of substantial technical and labor resources and facilities, would be capable of attacking the new questions of culture history and process that cannot be effectively approached through the traditional channel of one-man-scholar university-based or museum-based archeology.

The Foundation for Illinois Archeology (FIA) is the modest but real beginning of such an institution. Unlike universities and museums, it does not conduct archeology as a secondary activity; the sole purpose of FIA is the development of large-scale archeological programs such as the Illinois Valley Archeological Program.

The aim of the foundation is to explore the capacities of archeology as an intellectual discipline. To assess archeology's potential contribution to human knowledge, we must ask the following questions.

1. Is archeology a science, and can its practitioners work effectively within the strictures of the scientific method?
2. Can archeologists develop an understanding of prehistoric social, political, and economic behavior, or must they confine themselves to simpler statements about technology, diet, and subsistence practices?
3. Can archeologists study the interdependence of cultural, environmental, and human biological systems and define the processes that account for change and stability in these systems throughout the long prehistoric record?

THE NORTHWESTERN ARCHEOLOGICAL FIELD SCHOOL

The new questions archeologists are asking should have—but largely have not—changed the way archeological field schools are conducted.

Traditionally, archeological field schools give the undergraduate or graduate student the opportunity to learn digging techniques by excavating a prehistoric site. These field schools usually involve one university-based archeologist and a dozen students who live in tents or in an abandoned farmhouse near the site that they excavate together for six to eight weeks. Most of the effort is devoted to the actual work of excavating, with washing and cataloging artifacts in spare time a frequent addition. Archeological field schools are low-overhead operations—small, intimate, tutorial training in digging technique, in which a small number of students assist an archeologist in recovering artifacts from a site.

It is generally true that in order for the archeologist to study the changing interdependence of prehistoric cultural and environmental systems, he must work with a number of "environmental scientists" on whose research he depends for an understanding of the paleoenvironment. This understanding is essential to the interpretation of man-land relationships in prehistory; without it, many archeologists argue, it is not possible to interpret culture change and stability. Yet, today, there exist almost no training programs in which the potential relationships between archeology and the natural sciences are explored, or in which the student may learn the techniques of zoological, botanical, or geological analysis that are crucial to the reconstruction of extinct environments.

Though archeologists today readily acknowledge the importance of collaborative research with their colleagues in the natural sciences, programs that explore and develop these links, acquaint students with their significance and train them in the methods of data recovery and analysis in these disciplines are almost nonexistent.

A major goal of the Northwestern University Archeological Field School, then, is to broaden the concept of the "field school" to include (1) data processing and analysis as major aspects of archeological research and (2) training in the goals and methods of those biological, physical, and social sciences that play an important role in the interpretation of the prehistoric record.

By adding these dimensions to the program, the Northwestern Archeological Field School is able to provide clinical training for students seeking a career in these interface disciplines, and to provide the archeological student with a perspective on the potentialities and limitations of these disciplines for contributing to the solution of his problems.

These objectives are achieved by operating analytical laboratories concurrently with the excavations. In the summer of 1972 we operated 10 Kampsville (Illinois) laboratories, each one under the direction of a collaborating scientist and manned by students who will analyze materials recovered from excavations in the surrounding region. The laboratories are:

Zoology laboratory.   Frederick C. Hill, Department of Zoology, University of Louisville.

Botany laboratory.   Richard I. Ford, Ethnobotanical Laboratory and Museum of Anthropology, University of Michigan.

Malacology laboratory.   Manfred E. W. Jaehnig, Department of Anthropology, Central Washington State College.

Central Data Processing laboratory.   James A. Brown

Flotation laboratory.   R. Bruce McMillan, Department of Anthropology, Illinois State Museum.

Survey laboratory.   Stuart Struever, Department of Anthropology, Northwestern University.

Computer laboratory.   James A. Brown, Department of Anthropology, Northwestern Univertity.

Human Skeletal laboratory.   Lynn Goldstein, Foundation for Illinois Archeology.

Artifact laboratory.   Kenneth Farnsworth, Museum of Anthropology, University of Michigan.

Artifact laboratory. John Nicholas, Foundation for Illinois Archeology.

In addition to these Kampsville-based research and training operations, the foundation collaborates with several disciplines that, to date, we have not been able to integrate into our Kampsville operation.

The individuals listed below are actively working together in the Illinois Valley Archeological Program but do not yet have a Kampsville laboratory. They include:

Pollen analysis.   James Schoenwetter, Department of Anthropology, Arizona State University.

Geology.   Karl W. Butzer, Department of Geography, University of Chicago.

Special botanical studies.   Irwin Rovner, Department of Anthropology, University of Wisconsin at Madison.

Physical geography.   Ira Fogel, Department of Geography, Stanislaus
   State College, California

The Northwestern University Archeological Field School operates
between June 1 and August 31. Beginning in 1971, we extended the
duration of our Kampsville-based operation by conducting a limited
program in April, May, and September. Beginning in 1973, we hope
to operate a full-scale program during the fall months, thus leaving
the period between January and March as the only time when the
Kampsville facility is not in use.

ACTIVE COLLABORATION:
A CONTROL ON DECISION-MAKING IN THE FIELD

Among the most important results of the intensive collaboration
among (1) archeologists with different skills; (2) archeologists and
various natural scientists; and (3) archeologists and experienced student research assistants, all of which characterize the research projects of the Illinois Valley Archeological Program, is the reduction of
"idiosyncratic decision-making." In short, active collaboration
reduces the frequency of bad research strategy decisions that are
translated into action.

Traditionally, a single archeologist and his students constitute the
research group. In this context, decisions by the archeologist often
become the basis for excavation strategy. Archeologists prize this
high degree of autonomy, but it is sometimes exceedingly costly.

The Koster Project involves three archeologists and six collaborators from other disciplines, plus more than a dozen experienced
graduate students. Through their intense, daily interaction in Kampsville, where all or most of these people are in full-time residence
during the three-month field season, they comprise a decision-
making group. Together they argue out important research strategy
decisions as the excavation and analytical programs proceed. While a
single collaborator may have final responsibility for a decision in a
particular situation, this decision is often the outgrowth of an interactive process involving from two to eight people. Initial decision ideas
are laid out and scrutinized before they become incorporated into
field or laboratory strategies. Those of us who have participated in
this process have come to value it.

The isolation of the research group for 60 to 90 days in a rural
village of 450 people is the key to this interaction. By operating the

research program out of Kampsville we maximize the opportunity for —and probability of—this interaction. By living and working here we eliminate most external stimuli while increasing the interaction potential. Between forming the initial decision ideas and carrying them out on the site or in the laboratory there may be from one to a dozen discussions among the investigators who have a stake in the decision. The ramifications of a decision idea are explored in terms of our research goals; alternative, more economical approaches are reviewed. This process allows us to play out the results of a decision without suffering the cost or consequences that accompany decisions acted out on a site or in a laboratory.

All of this may sound obvious, but in fact the careful scrutiny to which major decisions at Koster are subjected before they become the basis for action is unusual in archeology. In archeology, as in the laboratory sciences, carrying out poor decisions may waste enormous resources. The chances of this occurring are substantially reduced when several contributors, each with somewhat different goals and research experience, consider a problem. This is one of the great strengths of long-term, multidisciplinary research as exemplified by the Koster Project.

THE ILLINOIS VALLEY ARCHEOLOGICAL PROGRAM AND THE DECISION TO DIG THE KOSTER SITE

Since its beginning in 1958, our long-term archeological program in the lower Illinois Valley has focused on the Woodland period. Particular attention has been given to the problem of the origins of cultivation and its relationship to the increased cultural complexity identified with the word "Hopewell" in the Middle Woodland period. The lower Illinois Valley region is particularly well suited to research on these problems. Struever (1968b) has described the applications of a systems model to research on these problems that is still continuing under Kenneth Farnsworth (n.d.) and others.

The work of Watson et al. (1969) in Salts Cave in northern Kentucky strongly suggests that the beginnings of cultivation in the Midwest are to be found in the preceding Archaic period. It therefore became logical to move our research emphasis back in time, specifically into the Late Archaic period.

The Koster site is an appropriate first step in the study of Late Archaic manifestations in the lower Illinois region.

First, we do not have an Archaic Chronology that is applicable to the lower Illinois Valley. Koster, with a minimum of 12 occupation levels, the earliest of which predates 5100 B.C., represents an economical first step in developing a chronological scheme for the Middle and Late Archaic periods in this region.

Second, since most of the Koster occupation layers appear to have been rapidly covered with a layer of slopewash soil, it is possible to treat each as a separate excavation and analysis problem. Indeed, the interbedding of sterile and cultural horizons at the site gives us an unusual opportunity to identify and treat as separate entities at least 12 sequential occupations representing an intermittent occupation of the site from at least 5100 B.C. to A.D. 1000.

PREREQUISITES TO THE KOSTER RESEARCH PROJECT

Treating each of these 12 occupations as a separate archeological problem is like excavating 12 single-component Archaic and Woodland habitation sites, except that these 12 components are layered one over another in 30 or more feet of deposit. This creates a complex problem of excavation and analytical strategy. Therefore, more than most sites, Koster presents a challenge that requires an organized, large-scaled, multidisciplinary approach.

The opportunities of deep stratification create practical difficulties in excavation and recovery that can easily interfere with the aims of the investigation. Since it is costly and laborious to work at depths over 20 feet, it might be supposed that a practical way of recovering data below such a depth would be to sink test shafts to recover a sample of data from each of the occupations. Such a procedure, however, might cost less but it would not yield information that would conform to the data requirements of our general model. The collections from such shafts would only be guides to the buried occupations and inferences drawn from it would depend on normative notions of the connection between cultural items and a cultural system. We are not interested in a search for diagnostic artifacts or in adding traits to a list. Test pits have already been dug and our combined experience at the site tells us that the density of distinctive artifacts is so low that it is easy to dig through an early occupation without recovering a point even though there is ample evidence of occupational debris.

Since we are interested in understanding what living surfaces or zones were like *within* the 12 occupations particularly with respect to activity variation, we must excavate each living surface extensively. Large excavation blocks are essential for achieving this since they provide us with adequate feature and artifact inventories and the sampling of several activity areas within each occupation.

GENERAL RESEARCH PROBLEMS AT KOSTER

Research at deeply stratified sites naturally centers around the stratification of occupations. But a good deal more must be known about the sequence of differences in activities and settlement types of specific traditions before the sequence can be projected to a statement of cultural change. One of the pitfalls facing investigators of well-stratified sites is the belief that changes in the formal variability of cultural items within the sequence simply represent changes in the cultural tradition or even a replacement of traditions. What might be thought of as developmental changes within a tradition may be no more than the appearance of alternate settlement types of a single stable tradition. For example, the superposition of cooking areas over a general processing area could result in tool assemblages differing to the point that they appear to be the products of different traditions. Indeed, this very problem has arisen in the interpretation of Mousterian industries (Binford and Binford 1966; Bordes and deSonneville-bordes 1970) and has been the subject of discussion elsewhere (Watson, LeBlanc, and Redman 1971:119).

Research at Koster properly hinges on establishing not only the cultural traditions that are represented but also the settlement types that are present. A tradition is conceived of as relating to a specific cultural system. Traditions are known from the formal organization of sets of cultural items such as lithic or ceramic industries. The analytical procedures of archeologists are relatively well prepared to discover and identify such traditions although the notion of how traditions conform to cultural systems is poorly developed (see Clarke 1968; Watson, LeBlanc, and Redman 1971).

If our knowledge of how to discover cultural traditions is relatively great, our knowledge of how to isolate settlement types and activity areas is correspondingly poor. Nonetheless the demands of a stratified site such as at Koster force us to come to grips with this difficulty. We may start by supposing that each of the occupations is a member of a specific settlement type belonging to one or more settlement systems. The task then becomes one of effective classification within one of the frameworks elaborated by Struever (1968b), Trigger (1968b), or Winters (1969).

A number of studies are available that systematically relate occupations to settlements and attempt to draft a settlement system, and it is our purpose here to outline a particular procedure for the Koster site that allows us to discover settlement types.

It has been recognized for some time that the evidence that establishes a settlement classification is not the same as that which demonstrates the connection between occupations and a cultural tradition (Hole and Heizer 1969). Each of these classifications looks at the collections of cultural data in different ways, and for this reason any attempt to confound them can only result in ambiguous results. It is this very ambiguity that Winters (1969) has skillfully exposed in Midwestern studies and others have exposed elsewhere. Settlement types cannot be derived directly from a tabulation of artifacts from individual occupations because types and lists belong to different orders of integration. Types are however derivable from the archeological evidence *after* establishing the distribution of necessary elemental components among occupations.

We are referring to a formal procedure of classification (Dunnell 1971). Although the formal demonstration lies at the basis of the discovery of settlement types, many investigators have chosen to establish types through the use of independent environmental indicators of such dimensions as season of occupation. The formal attributes of settlement size, clusters of specific artifacts, distribution of the remains of animal and plant species, and differences in the kind and number of structures and other features are among those that reflect differences in overall use of the space within a settlement. It is undeniable that a strong strategy makes use of the contributions of natural science specialists as a control, and that in the final analysis the more dependent a settlement classification is on culturally external data the more satisfactory it is.

THE KOSTER RESEARCH STRATEGY

We will give a brief outline of the research strategy. It is essentially directed at the extraction of the processes in the evolution of Archaic period cultural systems at Koster as this evolution is represented first in cultural behavior within a series of superimposed settlements and second in the systems' environmental contexts. In regard to the first concern our study is reduced to an examination of the behavior over a series of activity areas allocated to settlement type. Our initial requirement is that we are able to extract a sufficient number of measures of this behavior both to isolate areas and to measure their differences.

Our procedure is to isolate areas of occupation described by the intersection of specific characteristics that in a particular example could be defined by high chert density, medium limestone and animal bone, and low density of igneous rock. Such areas are not thought of as primary activity areas of the simple undifferentiated sort (e.g., meat roasting area, flint knapping area), rather they may be more properly termed aggregate activity areas to avoid the implication that there is a correspondence of such areas with simple activity sets, homogeneous tool kits, or specific feature types.

The aggregate activity areas as they are defined quantitatively can be mapped into a classification applicable to Koster. The classification would be appropriately tested outside Koster on a series of controlled Archaic site surface collections from the study area.

It is highly desirable to discover aggregate activity areas in an early phase of the investigation if such discovery is to become more than the final product of research. In the strategy outlined here aggregate activity areas are conceived of as units within which analysis of distributions of artifacts, debris, and environmental indicators should take place. In fact such areas can greatly facilitate analysis by dividing occupations into units from which data samples can be taken.

Collecting Scale

There are several procedures for differentiating among aggregate activity areas. Within a single excavation one could properly recover observations specific to any procedure or to all procedures. However, it is neither practical nor possible to recover *all simultaneously*. The reason for this lies in the simple disparities in scale of the collecting units appropriate to different types of observations. For instance, the size of the arbitrary recording units for collecting measures of density lie on a scale. The differences between a region, a site, a block or section within a site, a ten-foot square, or a small feature are obvious. Another type of measurement that is scaled is location that can be measured with coordinates provided at a scale of county, section, and locally with tape in feet and inches. Differences in scale have also been recognized in conceptual categories of cultural data, specifically in settlements where it is appropriate to differentiate among complex features such as dwellings and individual bounded disturbances of the subsoil (Binford 1964; Trigger 1968b).

Although scale has been recognized in cultural phenomena and in the mode of observation and measurement, it has yet to influence the collecting procedures of more than a small proportion of archeologists. Simply being explicitly aware of objectives before setting out into the field is not sufficient. It is imperative that more than passing attention be given to the scale of the collecting unit in order to make the achievement of an objective more effective (Watson, LeBlanc, and Redman 1971).

The adjustment of data collecting units and the procedure associated with it calls into operation a process of "problem optimizing." The form, number of observations, and observation scale is made consistent with the requirements of the objectives, while taking into consideration the opportunities presented in the site and study area (Binford 1968).

In contrast to this operating procedure is "site optimizing," wherein a "salvage" rationale is invoked to record all data that can be conceived or that is practical to recover within the limits of time and resources. Site optimizing is often considered to be a basic procedure that does not require the investigator to have specific goals and problems. Underlying this procedure are the notions that the data speak for themselves and that the contribution of a body of data on which others can build justifies itself. This simple inductive strategy rationale has been effectively discredited (Watson, LeBlanc, and Redman 1971), but the notion that "someone will be able to do something with this that I can't" still remains with us. This last notion suffers from the same faults as a strictly inductive strategy of research—differing amounts of available time, manpower, and resources ensure a large degree of noncomparability among excavations. For practical purposes this is a very inefficient strategy. Site optimizing is not only nongoal-directed but simply undirected.

Actually, "current practice" defines most of what is regarded as worthy of investigation and what is useful to observe. What were formerly discarded and unobserved are today regarded as useful data. As an example, the collecting and weighing of limestone, chert, and other lithic debris would not have been done 20 years ago. With more phenomena becoming relevant to observe, the archeologist and his coinvestigators have to choose which observations to make. No investigator—or group of investigators—can "do everything," since we have come to the point where making one observation destroys data for a different observation.

Just as there are different standards of field excavation among archeologists, there are different levels at which investigators have aimed their archeology. Some have investigated gross village or settlement morphology (cf. Adams 1968); others have investigated artifact clusters within small specialized settlements (Binford and others 1970); while others have fastened attention on microstructure (Wheat 1972). This is a matter of scale, and it is important to point out that it is practical to investigate settlement type distributions without collecting data on the specific context of sets of artifacts. What is little appreciated is that though specific artifact contexts in a set of sites or occupations *can* improve knowledge of settlement types, such information is not necessary. In fact, an adequate understanding is possible from a consideration of settlement types, for example, by collecting data on their components—which we have defined as activity areas.

Some would object by saying that we need more accurate information on the activity areas. This knowledge should really be preceded by more accurate knowledge respecting artifacts, so that an investigation of levels of activity and organizations of behavior would be conceived of as learning about the most basic element first, and then grouping or pooling knowledge at successively higher levels until we can talk of cultural systems or traditions. Stated in this manner we can expect little to emerge simply because the essential role of a theory or a model in determining what to observe is lacking. There are explicit decisions that need to be made to determine which component observations are significant or relevant. This point of view implies that useless observations are not only possible but even likely if objectives are not clear. Objectives in an observation-making context cannot be separated from attention to the scale at which the observing is being done. What we have argued for here is that there should exist in the initial data collecting phase a recognition of the congruence of a unit of analysis, which in the Koster investigation is an aggregate activity area, with the collecting unit.

Part of the appeal of an inductively oriented site optimization collecting approach is that it appears to parallel the logical priority of elements to a class (e.g., attributes to a type). But one need not explicitly recognize ceramic or lithic attributes to understand what pottery or chipped stone tools are. A thorough and explicit definition of attributes becomes important when categories among the artifact domains (pottery, chipped stone) are to be established. These attributes are at the next lower scale than the category described within the domain and do not include elements of different scale. To differentiate a domain all that is necessary is to recognize the attribute components.

At the general level, in order to decide which elements (or components) in combination encode the maximum amount of information in a technical sense, one needs to know of the "behavior" of the class of items or its range of expression with respect to some other order of observations. After this decision is made, it remains to be decided how these elements are to be counted or measured (Dunnell 1971).

In retrospect, part of the reluctance to adhere to the collecting scale dictated by a problem orientation resides in the insecurity that comes from destroying the very bit of prehistory that is being observed. However, if advances are to be made in our knowledge of cultural behavior in an investigation such as Koster, a problem-oriented observation procedure must prevail.

Stepwise Operating Procedure

In the absence of adequate prior knowledge of the distribution of activity areas, excavation at a site such as Koster entails excavation of units of an appropriate scale to record the variation among and between activity areas. Scales can maximize the range in behavior by selecting large collecting units, thereby insuring extensive coverage, or they can maximize the detail in behavior by selecting small units or measuring proximal distances among cultural items.

At Koster the size of the primary collecting unit was selected to allow recovery of large areas of an occupation (hence different activity areas if present) and at the same time to provide some control of objects in space. The standard collecting unit is a six-foot square of three-inch thickness (i.e., a level), which is also the minimum square area that a single excavator can work in at any depth. A supplementary collecting unit exists in the form of features, which are isolated and bounded aggregates of items and soil matrix.

Detail is lost in this collecting procedure, but questions that can be asked of the microarrangements of items and features can be fruitfully posed only after an analysis of the data recovered from the primary collecting units. Only after organizing the behavior on the scale of the primary collecting unit can one recognize potentially minimal components to the behavior and initiate a supplementary program to recover and measure these components. What is advocated here is a stepwise analytical and observation procedure from coarser to finer scale as the unexplained portion of the analysis at the initial level gives way to examination of specific detail with observations appropriate to it.

IMPLEMENTATION OF THE KOSTER RESEARCH STRATEGY

In the excavation of a site like Koster, involving 40 or more excavators and a heavy artifact and debris yield from 12 occupation levels, it becomes particularly necessary to process the excavated materials while the excavations are underway.

Every archeologist is aware that the large labor reservoirs of the summer are purely seasonal, and with the arrival of fall the manpower available for processing materials excavated during the previous summer may be only 10 to 20% as large as the manpower involved in the excavations themselves. Frequently the washing, cataloging, and analysis carried out by the small laboratory group during the nine months of the academic year do not complete the processing of the materials recovered by a much larger crew in the previous summer.

In addition, many archeologists are familiar with the problem of discovering, perhaps after five or six months of artifact analysis, that they should have focused greater attention on a specific locality within the site during the previous summer's excavations. By the time they have learned enough from their data to discover this, it is too late to redirect their field efforts to increase the yield from the locality in question.

By defining a number of intuitive functional categories of artifacts and debris in the Central Data Processing Lab, and quantifying the materials recovered from each excavation unit in terms of these categories, it becomes possible to immediately establish both individual activity areas and the larger "aggregate activity areas," analysis units that become the basis for defining subsequent excavation and even overall research goals.

Both the limited human resources available for laboratory work during the academic year and the lack of immediate feedback for directing excavation strategy are two major reasons for investing great effort in artifact processing during the excavation season itself. The data flow system devised for the Koster Project reflects some of the advantages of combining excavation and processing activities (Figure 1).

At Koster we maintain two standard controls on data recovery: (1) screening and (2) flotation. The entire site matrix is processed through half-inch mesh table screens. The screen-recovered artifacts and debris, together with those found through trowel work, are bagged, and at the end of each day they are trucked to a storage shed in the village of Kampsville, nine miles away.

A half-bushel basket of screened soil is saved from each excavation unit and will be subjected later to flotation processing.

The screen- and trowel-recovered materials are hand washed in Kampsville into compartmented drying racks. The racks containing the washed material are placed in a simple drier in a nearby building. The dried materials are then brought into the Central Data Processing Lab where they are sorted into a group of 30 to 40 intuitive functional categories (fire-cracked igneous cobbles, mussel shells, large mammal bones, grooved axes, etc.). The sorted material from each excavation unit is quantified by counting and weighing, and this information is plotted on master sheets. The data on these master sheets are then fed into a CDC 6400 computer in Evanston, Illinois, through a terminal set up in a building adjacent to the Data Processing Lab.

The artifacts and debris themselves are bagged in the Central Data Processing Lab and then taken to various recipient laboratories. Recipient laboratories for the Koster Project include Botany, Zoology, Malacology, Artifact, Osteology and Pollen Labs (Fig. 1). Of these, the first four are located within two blocks of the Central Data Processing Lab. Thus far, we have not been able to establish a Pollen Lab in Kampsville; and the skeletal lab is a preliminary facility that prepares material to be sent to Jane Buikstra's Osteology Lab in Evanston. The soil samples containing pollen are sent to James Schoenwetter's Palynology Lab at Arizona State University.

In the Kampsville Botany, Zoology, Malacology, and Artifact Labs a full-time instructor and full-time experienced student research assistants catalog and formally identify the excavated materials. By the end of the 1971 field season, zoologist Frederick C. Hill and his assis-

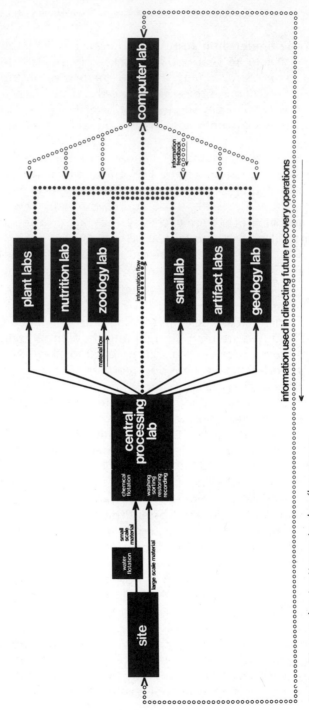

Fig. 1. Diagram showing Koster site data flow system.

tants had identified more than 45,000 excavated animal bones and mussel shells. Richard Ford and Nancy Asch's Botany Lab, Manfred Jaehnig's Snail Lab, and Thomas G. Cook's Artifact Lab all were able to complete a major part of the formal analysis before the excavation season came to an end. In each of these labs from two to four research assistants, each working about 50 hours a week, were able to complete a prodigious amount of the basic identifications before summer's end. This left the more interesting prospects of data manipulation and interpretation for the fall and winter months. With a major portion of the time-consuming identifications completed during the excavation season, it became practical for the various collaborating archeologists and natural scientists to complete their analyses with greatly reduced manpower during the following academic year. This allowed Nancy Asch, Richard Ford, and David Asch (1972) to complete and publish by April 1972 a monograph on the macroplant remains recovered from the Archaic levels at Koster during the 1969 and 1970 field seasons.

While all of this is happening to the trowel- and screen-recovered remains, a second processing system recovers quantities of small-scale debris that had escaped the screens at the Koster site.

During the 1971 field season some 4,700 half-bushel soil samples, one from each excavation unit, were put through a water separation and chemical flotation system. First, the artifacts, plant, and animal remains were separated from their soil matrix by using the water separation method described by Struever (1968a). This process, carried out in a stream four miles south of the Koster site, separates animal bone and plant remains as one fraction and stone artifacts and debris as a second fraction. Both fractions are then dried. The stone artifact and debris fraction is then bagged and taken to the Kampsville Central Data Processing Lab for quantification (similar to the screen-recovered artifacts), and thence to the Artifact Lab for analysis. The bone and plant remains fraction is sent to a chemical flotation room in Kampsville where the carbonized plant remains are floated free of the bone in a zinc chloride solution. The separated plant and bone subfractions are rinsed and dried, then quantified in the Central Data Processing Lab, and finally sent to the Kampsville Botany and Zoology Labs respectively.

Since a plan is no stronger than its weakest link, most plans for processing excavated data fall short in the vast amount of time required to clerically handle the data to get it into acceptable form. In fact most of the time put into large-scale archeological research can be assigned to clerical efforts. Given this situation it is obvious that the data-processing advances of computer technology should be enlisted. And moreover, the customary handling of data should be completely revised to take advantage of remote terminal access from a laboratory located on the site. Such computer use is planned for the Central Data Processing Lab to facilitate observation correction, progress of ongoing research, and information feedback to field operations. These three essential uses expand the scope of conventional data processing to provide information to field operations that can rarely be enjoyed otherwise.

It then becomes necessary to organize the identification output to feed into separate data files that correspond to specific analytical problems. We have planned to maintain a basic file of debris measures standardized by recorded unit volume and a series of other files recording counts of artifacts, animal bones, plant remains, and snail species. Each file is designed to facilitate a specific analytical task and the basic file carries the additional burden of discovering the aggregate activity areas and refining the vertical distribution of discrete occupations among a series of primary collecting units.

In addition to the feedback utility of processing excavated materials while you dig, there is the enormous psychological gain resulting from the completion or near-completion of the most tedious steps in the analysis of artifacts and debris. With the formal identifications largely completed during the summer, this leaves the happy prospect of data manipulation during the academic year. In short, in-field data processing makes completion of an archeological research project a feasible goal. Since the various collaborating archeologists and natural scientists reside in Kampsville for almost three months, it sharply increases the level of interaction and therefore increases the likelihood that the multidisciplinary effort will be a truly collaborative one. In such an effort as this the resulting publication is likely to contain major efforts at synthesis and not simply a series of unconnected articles by various specialists.

17. THE NATURE AND NURTURE OF ARCHEOLOGY: A PROSPECT

WALTER W. TAYLOR

Department of Anthropology
Southern Illinois University
Carbondale, Illinois

I believe that it is well recognized that archeological research within the last decade or so has become an immensely complex, widely ramified, and long, drawn-out undertaking. This has happened because, among other things, the archeologists have come to see that their raw data, the empirical evidence that they produce in the field, consist not merely of artifacts to be described, compared, and fitted into taxonomies, but also contain, however latent and in need of development, a vast amount of significant information about the past, both cultural and natural. The revelation and exploitation of this information has become an acknowledged obligation on the conscientious, modern archeologist, with the result that he feels more and more obligated to go beyond his own competencies and his own discipline in search of techniques and expertise that will assist him in realizing more fully the potentials of his material.

While it was once accepted practice to retain and describe only the artifactual materials from archeological excavations, and often only the more complete specimens at that, now not only the artifacts but also the full range of nonpurposive by-products of cultural activity, the chipping debris, food wastes, both wild and domestic pollen, even fecal matter, are grist to the archeological mill. The natural environment itself, as a distinct but conjunct and highly pertinent factor, comes under study as the effective setting of culture. It is no longer enough for the archeologist to say that a certain projectile point is made of chert—now we expect to be told the source of the chert and to have inferences drawn as to the cultural significance of finding chert from that source in that site in that region. It is now accepted in certain quarters to manipulate our empirical data in such ways as to support inferences about social organization, kinship and rules of residence, cultural values, and structuralizing configurations.

This change in viewpoint and the consequent expansion of expectancies and explicit goals have brought about a tremendous proliferation of the techniques and expertise that are necessary to modern archeological research. For many archeologists, it has become a serious matter of conscience to push the data as far as possible, to wring them as dry as science, all science, and controlled imagination can possibly be made to wring them. This compulsion (where it indeed exists) has put a considerable and often stultifying burden on modern archeology. In addition to the basic, conventional skills expected of him, today's archeologist is now expected to be aware of, and conversant with, if not proficient in, a host of methods, techniques, and tangent fields of knowledge, all of which continue to expand with every new insight, every new question asked of the data by every eager archeologist anywhere.

At least two results have emerged from this trend. The first and closest to home is that, as Stuart Struever has said on several occasions, the day of one-man archeological research appears to be virtually at an end, at least for projects that are more than minimally ambitious. One archeologist cannot hope to be competent in all the currently available and utilizable fields, nor does he have the time to pursue so many specialized investigations. Team attacks would seem to be the only solution. Such teams might be organized and led by archeologists, but of necessity they will be interdisciplinary, or at least multidisciplinary, and will require, again as Struever has pointed out, an appreciable reorganization of archeological research. I shall return to this topic later in my discussion.

The second result is that institutional administrators, and even fellow scientists in many instances, have not kept up with the realities of modern archeological research. This applies particularly to fund-granting institutions, whose personnel is rarely trained in archeology, but also to academic and even research institutions, where more current and sympathetic attitudes might be expected. By and large, in my personal experience, administrative personnel still appear to think in terms of the "old archeology." If they listen at all to the archeologists' cries for "more," for more research time, more assistance and collaboration, more elaborate technical resources, and more money, they often look upon them as special pleading and sometimes as mere pretensions to virtuosity and self-serving innuendo.

Therefore, if we are to remedy this problem of archeology, our first task is surely one of communication. We must make the administrators aware of the expansion of our research field and convince them that this is natural, necessary, and justified, not merely empire building and self-indulgence. They must be led to realize that our need for assistance, especially for outside expertise, is not due to laziness or a culpable incompetence, but rather that it is due to entirely defensible demands of our evolving goals. And then we must convince them that those goals and the price of reaching them are justifiable in terms of the scientific and humanistic importance of what we can produce. Unless we can convince the administrators of these things, unless we can erase the long-standing, persistent, and still all-too-common image of archeologists as what Ernest Hooton once called "the senile playboys of science rooting in the rubbish heaps of antiquity," any practical remedies we may propose will be futile—the money, time, personnel, and facilities to implement them will not be forthcoming in the quantity, quality, and diversity that the "new archeology" requires.

On the other hand, there are some practical ways through which we can make a start toward easing our troubles by helping ourselves and if carried out, they can make our representations to the administrators more effective and, hopefully, more productive. I shall discuss only two. I am sure that there are others.

A number of years ago during the conference held in Chicago on identification of archeological materials, I presented and later published a paper proposing a Clearinghouse or Central Agency, "a purely service organization . . . to perform inter- and intra-disciplinary services which [the archaeologist] . . . is not performing and can hardly be expected to perform . . . . What is needed is some central agency which will cooperate with, and facilitate the work of, the various parties to these interdisciplinary studies without coercing the independent investigations of any of them." I went on to suggest that this organization should not employ and house a stable of specialists but should act as a middleman between the archeologist and the suppliers of expertise, and I detailed some of the ways in which the organization might operate and some of the services that it might provide.

The suggestion was well received by many, but not all, of the conferees. In fact, a short time later the National Science Foundation came to me with the suggestion that I draw up a formal proposal for just such an organization. However, after the proposal was submitted, it was turned down by the archeologists to whom it had been referred for evaluation. I have never learned the reasons for this rejection, which seemed to many of us to be so self-detrimental, but I have heard faint rumblings to the effect that the referrees were afraid that the archeologists' "independence" might be compromised by such an organization. In any event, it is perhaps significant, possibly even characteristic, that it was the archeologists themselves, or a certain number of them, who killed that opportunity for assistance in our struggle for better and more abundant data to implement our ever-broadening research horizons. I would like to suggest that it may be time once again to consider such an agency, one with updated specifications but with the original mission of helping us solve the problem of our still present and ever-growing need for expertise.

My second proposal has also been anticipated—but more recently and by other archeologists. In fact, it has already begun to function. I refer to the inauguration, only in April 1971, of the Southwestern Anthropological Research Group, whose first publication has just come from the Prescott College Press, edited by George Gumerman. In essence, the group is a loose federation of anthropologists independently pursuing their own researches but, at the same time, devoting a portion of their energies to a group project that is tangent to, or within the range of, their own work. There is the explicit premise that the usual interdisciplinary approach, in practice at least and almost of necessity, is limited in geographic scope and is still essentially a "one-man" project in the sense in which Streuver has described. The concept of the research group, on the other hand, is that of a "large team of archeologists working . . . with the same hypotheses . . . and collecting data in a standardized manner." Here we have a concept that is promising because it is above all simple: that through joint attack on a project jointly conceived we can widen our research horizon from the standpoint of theory and method as well as of geographical coverage, and we can increase and broaden available expertise—and all with minimal, if any, increase in funding. Of course there are problems, and there will be more. But to me this is a very exciting and promising development in American archeology. I wish it well and dare to hope, even in these days of zero population growth, that it may have many and vigorous progeny!

In closing, let me epitomize. Archeology is in trouble. The requirements of our research have vastly proliferated, while our resources have failed to keep pace. Many of the problems that are restricting our activities seem to be due to the fact that many administrators do not believe that we really need (and can justify) what we say we need in order to do what we say we can do. Basically and most simply, the problem is one of communication, so that we can halt and then reverse the trend that is widening the gap between what we are able to do intellectually and technically and what we are able actually to accomplish operationally. I have suggested two lines of action:

1. To modernize the image of our discipline among "those in charge" and make them more aware of the real need we have for broadened support.
2. To help ourselves by economizing and making fuller use of the resources that we do have, among other ways, by pooling our intellectual and technical potential through group action and a reduction of duplication.

Perhaps if we can accomplish the latter through our own efforts, we can reassure "those in charge" of our seriousness and good faith—and of our worthiness to receive a more appropriate share of their moral support and financial bounty.

18. THE RECONCILIATION OF THEORY AND METHOD IN ARCHEOLOGY

GEORGE J. GUMERMAN

Center for Man and Environment
Prescott College
Prescott, Arizona

For years archeologists have been castigated for their lack of concern about articulating the theoretical basis that underlies their work. Today, however, there is no dearth of theory in American archeology. The situation of inadequate theory formulation and the virtual nonexistent examination of organizing principles by archeologists that anthropologists such as Kluckhohn deplored as early as 1940 (pp. 43–44) should no longer be an overriding concern. The major archeological journals seldom have an issue without at least one article devoted to the examination of theoretical concepts, and several excellent volumes expounding archeological theory and method have been published in the recent years (e.g., Clarke 1968; Watson, LeBlanc, Redman 1971; Dunnell 1971). In spite of this flowering of archeological theory, however, the majority of the published results of archeological endeavors bear too great a similarity to the survey and site reports of the 1940s and 1950s. The result is that aspects of Kluckhohn's famous 1940 criticism about Middle American archeologists are still applicable to many archeologists regardless of their area of specialization. Kluckhohn (p. 42) noted that:

> I should like to record an overwhelming impression that many students [of Middle American prehistory] are but slightly reformed antiquarians. To one who is a layman in these highly specialized realms there seems a great deal of obsessive wallowing in detail of and for itself. No one can feel more urgently than the writer the imperative obligation of anthropologists to set their descriptions in such a rich context of detail that they can properly be used for comparative purposes. Yet proliferation of minutiae is not its own justification.

The present contradiction is that in spite of the florescence of archeological theory, much current archeology is still "on the intellectual level of stamp collecting" that Kluckhohn deplores. Articles and monographs are usually either theoretical in orientation or are description-based culture history. With a few outstanding exceptions, theoretical concepts are usually tested by application to previous excavations that were undertaken for other purposes, or by short surveys and limited test excavations. Rarely are the theoretical articles based on or followed up by major excavation programs. In short, there is too little application of archeological theory to archeological method.

In part, this lack of reconciliation is a result of theoretical articles that stress a concern for the formulation and testing of general laws concerning the operation of entire cultural systems in contrast to the problems encountered in single site excavations or at best in the establishment of phase sequences (Struever 1968b). Hole and Heizer (1969: 269–270) have expressed in brief form the thrust of current archeological goals concerning the reconstruction of extinct cultural systems:

> The process of making [archeological] inferences may become quite complex, but the goal, of course, is to attempt to explain how a cultural system works.
>
> In examining cultural subsystems we focus our atttention for the first time on people, not as individuals, but as members of once-living communities. However, we are not able to comprehend people in all of their facets. We can say little about politics or theology, but we can perceive some of the ways to reconstruct how they were organized. All things are made up of organized parts; it is one of our jobs as social scientists to try to discover the principles of organization that make viable societies of collections of people. As archeologists we must try to reconstruct the organization of the people whose remains we can handle, count, measure, and draw. It is becoming more and more apparent that principles of organization are the basic keys in our understanding of any class of phenomena, including people. This

position is taken by general system theorists, and has been echoed in various forms by anthropologists for many years.

It is probably fortunate that organization has emerged as the focal point of behavioral studies, because archeologists are able to find information in prehistory that relates to organization. The sites, the artifacts in them, and especially the way in which sites and artifacts occur, give clues to the organization of the society that left them.

The goals of understanding the organizing principles of extinct cultural systems are, of course, more difficult and time consuming than developing a phase sequence or excavating a single site presumed to be representative of a culture or subculture. Nevertheless archeological theorists have suggested a number of ways in which the goals of archeologists can be met.

It has become quite obvious that to view a culture as a system calls for archeologists to structure their research within a deductive framework that necessitates an orientation toward the generation and testing of well formulated theories (Fritz and Plog 1970; Tuggle and others 1972). A primarily inductively oriented research strategy does not allow the necessary control of information and how it is collected to test general laws concerning the organization of cultural systems. However, the restructuring of research strategy toward a hypothetico-deductive model will not alone ensure the attainment of modern archeological goals. The concern with the organization of complete cultural systems in Hole and Heizer's statement is obviously a desirable and necessary trend, and yet there has been concern expressed that these goals, no matter how necessary, may not be obtainable. As Struever (1968c: 132) has demonstrated, personnel and financial resources are too restricted to devise the means necessary for testing significant laws concerning extinct cultural systems:

> Research is not executed by one [archeologist], but the extent and sophistication of problems conceived, of excavation and analytical methods used to solve these problems, and the capital outlays in equipment and facilities seldom exceed the resosurces or resourcefulness of a single investigator or the longevity of his personal interest. The scope of the problems investigated, then, is limited by the personal commitment of a single archeologist and by the restrictions imposed on or by the funding organizations in providing capital to carry out the project.

Simply stated, funds are not available to field large research teams to test the many theories that have been advanced concerning the functioning of entire cultural systems. The dichotomy between method and theory lies, in large part, in the financial inability to test current theory; yet, there is no absence of field work. On the contrary, the pace of archeological survey and excavation has increased greatly in the last decade, and there are many more individuals involved in the profession than in previous years.

The major increase in archeological activity, however, has been in the realm of salvage or emergency archeology while the funding, and consequently the activity, in other types of archeology has remained static or even declined in the last several years. Without doubt, funds are much more readily available for salvage archeology than for problem-oriented archeology. It has been estimated that in California there are one hundred times more funds available for salvage archeology than for nonsalvage work (Heizer 1966: 58). Because funding is more easily available for the excavation of endangered sites, Heizer (1966) predicted that salvage archeology would divert critically needed professional resources from theory-testing investigations to salvage archeology. This has not been the case. Funds used for contract salvage archeology programs have not been channeled from problem-oriented or theory-testing archeological projects. Salvage programs are usually operated with funds from state and federal agencies and from private industry that does not ordinarily finance archeological research. Recent products of graduate schools of anthropology are presently having difficulty obtaining professional positions so that salvage-oriented programs do not appear to be diverting needed personnel.

The problem of the reconciliation of archeological method with theory would appear to lie in the utilization of funds from salvage-oriented projects to formulate and test theoretical concepts, certainly a formidable, but not impossible, task. The conflict between salvage archeology with its tendency toward fact gathering inductive-oriented research and problem-oriented deductive, interdisciplinary team type of archeology has been adequately detailed by King (1971). While salvage archeologists continue with fact collection and "filling in the blanks on the archeological map" other archeologists are developing sophisticated, and often convoluted, hypotheses for the discovery of laws of the sociocultural process that they have not the time, money, or effort to test by large-scale excavation. It is necessary to meld the majority of the archeology done today, that is, salvage archeology, with some of the better theory, and to accomplish this requires that salvage archeology be considered as comprising two major types.

The first type of salvage archeology consists of those projects that involve large land masses when the archeologist has at least several months notice before the modification of the land takes place and a number of years in which to do the excavation, analysis, and writing. Most commonly these projects involve the damming of river systems or strip mining operations. The second type of salvage project is the small one, often lasting only a few days. Usually the time between notification of the archeologist and beginning of construction is short, often nonexistent, and the project covers only a small area and lasts for a short time. Examples of this type include building site locations, short access roads, and small areas being developed for agriculture. It should be noted that linear salvage archeology, that is, highway, power, and pipeline right-of-way projects, do not necessarily fall under the rubric of small-scale projects, since some construction covers considerable distance and requires years of excavation and analysis.

Obviously, the two types of salvage archeology demand different methodologies to orient them to theory-testing programs and, of course, the large-scale project is the one most easily adaptable to hypothetico-deductive research.

King (1971:260) has suggested that the huge salvage contracts that require large sums and a number of years to accomplish not be awarded without a long-range deductively oriented research program. Currently large salvage projects are often awarded to a number of different institutions working in the same area with no well-articulated research strategy and little coordination between institutions. Only by orienting integrated aspects of the large salvage efforts toward theory testing can the goals of explaining the organization and operation of cultural systems be attempted.

Even more importantly, means currently exist in the American Southwest, and could be developed elsewhere, to bring data from large salvage-oriented programs to bear on archeological theory testing. The means of integrating large-scale salvage programs toward hypothetico-deductive research lies in organizations such as the Southwestern Anthropological Research Group (SARG).

In 1971 SARG was formed to assist archeologists working in the Southwest to aim at least a part of their efforts at developing and testing a common research design (Gumerman 1971). The problem that the SARG associates are attempting to solve involves the explanation of settlement distribution, but this itself is not of importance here. The significance of the group is that it is attempting to answer

basic questions that concern all archeologists by having all participants contribute to the research design, collect data in a compatible
format, computer program the data, and test the design in different
areas of the Southwest. No person or institution will abandon individual research interests but all participants will expend the extra
effort and absorb the added expense to collect data that the group
requires. A data retrieval system will be established that will allow the
collected information to be available to all. The group will meet
annually to discuss mutual problems and to modify the research
design; it is expected that this will be a long-term project lasting for a
number of years.

The importance of SARG is that it enables data collected from
large salvage contract projects, as well as from nonsalvage archeology, to be programmed for modifying and testing hypotheses generated by the group. Needless to say, each individual salvage excavation or survey program may still be primarily inductive, and the
reports will probably still be descriptive for the most part. Nevertheless, a part of the project will be directed to the testing of theory
related to cultural systems and of concern to most people working in
a large culture area. An example can best illustrate the relationship of
a large salvage archeological project to hypothetico-deductive
research and to the testing of research designs of the SARG type.

Archeological salvage operations have been conducted on Black
Mesa in northeastern Arizona since 1967 in areas slated for coal strip
mining. It was apparent that the archeology program would last for a
number of years, and yet the first year was spent in survey and excavation mostly with an approach directed to the collection of data,
that is, with a basically inductive approach since little was known
about the area (Gumerman 1970). Since 1968, however, the direction
of the Black Mesa program has been more hypothetico-deductive
with attempts at well-formulated research strategy and theory testing.
This approach is applicable because it is a long-term project and
because the study area is not one which covers a narrow right-of-way
but instead has an areal expanse of 65,000 acres. The implementation
of SARG methodology now means that data collected on Black Mesa
will have even greater potential for theory testing. The Black Mesa
salvage effort will no longer be restricted solely to the testing of
theories that can be generated about the prehistoric populations of
that area but can be directed to the testing of some of the most
recently formulated theories concerning cultural systems. SARG
allows the Black Mesa salvage effort to be interrelated with compa-

rable salvage and nonsalvage programs throughout the Southwest on a much wider scale than was formerly conceivable.

The large salvage project can, as illustrated, be oriented to theory testing concerning the operation of cultural systems. The application of small salvage projects to a hypothetico-deductive approach, however, is not so easy, and King (1971) feels the single small site excavation on a highway or powerline right-of-way is beyond the scope of such methodology. He states that "Any hope that we might be able to develop a set of hypotheses as a bag of tricks from which we could select a guiding proposition whenever we found a site in danger, is probably doomed to disappointment" (p. 251). The problem may not be as great as King envisions and means can be developed to relate archeological method to theory using funds from salvage archeology.

The small project, the survey of a 2-mile-long, 50-foot-wide right-of-way or the excavation of a one-room farmhouse is not so easily adaptable to present SARG methodology. SARG is primarily designed for the collection of data regarding settlement patterns and as a result demands a rigorous data collection procedure in a relatively large area, not in a narrow right-of-way selected for the purpose of pipeline or highway construction. In order to direct the small-scale salvage job to hypothetico-deductive theory testing, it will be necessary to devise the theories before any work is even contemplated.

Traditionally, small-scale salvage methodology has been to develop a set of techniques for an archeological culture area that can be adapted to most types of sites in the region. Data is collected in similar ways and information recorded on general architecture or feature forms because it is not possible to determine when the necessity for excavation will arise. Because the archeologist is not certain where, when, or what type of site he will be excavating, preparation for the project has to be made beforehand, and consequently these factors almost dictate an inductively structured research program. Methods are perfected but theory is usually ignored or inadequately formulated. As a consequence, the salvage archeologist on small projects has worked with the usually poorly stated assumption that the work he will be doing is within the confines of a specific archeological culture zone and that the planned work will add something, in terms of empirical data, to the general fund of knowledge of that culture zone. The work proceeds with these assumptions in mind and when the report is completed, if ever, it is primarily descriptive, with a page or two of conclusions. In addition, the descriptions usually record the precise type of data that have traditionally been recorded by previous archeologists. Interpretations, when they occur, are usually concerned with explaining the degree of variability from the "norm," that is, the material remains and the architecture are compared with those from other sites in the region that have been excavated previously and are considered the "norm" by virtue of their having been excavated earlier. Seldom is an attempt made to explain variability in sites excavated as small salvage projects. Often the field archeologist is well trained in method, but knows little about the particular culture zone in which he is working, with the result that the site is excavated mechanically and data is collected "by the book" rather than to test specific theories. The attempt, therefore, at comparing the site to nearby excavated sites is done inductively from published reports after the excavations are completed.

Small scale archeological excavations can, however, be related to understanding cultural systems by devising research strategies for cultural or subcultural zones prior to the probability of the necessity of salvage archeology. Generally, enough is known about most areas so that specific questions about the regions can be raised other than the usual ones of what are the material remains and who lived in the area and when. It is essential that specific questions be asked about individual areas prior to the announcement of construction possibilities.

In some areas of the United States, a framework already exists for devising research strategies about individual culture zones. The Arizona State Museum has divided southern Arizona into 29 different archeological zones primarily for purposes of administering the National Environmental Policy Act of 1969, that is, for preparing environmental impact statements.

The archeological zone concept will enable the archeologist to provide the appropriate federal agency and the contracting firms with more accurate information—essentially, what is known and unknown about the area and what the general character of the archeological manifestations are in areas scheduled for construction. In order to orient the small-scale salvage project in a hypothetico-deductive manner, it will be necessary to adopt the concept of the archeological zone and to devise theories for testing in these individual zones. It should be emphasized that these archeological zones are not smaller equivalents of the traditional culture area (Kroeber 1947). Instead, they reflect what appear to be regionally distinct variations of archeological manifestations. In addition, like all classificatory systems, the zones themselves and their boundaries cannot be considered immutable but will probably change as salvage archeology continues. These research designs structured for the zones need not be solely of a culture-history nature tied only to the archeological zone itself but should also be concerned with culture process. Again a short example will clarify the scheme.

A north-south highway or powerline being constructed from Phoenix in south central Arizona to Flagstaff in northern Arizona will pass through several major environmental zones and a number of archeological zones. Theories involving culture-history and environment can be easily formulated for testing. For example, instead of simply asking what is the nature of the archeological manifestations in the different areas, the questions may be sharpened by devising research strategies for answering such questions as: How did the subsistence base differ in the diverse environmental regions? What was the character of interaction, if any, between zones, and are the cultural manifestations of each zone coterminous with the subenvironmental regions? In this way, by devising a deductively oriented research program to answer these questions prior to the commencement of survey and excavation, data can be collected in such a manner that the theories are testable within the framework of salvage archeology.

Theories concerning the organization of cultural systems can also be formulated. The north-south highway will traverse several environmental transition zones between major environments. Ecologists have demonstrated that these transition zones or edge areas contain many of the species of plants and animals found in the contiguous major environmental zones, and there are often a number of organisms found only in the edge area (Odum 1965). There is an excellent possibility that there is a tendency for increased variety in cultural systems as well as in ecosystems in these biological tension zones or edge areas. The use of the edge area concept to explain cultural variability has been attempted in the Great Lakes region with only partial success because of the difficulty in distinguishing the edge area (Fitting 1966; 1970). Because the edge area is easily definable in central Arizona, Gumerman and Johnson (1971:84) feel

> that the concept of the [edge area] as a heuristic device provides an ideal construct for the study of factors affecting the occurrence and distribution of human habitation in a biological tension zone. The edge area may, in addition, result in and explain what are

called sub-cultures, or regional cultural variants. It may also explain other differences between the major environmental zone and the [edge area], such as differences in population density, settlement pattern, and differences and diversity in subsistence patterns. It also may explain site locations in defensive situations due to warfare over the natural resources of the edge area. In other words, the use of the [edge area] concept in archeology may help anthropologists to understand the zones between culture areas.

A number of hypotheses concerning culture process can be framed for testing from the above statements. For example, the edge area as opposed to the surrounding major environmental zones tends to have increased variety and diversity of plant and animal communities. Because of this diversity, human communities in an edge area will exhibit more diversity in subsistence patterns because of the necessity to develop more varied techniques to exploit the greater variation of plant and animal species.

Certainly, single small-scale efforts will not provide enough information to satisfactorily test broadly framed theories such as cultural adaptation to an edge area. Nevertheless, data that bear on the questions posed above can be collected. Eventually, enough work may be done in the different archeological zones so that the theories can be satisfactorily tested. It is doubtful that enough data can be collected to *demonstrate* laws of cultural process, but it should be possible to *suggest* the existence of certain principles.

If there are doubts that areas affected by construction, and hence by salvage archeology, are too constricted and isolated to provide answers to specific regional and general questions, the quickening pace of construction in this country and a glance at Figure 1 should dispel these doubts. Figure 1 represents the larger areas of survey and excavation in Arizona since the 1953 excavations along the El Paso Gas pipeline right-of-way, the first large-scale salvage archeology project in Arizona. Literally, hundreds of smaller projects lasting a day or two have been left off the map. With rare exceptions, such as the Glen Canyon program in northeastern Arizona, few of these projects have been oriented toward hypothetico-deductive research. Work in the immense area covered by 20 years of salvage archeology could have answered numerous questions if it had been organized to collect information to test specific theories. The orientation of these salvage archeological projects toward theory testing could have provided an opportunity for integration of archeological method and theory. Admittedly, the examples I have presented are oversimplified and the implementation of these programs

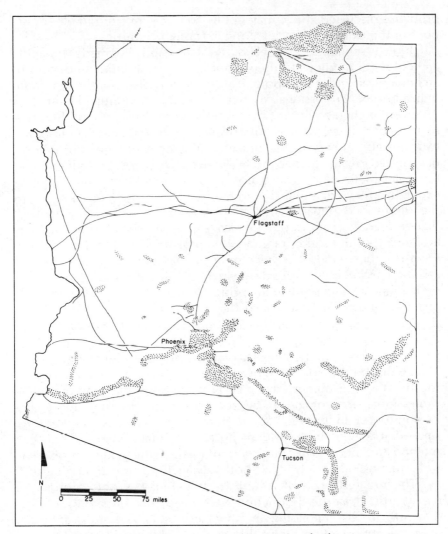

Fig. 1.   Salvage archeology in Arizona in the last 20 years of either site survey or excavation. The stippled areas represent projects involving large land areas and the lines
represent survey or excavation programs along a narrow right-of-way such as for
highway or powerline construction.

may be more feasible in the American Southwest because of our vast
knowledge about the archeological manifestations in the region, and
because it is an area of extremely rapid population growth necessi-
tating a large amount of salvage archeology. The solutions to the

problems discussed above may not be so easily initiated in other portions of the United States, let alone in foreign countries.

It is essential, nevertheless, that attempts be made to apply archeological methods to theory not only for the ultimate benefit of archeological and anthropological goals, but also for the optimum utilization of professional archeologists. The curious dilemma in American archeology of method unrelated to theory about the organization of cultural systems not only involves the reconciliation of the two, but also concerns the future employment situations of numerous professionally trained archeologists. The present reduction in the availability of teaching positions in American universities is common knowledge and the archeologist has not been immune to the diminished departmental employment. Recent graduates with higher degrees in anthropology have experienced difficulty obtaining academic positions, the traditional employment for the archeologist. On the other hand, it is becoming increasingly difficult to recruit *qualified* archeologists for salvage archeological programs. Numerous permanent or semipermanent positions have been filled by poorly qualified archeologists because those who are qualified have been trained to deal with hypothetico-deductive research problems, and disdain, often rightfully so, the primarily inductively structured research of salvage archeology. It is necessary, therefore, that salvage archeology become oriented in a hypothetico-deductive manner both for the sake of problem solving and for the best utilization of trained professional archeologists. The solution is *not* to train more archeologists for inductively oriented research in salvage archeology, since that would simply widen the already increasing gap between method and theory. The solution is to organize the general research in order to most effectively utilize both salvage funds and archeologists.

The greatest crisis in American archeology is not, contrary to recent articles, in site destruction wrought by the spreading subdivision and in the increasing numbers of vandalized sites, although these are important problems that must be addressed (Davis 1972). As archeologists, we must recognize that we do not need to keep adding to research collections so that so-called representative samples are available for every conceivable type of artifact from every culture area. Nor is it necessary to excavate every endangered site. Rather we must devise research designs for theory testing and use funds from salvage programs to excavate in a manner that will test those theories.

It has often been implied that many of the wrongs of American archeology, like all other wrongs, could be cured by the infusion of large sums of money. While archeological research must be funded at a higher level than it is currently, this should not be simply to save more sites and artifacts from destruction. Additional funds should go toward the restructuring of archeological salvage research into a hypothetico-deductive framework and to help with analysis and publication of both data and the testing of laws bearing on cultural systems. Funding agencies have to be made aware of the necessity in modern archeology of preexcavation and postexcavation expenses. No matter how impressive the pictures are of archeologists racing against the bulldozer or the rising waters of a newly constructed dam, archeological funds are being misspent if they are not oriented in some degree to theory testing. The crisis in American archeology is not simply to save the endangered site but to meld method with theory in order to deal with the problems that archeologists have said are their concern.

19. THE GOALS AND STRUCTURE
OF ARCHEOLOGY AND THEIR
RELATION TO STUDENT TRAINING

FRANK HOLE

Department of Anthropology
Rice University
Houston, Texas

This volume deals with many aspects of archeology and the structure of archeological research. There are good reasons for these concerns, for we have fundamental shifts in ideas of how archeology can contribute to understanding human history and a plethora of recently developed techniques for eliciting and analyzing data. Today we are faced with the problem of using these new ideas and methods effectively. In view of the unprecedented surge of science and technology in most fields during the last two decades, it is not surprising that many archeologists have turned to an explicitly scientific approach. What is surprising is that the impact of science on archeology was delayed and, except in the multitude of technical applications, has not yet resulted in many substantive results.

Inasmuch as the philosophical issues concerning the use of a strictly scientific approach have been debated at length in this volume and elsewhere, I shall turn my attention to some matters that have not been accorded much publicity recently. Briefly, I shall consider the chief goals of archeology, the manner in which these goals are actually achieved, and the kind of talents and training needed to carry out one of the most fundamental of archeological tasks—excavation.

GOALS AND STRUCTURE OF ARCHEOLOGY

Let us look for a moment at what archeology is and what is involved in doing it. Archeology deals with the past, and one of its most important activities has always been to get things out of the ground that will inform us of the past. In this concern archeology is like history and its ends are very similar. History is usually considered one of the humanities—among those branches of learning that have "primarily a cultural character"—and many view archeology as a humanity. However in American archeology we are still riding the crest of science (it has subsided in some other fields), and the humanistic nature of archeology has been played down.

In the minds of most, scientists included, archeology is a form of history. If it were not, why would there be such concern with finding the origins of man, or sites prominent in Biblical history, or the origins of civilization? If it were not, of what good would be the museums full of artifacts, and descriptive reports that are abstracted and incorporated into the texts we use in classroom teaching? This is not to deny, however, that history can be elicited through archeology most economically by the systematic kind of investigations we call science. Science is a process of reasoned thinking and experimentation (in our case excavation and analysis). In this sense science can be considered an approach to enable us to get at history more economically and accurately.

There are those who would disagree with this viewpoint, who would maintain that science is its own goal, that the real end of archeology is to discover laws about the behavior of man. While this is certainly a possibility, it is nevertheless true that we can hardly discover the laws until we have determined, or have the means of determining, what happened in the past. Thus an accurate assessment of archeological remains is a prerequisite to scientific inference and to the testing of hypotheses.

Whatever the ultimate aims of archeology, it is clear that a fundamental shift has developed in the way archeology will be done in the future. During the last decade or more, several major projects have been carried out by teams of specialists equipped to deal with a range of information and techniques that pertain both directly and indirectly to archeology. The team leader has become more a coordinator than a doer, while the technical aspects of field work and analysis have been carried out by specialists. Clearly it is impossible for one person to do everything effectively. Recognition of this fact has already begun, and should continue in the future, to afford archeologists new opportunities for specialization. One might imagine meticulous field workers digging for remains, ceramacists analyzing pots, and zoologists measuring bones, according to the overall goals of the project, each worker responsible for his specialty and no more. A research lab in any scientific field that is not filled with such technicians under the supervision of a scientist is practically inconceivable. While this notion has come to archeology in a limited way and will surely develop further in the future, the very idea is anathema to many.

Perhaps it is here that the differences between archeology and history are most apparent. History can be done by a person who reads with perception. A library of books and documents brings extant knowledge together in a standard script so that matters of interpretation depend largely on the skill and theoretical orientation of the historian. Archeology, on the other hand, depends on analysis of data dug from the earth—data that are neither in common script nor readily comprehensible. Moreover many of the data are not of cultural origin: they consist of geographic, climatologic, botanic, zoologic, physical, and chemical entities and relationships. The technical studies of these data must be cast into a framework that relates them to man's activities. Obviously this is not like the usual historical research that emphasizes cultural affairs. Thus while archeology is like history in many of its interests, its methods of obtaining data are different, and in some respects it is vastly more complicated and more liable to interpretative error.

In view of this we must recognize that prehistoric archeology is not just illiterate history. To my mind archeology is still basically a historical activity as far as its goals are concerned, but the historical interests are best served by approaching them scientifically through the integration of teams of related specialists. Thus there is a growing need for persons who are trained in special techniques that can serve archeology—who can actually do the many things required in archeology.

DOING ARCHEOLOGY

What is involved in doing archeology? Archeology is a process that progresses sequentially through a series of steps and then returns to the starting point. It is a cycle whose most important step is the conception of a problem to investigate, for this determines how the ensuing steps will be carried out and what the nature of the conclusions will be. The range of problems one can investigate is nearly limitless: problems may be strictly historical or scientific; they may emphasize narrow interests, or they may be of global importance, and their investigation may involve simple or complex projects. Historical problems are concerned with the history of a site, of a people, or even of mankind. Scientific problems investigate the relationships among variables in the attempt to reach an understanding of why events happened or of general laws of human behavior. This is the theme of "new archeology."

Once a problem has been selected the next step in the cycle is to design an appropriate field project or experiment that requires survey, excavation, or lab work. This step is no less crucial than the first because the worth of the results will depend on whether the field work or experimentation has been set up and carried out properly. Since field work is the part of archeology most people see and since it is also one of the most difficult tasks technically, most of the remainder of this essay will be devoted to the topic. Following the field work, is the analysis of material; this in turn is followed by publication. At this point the archeological cycle is completed, and it is time to plan another project.

Many people need to be reminded that archeology is complicated and requires diverse skills—scientific, aesthetic, administrative, practical, clerical, editorial, and so on. There are very few persons who have all the requisite skills to take a project from its conception to its completion, and there is probably no one who can handle a large or complex project entirely on his own. It should be clear too in this sense that it is not true (to paraphrase a colleague) that archeology is science or it is nothing. Archeology is a lot of things, of which scientific interests are only a part. The fact seems inescapable that the process of doing archeology is basically a series of technical operations whether the ultimate goals are scientific or historic.

TALENTS, SKILLS, AND TRAINING

Archeology requires diverse skills. To suggest the range, I offer a simple and by no means exhaustive list. For convenience I have

TABLE 1. AN OUTLINE OF SOME OF THE JOBS REQUIRED TO CARRY OUT AN
ARCHEOLOGICAL PROJECT

Scientific
  Theoretician
  Integrator
  Evaluator

Administrative
  Executive director
  Expeditor
  Foreman
  Politician
  Secretary
  Accountant

Field Work
  Dirt archeologist
  Stratigrapher
  Detective
  Photo interpreter
  Explorer

Analytic
  Research assistant
  Statistician
  Computer programmer

Ancillary Scientific
  Botanist
  Ethnologist
  Geographer
  Geologist
  Palynologist
  Zoologist

Technical
  Surveyor
  Draftsman
  Photographer
  Restorer
  Carpenter
  Machine operator
  Mechanic

Editorial
  Writer
  Editor
  Layout and design

grouped these skills into seven categories with their usual job titles
(Table 1).

It is beyond the scope of this chapter to delve fully into the
implications of all these jobs and their requisite skills, but the point
should be obvious. A certain amount of talent and training is necessary for a person to do any of the jobs effectively. For that reason I
shall discuss one set of skills and suggest some implications for the
training of students. The skills I refer to are those of digging, the
heart of archeological field work.

It is usually assumed that a professional archeologist is competent to dig even if he cannot do technical studies of ceramics or bone
or most of the other jobs listed above. My purpose here is to suggest
that perceptive digging is no less an art than faunal analysis and that it
requires a special sort of person whose natural abilities have been
deliberately sharpened to carry it out successfully. Finally I suggest
that the training of students in digging has not formally recognized
the combination of qualities that need coordinated education. We
might usefully conceptualize several kinds of talents desirable in
archeology that run a continuous gamut from tactile-sensual to cere-
bral, recognizing that there is no strict line dividing one from the
other and that some persons may come equipped to exploit the
entire range. The reason for this conceptualization is that perceptive
digging is basically a sensual experience that integrates visual, audi-
tory, tactile, olefactory, and even gustatory information. Most persons, even many good field archeologists, do not explicitly recognize
this and consequently, to my knowledge, have never formally taught
the effective integration of these various inputs of data. Before I discuss how one might teach sensual archeology, let me elaborate on
why I think digging is basically a sensual process.

I have often watched students dig through strata, walls, and
other features without any apparent recognition of the fact. Floors of
hard-packed earth, especially when they are marred by burrows or
broken from use are notoriously hard for students to comprehend.
Yet a supervisor will take a trowel and scrape down to a surface he
confidently asserts is the floor while the student stands by in absolute
bewilderment. The supervisor is likely to tell the student that the
floor is obvious. Often he will say he can see or feel it but the typical
student remains unconvinced and unable to find the floor by himself.
The average supervisor will not be able to convey further information
and either tells the student to scrape the whole area down to the
same level or does the job himself.

The point is that finding a floor, a pit, or a wall is not just a matter
of seeing or feeling. What the supervisor perceives as he carefully
trowels the earth is a multiple set of sensory data to which he is
attuned and which he integrates into the concept, "floor." In the first
place, an archeologist must train himself to be aware of differences:
this is the basis of any analysis, and he is in fact analyzing the soil as
he digs. Differences take many forms. An archeologist may see color
changes or differences in the texture or moisture content of the soil;
he may feel the differences if he holds his tool properly. Hearing and

feeling are closely related, and it is not trivial to mention that a low noise level on a site is necessary for sensitive work. Sometimes too a trained excavator will smell the soil, rub some between his fingers, and even taste it, for on the tongue different soils have a singular feel and taste. In short, based on a variety of sensory perceptions, a skilled excavator builds up a picture of differences and changes that enable him to begin to interpret what they mean. Do they represent a rodent burrow, burned earth, a wall, a floor, or a pit? Usually such inferences are easy to make once the essential fact has been established that something in the soil has changed. Thus while most neophytes would have no difficulty inferring that a flat surface between walls is a floor, they might have considerable difficulty in finding the floor in the first place.

What this means in practical terms for persons who wish to learn or to teach how to dig is that they need to become accustomed to integrating a full range of sensory data so that the hand, the eye, the ear, and the nose work together, literally sniffing out from the background matrix those differences that have pattern. To compound the problem, it is necessary for the excavator to dismiss irrelevant differences and to retain significant ones. Students often find themselves laboring fruitlessly over the insignificant, afraid to move when they are unable to comprehend or are too timid about making a mistake. The skilled excavator probes and explores, taking care to preserve a portion of what confuses him until he has ascertained its contextual pattern. In other words, he keeps moving, knowing that unless he can establish a pattern in what he finds he will have no useful information. In addition to comprehending sensory data then, the archeologist must employ a sense of configuration or pattern, basically the integration of data in three dimensions. In short the skilled excavator must have well-developed sensory perception, the ability to integrate sensory data for purposes of discrimination, and the ability to recognize three dimensional patterns.

The implications for teaching are obvious. Instead of starting students with a shovel or trowel, teach them first to sense shape, texture, color, smell, and taste through a series of experiments with, and manipulations of, physical things. Second, they should be taught to discriminate subtle differences among apparently similar sets of physical phenomena and, finally, to offer a reasoned interpretation of the differences they observe. If care has been taken to ensure that the demonstration material actually fulfills the dual objectives of testing student's abilities and of having relevance to archeological situations then students who are unable to deal effectively with laboratory examples may find it impossible to deal with real archeological situations.

In this connection it is imperative for instructors to analyze their own procedures and to learn to verbalize their own methods of discrimination. Some instructors will find that they are as inept as their students; while this may be a sobering experience it will caution them to work diligently to sharpen their own skills before teaching or undertaking additional field work.

Some persons are better suited as field archeologists than others, and some students progress very rapidly from fumbling inexperience to becoming skilled and perceptive excavators. If formal instruction has been essentially equal, this suggests that special talents may be required for digging that not every person shares equally. This is like saying that some persons have an ear for music, an eye for composition, or natural coordination. While all these "natural" talents may be enhanced through intensive training, it has never been shown that a tone-deaf singer can become an operatic star.

Students who are unable to deal perceptively with sensual data can be taught other skills that are just as necessary on an excavation (photography, recording, map-making, etc.), or they can be steered in the direction of analysis, editorial work, or interpretive educational presentation, which do not employ strictly sensory skills. While this may sound harsh, I have the distinct feeling that some persons ought to be kept out of the trenches just as some persons ought to be kept out of chemistry labs, classrooms, or the cockpits of jet aircraft.

I do not think it would serve any useful purpose to bar persons who lack sensual acuity from all field work; indeed it might be detrimental because archeology must be a closely integrated activity: while it is not necessary for the editor or programmer to see how the artifacts came out of the ground, it is imperative for anyone handling primary data to know the circumstances under which they were gathered. The same is true of the person who conceptualizes the project and integrates the data; he must see how his ideas are translated into field work and how the data he integrates were derived.

Archeology is not an easy art and to do it well requires both theoretical knowledge and considerable practical experience. An appreciation of the nature of excavation and archeological data is one of the most important things we can teach a beginning student.

CONCLUDING REMARKS

Using a specific example like digging it is easy to make a convincing argument that serious thought ought to be given to its teaching. It would also be easy to demonstrate that many of the other skills necessary in archeology today must be dealt with separately and with prolonged instruction. It is fruitless for any one person to try to master all aspects of the field. We are thus left with the inescapable conclusion that specialization is necessary. But will it come?

While theoretically specialization within archeology may seem desirable, some would accord its development only a low probability, partly for economic reasons. At a time when specialization is recognized as necessary for rapid and productive science, we are faced with shortages of funds that might have supported the diversification. On the other hand there is a compelling factor that we cannot ignore and which, to my mind, is likely to prevail and thus encourage a shift toward greater specialization: overpopulation. Archeology, like many fields, is currently producing more doctorates than can be absorbed readily in the market or supported as directors of independent projects. In keeping with the general principle (expressed since Darwin's time) that increasing density results in specializations that are contributory and mutually supporting. Since money to fund projects is limited and as sites themselves become scarcer, many archeologists will find themselves prevented from digging their "own site." Through processes such as these the adaptive strategy best suited to the circumstances appears to be specialization. This, I submit, will take place whether the rationale is the need for doing effective science or merely the longing for survival.

20. GETTING ROUND ARCHEOLOGISTS OUT OF SQUARE HOLES

RICHARD B. WOODBURY

Department of Anthropology
University of Massachusetts
Amherst, Massachusetts

It is only about twenty-five years since Walter W. Taylor wrote,

Archeology *per se* is no more than a method and a set of specialized techniques for the gathering of cultural information. The archeologist, as archeologist, is really nothing but a technician [Taylor 1948:43].

He also urged that archeologists interested in anthropology rather
than in such fields as mythology, architecture, or ceramics, should
attempt "to interpret the concrete, empirical findings of archeology
in terms of culture itself, of cultural behavior, and of the nonmaterial
results of cultural behavior" (Taylor 1948:96). Unfortunately, no one
has yet made a convincing application of the approach that Taylor
offered. But the direction in which he urged archeology to move has
been followed, that is, the incorporation of anthropological concepts
and insights into archeological research. Today's archeologists are
likely also to regard themselves as anthropologists (or, less often,
historians), and to view the techniques of archeology as only a small
part of their research strategies. Processual archeology has been
making broader scientific hypotheses amenable to archeological

study, in contrast to the relatively limited and specific questions of cultural history that occupied most of archeology's attention only a few years ago.

But paradoxically, archeology's dependence on a large number of technical activities has been increasing. For example, Hole and Heizer (1969:27) quote with apparent approval the observation of Sir Mortimer H. Wheeler in 1956 that the staff of a major archeological excavation can be expected to include "a director, a deputy director, a supervisor for each area under excavation, a trained foreman, a small-find recorder, a pottery-assistant, a photographer, a surveyor, a chemist, a draftsman" and sometimes an epigraphist or numismatist. Hole and Heizer comment that Wheeler might have added the need for a botanist, a zoologist, and a geomorphologist in many field programs. And this is far from an exhaustive list. To plan research for such a team and coordinate their efforts requires a high level of anthropological training and experience in field investigations. As Binford has written (1964:440): "Field work must be conducted in terms of a running analysis and against a backdrop of the widest possible set of questions to which the data are potentially relevant. This is no technician's job. This is the job of an anthropologist specialized in the collection and analysis of data concerning extinct cultural systems."

It is instructive to compare Flinders Petrie's careful discussion of "Preservation of Objects" (in the field, that is) in his excellent little book, *Methods and Aims in Archeology* (1904), with more recent books on the subject. Petrie was able to discuss fairly satisfactorily in only 20 pages the field techniques available for preserving stone, pottery, textiles, wood, ivory, papyri, beadwork, stucco, gold, silver, copper, bronze, lead, and iron. Fifty years later Wheeler, in *Archaeology from the Earth*, did not even attempt to detail the work of the field laboratory, but referred readers to such authors as Plenderleith, whose *Conservation of Antiquities and Works of Art* (1956) devotes over 300 pages to the topics earlier covered in 20. More recently, *Science in Archaeology*, by Brothwell and Higgs, has added many additional specialized techniques about which the archeologist must be at least minimally informed. This "methods explosion," as Struever aptly calls it (1968c:149) poses both a tremendous challenge to archeology's traditional modes of operation and an opportunity for a major advance in its ability to achieve sound results of broad significance.

There are two aspects to the problem that is posed by these new potentialities. One is the financial and organizational, which Struever (1968c) has commented on with insight and persuasiveness, pointing out that the days of inexpensive, one-year field research programs are over, and long-term funding is needed, together with institutional arrangements that can bring together the requisite skills on more than an *ad hoc* basis. The other aspect of the problem, which I shall briefly discuss here, lies in the area of first training and then employing individuals able to carry out the many highly technical activities that archeology is now in a position to make good use of. It need hardly be argued that the archeologist who plans and directs a research program will rarely be able to carry through most of the specialized investigations in the field and laboratory that may be essential to his program. It is the rare archeologist who is not only an anthropologist but also happens to have had substantial training in metallurgy, or zoology, or pedology, for example, and can therefore undertake some of the analyses that lie within these specialties. But it is equally rare for the undergraduate in an anthropology department, once he or she has indicated an interest in archeology as a subfield, to be directed toward a career in a specialty like archeological surveying and drafting, or dendrochronology, or textile preservation and analysis, much less archeological zoology or electronics. And if thus directed, it would be difficult to justify this specialized training, as things now stand, with assurances of future employment in ongoing programs where these skills would be used appropriately. Instead, we often advise students to secure at least a basic familiarity with all aspects of anthropology, plan on graduate work in an anthropology department with a good archeology faculty, and only when they falter at the master's level do we tell them that their poor prospects of securing a Ph.D. in anthropology make a career in archeology almost out of the question. Thus we lose the potential archeological technician as well as the anthropological archeologist.

This problem is easier to describe, of course, than to solve. In general, schools do not train people for nonexistent jobs, and conversely jobs for which there are no trained candidates seldom appear in tables of organization, since jobs long unfilled are an institutional anathema. The situation has been worsened by the gradual shift of archeology from the museum base from which so much of it operated in the first half of this century to the university base from which most of it now operates. Most museums that were major centers of archeological research a few decades ago are still active and some have expanded, but their archeological staffs are now heavily outnumbered by the archeologists in anthropology departments of universities. By way of illustration of this, it can be noted that of 93 archeological research projects funded by the National Science Foundation between July 1967 and March 1969, 79 originated in colleges or universities, 5 in museums, and 9 in independent research institutes (Division of Social Sciences, N.S.F., annual and quarterly Grant Lists). A few applicants, of course, are based in university museums and their proposals are submitted through a university, but their identification and the adjustment of these figures accordingly would bring only a slight shift in the totals, and many archeologists associated with university museums are supported in whole or part by the budgets of teaching departments.

A significant difference between museums and teaching departments has been that traditionally museums have had nonprofessional staffs, including technicians with little or no graduate training, who were available to carry out the sort of laboratory analyses on which archeology depended. Such positions are extremely difficult to support in the laboratory facilities that can be developed by university teaching departments, since budgets must be strongly focused on teaching, with research funded mainly from intermittent outside sources. Therefore, with a decreasing fraction of archeological research based in our museums, even such technical support as was available in the past has become less common.

Nevertheless, the rational and effective organization of future archeological research makes it essential that we depend on increasing numbers of well-trained and experienced experts in various indispensable ancillary technical activities. A way must be found, as Struever has said, to design and support the essential institutional structures for making use of the resources potentially available to archeology.

But this will also require a change in educational attitudes and practices as well as in institutional structuring. We must find ways to provide two educational routes to careers in archeology rather than the single traditional path. It has long been obvious that not every student with an interest in archeology should be encouraged to aim for the Ph.D. in anthropology, to apply fully their particular archeological talents. Too often we have awarded the master's degree as a second choice degree, implying failure to achieve the doctorate. Those individuals who show promise of becoming technically skillful in one of the supporting specialties of archeology deserve separate educational programs that will be appropriate to careers as archeological technicians, able to play essential roles in major research programs. They will need a combination of courses and experience that we have not precisely defined, much less made regularly available in our curricula. Above all, we must make it clear that such individuals are pursuing a worthwhile program with its own goal, and not merely dropping by the wayside while others continue to the doctorate.

This may be a particularly appropriate moment to expand the opportunities for training and employing archeological technicians, for, as William Clewlow has pointed out (personal communication) the attractiveness of the Ph.D. and the academic life has somewhat faded in the eyes of many students in the last few years. I know that some of them see the criteria for advancement and the preoccupations of their professors as superficial or even fraudulent. They might welcome "working with their hands," as is required in the technical occupations that archeology needs. At the same time this work can be associated with potentially meaningful research on social, cultural, and ecological problems.

Anthropology as a whole has been attracting a growing proportion of undergraduate majors, as shown by the figures of the Behavioral and Social Sciences Survey Committee of the National Academy of Sciences. The number of bachelor's degrees awarded in anthropology rose from 350 in 1957 to 1825 in 1967, more than a fivefold increase (Smith and Fischer 1970:107). In the same period bachelor's degrees in the social and behavioral sciences as a whole increased about two and one-half times and for all fields of academic study the number less than doubled. Forty-nine Ph.D. degrees were awarded in anthropology in 1957, and 163 in 1967, also a more rapid increase than for the social sciences as a whole (Behavioral and Social Sciences Survey Committee 1969:138-150).

Since we do not hope or wish to stem this growth completely, and we cannot expect that traditional careers will fully absorb these growing numbers, it is essential to discover new ways to make good use of some of this enormous human potential for the support of anthropology. For a substantial number of students of anthropology whose primary interest is archeology, careers in the technical aspects of archeology could be more successful and satisfying than in the broader problem-posing and hypothesis-testing aspects.

Two distinct and equally "respectable" kinds of archeological training can be developed, provided we rethink our educational values so that the bachelor's and master's degrees are meaningful stopping places and not mere stepping-stones to the only acceptable goal, the Ph.D. The exact content of these training programs for archeological technicians will require careful planning, and I know of only one substantial start along these lines. From Raymond H. Thompson I recently learned that the University of Arizona's Department of Anthropology, in conjunction with the Arizona State Museum, is providing training in several anthropological fields, including archeology, directed toward the specific career goals of today's students rather than the traditional subdivisions of anthropology. The program already includes training at the master's level for work in ethnic programs, community action programs, junior college teaching, several kinds of museum work, historical archeology, and such archeological research techniques as lithic analysis and tree-ring dating (the last at the university's Laboratory of Tree-Ring Research). Each student receives a basic core of "traditional" anthropology, comprising about a third of the graduate work, with the remainder devoted to training in a particular specialty.

By providing a variety of "career tracks" this University of Arizona curriculum is producing people trained for and oriented to middle level anthropological jobs. This has resulted in the awarding of an increased number of master's degrees, in contrast to the practice of many departments that wish to emphasize the Ph.D. more than the M.A. or M.S. The need for the kind of training Arizona is providing is demonstrated by the fact that jobs are developing for these people, in fact, developing more rapidly than qualified people are becoming available. This is partly a result, as Thompson pointed out to me, of the new attitudes at state and federal levels about the importance of archeological and historical preservation and interpretation, and also a result of the rapid development of legislation requiring more extensive consideration of environmental impact (including the impact on historical and archeological materials) of all kinds of proposed construction and resource use.

Within the field of archeology, Arizona added a new course in 1972-1973, "Archeological Resources Management," to include such topics as current legislation for archeological financing and protection, the planning of salvage work, the costs of archeological survey, stabilization, conservation, and other matters essential to archeologists who will be professionally responsible for programs that are oriented to public archeological needs and not primarily to research.

Many additional college and university programs like this—and different from it, also—will be needed if we are to successfully staff the archeological work of the next two or three decades. They must serve both our growing public archeological programs of preservation and interpretation and the research programs of universities and institutes. These programs will need people who are not now available in sufficient numbers, with a large repertoire of skills that we already know something about and others that are just appearing. More difficult than identifying the necessary technical skills and training for them will be fitting these people into a new social structure for archeological research. No longer can each special kind of analysis be carried out by a colleague in another field who temporarily lays aside his own research and teaching to examine coprolites or animal bones, or design a magnetometer survey, or run spectrographic analyses. The *ad hoc* recruitment of temporary research teams based in many different institutions has never been the best solution to the staffing of archeological research. But to improve on it in a major way we need a bootstrap operation, both to create the trained personnel in numerous specialties and to create the positions they will occupy. This will not be easy, but it will hardly be to the credit of archeology if we look back on the 1970s as the decade when many promising new archeological techniques had to be increasingly ignored for lack of people to carry them through, while at the same time more and more people sought training and careers in archeology.

FIVE

COMMENTARIES

The three chapters in this section discuss the contributions to this volume. The commentaries by Robert McC. Adams (Chapter 21) and William A. Longacre (Chapter 22) respond to the papers presented at the 1971 American Anthropological Association symposium "Archeology's Future: Roles and Relevance" (i.e., Chapters 2, 5, 7, 8, 17, and 20 of this volume). Albert C. Spaulding's discussion (Chapter 23) is a commentary on this complete volume.

Robert McC. Adams suggests that we must maintain diversity within archeology if it is to continue as an active discipline. Specifically, he asserts that archeology has a significant amount to learn from an understanding of the work of modern historians. He cites the development of the "new" economic history as a phenomenon parallel to the development of the "new" archeology. Adams points out that these historians have accomplished the transformation with greater self-awareness and on a sounder data base than contemporary archeologists. Contrary to some of the chapters in this volume, Adams proposes that archeology should maintain a mixture of objectives and continue to include both large-scale multidisciplinary research teams and one-man operations.

William A. Longacre summarizes and critically evaluates the same six chapters and suggests modifications. Longacre raises three important issues on which he is in disagreement with some of the views stated by other authors: there is a necessity for multidisciplinary collaboration in which the collaborators are considered as partners and not as consultants. The theoretical divergence present among archeologists is healthy and should remain. Archeology as a social science can and should be in part a generalizing discipline.

Albert C. Spaulding's comments on specific aspects of some of the chapters are a point of departure for a discussion of what he considers to be the major "pressure points of disharmony" within the field of archeology. He critically evaluates the trends within archeology in order to "clarify the issues and perhaps lessen the discord." Spaulding's discussion divides the chapters in this volume and the problem areas of archeology into four major categories. The first is the intellectual foundations of the discipline. The question here is whether archeologists should follow the methodology of history or science, or both. Spaulding asserts that history is worthwhile, but does not go far enough and that an explicitly scientific approach is necessary for maximum understanding of human behavior. A secondary dispute concerning the intellectual foundations of archeology is between what Kent V. Flannery (Chapter 4) characterized as the law and order people, and the systems people. Spaulding does not see the conflict as drawn by Flannery as one of linear causality versus multivariate systems. Instead he interprets it as a differing emphasis and level of complexity in testing ideas.

Spaulding considers the conflict that exists over intellectual commitments, especially those of archeological field work. Should one attempt to collect all of the data or be specialized and try to answer a specific question? Clearly the extreme of neither position is entirely tenable. He also urges archeologists to attempt to contribute general insights and models as well as borrow them from other disciplines.

Spaulding concludes with a brief discussion of the relevance of archeology. After acknowledging the relevant aspects of archeology that are outlined by authors in this volume Spaulding ponders (as did Einstein) the question: "Why do we devise theories at all?" The answer is simple yet persuasive: "Because we enjoy comprehending."

21. DISCUSSION

ROBERT McC. ADAMS

Oriental Institute
University of Chicago
Chicago, Illinois

A number of contributors, including Patty Jo Watson (Chapter 8) and Bruce G. Trigger (Chapter 7), have made a plea for the maintenance of diversity as a condition of archeology's continuing viability. I find that position persuasive, and would like to support it with further arguments and to outline some of its additional implications.

Like Watson and Trigger, I feel that a scientific study of human behavior requires *both* idiographic and nomothetic elements, and that it is grossly inaccurate and diversionary to equate history with particularizing and then to contrast it with the scientific disciplines. Trigger's suggestion that this false opposition originated in the relative absence of continuity between the prehistoric American aborigines and the European colonists is intuitively reasonable, but we should be less concerned with the etiology of the disease than with its eradication. American archeology is a relatively small discipline, with a brief developmental span and a supply of data that will always be limited to and contingent on its applicability to general theoretical problems. Change through time is its principal axis of investigation. In this respect archeology cannot sustain itself intellectually on its own findings, on systems theory smuggled in from biology, and on the limited body of time-oriented findings that ethnology and social anthropology have offered. Unless the horizons of many archeologists widen to include more of the current work of historians, their own field is likely to wither.

Here is an example from the work of a vigorous and growing group that styles itself as cliometricians or—interestingly enough— "new" economic historians. An article that served as its call to arms has a decidedly familiar ring for American archeologists:

> ... the fundamental methodological feature of the new economic history is its attempt to cast all explanations of past economic development in the form of valid hypothetico-deductive models. This is another way of saying that the new generation seeks to continue an effort that was underway long before it appeared on the scene: namely, the construction of economic history on the basis of scientific methods [R. W. Fogel, "The new economic history: its findings and methods," *Economic Historical Review* 19(1966); reprinted in R. W. Fogel and S. L. Engerman (eds.), "The Reinterpretation of American Economic History" (New York, 1971)].

This intriguing parallelism in outlook and program between quite independent Young Turk movements in archeology and history should interest historians of contemporary science, but more important, this is an example of an enormously fruitful source of innovative ideas, hypotheses, generalizations at all levels, and methods for testing them, of which American archeology's insularity with respect to the field of history as a whole has kept it virtually in ignorance. To pursue the example further, another article speaks of the new economic history's

> ... unabashedly developmental interest. Cliometricians have been concerned with rates of growth rather than levels, with economic aggregates rather than persons, and with production rather than distribution. This has meant an inevitable shift of focus from earlier writings in which the description of the institutional structure was the central objective, and in which much attention was bestowed upon distributional problems reflected in the farmers' discontent, the rise of unions, business concentration, and government regulation. A parallel list of topics covered by the new economic historians would read agricultural productivity, investment in human capital, industrial supply and demand responses, and government promotion of social overhead investment [A. Fishlow and R. W. Fogel, "Quantitative economic history: an interim evaluation" *Journal of Economic History* 31 (1971):18; cf. Habakkuk 1971:305–322)].

Obviously there are not merely parallelisms but structural identities, taking into account the huge disparities between historic and prehistoric data, between what these historians have already done and what the new archeologists still largely aspire to do. Note also that the same article concedes that its approach embodies a gradualist bias, a lack of easy adaptability to problems of handling dynamics and discontinuities, and a nearly absolute neglect of phenomena like entrepreneurship that have a large motivational component (Fishlow and Fogel 1971:31). Those biases also are a pervasive characteristic of archeology, although for the most part we have lacked the insight (or the candor) to recognize them. Archeologists have much to learn from a discipline that has already crossed and recrossed the same terrain with the advantage of far more adequate and diversified data.

Charles Erasmus offers a somewhat similar criticism, extending it to anthropology as a whole rather than confining it to archeology alone:

Explanations in anthropological studies of cultural evolution rely heavily on situational factors viewed as enhancing group survival. Goal-intention explanations are seldom employed unless the writer is basing his model in part on behavior personally observed and not simply on documents and oral history. Studies which are highly "systemic" in their explanatory analyses achieve a high degree of internal consistency by employing limited and unreliable case materials ["Explanation and reconstruction in cultural evolution," *Sociologus* 19(1969):36].

Gradualist, situationalist biases have been, and continue to be, suffused through the new and the old archeology. A wide discrepancy exists, for example, between the dynamism and complexity of some of the major anthropological studies of social process that are currently available, such as Edmund Leach's "Political Systems of Highland Burma" (London, 1954) and the assumption of a steady, inexorable progression toward chiefdom status or statehood with which archeologists generally have been content when they reconstruct the prehistoric record. The variability and instability of closely examined cases like Kachin society strongly suggest that we must deal not with sites but with regions, whose components oscillate in size and structure at different rates through time, interacting differentially with one another in response both to the character of internal leadership and to external pressure.

Similar conclusions emerge from other recent social anthropological studies of state formation. Deep, rapid oscillations in political integration were characteristic of eighteenth- and nineteenth-century West African kingdoms, for example, with small-scale, centralized polities coalescing and quickly disintegrating under the principal stimulus of trade in slaves and guns. Regiments of musket-men, recruited from among prisoners and slaves and cross-cutting the lines of traditional kin loyalties, were an important instrument of aggrandizement among these forest dynasties. But as Jack Goody insists, this innovation and the polities that gave rise to it must be placed within the context of a wider, shifting network of social interactions between state systems and acephalous peoples ("Technology, tradition and the state of Africa," (London, 1971 pp. 18–20, 50, 54–57). With almost identical substantive findings, Henry Rosenfeld's analysis of interactive patterns between Arabian nomads and oasis-dwellers also takes as its starting point a regionally differentiated, rapidly shifting framework of "tribes" and emergent polities ("The social composition of the military in the process of state formation in the Arabian desert," *Journal of the Royal Anthropological Institute* 95 (1965):75–86, 174–194).

These are only a few of the many available leads that would bring archeological constructs of social and cultural change into closer congruence with what happens in the "real world." As Irving Rouse observes in Chapter 2, archeology is and must be an empirical science. We need to make a greater effort to adjust archeological models of change to what is actually known of the processes those models purport to describe.

The failure of the new economic history to come to grips with problems of entrepreneurship has already been mentioned. There is a close archeological cognate, the field of long-range diffusion insofar as it rests not on a sequence of group-to-group transfers of objects but on the goal-directed behavior of long-distance traders and other agents. Studies of entrepreneurs have a substantial place in traditional economic history. In American archeology, however, few would dispute Gordon R. Willey's recent comment that the field has "turned away" from such problems, "even though they arouse the most intense partisanship because they carry with them crucial implications. In spite of some attempts to systematize an approach to long range diffusionistic comparisons . . . , most of us still come down to very impressionistic resolutions of specific cases" (review of J. A. Ford, "A comparison of formative cultures in the Americas," *American Journal of Archaeology* 75 (1971):117).

Willey observes that what is needed is the elaboration and testing of "processual" models of diffusion like those that Kent V. Flannery offered for the spread of Olmec influence ("The Olmec and the valley of Oaxaca," pp. 79–110 in *Dumbarton Oaks Conference on the Olmec* (Washington, D.C., 1968), and William I. Rathje on the lowland Classic Maya ("The origin and development of lowland Classic Maya civilization," *American Antiquity* 36 (1971):275-285). Until this is done on a wider scale and more systematically, archeology will continue to impale itself needlessly on the horns of false dichotomies like diffusion versus independent invention. Those particular terms may now have passed out of fashion. A more up-to-date and no less spurious version is emerging, however, that seems to pit analysts of local ecological settings against specialists in art styles or trade wares. Hence it is not enough to lament the absence of processual accounts of diffusion. We need to reorganize our priorities and then begin the long and difficult job of constructing such accounts ourselves or borrowing them from the historians and then testing them.

There are many strategies and priorities different from those I have been elaborating, and I would not impose my perception of our greatest needs and opportunities on the field at large. But too often we find ourselves arguing acrimoniously over who is and who is not "scientific" at a time when an explosion of methodological and conceptual possibilities has opened new realms of interpretation for adherents of almost any school. Lewis R. Binford, who has contributed perhaps as much as any single individual to our awareness of these possibilities, nevertheless finds it necessary in a recent review to condemn a colleague for not offering strategies that will lead in the direction he favors, toward "theory and the generation of time-less and spaceless, lawlike propositions" (review of "Reconstructing Prehistoric Pueblo Societies," W. A. Longacre, ed., *Science* 172(1971): 1226). The same issue of *Science* carried a splendid rejoinder, addressed to another writer, by Karl W. Deutsch, John Platt, and Dieter Senghaas:

> His notion of "real" science is centered on "explanatory theory," while our operational definition of a major advance called for the discovery of a demonstrable new fact or relationship, or of a repeatable new method or operation, and, in any case, for a major impact on social science. In the work of Maxwell, Hertz, and Marconi, it seems that (he) would have looked for their "explanatory theory," which was the "ether" theory, long since discarded. We would look at Maxwell's equations, Hertz's waves, and Marconi's wireless telegraphy, all of which remained lasting and cumulative contributions even though the accompanying explanatory theories have changed [*Science* 172 (1971):1192].

I have been propounding the general view that archeology must widen its intellectual range, particularly by intensifying its intellectual inputs from history. This is really not a very bold or imaginative position; after all, who would deny the possibility of interdisciplinary stimuli from almost any direction? But as Patty Jo Watson observes in Chapter 8, the "Image of the Limited Good" now rears its head. With the vast proliferation of methodologies and realms of interpretation from the natural sciences for which the archeologist has become responsible, how much more can he be expected to control and assimilate?

Here I must take a more exposed, or certainly more debatable, position. In Chapter 17, Walter W. Taylor alludes briefly to the growing masses of nonartifactual data that were never previously recognized as such, as well as to the increasing sophistication of the ways in which data must be manipulated quantitatively in order to support inferences about subsistence and social organization. He speaks of the "stultifying burden" for many archeologists of the compulsion "to push the data as far as possible, to wring them as dry as science, all science, and controlled imagination can possibly be made to wring them." If the burden is already stultifying, how can we expect to add a generous component of history to it?

Part of the answer is likely to be that the Image of the Limited Good is, after all, only an image. Fields that are seen as sharply opposed alternatives in fact often turn out to be mutually supportive and additive. But to the degree that this is not so, the remainder of the answer is for me inescapable: the field must widen its awareness of the discipline of history at any cost. This means that more students and professionals in archeology should turn their training and interests away from the manipulation of paleoenvironmental data and toward the comparative understanding of historically documented human societies. And in so doing they will be every bit as "scientific" in their approach to the discipline, in any meaningful sense of that term, as any of their colleagues.

Taylor concludes, in my judgment very accurately, that "archeology is in trouble." He speaks of the proliferating requirements of our research, while our resources have failed to keep pace. He feels that we must find new ways to convince academic and foundation administrators that archeological expansion is "natural, necessary, and justified, not merely empire building and self-indulgence. . . . And then we must convince them that these goals and the price of reaching them are justifiable in terms of the scientific and humanistic importance of what we can produce."

This prescription calls for a real tour de force of persuasion. Particularly in a time of budgetary cutbacks throughout the research world, it is doubtful that anyone who is not an archeologist will agree that it is imperative to wring all archeological data dry. How do we propose to adjust the cost and scale of our projects to the importance of their central themes or problems for the social sciences? Are we prepared to say that archeologists must work either at a minute scale on highly specialized issues or else in costly, long-term, multidisciplinary aggregates? A significant reason for the growing importance of archeological reconnaissance as a method is that to a large degree it permits individuals or small teams to avoid both ends of this dilemma.

In short, I have argued for a wider *mix* of archeological objectives and activities, with the epistemological basis of the approaches constituting that mix being subordinated to their efficacy in the production of new knowledge. Biologists say that the condition of "balanced polymorphism" within a species heightens its evolutionary potential to take adaptive advantage of new niches or changed circumstances. For archeology, this means that paleoenvironmental work must continue, but that not all work with a historical focus and lacking an ecological orientation can be regarded as scientifically primitive. Similarly, all large-scale, multidisciplinary projects should not be abandoned. But neither are they innately superior for the production of new knowledge, so they should not drive out small-scale, more narrowly focused, one-man operations.

In scale, as in approach, methodology, and choice of problem, the password for American archeology's cumulative growth is *diversification*.

22. COMMENT

WILLIAM A. LONGACRE

Department of Anthropology
University of Arizona
Tucson, Arizona

I salute the contributors for their interesting and provocative chapters. As some of them have reminded us, it is precisely this kind of interchange that is so important in the avoiding of a tendency toward splintering and a breakdown in communication that we all agree would be so deterimental in achieving our professional goals. I shall comment specifically on Chapters 2, 5, 7, 8, 17, and 20.

I was initially surprised at the broad range of concern expressed by these chapters with respect to relevance and the future of archeology. My expectations for these chapters were much narrower in scope than the reality of topics and concerns reflected in them. I anticipated much more concern with relevance as it is popularly thought of today, the relevance of archeology to our own society, now and in the immediate future. Only John M. Fritz (Chapter 5) has addressed himself specifically to this aspect, and I will comment on his chapter somewhat later.

Bowing to admittedly base archeological instincts, I am tempted to classify these six chapters into three groupings. Two of the authors focus on the future research directions of our discipline as they sense them and have provided sage advice with respect to easing the path toward carrying these endeavors. I refer to Walter W. Taylor (Chapter

17) and Richard B. Woodbury (Chapter 20). Both of them are in essential agreement, I feel, about the immediate research thrust of our field. They see a growing need for a multidisciplinary effort for the solution of anthropological problems, an enterprise that they suggest is central to the immediate future of archeology. Taylor calls for the need to communicate with force the necessity for this enlarged basis of research to the power elite—the "establishment," if you will. He sees this as an imperative task of communication and education in order to gain the critical support of university administrations for larger-scale operations and funding than is traditionally thought of in popular ideas about the doing of archeological research. As one possible solution, Taylor suggests a sort of "clearing-house of expertise"—a liaison between the archeologist and other experts in a broad range of specialties on which the prehistorian relies for assistance in interpretation. I would argue that this may not be the best solution. I feel that the best interdisciplinary research is just that—*research*, conceived of and carried out by researchers, partners in a scientific enterprise designed to test specific hypotheses or solve particular problems together. It requires the active involvement of the co-researchers—developing the research design and planning the appropriate data gathering and attendant practical field operations. This has to be a team effort from the onset. I realize that Taylor's suggestion does not preclude this approach, but I wish to emphasize this at this time. The success of this approach is demonstrated in work that is familiar to us all.

He also supports team efforts in the solution of broad anthropological problems such as the Southwestern Anthropological Research Group's approach. Of course, I concur and emphasize this suggestion on the basis of my own experience. It is an efficient approach to problem solving, bringing to bear a variety of expertise, and encouraging an exciting and enjoyable interaction among anthropologists working on broadly similar problems.

Woodbury presents similar arguments with respect to archeology's future. He sees the need for the training and support of technical specialists within archeology. I call your attention to a current academic experiment along these lines at the University of Arizona. We have been operating a one-year, career-oriented Master's Program designed to provide technical training in a variety of specializations—from junior college teaching to museology, or geochronology, dendrochronology, or National Parks Service preparation. As Woodbury points out, there are problems in the support of such technically trained specialists that must be overcome among the somewhat rigid administrations—especially at the university level.

These two chapters, then, focus explicitly on the more immediate future of archeology in terms of what these senior members of our group recognize as the modern thrust of our discipline.

The second group of chapters (those by Irving Rouse, Bruce G. Trigger, and Patty Jo Watson) adopts a more philosophical point of view, exploring what the authors feel is a growing tendency toward schism in archeology. Their concern is with a resolution of conflict, a coming together, an intensification of communication, a more efficient use of our energy. I have mixed reactions toward these chapters. On the one hand, I share their discomfort from stressful interaction—especially at a personal level. I agree that our common interests override the relatively minor conflicts we enjoy. On the other hand, I am convinced that there are real points of divergence at a theoretical and methodological level in our profession. I would not like to see these minimized as I think this would be detrimental. The stimulation that these differences provide—the excitement and interest that we are currently enjoying is basic to the surge in research excellence, teaching, and general creativity in archeology today. I would hate to see that lessened. Let me turn to more specific comment and reaction. Irving Rouse shows his interest and skill in classifications in his division of the archeological world into three classes. Normally I do not protest nomenclature that I find fault with as long as the proponent makes his meaning clear. I know that Rouse has thought deeply—even agonized over his choice of label for the three types of archeology he discusses. My discomfort over his classifications can be focused by reference to his terminology, however. First, Rouse has (as has Watson) emphasized the relevance of the various approaches to archeology. He has done this skillfully and incisively, and I hope my comments do not distract from his valuable efforts.

The labels themselves have been used and have come to be associated with specific archeological endeavors that have somewhat different meanings from those defined by Rouse. Thus, analytic archeology brings to mind the artifact-oriented systems theory approach expounded by David L. Clarke in his book, *Analytical Archaeology* (1968).

Experimental archeology has come to mean technical experimentations with raw materials and other facets of material culture to get at processes of manufacture, wear, and deposition. This term brings to mind the work of Crabtree, Bordes, and Tixier in lithic technology, and other such studies.

I find I must disagree with his rejection of the label "scientific archeology" as proposed by Watson, LeBlanc, and Redman (1971) in their recent book. But perhaps one could call this "deductive archeology" and contrast this with Rouse's "synthetic archeology" or "inductive archeology." These terms mask the truth, too, because there are inductive and deductive facets in both approaches to the doing of archeology. I am more sympathetic to the term scientific archeology because of the focus on the explicit and rigorous application of the scientific method, which I would characterize as the setting up of a hypothesis, the deduction of consequences (observational predictions or test implications), and the testing of the hypothesis and its alternatives against independent data. In the testing, of course, there is an interplay between deduction and induction. Also disagreeing with Rouse, I think this is what Chamberlain had in mind in his method of Multiple Working Hypothesis rather than the consideration of various plausible explanations for already gathered evidence and selection of the one most plausible on the basis of best fit. This is not a test but a statement of plausibility that, in order to be tested, would have to be evaluated against independent data utilizing the scientific method as I outlined it above. At best, this seems to be an inefficient method. I wonder, too, if the utilization of "scientific expertise" in the doing of archeology necessarily makes it scientific.

All of us sense the interrelationship among the various approaches to archeology—all of us also recognize the differences. Rouse has done a valuable job in articulating these facets and has done much to facilitate communication and understanding. I am especially glad to see this development and the excellent contributions toward an understanding rapprochement by Rouse, Watson, and Trigger. If their efforts and others in a similar vein help ease the hostility and *ad hominen* arguments that typified the late 1960s, then their contributions will be especially valuable. I am impressed with their ability to plumb the interrelations among the kinds of archeology, while at the same time keeping the healthy differences in full focus. Emphasis on the commonality and the profound differences keeps the excitement alive and promotes communication within the discipline—all essential if we are to advance the frontiers of knowledge, method, and theory of archeology.

Watson emphasizes the need for different approaches to problem solving in archeology. As usual, she has presented a thoughtful and lucid statement encouraging continued debate, communication, and rapprochement.

Like Trigger, she argues that history and science are really not that different—in fact perhaps only different in emphasis. Like Rouse, she calls for a "maximum, sympathetic interaction . . . between particularists and generalists who understand each other's problems and respect each other's concerns and methods."

I fully concur with that eloquent statement. Both sides in the theoretical and methodological debate that has caused such ferment in our discipline must exhibit more tolerance and respect for each other's interests and work. This is not to discourage constructive criticism, not only useful but critical to our continued growth. Watson gives some examples, including the paper by Richardson and Allen (1971). These authors, pointing out the cognitive nature of descent, argue that archeology cannot possibly uncover it. Their criticism of my own work is proper, and they and other colleagues and students have caused me to reject my view and claim that I had dealt with prehistoric lineality and descent. I disagree with Allen and Richardson in that I am more optimistic about our ability to get at descent. But I think we will have to test alternative hypotheses through biological data as well, rather than simply through pot sherds and arrowheads, as in the past.

My reaction to Trigger's provocative chapter is more complex. Perhaps this is because I am still a little unclear about what exactly he is arguing. I suspect there is a communications problem here. For one thing, I view archeology as an integral part of anthropology— involving a much more fundamental kinship with other kinds of anthropology than just the sharing of general concern with the behavior of man and his works. The various kinds of anthropology are bound together by the sharing of specific goals that in turn are translated into shared interest in the solution of problems of concern to anthropology; differences lie more noticeably in techniques that are applied. Thus, to argue that one kind of anthropology is law consuming and another is law creating makes little sense to me and denies the larger context of the discipline.

But perhaps Trigger would argue that anthropology as a whole is at least relatively idiographic within the realm of social sciences. If so, he would be reinforcing the paradigm that stresses the nonexistence of laws to cover cultural things—a paradigm that was gradually accepted in American anthropology during the 1930s and 1940s and that can be found in the writings of Boas. By 1940, he was able to state: "On account of the uniqueness of cultural phenomena and their complexity, nothing will ever be found that deserves the name of a law" (Boas 1940:311).

Closely tied to this belief is the paradigm that one negative example falsifies a law. To be a law, the relationship expressed by the statement must be universal, what Trigger calls a covering law. He intimates that this kind of law holds in the physical sciences but not for natural history and archeology, that we must be idiographic.

He takes some of us to task for our inaccurate portrait of modern historical research, and rightly so. But his view of the role of theory in the physical sciences is a little out-of-date as well. The so-called covering law paradigm does not hold for the physical sciences today any more than it does for anthropology.

We might do better to speak of "probabilistic causality." As Marvin Harris put it: "In expressing the principles of uniformitarian relationships, we speak only of *similar* variables under *similar* conditions tending to give rise to *similar* consequences" (1971:594).

This issue is raised in post-Einsteinian physics in Hersenberg's principle of indeterminacy: probability versus certainty.

Trigger argues that archeologists do, and indeed must, rely on outside sources for laws or general theory because of the nature of our data and our focus.

Michael Schiffer in papers presented in 1970 and 1971, has presented persuasive arguments to the contrary. He points to the broad use of laws and lawlike statements in archeological interpretation. Some are indeed adopted or adapted from other disciplines, like the law of superpositioning and uniformitarian theory—but others are archeologically specific.

Most of these, he suggests, tend to be truisms held by practicing archeologists or "common sense propositions" (1970:3). In some part, our evaluation of inferences about the past is often based on our faith in certain of these lawlike relationships, seldom made explicit through what the Binfords (1968:2) had called "arguments of relevance." Examples include the presence of domesticates in a site (all things being equal) revealing the practice of agriculture, or the common occurrence of particular styles in a prehistoric site reflecting the peoples cognitive model for doing things—the mental template.

Recently, broader statements, essentially untested, have appeared; for example: the materials in an archeological site are patterned and their structure is determined primarily by the organization and behavior of the (now-extinct) society that produced them.

If one is interested in testing hypotheses about behavioral or organizational aspects of extinct societies, one can deduce from the implications of this "law" test predictions for the patterned array of material in a site *vis à vis* aspects of sociopolitical organization.

As Lewis and Sally Binford stated it:

Archeological theory consists of propositions and assumptions regarding the archeological record itself—its origins, its sources of variability, the determinants of differences and similarities in the formal, spatial, and temporal characteristics of artifacts and features and their interrelationships [1968:2].

In conclusion, I feel that archeology as anthropology is at least in part a generalizing science. This statement follows from the acceptance of the argument that archeology is a viable social science and that archeology, as a kind of anthropology, is therefore not necessarily a totally idiographic enterprise. This, of course, is not to deny that archeology can be idiographic in its research depending in large measure on the beliefs and interests of individual archeologists, a point most clearly made by Rouse.

The third subject dealt with in these chapters is the relevance and, by extension, the future of archeology. I agree with John M. Fritz (Chapter 5) in this matter. His lucid and tightly reasoned statement suggests that the answer lies primarily in the generalizing social science contributions of our discipline as a part of the larger contributions of anthropology. This certainly does not deny the value of other areas of contribution, but I am convinced that his appraisal is correct.

23. ARCHEOLOGY IN THE ACTIVE VOICE: THE NEW ANTHROPOLOGY

ALBERT C. SPAULDING

Department of Anthropology
University of California
Santa Barbara, California

The chapters in this volume represent the thinking of new, middle-aged, and old North American archeologists on the current condition of the intellectual foundations, research methods, and relevance of the enterprise commonly known as archeology. Most readers will be aware that the occasion for this stock-taking is the completion of approximately 10 years of vigorous questioning of the customary habits of thought and action of archeologists. The body of concepts and recommendations produced in this period is the "new archeology." As is the case with most intellectual turning points, the new archeology has antecedents, and they extend back at least to Kluckhorn (1940), Taylor (1948), and Steward and Setzler (1933). But the existence of antecedents does not preclude originality; the new archeology is indeed new in its full-bodied insistence on the scientific model with explicit theory, rigorous logical analysis, and hypothesis-guided research. Perhaps more important is a shift in presuppositions on the nature of human social behavior and the relationship of archeological data to this social behavior. Briefly, the new archeologists do not accept limitations on our ability to generalize on past human behavior based on (1) a conviction that the behavior was (and

337

is) inherently idiosyncratic because of the special character of human nature and (2) a conviction that the archeological record is so deficient and capricious that we cannot hope to proceed far in our understanding of past societies. Instead, they argue that we must assume the operation of general laws and processes at all levels of human cultural development and that the archeological record reflects this lawfulness, thus providing the logical justification for the application of scientific method. These notions have a very great merit: whether they are right or wrong, they set forth a factual claim that can be tested by research. Certainly we will never know how deep our understanding can be unless we try to increase it by searching for order in the empirical data. Unfortunately, this development has been accompanied by "hostility and *ad hominem* arguments that typified the late 1960s" (William A. Longacre, Chapter 22), and not all of this unpleasantness can be attributed to the snarling resistance of those whose comfortable habits are threatened by the pure light of reason. It is my purpose here to discuss what I take to be the pressure points of the disharmony in an attempt to clarify the issues and perhaps to lessen the discord. I am pleased that a number of the chapters (in particular, that by Watson) exhibit the same attitude. Apparently others share my view that we have had more than enough of shrill preaching on the one hand and postures of amused condescension on the other. My discussion will be conducted under four major categories: intellectual foundations, implications for research, the place of archeology in the intellectual disciplines, and the relevance of archeology.

In this volume, a number of chapters are specifically directed to the intellectual foundations, and most at least touch on the subject. In broad terms, we have conflicting claims for archeology as history (or as a humanity) and for archeology as a science, with various interpretations of the implications of each claim. We may note that the arguments have a familiar ring because similar disputes have come up in connection with other aspects of social science. In fact, Adams (Chapter 21) points to a striking parallel (or identity) within history itself—the new economic history with its call for explanation "in the form of valid hypothetico-deductive models" (Fogel 1966). Again in broad terms, we can distinguish at least three main contenders for truth: (1) archeology is concerned with the activities of past humans, and this concern places it squarely within the domain of history with its special resources and limitations, particularly its distinctive mode of explanation; (2) archeology is an attempt to explain past human activities, the only valid form of explanation is nomological in character, and the only procedure we have to produce the valid laws required for nomological explanation is the scientific method; and (3) history and science are indeed distinctive fields of inquiry but each has its special merits and archeology should draw on the methods of both for maximum comprehension of past human behavior.

1. Clearly archeology and history are linked by a common interest in past human activities and their chronological relationships, and in this sense archeology is history; in fact, the two fields overlap in subject matter, as Robert J. Braidwood (Chapter 3) emphasizes. If history possesses a special mode of understanding, then surely archeology should attempt to apply it. At this point, we are starting down a well-worn path, and there is no escape from the journey. There is an extensive literature expounding adroitly the thesis that history does have a special, an irreducibly historical, kind of explanation of its data. This thesis is associated with statements on the emergent quality of human behavior, sometimes including references to rationality, free will, moral and esthetic values, the fundamental complexity of human affairs, and the like. Science, it is alleged, simply cannot cope adequately with the complexity and uniqueness of the events with which history is concerned because of the scientific commitment to the rigidly deductive covering law or nomological conception of explanation. And further, even within science there are disciplines (characteristically nonexperimental disciplines), exemplified by historical geology and paleontology, that deal with individual events in all their complexity, and in these disciplines the peculiarly scientific kind of explanation by deduction from universal laws must be supplemented by the peculiarly historical kind of explanation. (For a critique of this view, see Watson 1969). There are, then, two kinds of intellectual disciplines: the idiographic disciplines represented by history itself and the historical sciences and the nomothetic disciplines represented paradigmatically by physics. The idiographic disciplines are particularizing: they attempt to explain particular events in all or, at any rate, some of their complexity. The nomothetic disciplines are generalizing: they seek understanding through the process of formulating laws and theories of ever-increasing scope that unite selected aspects of individual events in increasingly broad classes as the process continues. Both disciplines conform to a basic standard of scrupulous objectivity, and this is the reason that we call them "disciplines." In this view, history enjoys a separate but equal

status with generalizing science; it is linked with science by the common standard of objectivity in the treatment of data, and it is distinguished from science by its ability to explain at least to some degree complex individual events by peculiarly historical kinds of explanations. (It would be more accurate to say non-nomological explanations rather than "peculiarly historical" explanations, but the context of our argument is history versus science, and in fact philosophers of history are prominent in the attack on the nomological concept.) Leading candidates for historical explanation as opposed to nomological explanation are (my account here is drawn from Hempel, 1965) the "how possibly" explanation (discussed by Bruce G. Trigger in Chapter 7), the genetic explanation, the explanation by concept, dispositional explanation, and explanation by reasons (or rational explanation). These claims for explanations free from the covering law requirement have a striking feature in common—they are all false.

2. I will not attempt a lengthy paraphrase of the logical analysis leading to this sweeping conclusion; I refer doubting readers to Brodbeck (1962) and Hempel (1965). Briefly, it can be shown that all of the candidates merely conceal or disguise the underlying regularity that makes possible explanation in the strong sense of an intelligible answer to a why-question about some aspect or aspects of an observed phenomenon (for example, why are large stone projectile points common in the Archaic Period of North America?). The nomological model asserts that all such explanations involve, explicitly or implicitly, a demonstration that the phenomenon to be explained is an instance of a general relationship (an empirical generalization or a scientific law), either an invariant relationship or a probabilistic or statistically nonrandom relationship. In the case of the invariant relationship, we speak of deductive-nomological explanations because the invariance allows us to deduce with logical certainty the occurrence of the particular event to be explained when we know that the event is indeed an instance of the invariant relationship. (Crudely, why did this object expand when it was heated? Because it is a piece of iron, and iron invariably expands when it is heated). If the covering law is statistical in nature, we cannot explain a particular event with logical certainty, but we can say something about the class of events to which it belongs. Thus we cannot deduce that a particular toss of an unbiased coin will result in a head, but we can say on the basis of mathematical probability theory that such an event will occur in about half of a large number of tosses and add that we need not

be surprised by its occurrence with this toss. Hempel accordingly recognizes two varieties of nomological explanation, deductive-nomological and statistical-nomological; both are nomological because the explanation is achieved by subsumption under, respectively, universal or statistical laws. Statistical explanation can be further divided into deductive-statistical and inductive-statistical types, but this distinction is not essential to the sketch of an argument that I am making.

3. Granted that the nomological model of explanation is correct, what are we to conclude about the archeology is history versus archeology is science controversy? Obviously, we flatly reject the notion that archeology should be history because history has a special kind of explanation peculiarly suited to the understanding of human behavior. If this is the case, what is the character of history, and what, if anything, can archeologists learn from historians? On the character of history, we must concede that historians do produce explanations, often very skillful and satisfactory explanations, of human behavioral events as opposed to merely providing objective and chronologically arranged descriptions of events. The explanations must be implicitly nomological in character because no other basis is possible for serious explanation; there are universal or statistical generalizations lurking somewhere in the background or there would be no explanations of historical events. It seems to me that the answer is that historians characteristically explain events by implicit references to well-known empirical generalizations on human dispositions, as other authors have concluded before me. The existence of this prior body of commonly accepted explanatory generalizations explains the idiographic character of history: the historian and his readers share the explanatory generalizations, and there is no real need to make them explicit for understanding; the primary need is rather for the historian to supply the facts that make it possible to apply the generalizations to historical events—to solve puzzles by acquiring new information. This view of the basic character of history provides a plain answer to the history versus science question. History is not an intellectual discipline separate from but equal to science. Instead, it is an incomplete discipline because it lacks the explicit and well-developed theory-building aspect that is a fundamental characteristic of true science. This is precisely what the hypothetico-deductive economic historians tell us: they argue that the data of economic history can be and should be used for scientific purposes (that is, theory building and testing) as well as for conventional historical pur-

poses. And this is also the assertion of the new archeologists: archeological data can and should be used for scientific in addition to
historical purposes. The phrase "in addition to" is crucial for understanding. There is nothing wrong with the historical discipline so far
as it goes; it gives us reliable information and illuminating explanations. Archeologists should be and in fact are historians in the sense
that they should be familiar with and do operate with the well-established explanatory principles of history, with common-sense
knowledge of human proclivities, and the history versus science argument turns into the question of whether or not history goes far
enough. Do we already know well enough how humans behave,
leaving to archeologists only the task of illustrating the behavior with
a full set of chronologically ordered materials from the past? Or is it
the case that the present and future data of archeology will yield significantly greater understanding if we are diligent in the search for
uniformities by means of the endless scientific process of hypothesis
formation, testing of the material implications of the hypothesis,
formation of new hypotheses, and so on? Are the present defi-
ciencies in our understanding solely a combination of lack of sufficient evidence and the incorrigibly stubborn chanciness of human affairs, or are they also to be attributed, at least in part, to our failure to
ask the right questions of the evidence and to conduct our research
in the light of these questions? No one, I think, has unequivocal
answers to these questions. We simply do not know what the result of
a fully scientific archeology of the future might be. But we do know
we will never approach an answer if we do not try to develop a scientific archeology, and we do know that a scientific archeology must incorporate the evidence and valid empirical generalizations of history.

The foregoing remarks comprise the main part of my own
Hempel-mongering. They are intended to provide—more accurately,
to point to—the principal intellectual reasons for concluding that an
explicitly scientific archeology is not only desirable but also necessary
if we aspire to a maximum understanding of human behavior in the
past. They also contained an admonition against neglecting the valid
results of research in the historical mode because there is no merit in
attempting to prove that the predecessors of the new archeologists
did not accomplish that which they obviously have accomplished on
the ground that they did not use the right words. The task is to recast
these accomplishments in the scientific mode and get on with the
business of new research in an explicitly scientific manner.

This work will be facilitated by the exercise of care in exposition and thinking by the new archeologists. In reading the unedited manuscripts of this volume, I accumulated 20 pages of critical comments on predominantly minor points—for instance, the contributors misspelled "idiographic" as "ideographic," a practice that does not suggest profound consideration of the philosophical underpinnings of our current debates. This careless error points to the existence of a considerable body of "mouthtalk" (in the sense of Service 1969). In this vein, I would suggest that archeologists who are genuinely concerned with intellectual foundations should investigate more thoroughly the connotation of such high-sounding terms as "model," "parameter," and other favorites. Above all, the investigation should consist of considerably more than consulting the works of other archeologists; as the example of "idiographic" shows, fellow archeologists (and even fellow social scientists) are not a reliable guide in these matters. As a final comment in the peevish vein, I suggest that solemn "explications" of the obvious (there are examples in this volume) should be leavened by an occasional smile of self-deprecation.

A more serious criticism of rampageous scientism is offered by Steven A. LeBlanc (Chapter 13). His warning against the strange notion that the data used in formulating a hypothesis cannot be used to test the hypothesis is not an idle exercise; the fallacy is exhibited in clear form in Chapter 14 by Leonard Williams, David H. Thomas, and Robert Bettinger. These authors state that: "Since hypothesis testing (verification) always necessitates data *independent* from those involved in the hypothesis formation (induction), the 13 randomly selected 500 square meter tracts [the tracts previously studied] were excluded from the 1971 survey. Thus no sites involved in forming the theory of Reese River settlement patterns were included in the sample selected to test this theory." The emphasis on "independent" is the authors'. According to this interpretation, the hypothesis would have been forever unverifiable if it had happened that it was formulated after all of the Reese River sites had been inspected, and we would also have to conclude that the sites previously studied were somehow not really Reese River sites. This example is an interesting one (I might almost say, with tongue in cheek, a paradigmatic model) because it is embedded in a useful and competent research program. I considered the scheme of making my contribution to this volume simply an analytical commentary on the Williams, Thomas, and Bettinger chapter but decided that such a commentary would be both unwise and unfair. It would be unwise because I wish to defend and encourage the main driving force of the new archeology, the attempt to develop a truly scientific archeology. It would be unfair because the chapter is not an egregious example of "Models for the Methodology of Mouthtalk" (the phrase is Service's 1969), it is simply a readily available example and on balance it is a good chapter because it presents some very worthwhile data on the piñon-juniper ecotone settlements of the Great Basin. Anticipating my next topic, we seem to have a case of runaway positive feedback among the new archeologists.

History versus science is the first major pressure point in contemporary archeology; the second is the conflict within science between the law and order people and the systems people described in Kent V. Flannery's spirited chapter. In Flannery's view, the opposition can be characterized as explanation through covering laws versus a systems theory framework; belief in linear causality versus belief in complex, multivariate, and mutual causality; reliance on statistical correlation as a revealer of laws versus simulation as a revealer of process; and belief in the present relevance of archeology to the modern world versus skepticism on present relevance and unwillingness to speculate on future relevance. The question of relevance seems to me to be an accidental inclusion in this context, and I will not discuss it here. The heart of the conflict is, instead, in how the systems theory framework is conceived and in the nature of the advances in understanding to be expected from the systems theory approach.

The putative conflict between a covering law approach to the understanding of cultural behavior and a systems theory approach is neatly disposed of by LeBlanc in Chapter 13. The systems framework is in no sense a logical alternative to law-seeking inquiry either in methods of hypothesis formulation and testing or in explanation. The kinds of relationship dealt with in the systems approach are in fact no more than complex examples of laws or proposed laws, and scientific explanations of individual cultural systems must be attained by subsumption under these covering laws. There is no escape from the covering law if we are to explain anything. Moreover, the existence of the complex relationships postulated by systems theorists can be established only through establishing the existence of the numerous lower level component relationships that, taken together, constitute the more complex systemic relationship. If there is a conflict between the law and order archeologists and the systems archeologists, it is not because the two approaches are contrastive in a logical sense. Everyone must be a "law" man or there will be no discernible order, systemic or otherwise. We must look elsewhere for the source of the differences that Flannery perceives, and the search will require some clarification of the nature of systems theory.

There are two levels of systems theory, general systems theory and just systems theory. Those who work with just systems theory simply apply concepts about systems to their investigations of whatever particular manifestations of systems they are concerned with (cultural systems in our case). On the other hand, as stated by Miller (1972), general systems theorists "accept the more daring and controversial position that—though every living system and every level is obviously unique—there are important formal identities of large generality across levels. These can potentially be evaluated quantitatively, applying the same model to data collected at two or more levels." I confine myself at the moment to just systems theory, that is, to cultural behavior considered as a system or set of systems and take as an entry Flannery's distinction between believers in linear causality and those who "prefer feedback models in which causality is multivariate and mutual."

The main issue here is the nature of cultural behavior, and there is no doubt of the general correctness of the systems view, the view of causality in culture as multivariate and mutual. Past and present cultures are systems in this reasonable sense; the various patterned activities comprising the repertory of a given culture do in fact mutually influence each other to some degree, and they also interact with the noncultural environment. A change in activity A causes a change in activity B, and the new state of activity B in turn causes a further change in activity A thus opening the door for the use of such concepts as homeostasis, positive and negative feedback, oscillation, and others. Flannery's linear causality people deal with only one aspect of these complicated reflexive relationships, the straightforward relationship of A causes B, B causes C, and so on. The systems people, in contrast, face up squarely to the complexity of things as they are (or were). Clearly all the virtue lies on the side of the systems people when the matter is put in this way. The linear causality people are guilty of sins of omission, and they had better mend their ways under penalty of the displeasure of all right-thinking archeologists. They should also purge themselves of the statistical naiveté, confusion of causality and correlation, and Mickey Mousism that Flannery detects (and so do I). But, regrettably, Flannery does not rest the case there; he goes on to contrast simulation and correlation, to cast suspicion on the existence of covering laws specific to human behavior, to voice skepticism of linear causality, and otherwise to exhibit symptoms of infection by general systems theory.

This remark seems to promise an incisive discussion of general systems theory and its implications for archeology, but that promise will be hard to keep, chiefly because I have never grasped just what general systems theory is. Put baldly, what important new insights on past cultural behavior are offered by the observation that thermostats, slime molds, and cultural systems exhibit feedback behavior? The existence of the analogy (or formal identity, if you prefer) is not in question; instead, the question is what further implications the analogy has for the archeologist. A very plain answer is given by Buck (1956). In his analysis, the general systems theory of that date consistently failed to explain the inferences that can be made from the analogy or analogies between systems other than the fact that they exist, and he concludes (p. 223) that general systems theory is not science at all. It is instead an example of a degeneration of programmatic science into "naive and low-grade speculative philosophy." More recently, Doran (1970:294) questioned the effectiveness of general systems theory (and the linked field of cybernetics) in archeology on the ground that the "terminology and concept framework within which facts and ideas are to be expressed seem dangerously vague. Although concepts such as dynamic equilibrium, positive feedback, Markov process, redundancy are all capable of mathematical definition, it is not these definitions which the proponents of systems theory have used, but rather the imprecise ideas which give rise to the definitions." The value of general systems theory and incorporated concepts from cybernetics is, then, essentially heuristic: no great new truths are revealed, but it can in fact stimulate archeologists to examine their data in new ways.

The vague, inconclusive character of the general systems (living systems division) and cybernetics approach ensures the reasonableness of Flannery's skepticism on the existence of an undiscovered set of covering laws specific to human behavior. Cultures are living systems, and the behavioral relationship within and among cultures can always be described in terms of the concepts of systems processes— positive and negative feedback, dynamic equilibrium, and so on. In this very broad sense, no living system can do anything that is not an example of a systems process, and obviously there are no valid gener-

alizations specific to human behavior. But the mere fact of the existence of broad analogies among living systems does not increase our
understanding of human living systems if our only conclusion from
the analogies is the fact of their existence. I am unaware of any
demonstration that further inferences important to the understanding of cultural systems can be drawn from the analogies of
general systems theory, and I doubt that there is any basis for further
inferences. Until we have such a demonstration, general systems
theory can make no progress, although it undoubtedly has some
heuristic value. One thing that is clear is that human cultural
behavior exhibits properties not found in other living systems, and it
is precisely this peculiarly human way of behaving that is our subject.
In this sense, it is not only reasonable but also necessary to search for
valid generalizations on these peculiarly human ways of doing things.
If we cannot attain such generalizations, there is no special science of
human behavior. We can only repeat endlessly that this or that chunk
of cultural behavior is an example of positive feedback or something
of the sort; we could also repeat endlessly the equally true generalization that humans, like other physical objects, when falling freely
near the surface of the earth accelerate at approximately 32 feet per
second per second. I conclude with Flannery but with my own
emphasis that we should be concerned with "a search for the ways
human populations (*in their own way*) do the things that other living
systems do." The phrase "in their own way" is the essence of the
matter.

I emerge from this line of argument with no great admiration for
either law and order archeologists or systems archeologists as
described by Flannery. In caricature, I reject both those who refuse
to consider anything but simple-minded one-way causal relationships
and those who keep promising us dazzling revelations on Upper
Paleolithic or Hopewellian cultures through contemplation of slime
molds. I do not reject the concept of cultural causality as characteristically multivariate and mutual, although I am by no means sure that
everything is so neatly articulated that there are no useful applications of the concept of linear causality. My rejections do not deny the
usefulness of working with simple correlations and associations to
achieve elementary and partial understanding of selected aspects of
the cultural process, and I further suppose that the complex ordered
assumptions needed for the mathematical models underlying digital
computer simulation of cultural process are in fact built up from
knowledge of these simpler relationships. And I am quite sure that

any genuinely new and broader understanding of cultural systems will result from explanations based on subsuming the manifestations of particular cultural systems under well-established covering laws dealing with the operation of cultural systems in a more general way. Further, I am quite sure that such powerful laws will contain ingredients not found in generalizations applicable equally to all or to any particular nonhuman living system.

In summary of the status of intellectual foundations, there is a major split between the historians and the scientists with the new archeology securely in the camp of the scientists and a secondary split in the scientific camp between those who emphasize systems theory, particularly general systems theory, and those who do not. The resolution of the history versus science conflict is easy. The historians are flatly in error in arguing for a logical distinction between science and history and on shaky ground in the factual claim that human behavior is either so obviously the product of well-known human dispositions or, above that level, so capricious that an active program of hypothesis formulation and testing is doomed to futility. The new archeologists are surely right in arguing that we will never know what we can learn about past human behavior in the absence of a vigorous program of hypothesis formulation, careful research in the light of the hypothesis formulated, and so on in the endless scientific spiral of interaction between theory and observation. The secondary split between the general systems people and other scientific archeologists seems to me to be much less important. This is the kind of division that will be resolved by research and theory construction, and I think the resolution will take the form of an elevation to a reasonable employment of systems concepts by those who like to proceed one step at a time and a deflation to a reasonable employment of systems concepts by those who are attracted by the overarching, ecstatic character of unrestrained general systems theory. These conclusions are sharply at odds with those expressed in several of the chapters of this volume, and they are in agreement with those of other chapters. We can say, at least, that we are not discussing dead issues, although I feel strongly that some of the issues should be dead.

Broad statements on basic intellectual commitments are all very well, but if the commitments are to lead to anything but talk they must have implications for archeological action. These implications have been recognized by the new archeologists, although there is a note of moderate desperation on the problems of assembling and organizing the required apparatus of multidisciplinary teams, of designing and acquiring the information-recording and- coordinating machinery needed, and of maintaining a scientifically oriented archeology in the face of pressing salvage problems. On these problems, I have little to add to the comments of Walter W. Taylor, Richard B. Woodbury, George J. Gumerman, Frank Hole, James A. Brown and Stuart Struever (see Section IV) and others in this volume. The major implications for action are now familiar to most of us from numerous statements: effective archeological research requires planning and execution in the light of clear hypotheses; the guiding hypothesis must be formulated in the light of the multivariate, systemic, reflexive causal relationships characteristic of cultural activities; and the resulting information should be treated as a base for inferences on the nonmaterial activities of the societies whose cultural systems are represented by the archeological data. A pervading but not logically necessary theorem is the conviction that the innovations in the environmental-technological relationship have a certain pride of place in the process of cultural transformation—that the trigger actions for change after a period of relative stability are usually new ways of dealing with the noncultural environment.

There is perhaps less difference in some respects between the field practices of the old and the new archeology than is supposed by certain spokesmen. There is, nevertheless, a real difference, and it cannot be explained away by defenders of the past who are annoyed by the millennial tone of recent writing. The elaborate organization of archeologists, paleolimatologists, palynological botanists, macrobotanists, zoologists, ecologists, and others described by Brown and Struever (Chapter 16) and their effective and active cooperation in field and laboratory studies is a far cry from asking a museum or university colleague to identify a few animal bones brought in from the field. The justification for such a gigantic enterprise is the underlying conception of the generally orderly, lawful, systemic character of human activities and the additional conviction that the order is reflected to a substantial degree in the form and locus and other depositional circumstances of the materials recovered. The new archeologists are willing (at least in theory) to face up to the difficult analytical procedures needed to detect and explain the order, beginning with carefully designed sampling programs in the field and culminating in computer-assisted statistical analyses of the form and context of the material. With this background, it is difficult to avoid intellectual paralysis (the stultifying burden, in Taylor's words); how does one go about collecting and interpreting *all* of the relevant data if practically everything may be relevant because of the pervasive interconnectedness of various kinds of human activities with each other and with the nonhuman environment? The answer, of course, in archeology and elsewhere is that one cannot proceed in all directions at once. Instead, one must gear his research to the confirmation or rejection of a hypothesis or hypotheses—he must conduct problem-oriented research.

Problem-oriented research as a method cannot be opposed. Nobody is willing to defend the converse, which is aimless digging and random comparison of artifacts. It is possible, however, to entertain some misgivings on some of the implications seen by some of the enthusiasts. The fundamental uneasiness comes from the fear that specialized field procedures will result in the destruction of data at least as important as that which is recovered. Archeology is not an experimental science in any reasonable sense: archeological deposits are finite in number and excavations cannot be repeated endlessly in the manner of experiments with balls rolling down an inclined plane. This fact seems to dictate a maximizing strategy for the conduct of excavations. We should observe everything that the current state of archeological theory indicates may have a significant relationship to past human behavior. We are thereby led to Taylor's stultifying burden, and, even worse, we are in the position of never doing field research at all because we cannot anticipate the observations that will be required by future theoretical developments. This is an old dilemma, which has been circumvented in the past by happy unconcern; by arguments from the salvage concept (any information is better than none); by the realistic recognition that we will never get anywhere if we do not start; and by the conviction that there is a ceiling on theoretical development, that we already have enough knowledge on general tendencies in human behavior and cannot hope to attain more by finicking excavation techniques. The last argument is an unadorned restatement of the historical position, and it is flatly rejected by those archaeologists, new or old, who are committed to the scientific position. But the scientific rejection of simpleminded historicism and its simpleminded inductive strategy does not justify an equally simpleminded problem-oriented approach —we do not throw away the potsherds because our hypothesis is concerned with projectile points. I believe that we will never circumvent the dilemma and, consequently, that our best research strategy must incorporate a base of generalized techniques and a superstructure of special techniques specifically designed to illuminate clearly formulated hypotheses. Brown and Struever (Chapter 16) are overly critical of the idea that "someone will be able to do something with this that I can't," but they are absolutely right in insisting on explicit hypotheses and the associated special research techniques if we are to justify the claim of a scientific archeology. There is no alternative to archeology in the active voice if our objective is to push our ability to explain past cultural behavior to the limit, whatever it may be.

These considerations bring us face to face with the ultimate problem. Where do we get the ideas that underlie the hypotheses to be investigated? There is no answer, so far as I know. There are no machines for generating useful ideas, and we can only attempt a vague description of the circumstances under which ideas arise. In simplest form, we can notice an apparent nonrandom relationship in a body of data, make a logical analysis to determine the variables involved, construct a hypothesis (either in the form of a frequency distribution or an invariant relationship), and attempt to confirm or reject the hypothesis by reanalysis of the data in hand if they are adequate to the purpose or by using the data in hand plus new data, if stronger evidence is needed. This is the process of inductive inference followed by hypothetico-deductive confirmation or rejection. The hypothetico-deductive aspect of the process is the essence of science and the new archeology. Inductive inferences can come from anywhere, but evaluation of the inferences can only be a matter of appeal to the data *via* the hypothetico-deductive route. In practice, we usually do not simply "notice" some putatively general relationship. Rather, we are struck by a resemblance between the data under consideration and data available from previous experience—we perceive an analogy and wish to explore its implications. If we are lucky, the analogy will lead to something beyond itself, to a more general understanding of the relationships of past and present data and so toward the goal of general laws of cultural behavior. The importance of analogy and analogic argument brings me to Bert Salwen (Chapter 10) and Mark P. Leone (Chapter 9) and the new anthropology.

One proposed source of fruitful analogies is the behavior of noncultural living systems and even nonliving systems—the general systems approach. I have taken a dim view of claims that this approach will produce basic new insights because the analogies drawn from noncultural systems fail at precisely the point of central interest to archeology, the peculiarly human aspects of systemic behavior, and I conclude that the chief value of the general systems approach lies in its logical analysis of the processes common to all living systems and the heuristic effect that appreciation of this analysis may have in the individual intellectual histories of archeologists. The second source of analogies is, in contrast, so fundamental that it is difficult to describe its importance. I refer, of course, to our knowledge of living cultural systems. The very identification of the subject matter of archeology, artifacts and their contexts, is a simple example of analogy drawn from our knowledge of existing human and animal behavior; our only way of connecting objects interpreted as relics of the past with human behavior is by analogy with directly observed behavior. And the archeological debt to knowledge of living cultures is not limited to the mere identification of artifacts as artifacts—it extends to every behavioral inference and to every explanation of similarities and differences of past cultures based on behavioral inferences. The ultimate theoretical entity of archeology is prehistoric man, recognizable because he shares dispositions, predilections, and attributes with the man we know by introspection and observation. Statements of this sort create distress in some archeological circles. They seem to deny a creative role for archeology, to assert that the only function of archeology is an endless task of illustrating ethnographically derived truths.

Leone concludes that after 10 years of the new archeology, clear demonstrations of archeological research as a prime mover in either social theory or evolutionary theory are lacking, although there have been resourceful attempts to apply complex models from ethnographically derived theory on social and economic organization and from demography and plant genetics. But these efforts have not resulted in significant modifications of the theories from which the models were derived; the models illuminate the archeological data, but the archeological data do not illuminate the models and so archeology seems to remain in a subordinate, incomplete condition, with no more than "increasing but undirected and unrealized promise," in Leone's phrase. My view of the situation does not differ greatly from that of Leone, but I am unable to work up a serious fit of despondency as a result. It seems to me that the subordinate position of archeology (and other studies of the past) is logically inescapable. Archeology is in fact a technique, just as Taylor argued (quoted by Richard B. Woodbury in Chapter 20), and archeologists are technicians who produce information about the past by collecting its relics. This fact allows us to bring together students of the Paleolithic of

France, of Greek statuary, of protohistoric Iroquois culture, and of nineteenth-century Nauvoo under the label "archeologist," despite their broad range of intellectual interests and backgrounds. Archeology as a technique is employed in the service of various intellectual disciplines (as is the technique of microscopy), but there is no reason for the practitioners to confine their efforts to technical matters—they need not be merely technicians.

The intellectual background of the new archeology is obvious: it is anthropology, and the new archeologists are anthropologists. They are also more than merely anthropologists, they are active anthropologists because they are engaged in an active program of theory development that includes the production and study of data from living or historically known cultures. They are engaged in this activity because the old anthropology has not developed a discipline of comparative and evolutionary technology adequate to the needs of paleoanthropology, and in this sense they are new anthropologists. I would argue further that even if we had on hand a developed theory of comparative and evolutionary technology based on direct observation of living cultures, archeologists as anthropologists would still play an active role. This is so because of the limited range of variables (including the variable of time) exhibited by living and historically known cultures. There are no direct observations on technologies and environments strictly comparable to those of southwestern France at the end of the Pleistocene, for example. For the same region, we can recall the puzzling alternations of the various kinds of Mousterian and point to Lewis R. Binford's suggestion (personal communication) that the Mousterian people, in contrast to their successors of the Upper Paleolithic and most or all directly observed peoples, had not developed "curating" behavior; instead of transporting a substantial outfit of tools and other gear from one activity locus to another, they manufactured the tools required for the activity at the locus and thus created the *appearance* of alternate territorial advances and withdrawals of several distinct cultures. This is a case of genuine theoretical extrapolation to a new order of things, and the scientific task of deducing further material implications to guide research designed to substantiate or reject the theory is, I submit, sufficiently challenging and important to satisfy the creative impulses of the most demanding among us. We have no need to apologize for or to try to explain away the primacy of observations on living behavior. Archeologists as anthropologists can and will, I think, play a leading role in the development of a science of cultural evolution. To this end, they will be active consumers of existing knowledge and theory on cultural behavior, producers of new observations and theory on the behavior of living cultures when the existing knowledge is inadequate to their needs, and providers of data and theory on cultural behavior in times and situations well outside the range of ethnography.

I conclude with a brief comment on the painstaking consideration of relevance by Fritz, Leone, Ford, and others. I have no serious quarrels with their expositions, but I would like to emphasize—apparently unfashionably—the following: "What, then, impels us to devise theory after theory? Why do we devise theories at all? The answer to the latter question is simply: because we enjoy 'comprehending,' i.e. reducing phenomena by the process of logic to something already known or (apparently) evident" (Einstein 1950).

REFERENCES

Adams, Robert McC.

1956   Level and Trend in Early Sumerian Civilization. Unpublished Ph.D. dissertation, Department of Anthropology, University of Chicago, Chicago.

1960   Factors influencing the rise of civilization in the alluvium: illustrated by Mesopotamia. Early civilizations, subsistence and environment. In *City Invincible: an Oriental Institute Symposium*, edited by Carl H. Kraeling and Robert McC. Adams. University of Chicago Press, Chicago.

1962   Agriculture and Urban Life in Early Southwestern Iran. *Science* 136:109–122.

1965   *Land Behind Baghdad: A History of Settlement on the Diyala Plains*. University of Chicago Press, Chicago.

1966a *The Evolution of Urban Society*. Aldine Publishing Company, Chicago.

1966b Trend and Tradition in Near Eastern Archaeology. *Proceedings of the American Philosophical Society* 110:105–110.

1968   Archeological Research Strategies: Past and Present. *Science* 160: 1187–1192.

Adams, Robert McC. and Hans Nissen

1972   *The Uruk Countryside*. University of Chicago Press, Chicago.

Adams, William Y.

1968   Settlement pattern in microcosm: the changing aspect of a Nubian village during twelve centuries. In *Settlement Archaeology*, edited by K. C. Chang, pp. 174–207. National Press, Palo Alto, Calif.

Aitken. M. J.

1961   *Physics and Archaeology*. Interscience Publishers, New York.

Allen, William L. and James B. Richardson III

1971   The Reconstruction of Kinship from Archaeological Data: The Concepts, the Methods, and the Feasibility. *American Antiquity* 36:41–53.

Andrews, E. D. and F. Andrews

1966   *Religion in Wood: A Book of Shaker Furniture*. Indiana University Press, Bloomington.

Arensberg, Conrad and Solon T. Kimball

1965   *Culture and Community*. Harcourt, Brace and World, New York.

Asch, Nancy B., Richard I. Ford, and David L. Asch

1972   Paleoethnobotany of the Koster Site: The Archaic Horizons. *Illinois State Museum, Reports of Investigations, 24.*

Ascher, Robert

1960   Archaeology and the Public Image. *American Antiquity* 25: 402–403.

1968   Time's arrow and the archaeology of a contemporary community. In *Settlement Archaeology*, edited by K. C. Chang, pp. 43–52. National Press, Palo Alto, Calif.

Bascom, Willard

1971   Deep-Water Archeology. *Science* 174(4006):261–269.

Bayard, Donn T.

1969   Science, Theory, and Reality in the "New Archaeology." *American Antiquity* 34:376–384.

Beckner, Morton

1959   *The Biological Way of Thought*. Columbia University, New York.

Behavioral and Social Sciences Survey Committee.

1969 *The Behavioral and Social Sciences: Outlook and needs.* National
      Academy of Science.

Berkhofer, R. F.

1969 *A Behavioral Approach to Historical Analysis.* Free Press, New
      York.

Berry, Brian J. L.

1967 *Geography of Market Centers and Retail Distribution.* Prentice-
      Hall, Englewood Cliffs, N.J.

Bibby, Geoffrey

1956 *The Testimony of the Spade.* Knopf, New York.

Binclarke, Lewis D. L.

n.d. New Analytical Archaeological Perspectives: A Logogenetic
      Inquiry into the Nature of Archaeological Theoretic Theoreticians.
      Phu Wiang University Press, Non Nok Tha, Thailand.

Binford, Lewis R.

1962 Archaeology as anthropology. *American Antiquity* 28:217–225.

1964 A consideration of archaeological research design. *American
      Antiquity* 29(4):425–444.

1965 Archaeological systematics and the study of cultural process.
      American Antiquity 31(2):203–210.

1968a Archeological perspectives. In *New Perspectives in Archeology*;
      edited By Sally R. and Lewis R. Binford, pp. 5–32. Aldine Publishing
      Company, Chicago.

1968b Post-pleistocene adaptations. In *New Perspectives in Archeology*;
      edited by Sally R. and Lewis R. Binford, pp. 313–341. Aldine Pub-
      lishing Company, Chicago.

1968c Some comments on historical versus processual archeology.
      Southwestern Journal of Anthropology 24:267–275.

1971 Review of *Reconstructing Prehistoric Pueblo Societies*; edited by
      W. A. Longacre. *Science* 172:1226.

1972 Book Review, *Archeological Inquiry Into Social Organization.*
      Science 176:1225–1226.

1973 Interassemblage Variability—The Mousterian and the "Func-
      tional" Argument. In *Explanation of Culture Change- Models in
      Prehistory*; edited by C. Renfrew. G. Duckworth & Co., Ltd.,
      London.

Binford, Lewis R. and others

1970 Archaeology at Hatchery West. *Memoirs of the Society for American Archaeology.* No. 24.

Binford, Lewis R. and Sally R. Binford

1966 A preliminary analysis of functional variability in the Mousterian of Levallois facies. In *Recent Studies in Paleoanthropology;* edited by J. D. Clark and F. Clark Howell. *American Anthropologist* 68(2, Part 2):238–295.

Binford, Sally R. and Lewis R. Binford

1968 Archeological Theory and Method. In *New Perspectives in Archeology;* edited by Sally R. and Lewis R. Binford, pp. 1–3. Aldine Publishing Company, Chicago.

Binford, Sally R. and Lewis R. Binford, eds.

1968 *New Perspectives in Archeology.* Aldine Publishing Company, Chicago.

Boas, Franz

1940 *Race, Language, and Culture.* Macmillan, New York.

Bohrer, Vorsila L.

1969 Paleoecology of the Hay Hollow site. Unpublished Ph.D. dissertation, Department of Anthropology, University of Arizona, Tucson.

Bolton, Reginald P.

1920 New York City in Indian Possession. Museum of the American Indian, Heye Foundation, Indian Notes and Monographs, 2(7). New York.

Bordes, Francois

1971 Physical Evolution and Technological Evolution in Man: A Parallelism. *World Archeology* 3(1):1–5.

Bordes, Francois and Denis de Sonneville-Bordes

1970 The Significance of Variability in Paleolithic Assemblages. *World Archaeology* 2:61–73.

Boulding, Kenneth

    1956   General Systems Theory—The Skeleton of Science. *Management Science* 2:197–208.

Braidwood, Robert J.

    1937   *Mounds in the Plain of Antioch: an Archeological Survey.* Oriental Institute Publications, No. 48. University of Chicago Press, Chicago.

    1960   The Agricultural Revolution. *Scientific American* 203(3):130–148.

    1971   *Archeology: View from Southwestern Asia.* Annual Report of the American Anthropological Association.

Braidwood, Robert J., Halet Çambel, Charles L. Redman, and Patty Jo Watson

    1971   Beginnings of Village-Farming Communities in Southeastern Turkey. *Proceedings of the National Academy Science U.S.A.*, 68: 1236–1240.

Braidwood, Robert J. and Gordon R. Willey

    1962   Conclusions and afterthoughts. In *Courses Toward Urban Life;* edited by R. J. Braidwood and G. R. Willey. Viking Fund Publication in Anthropology, 32. Aldine Publishing Company, Chicago.

Breasted, James H.

    1933   *The Oriental Institute.* University of Chicago Survey, Vol. 12. University of Chicago Press, Chicago.

Brodbeck, May

    1962   Explanation, prediction, and imperfect knowledge. In *Scientific Explanation, Space, and Time;* edited by H. Feigl and G. Maxwell, *Minnesota Studies in the Philosophy of Science,* 3:231–272. University of Minnesota Press.

Brothwell, Don R. and Eric Higgs, eds.

    1969   *Science in Archaeology: A Survey of Progress and Research.* Revised and enlarged edition. Thames and Hudson, London.

Brothwell, Don R. and R. Spearman

1963 The hair of earlier peoples. In *Science and Archaeology;* edited by D. Brothwell and E. Higgs, pp. 427–436. Thames and Hudson, London.

Bruwer, J.

1965 *Zimbabwe: Rhodesia's Ancient Greatness.* H. Keartland, Johannesburg.

Buck, R. C.

1956 On the logic of general behavioral systems theory. In *The Foundations of Science and the Concept of Psychology and Psychoanalysis;* edited by Herbert Feigl and Michael Scriven. *Minnesota Studies in the Philosophy of Science,* Vol. 1, pp. 223–238. University of Minnesota Press.

Buckley, Walter

1967 *Sociology and Modern Systems Theory.* Prentice-Hall, Englewood Cliffs, N.J.

Butzer, Karl W.

1971 *Environment and Archeology, an Ecological Approach to Prehistory.* 2nd ed. Aldine-Atherton, Chicago.

Byers, D. S., ed.

1967a *The Prehistory of the Tehuacan Valley, Vol. One: Environment and Subsistence,* Peabody Foundation. Andover, Mass., and University of Texas Press, Austin.

1967b *The Prehistory of the Tehuacan Valley, Vol. Two: The Non-Ceramic Artifacts,* Peabody Foundation. Andover, Mass., and University of Texas Press, Austin.

Caldwell, Joseph R.

1959 The New American Archeology. *Science* 129:303–307.

Carr, E. H.

1962 *What is History?* Random House, New York.

Ceram, C. W.

1954 *Gods, Graves, and Scholars.* Knopf, New York.

Chamberlain, Thomas C.

1944 The Method of Multiple Working Hypotheses. *Scientific Monthly* 59:357–362.

1965 The Method of Multiple Working Hypotheses. *Science* 148(3671): 754–759. Washington, D.C.

Chang, Kwang-Chih

1958 Study of the Neolithic Social Grouping: Examples from the New World. *American Anthropologist* 60(2):298–334.

1968 *Settlement Archaeology*. National Press, Palo Alto, Calif.

Chenhall, Richard G.

1971 Positivism and the Collection of Data. *American Antiquity* 36: 372–373.

Chomsky, Noam

1962 Explanatory models in linguistics. In *Logic, Methodology and Philosophy of Science*; edited by Ernest Nagel, Patrick Suppes, and Alfred Tarski, pp. 528–550. Stanford University Press, Stanford, Calif.

Clark, John Grahame D.

1957 *Archaeology and Society: Reconstructing the Prehistoric Past*. Barnes & Noble, New York.

1970 *Aspects of Prehistory*. University of California Press, Berkeley.

1972 *Star Carr: A Case Study in Bioarchaeology*. McCaleb Module. No. 10, Addison-Wesley, Reading, Mass.

Clark, P. and F. Evans

1954 Distance to Nearest Neighbor as a Measure of Spatial Relationships in Population. *Ecology* 35;445–453.

Clarke, David L.

1968 *Analytical Archaeology*. Methuen, London.

Cook, Sherburne F. and Robert F. Heizer

1965 The Quantitative Approach to the Relation between Population and Settlement Size. *University of California Archaeological Survey, Reports*. No. 64. Department of Anthropology, University of California, Berkeley.

1968   Relationships among houses, settlement areas, and population in aboriginal California. In *Settlement Archaeology;* edited by K. C. Chang, pp. 79–116. National Press, Palo Alto, Calif.

Cotter, John L.

1970   Colonial Williamsburg. *Technology and Culture* 11(3):417–427.

Crabtree, Don E.

1966   A Stoneworker's Approach to Analyzing and Replicating the Lindenmeier Folsom, *Tebiwa* 9(3):3–39.

Creese, Walter

1946   Fowler and the Domestic Octagon. *The Art Bulletin* 28(2):89–102.

Dalibard, James

1970   Architectural Recording as Above-Ground Archeology. *Abstracts: Third Annual Meeting, Soceity for Historical Archeology*, p. 15. Bethlehem, Pa.

Daly, Patricia

1969   Approaches to Faunal Analysis in Archaeology. *American Antiquity* 34(2):146–153.

Daniel, Glyn E.

1950   *A Hundred Years of Archaeology.* Duckworth, London.
1962   *The Idea of Prehistory.* Penguin Books, Baltimore.
1971a Editorial. *Antiquity* 45:1–2.
1971b Editorial. *Antiquity* 45:85–87.

Daniels, George H.

1970   The Big Questions in the History of Technology. *Technology and Culture* 11(1):1–21.

David, Nicholas

1971   The Fulani Compound and the Archaeologist. *World Archaeology* 3(2):111–131.

David, Nicholas and Hilke Hennig

1972 *The Ethnography of Pottery: A Fulani Case Seen in Archaeological Perspective.* McCaleb Module. No. 21. Addison-Wesley, Reading, Mass.

Davis, Hester A.

1972 The Crisis in American Archaeology. *Science* 175(4019):267–272.

Deetz, James

1965 The Dynamics of Stylistic Change in Arikara Ceramics. *Illinois Studies in Anthropology.* No. 4. University of Illinois Press, Urbana, Ill.

1970 Archeology as a Social Science. *Bulletin of the American Anthropological Association* 3(3, Part 2):115–125.

Deetz, James and Edwin Dethlefsen

1965 The Doppler Effect and Archaeology: A Consideration of the Spatial Aspects of Seriation. *Southwestern Journal of Anthropology* 21:196–206.

1966 Death's Heads, Cherubs and Willow Trees: Experimental Archaeology in Colonial Cemeteries. *American Antiquity* 31:502–510.

Dethlefsen, Edwin and James Deetz

1967 Eighteenth Century Cemeteries: A Demographic View. *Historical Archaeology 1967* pp. 66–68. Detroit, Michigan.

Deustua, Patricia N.

1969 The 1968 Season at the Wort Farm Site, Staten Island. *Staten Island Institute of Arts and Sciences, Proceedings* 24(3):58–60. Staten Island, N.Y.

Deutsch, Karl W., John Platt, and Dieter Senghaas

1971 Letter. *Science* 172:1192.

Dodson, Peter

1971 Sedimentology and Taphonomy of the Oldman Formation (Campanian), Dinosaur Provincial Park, Alberta (Canada). *Palaeogeography, Palaeoclimatology, Palaeoecology* 10:21–74. Amsterdam.

Doran, James

    1970   Systems Theory, Computer Simulations and Archaeology. *World Archaeology*, 1(3):289–298.

Dowman, Elizabeth A.

    1970   *Conservation in Field Archaeology*. Methuen, London.

Dray, W.

    1957   *Laws and Explanation in History*. University Press, Oxford.

Dunnell, Robert C.

    1971   *Systematics in Prehistory*. Free Press, New York.

Eggan, Fred

    1950   *Social Organization of the Western Pueblos*. University of Chicago.

Einstein, Albert

    1950   On the Generalized Theory of Gravitation. *Scientific American*, 182(4):13–17.

Elton, G. R.

    1969   *The Practice of History*. Collins, London.

Erasmus, Charles

    1969   Explanation and Reconstruction in Cultural Evolution. *Sociologus* 19:20-36.

Evans, Robin

    1971a Bentham's Panopticon. An Incident in the Social History of Architecture. *Architectural Association Quarterly* April–June:21–37.
    1971b The Rights of Retreat and the Rights of Exclusion: Notes Toward the Definition of Wall. *Architectural Design* 41:335–339.

Evenari, Michael, Leslie Shanan, and Naphtali Tadmor

    1971   *The Negev: The Challenge of a Desert*. Harvard University Press, Cambridge, Mass.

Fagan, Brian M.

1970   Review of A. J. Bruwer: *Zimbabwe: Rhodesia's Ancient Greatness.* *Antiquity* 44(176):320–322.

1972   *In the Beginning: An Introduction to Archaeology.* Little, Brown, Boston.

Farnsworth, Kenneth B.

n.d.   An Archeological Survey of the Macoupin Valley. *Illinois State Museum, Reports of Investigations,* in press.

Finley, M. L.

1971   Archaeology and History. *Daedalus* 100:168–186.

Fishlow, A. and R. W. Fogel

1971   Quantitative Economic History: An Interim Evaluation. *Journal of Economic History* 31:18.

Fitting, James E.

1966   Archaeological Investigations of the Carolinian-Canadian Edge Area in Michigan. *The Michigan Archaeologist* 12(4).

1970   *The Archaeology of Michigan.* Doubleday, New York.

Flannery, Kent V.

1965   The Ecology of Early Food Production in Mesopotamia. *Science* 147:1247–1256.

1967   Culture History Versus Cultural Process: a Debate in American Archaeology. *Scientific American* 217(2):119–122.

1968a The Olmec and the Valley of Oaxaca. *Dumbarton Oaks Conference on the Olmec.* Washington, D. C. pp. 79–110.

1968b Archeological systems theory and early Mesoamerica. In *Anthropological Archeology in the Americas*; edited by Betty J. Meggers, Theo. Gaus' Sons, Brooklyn, N.Y.

1969   Origins and ecological effects of early domestication in Iran and the Near East. In *The Domestication of Plants and Animals*; edited by Peter J. Ucko and G. W. Dimbelbly. Aldine Publishing Company, Chicago.

1972   The Cultural Evolution of Civilizations. *Annual Review of Ecology and Systematics* 3:399–426.

Fleming, Ronald L.

1971 After the Report, What?: The Uses of Historical Archaeology, A Planner's View. *Historical Archaeology* 5:49–61. Lansing, Mich.

Fogel, R. W.

1966 The New Economic History, Its Findings and Methods. *Economic Historical Review.* 19:642–56; reprinted in R. W. Fogel and S. L. Engerman (eds.), *The Reinterpretation of American Economic History*, Harper and Row, New York, 1971.

Foley, Vincent P.

1968 On the Meaning of Industrial Archeology. *Historical Archeology 1968.* pp. 66–68. Mason, Michigan.

Fontana, Bernard L.

1968 A Reply to "Some Thoughts on Theory and Method in Historical Archaeology." In *Historical Archaeology Forum-1968*; edited by Stanley South, Box 1881, Raleigh, N.C.

Ford, Richard I.

1968 Jemez Cave and Its Place in an Early Horticultural Settlement Pattern. Manuscript presented at Thirty-Third Annual Meeting, Society for American Archeology, Santa Fe, N. Mex.

Forrester, Jay

1969 *Urban Dynamics.* M.I.T. Press, Cambridge, Mass.

Foster, George M.

1960 Life-Expectancy of Utilitarian Pottery in Tzintzuntzan, Michoacan, Mexico. *American Antiquity* 25:606–609.

Fox, Feramorz Young

1932 The Mormon Land System: A Study of the Settlement and Utilization of Land Under the Direction of the Mormon Church. Ph.D. dissertation, Northwestern University, Evanston, Ill.

Fraser, Douglas

1968 *Village Planning in the Primitve World.* George Braziller, New York.

Freeman, Leslie G., Jr.

1968 A theoretical framework for interpreting archeological materials. In *Man the Hunter*; edited by Richard Lee and Irven DeVore, pp. 262–267. Aldine Publishing Company, Chicago.

1971 Introduction to "New Research in Paleoanthropology." *American Anthropologist* 73(5):1195–1197. Washington, D.C.

Friend, Joseph H. and David R. Guralnik, eds.

1957 *Webster's New World Dictionary*. World Publishers, Cleveland.

Fritz, John M.

1968 Archeological Epistemology: Two Views. Unpublished master's thesis, Department of Anthropology, University of Chicago, Chicago.

Fritz, John M. and Fred T. Plog

1970 The Nature of Archeological Explanation, *American Antiquity 35*: 405–412.

Gjessing, Gutorm

1963 Archaeology, nationalism, and society. In *The Teaching of Anthropology*; edited by David G. Mandelbaum, Gabriel W. Lasker, and Ethel M. Albert. *American Anthropological Association Memoir* 94:261–267.

Glob, P. V.

1971 *The Bog People: Iron-Age Man Preserved*; translated by R. Bruce-Mitford. Ballantine Books, New York.

Goody, Jack

1971 *Technology, Tradition and the State of Africa*. Oxford University Press, London.

Gordon, D. H.

1953 Fire and the Sword: the Technique of Destruction. *Antiquity 27*: 149–153.

Gould, Richard A.

1968 Living Archeology: the Ngatatjara of Western Australia. *Southwestern Journal of Anthropology* 24(2):101–120.

Greig-Smith, P.

1964   *Quantitative Plant Ecology.* 2nd ed. Plenum Press, New York.

Gumerman, George J.

1970   Black Mesa; Survey and Excavation in Northeastern Arizona, 1968. *Prescott College Studies in Anthropology.* No. 2. Prescott College Press, Prescott, Ariz.

1971   The Distribution of Prehistoric Population Aggregates. Proceedings of the First Annual Southwestern Anthropological Research Group. George J. Gumerman editor. *Prescott College Anthropology Reports* 1. Prescott College Press, Prescott, Ariz.

Gumerman, George J. and R. Roy Johnson

1971   Prehistoric human population distribution in a biological transition zone. In *The Distribution of Prehistoric Population Aggregates.* Proceedings of the First Annual Southwestern Anthropological Research Group. George J. Gumerman editor. *Prescott College Anthropology Reports* 1. Prescott College Press, Prescott, Ariz.

Habakkuk, John

1971   Economic History and Economic Theory. *Daedalus* 100:305–322.

Haggett, Peter

1965   *Locational Analysis in Human Geography.* Edward Arnold, London.

Hanson, John A. and Michael B. Schiffer

n.d.   The Joint Site: A Preliminary Report. *Fieldiana: Anthropology,* in press.

Harary, Frank, Robert Z. Norman, and Dorwin Cartwright

1965   *Structural Models: An Introduction to the Theory of Directed Graphs.* Wiley, New York.

Hardoy, Jorge

1968   *Urban Planning in Pre-Columbian America.* George Braziller, New York.

Harris, Marvin

    1968   *The Rise of Anthropological Theory.* Thomas Y. Crowell, New York.

Harris, W. T., ed.

    1918   *Webster's New International Dictionary.* Revised. G. & C. Merriam Company, Springfield, Mass.

Harvey, David

    1969   *Explanation in Geography.* Edward Arnold, London.

Hawkes, Christopher

    1954   Archeological Theory and Method: Some Suggestions from the Old World. *American Anthropologist* 56(2):155–167.

Hawkes, Jacquetta

    1968   The Proper Study of Mankind. *Antiquity* 42:255–262.

Heidegger, Martin

    1971   The thing. In *Poetry, Language, and Thought.* Translated and with an introduction by Albert Hofstadter. Harper and Row, New York.

Heider, Karl G.

    1967   Archaeological Assumptions and Ethnographical Facts: A Cautionary Tale from New Guinea. *Southwestern Journal of Anthropology* 23(1):52–64.

Heizer, Robert F.

    1966   Salvage and Other Archaeology. *The Masterkey* 40(2):54–60.

Hempel, Carl G.

    1942   The Function of General Laws in History. *Journal of Philosophy* 39:35–48.

    1949   The Function of General Laws in History, *Readings in Philosophical Analysis;* edited by H. Feigl and W. Sellars, pp. 459–471. Appleton-Century-Crofts, New York.

    1959   The Logic of Functional Analysis. In L. Gross, ed., *Symposium on Sociological Theory,* pp. 271–307. Harper and Row, New York. Reprinted in Carl G. Hempel, *Aspects of Scientific Explanation,* 1965, pp. 297–330. Free Press, Glencoe, Ill.

1965   Aspects of Scientific Explanation. In, *Aspects of Scientific Explanation and Other Essays in the Philosophy of Science*, by Carl G. Hempel, pp. 331–496. Free Press, New York.

1966   *Philosophy of Natural Science*. Foundations of Philosophy Series, Prentice-Hall, Englewood Cliffs, N.J.

Hempel, Carl G. and Paul Oppenheim

1948   Studies in the Logic of Explanation. *Philosophy of Science* 15(2): 135–175.

Hevly, Richard H.

1964   Pollen Analysis of Quaternary Archaeological and Lacustrine Sediments from the Colorado Plateau. Unpublished Ph.D. dissertation, Department of Anthropology, University of Arizona, Tucson.

Hill, James N.

1966   A Prehistoric Community in Eastern Arizona. *Southwestern Journal of Anthropology* 22:9–30.

1968   Broken K Pueblo: patterns of form and function: In *New Perspectives in Archeology;* edited by Sally R. and Lewis R. Binford, pp. 103–142. Aldine Publishing Company, Chicago.

1970   Broken K Pueblo: Prehistoric Social Organization in the American Southwest. *Anthropological Papers of the University of Arizona* No. 18. University of Arizona Press, Tucson.

1971   Seminar on the explanation of prehistoric organizational change. *Current Anthropology* 12(3):406–408.

Hole, Frank

1962   Archeological Survey and Excavation in Iran 1961. *Science* 137: 524–526.

Hole, Frank, Kent V. Flannery, and James A. Neely

1969   Prehistory and Human Ecology of the Deh Luran Plain. *Memoirs of the Museum of Anthropology, University of Michigan* 1.

Hole, Frank and Robert F. Heizer

1969   *An Introduction to Prehistoric Archeology*. 2nd ed. Holt, Rinehart and Winston, New York.

Horwitz, Jonathan

1971 Wort's Farm Excavation, 1969. *Staten Island Institute of Arts and Sciences, Proceedings* 26(2):35–44. Staten Island, N.Y.

Howell, F. Clark

1968 *Early Man.* Revised. Life Nature Library, New York.

Howells, W. W.

1960 Estimating Population Numbers Through Archaeological and Skeletal Remains. *Viking Fund Publications in Anthropology* 158–176.

Hudson, Kenneth

1966 *Industrial Archeology: An Introduction.* 2nd Edition. John Baker, London.

Huey, Paul

1970 Some Technical Problems and Cultural Implicatione in Urban Archaeology Paper delivered at the third Annual meeting of the Soceity for Historical Archaeology, Jan., 1970. Bethlehem, Pa.

Hull, David L.

1968 The Operational Imperative: Sense and Nonsense in Operationalism. *Systematic Zoology* 17:438–457.

Isaac, Glynn

1971 Whither Archaeology? *Antiquity* 45:123–129.

Jacobsen, Thorkild and Robert McC. Adams

1958 Salt and Silt in Ancient Mesopotamian Agriculture. *Science* 128 (3334):1251–1258.

Jennings, Jesse D.

1957 Danger Cave. *Society for American Archaeology, Memoir* 14. Salt Lake City.

1964 The Desert West: *In Prehistoric Man in the New World*; edited by J. D. Jennings and Edward Norbeck, pp. 149–174. University of Chicago Press, Chicago.

1968 *Prehistory of North America.* McGraw-Hill, New York.

Jewell, P. A. and G. W. Dimbleby, eds.

1966 The Experimental Earthwork on Overton Down, Wiltshire, England: The First Four Years. *Proceedings of the Prehistoric Society for 1966* 32:313–342. Cambridge, England.

Kemeny, John G.

1959 *A Philosopher Looks at Science.* Van Nostrand-Reinhold, New York.

Kidder, Alfred V.

1926 The Mimbres Excavations, Season of 1926. Unpublished manuscript.

1949 Introduction. In *Prehistoric Southwesterners from Basket Maker to Pueblo;* by Charles Amsden. Southwest Museum, Los Angeles.

Kim, Won-Yong

1966 Fieldwork Planned and Begun. *Current Anthropology* 7:99.

King, Blanche Busey

1939 *Under Your Feet.* Dodd, Mead, New York.

King, Leslie J.

1969 *Statistical Analysis in Geography.* Prentice-Hall, Englewood Cliffs, N.J.

King, Thomas F.

1971 A Conflict of Values in American Archaeology. *American Antiquity* 36(3):255–262.

Kluckhohn, Clyde

1940 The conceptual structure in Middle American studies. In *The Maya and Their Neighbors;* edited by C. L. Hay et al. University of Utah Press, Salt Lake City.

1961 *Mirror for Man.* McGraw-Hill, New York.

Kroeber, A. L.

1947 *Cultural and Natural Areas of Native North America.* University of California Press, Berkeley, Calif.

1952 *The Nature of Culture.* University of Chicago Press, Chicago.

Kuhn, Thomas S.

1970   The Structure of Scientific Revolutions. Revised edition. University
       of Chicago Press, Chicago.

Kushner, Gilbert

1970   A Consideration of Some Processual Designs for Archaeology as
       Anthropology. American Antiquity 35:125–132.

Layard, Austen H.

1853   Discoveries Among the Ruins of Nineveh and Babylon. Harper &
       Brothers, New York.

Leach, Edmund R.

1954   Political Systems of Highland Burma. Beacon Press, Boston.

LeBlanc, Steven A.

1971   Computerized, Conjunctive Archeology and the Near Eastern
       Halaf. Unpublished Ph.D. dissertation, Department of Anthropol-
       ogy, Washington University, St. Louis, Missouri.

Lee, Richard B.

1968   What hunters do for a living, or, how to make out on scarce
       resources. In Man the Hunter; edited by Richard B. Lee and Irven
       DeVore, pp. 30–48. Aldine Publishing Company, Chicago.

Lee, Richard and Irven DeVore, eds.

1968   Man the Hunter. Aldine Publishing Company, Chicago.

Leone, Mark P.

1968a Economic Autonomy and Social Distance: Archaeological Evi-
       dences. Unpublished Ph.D. dissertation, Department of Anthro-
       pology, University of Arizona, Tucson.
1968b Neolithic Economic Autonomy and Social Distance. Science 162:
       1150–1151.
1969   Modern Cultural Patterns in East-Central Arizona. Unpublished
       manuscript read at the 1968 Pecos Conference, Prescott, Ariz.
1971   Review of New Perspectives in Archeology; edited by Sally R. and
       Lewis R. Binford. American Antiquity 36(2):220–222.
1972   Archaeology as Technology. Paper delivered at Department of
       Anthropology Colloquium, New York University, New York.

Leone, Mark P., ed.

    1972 *Contemporary Archaeology: A Guide to Theory and Contributions.* Southern Illinois University Press, Carbondale, Ill.

Levi-Strauss, Claude

    1963 Do dual organizations exist? In *Structural Anthropology.* Translated by Claire Jacobson and Brooke Grundfest Schoepf, pp. 132–163. Basic Books, New York.

Lloyd, Seton

    1947 *Foundations in the Dust.* Oxford, London.

Longacre, William A.

    1964 Archaeology as Anthropology: A Case Study. *Science* 144(3625): 1454–1455.

    1968 Some Aspects of Prehistoric Society in East-Central Arizona. In *New Perspectives in Archeology*; edited by Sally R. and Lewis R. Binford, pp. 89–102. Aldine Publishing Company, Chicago.

    1970 Archaeology as Anthropology: A Case Study. *Anthropological Papers of the University of Arizona.* No. 17. University of Arizona Press, Tucson.

Longacre, William A., ed.

    1970 *Reconstructing Prehistoric Pueblo Societies.* University of New Mexico Press, Albuquerque.

Longacre, William A. and James E. Ayres

    1968 Archeological lessons from an Apache wickiup. In *New Perspectives in Archeology*; edited by Sally R. Binford and Lewis R. Binford, pp. 151–159. Aldine Publishing Company, Chicago.

Loud, Llewellyn L. and M. R. Harrington

    1929 Lovelock Cave. *University of California Publications in American Archaeology and Ethnology* 25:vii–183.

Lynch, Kevin

    1960 *The Image of the City.* M.I.T. Press, Cambridge, Mass.

MacNeish, Richard S.

    1964 Ancient Mesoamerican Civilization. *Science* 143(3606):531–537.

MacNeish, Richard S. and F. A. Peterson

1962 The Santa Marta Rock Shelter, Ocozocoantle, Chiapas, Mexico. *Papers, New World Archaeological Foundation.* No. 14. Brigham Young University, Salt Lake City, Utah.

Martin, Paul S.

1963 *The Last 10,000 Years, a Fossil Pollen Record of the American Southwest.* The University of Arizona Press, Tucson.

1967 Pleistocene overkill. In *Pleistocene Extinctions: the Search for a Cause;* edited by Paul S. Martin and H. E. Wright, pp. 75–120. Yale University Press, New Haven, Conn.

Martin, Paul S.

1971 The Revolution in Archaeology. *American Antiquity* 36(1):1–8.

McLuhan, Marshall

1964 *Understanding Media.* McGraw-Hill, New York.

McNeill, William H.

1963 *The Rise of the West.* University of Chicago Press, Chicago.

Meehan, Eugene J.

1968 *Explanation in Social Science: A System Paradigm.* Dorsey Press, Homewood, Ill.

Michael, Henry N. and Elizabeth K. Ralph

1971 *Dating Techniques for the Archaeologist.* M.I.T. Press, Cambridge, Mass.

Milgram, Stanley

1970 The Experience of Living in Cities. *Science* 167(3924):1461–1468. Washington, D.C.

Miller, James G.

1972 Living Systems: The Organization. *Behavioral Science* 17(1).

Movius, H. L., Jr., N. C. David, H. M. Bricker, and R. B. Clay

1968 The analysis of certain major classes of Upper Paleolithic tools. *American School of Prehistoric Research.* Peabody Museum, Harvard University, Bulletin No. 26.

Mumford, Lewis

    1970   *The Myth of the Machine: The Pentagon of Power.* Harcourt Brace Jovanovich, New York.

Murdock, George Peter

    1957   World Ethnographic Sample. *American Anthropologist* 59(4): 664–687.

Murra, John V.

    1968   An Aymara Kingdom in 1567. *Ethnohistory* 15(2):115–151.

Naroll, Raoul

    1962   Floor Area and Settlement Population. *American Antiquity* 27(4): 587–589. Salt Lake City, Utah.

Neumann, George K.

    1952   Archeology and race in the American Indian. In *Archeology of Eastern United States*; edited by James B. Griffin, pp. 13–34. University of Chicago Press, Chicago.

Northrop, F. S. C.

    1947   *The Logic of the Sciences and the Humanities.* Meridian Books. World Publishing Company, Cleveland.

Odum, E. P.

    1965   *Fundamentals of Ecology.* W. B. Saunders Company, Philadelphia, Pa.

Onions, C. T., ed.

    1965   *The Shorter Oxford English Dictionary on Historical Principles*; 3rd ed., revised with addenda. Clarendon Press, Oxford.

Oppenheim, A. L.

    1960   Assyriology—Why and How? *Current Anthropology* 1:409–423.

Pallis, Svend A.

    1956   *The Antiquity of Iraq.* Munksgaard, Copenhagen.

Pallottino, Massimo

1968 The Meaning of Archaeology. Harry N. Abrams, New York.

Pannell, J. P. M.

1966 The Techniques of Industrial Archaeology. David and Charles Ltd. Newton Abbot, England.

Park, Robert E., Ernest W. Burgess, and Roderick D. McKenzie

1925 The City. University of Chicago Press, Chicago.

Parsons, Jeffrey R.

1971 Prehistoric Settlement Patterns in the Texcoco Region, Mexico. Memoirs of the Museum of Anthropology. University of Michigan, No.3.

Pelto, Pertti J.

1970 Anthropological Research: The Structure of Inquiry. Harper and Row, New York.

Phillips, Philip

1958 Application of the Wheat-Gifford-Wasley Taxonomy to Eastern Ceramics. American Antiquity 24:117–130.

Plog, Fred T.

1968a Archaeological Survey—A New Perspective. Unpublished master's thesis, Department of Anthropology, University of Chicago, Chicago.

1968b The Explanatory Approach: A Test Case. Manuscript presented 9 May, Thirty-Third Annual Meeting, Society for American Archaeology, Santa Fe, N.M.

1969 An Approach to the Study of Prehistoric Change. Unpublished Ph.D. dissertation, Department of Anthropology, University of Chicago, Chicago.

n.d. Application for a National Science Foundation grant (1970).

Polanyi, Karl, Conrad M. Arensberg, and Harry W. Pearson

1957 Trade and Market in the Early Empires. Free Press, Glencoe, Ill.

Proshansky, Harold M., William H. Ittelson, and Leanne G. Rivlin, eds.

1970 *Environmental Psychology: Man and His Physical Setting.* Holt, Rinehart and Winston, New York.

Przeworski, A. and H. Teune

1970 *The Logic of Comparative Social Inquiry.* Wiley, New York.

Rappoport, Amos

1969 *House Form and Culture.* Prentice-Hall, Englewood Cliffs, N.J.

Rathje, William E.

1971 The Origin and Development of Lowland Classic Maya Civilization. *American Antiquity* 36:275–85.

Redfield, Robert

1963 *The Primitive World and Its Transformations.* Cornell University Press, Ithaca, N.Y.

Redman, Charles L.

1969 Context and Stratigraphy: The Need for Observations. Unpublished master's thesis, Department of Anthropology, University of Chicago, Chicago.

1973 Multisage Field work and Analytical Techniques. *American Antiquity* 38(1):61–79.

Redman, Charles L. and Patty Jo Watson

1970 Systematic, Intensive Surface Collection. *American Antiquity* 35:279–291.

Reps, John W.

1969 *Town Planning in Frontier America.* Princeton University Press, Princeton, N.J.

Rescher, Nicholas

1970 *Scientific Explanation.* Free Press, New York.

Ricks, Joel E.

1964 *Forms and Methods of Early Mormon Settlement in Utah and the Surrounding Region, 1847–1877.* Utah State University Press, Logan, Utah.

Robbins, M. C.

1966 House Types and Settlement Patterns: An Application of Ethnology to Archaeological Interpretation. *Minnesota Archaeologist*
28(1):3–26.

Rosenfeld, Henry

1965 The Social Composition of the Military in the Process of State
Formation in the Arabian Desert. *Journal of the Royal Anthropological Institute* 95:75–86, 174–194.

Rouse, Irving

1952 Porto Rican Prehistory. *New York Academy of Sciences, Scientific
Survey of Porto Rico and the Virgin Islands* 18(3–4):307–578. New
York.

1964 Archaeological approaches to cultural evolution. In *Explorations
in Cultural Anthropology*; edited by W. Goodenough, pp.
455–468. McGraw-Hill, New York.

1970 Classification for What? *Norweigian Archaeological Review* 3:
4–12. Oslo.

1972 *Introduction to Prehistory: A Systematic Approach.* McGraw-Hill,
New York.

Rowe, John H.

1962 Worsaae's Law and the Use of Grave Lots for Archaeological Dating. *American Antiquity* 28:129–137.

Ruppert, Karl, J. E. S. Thompson, and T. Proskouriakoff

1955 *Bonampak, Chiapas, Mexico.* Carnegie Institute of Washington,
Publication 602.

Rutsch, Edward S.

1968 A Petrological Study of Aboriginal Projectile Points from Staten
Island. *Staten Island Institute of Arts and Sciences, Proceedings*
23(3):75–81. Staten Island, N.Y.

1970a An Analysis of the Lithic Materials Used in the Manufacture of
Projectile Points in Coastal New York. *New York State Archeological Association, Bulletin* 49:1–12. Ann Arbor, Mich.

1970b A Report on the Black River Reservation Site Survey. *Archeological Society of New Jersey, Bulletin* 26:22–25. Trenton, N.J.

1972 Archaeological Investigations at Fort Nonsense. *Northeast Historical Archaeology* 1(3). Providence, R.I.

Sackett, James R.

1966   Quantitative analysis of Upper Paleolithic stone tools. In *Recent Studies in Paleoanthropology*; edited by J. Desmond Clark and F. Clark Howell. American Anthropologist Special Publications 68(2, Part 2):356–394.

Salwen, Bert

1968   Muskeeta Cove 2: A Stratified Woodland Site on Long Island. *American Antiquity* 33(3):322–340. Salt Lake City, Utah.

Sanders, James A., ed.

1970   *Near Eastern Archaeology in the Twentieth Century* (Essays in Honor of Nelson Glueck), Doubleday, New York.

Sanders, William T.

1968   Hydraulic agriculture and regional symbiosis. In *Anthropological Archeology in the Americas*; edited by Betty J. Meggers. Anthropolitical Society, Washington.

Schiffer, Michael B.

1970   Cultural Laws and the Reconstruction of Past Lifeways. Unpublished paper presented at the 35th annual meeting of the Society for American Archaeology, Mexico City, May 1970. Manuscript on file: Arizona State Museum Library, University of Arizona, Tucson.

1971   Archaeology as Behavioral Science. Paper presented at the 36th Annual Meeting of the Society for American Archaeology in Norman, Oklahoma.

1972   Archaeological Context and Systemic Context. *American Antiquity* 37:156–165.

n.d.   Behavioral Chain Analysis: Activities, Organization and the Use of Space. *Fieldiana: Anthropology*, in press.

Schuyler, Robert L.

1970   Historical and Historic Sites Archaeology as Anthropology: Basic Definitions and Relationships. *Historical Archaeology* 4:83–89.

1972   Archaeological Dig. *City College Alumnus* 67(5):12–13. New York.

Semenov, S. A.

1964   *Prehistoric Technology*. Adams and Dart, Bath, Great Britain.

Service, Elman R.

    1969   Models for the Methodology of Mouthtalk. *Southwestern Journal of Anthropology* 25:68–80.

Siegel, Sydney

    1956   *Nonparametric statistics for the behavioral sciences.* McGraw-Hill, New York.

Smith, Allen H., and J. L. Fischer, eds.

    1970   *Anthropology.* Prentice-Hall, Englewood Cliff, New Jersey.

Sneath, P. H. A.

    1962   The construction of taxonomic groups. In *Microbial Classification;* edited by G. C. Ainsworth and P. H. A. Sneath, pp. 289–332. Cambridge University Press, Cambridge, Mass.

Snedecor, George W. and William G. Cochran

    1967   *Statistical Methods.* Iowa State University, Ames.

Sommer, Robert

    1969   *Personal Space: the Behavioral Basis of Design.* Prentice-Hall, Englewood Cliffs, N.J.

Soto, Alvaro and Carol Szarek

    1971   Interview with Rodney Needham. *The Piltdown Newsletter* 2(2): 1–4. Department of Anthropology, University of California, Riverside, Calif.

Spaulding, Albert C.

    1953   Review of "Measurements of Some Prehistoric Design Developments in the Southwestern States," by James A. Ford. *American Anthropologist* 55(4):588–591.

    ✓ 1960   The dimensions of archaeology. In *Essays in the Science of Culture in Honor of Leslie A. White;* edited by Gertrude E. Dole and Robert L. Carneiro, pp. 437–456. Thomas Y. Crowell, New York.

    ✓ 1968   Explanation in archeology. In *New Perspectives in Archeology;* edited by Sally R. Binford and Lewis R. Binford, pp. 33–40. Aldine Publishing Company, Chicago.

Spencer, Joseph Earle

1937 *The Middle Virgin River Valley, Utah: A Study in Culture Growth and Change.* Unpublished Ph.D. dissertation, University of California, Berkeley.

Spier, Leslie

1917 An Outline for a Chronology of Zuni Ruins. Anthropological Papers of the American Museum of Natural History. Vol. 18

Stanislawski, Michael B.

1969 What good is a broken pot? *Southwestern Lore* 35:11–18.

Steiger, W. L.

1971 Analytical Archaeology? *Mankind* 8:67–70.

Steward, Julian H.

1938 Basin-plateau aboriginal sociopolitical groups. *Bureau of American Ethnology*, Bulletin 120.

1949 Cultural Causality and Law: A Trial Formulation of the Development of Early Civilization. *American Anthropologist* 51(1):1–27.

1955 *Theory of Culture Change.* University of Illinois Press, Urbana.

Steward, Julian H. and Frank M. Setzler

1938 Function and Configuration in American Archaeology. *American Antiquity* 4(1):4–10.

Struever, Stuart

1968a Flotation Techniques for the Recovery of Small-Scale Archaeological Remains. *American Antiquity* 33:353–362.

1968b Woodland subsistence-settlement systems in the lower Illinois Valley. In *New Perspectives in Archeology*; edited by Sally R. and Lewis R. Binford, pp. 285–312. Aldine Publishing Company, Chicago.

1968c Problems, methods and organization: a disparity in the growth of archeology. In *Anthropological Archeology in the Americas*; edited by B. J. Meggers, pp. 131–151. Anthropological Society of Washington.

Struever, Stuart, ed.

1971 *Prehistoric Agriculture.* Natural History Press, New York.

Swanton, John R.

1911   Indian Tribes of the Lower Mississippi Valley and Adjacent Coast of the Gulf of Mexico. *Bureau of American Ethnology, Bulletin,* No. 43. Washington, D.C.

Taylor, Walter W.

1948   A Study of Archeology. *Memoir.* No. 69. American Anthropological Association. 50(3)Part 2.

The Editors of *The Progressive* and the Editors of the College Division of Scott, Foresman and Company.

1970   *The Crisis of Survival.* Scott, Foresmen, Glenview, Ill.

Thomas, David Hurst

1969   Regional sampling in archaeology: a pilot Great Basin research design. *University of California Archaeological Survey Annual Report,* 1968–1969, 11:87–100. Los Angeles.

1970   Archeology's operational imperative: Great Basin projectile points as a test case. *University of California Archaeological Survey Annual Report,* 1969–1970, 12:27–60. Los Angeles.

1971   *Prehistoric Subsistence-Settlement Patterns of the Reese River Valley, Central Nevada.* Unpublished Ph.D. dissertation, Department of Anthropology, University of California, Davis. University Microfilms, Ann Arbor, Mich.

1972   A computer simulation model of Great Basin Shoshoenean settlement patterns. In *Models in Archaeology;* edited by David L. Clark, pp. 671–704, Methuen, London.

1973   An empirical Test of Steward's Model of Great Basin Settlement Patterns. *American Antiquity,* 38:155–176.

Thompson, Raymond H.

1958   Modern Yucatecan Maya Pottery Making. *Memoirs of the Society for American Archaeology.* No. 15. *American Antiquity* 23(3) Part 2.

Trigger, Bruce G.

1968a *Beyond History: The Methods of Prehistory.* Holt, Rinehart and Winston, New York.

1968b The determinants of settlement patterns. In *Settlement Archaeology,* edited by Kwang-Chih Chang, pp. 53–78. National Press, Palo Alto, Calif.

1970   Aims in Prehistoric Archaeology. *Antiquity* 44:26–37.

Tuggle, H. David

　1971　Trigger and Prehistoric Archaeology. *Antiquity* 45:130–132.

Tuggle, H. David, Alex H. Townsend, and Thomas J. Riley

　1972　Laws, Systems, and Research Designs: A Discussion of Explanation in Archaeology. *American Antiquity* 37(1):3–12.

Washburn, Sherwood L. and C. S. Lancaster

　1968　The evolution of hunting. In *Man the Hunter;* edited by Richard Lee and Irven DeVore, pp. 293–303. Aldine Publishing Co.,

Watson, Patty Jo

　1971　The Aims of Prehistory and the Search for Explanation in Archeology. Paper presented at the 36th Annual Meeting of the Society for American Archaeology in Norman, Oklahoma, May 1971.

Watson, Patty Jo et al.

　1969　The Prehistory of Salts Cave, Kentucky. Illinois State Museum Reports of Archeological Investigations Number 16. Springfield, Ill.

Watson, Patty Jo, Steven A. LeBlanc, and Charles L. Redman

　1971　*Explanation in Archeology: An Explicitly Scientific Approach.* Columbia University Press, New York.

Watson, Richard A.

　1966　Discussion: Is Geology Different: A Critical Discussion of *The Fabric of Geology. Philosophy of Science* 33:172–185.

　1969　Explanation and Prediction in Geology. *Journal of Geology* 77:488–494.

　1970　Inference in Archeology. Paper read at the 35th Annual Meeting of the Society for American Archaeology, Mexico City, May 1970.

Wauchope, Robert, ed.

　1956　Seminars in Archaeology: 1955. *Memoirs of the Society for American Archaeology,* 11.

Whallon, Robert Jr.

　1973　Spatial Analysis of Occupation Floors: The Application of Dimensional Analysis of Variance. In *Explanation of Culture Change:*

Models in Prehistory, edited by C. Renfrew. G. Duckworth & Co. Ltd., London.

Wheat, Jo Ben

1972 The Olsen-Chubbuck Site: A Paleo-Indian Bison Kill. *Memoirs of the Society for American Archaeology,* 26.

White, Leslie A.

1949 Science is sciencing. In *The Science of Culture, a Study of Man and Civilization,* pp. 3–21. Grove Press, New York.

1959 *The Evolution of Culture.* McGraw-Hill, New York.

Whiting, John W. M., and Barbara Ayres

1968 Inferences from the Shape of Dwellings. In *Settlement Archaeology,* edited by K. C. Chang, pp. 117–133. National Press, Palo Alto, Calif.

Willey, Gordon R.

1953 Prehistoric Settlement Patterns in the Viru Valley, Peru. *Bureau of American Ethnology, Bulletin.* No. 155. Washington, D.C.

1956 Prehistoric Settlement Patterns in the New World. *Viking Fund Publications in Anthropology,* No. 23. Wenner-Gren Foundation for Anthropological Research. New York.

1966 *Introduction to American Archaeology, Volume 1: North and Middle American.* Prentice-Hall, Englewood Cliffs, N.J.

1971a *Introduction to American Archaeology, Vol. 2. South America.* Prentice-Hall, Englewood Cliffs, N.J.

1971b Review of J. A. Ford, A Comparison of Formative·Cultures in the Americas. *American Journal of Archaeology* 75:117.

Willey, Gordon R. and Charles R. McGimsey

1954 The Monagrillo Culture of Panama. Papers of the Peabody Museum of Archaeology and Ethnology of Harvard University. XLIX(2).

Willey, Gordon R. and Philip Phillips

1958 *Method and Theory in American Archaeology.* University of Chicago Press, Chicago.

Williams, Lorraine

    1968   The Wort Farm: A Report on the 1963–64 Excavations. *Staten Island Institute of Arts and Sciences, Proceedings* 23(2):39–52. Staten Island, N.Y.

Wilmsen, Edwin N.

    1970a Review of *Man in Prehistory* by Chester Chard. *American Anthropologist* 72(3):689–691.

    1970b Lithic Analysis and Cultural Inference: a Paleo-Indian Case. *Anthropological Papers*, No. 16. University of Arizona Press, Tucson.

Wilmsen, Edwin N. and J. Thomas Meyers

    1972   Mercury Content of Prehistoric Fish. *Ecology of Food and Nutrition* 1(3):179–186.

Wilson, John A.

    1964   *Signs and Wonders upon Pharoah*. University of Chicago Press, Chicago.

    1968   A Century of Near Eastern Archeology and the Future. In *The Role of the Phoenicians in the Interaction of Mediterranean Civilizations*: edited by W. Ward, pp. 113–122. American University Centennial Publishers, Beirut, Lebanon.

Winters, Howard D.

    1969   The Riverton Culture: A Second Millennium Occupation in the Central Wabash Valley. *Illinois Archaeological Survey, Monograph* 1.

Wittfogel, Karl A.

    1955   Developmental aspects of hydraulic societies. In *Irrigation civilization: A Comparative Study*, edited by Julian E. Steward, Organization of the American States, Washington, D.C.

Wolf Rackl, Hanns

    1968   *Diving into the Past: Archaeology Under Water*. Translated by R. J. Floyd. Scribner's, New York.

Woolley, Sir Leonard

    1953   *A Forgotten Kingdom: Being a Record of the Results Obtained from the Excavation of Two Mounds, Atchana and Al Mina, in the Turkish Hatay*. Penguin Books, Baltimore.

Wright, G. A.

1971   Origins of Food Production in Southwestern Asia: A Survey of
        Ideas. *Current Anthropology* 12:447–477.

Zubrow, Ezra

1969   *Population, Climate and Contact in the New Mexican Pueblos.*
        Unpublished master's thesis, Department of Anthropology, Uni-
        versity of Arizona, Tucson.

1971a   Carrying Capacity and Dynamic Equilibrium in the Prehistoric
        Southwest. *American Antiquity* 36(2):127–138.

1971b   A Southwestern Test of an Anthropological Model of Population
        Dynamics. Unpublished Ph.D. dissertation, Department of An-
        thropology, University of Arizona, Tucson.

INDEX